MO . 5 . ½ . MO . 5 . ½ .

CLASSICAL ARCHITECTURE IN BRITAIN

CLASSICAL ARCHITECTURE IN BRITAIN
THE HEROIC AGE

GILES WORSLEY

Published for
THE PAUL MELLON CENTRE
FOR STUDIES IN BRITISH ART
by
YALE UNIVERSITY PRESS
NEW HAVEN AND LONDON

Set in Linotron Bembo by Best-set Typesetter Ltd, Hong Kong
Printed in Singapore by C.S. Graphics PTE Ltd

Library of Congress Cataloging-in-Publication Data
Worsley, Giles.
Classical architecture in Britain : the Heroic Age / Giles Worsley
Includes bibliographical references and index.
ISBN 0–300–05896–9
1. Classicism in architecture–Great Britain.   2. Architecture.
Modern–17th–18th centuries–Great Britain.   3. Architecture,
Modern–19th century–Great Britain.   4. Architecture–Great Britain.
5. Palladio. Andrea, 1508–1580—Influence.   I. Title.
NA966.5.C55W67   1994
720′.941—dc20   94-19211

A catalogue record for this book is available from
The British Library

Frontispiece: Thomas Worsley, the Samson Hall,
Hovingham Hall, Yorkshire, 1755.

Endpapers: Double-page spread from Andrea Palladio,
I Quattro Libri dell'Architettura, (Venice 1570).

For Thomas Worsley
Architect and Rider of the Great Horse

1   Robert Morris, frontispiece to *An Essay in Defence of Ancient Architecture* (1728).

CONTENTS

ABBREVIATIONS

AH	*Architectural History*
Architecture in Britain	John Summerson, *Architecture in Britain, 1530–1830*, 6th edn (Harmondsworth, 1977)
BCISAP	*Bolletino del Centro Italiano di Studii Andrea Palladio*
BDBA	Howard Colvin, *Biographical Dictionary of British Architects, 1600–1840*, 2nd edn (London, 1978)
BM	*Burlington Magazine*
CL	*Country Life*
GGJ	*Georgian Group Journal*
RCHM	Royal Commission on the Historical Monuments of England
RIBA	Royal Institute of British Architects
VB	Colen Campbell, *Vitruvius Britannicus*, vol. I (London, 1715), vol. II (London, 1717), vol. III (London, 1725); John Woolfe and James Gandon, *Vitruvius Britannicus*, vol. IV (London, 1767), vol. V (London, 1771)

ACKNOWLEDGEMENTS

IT IS TWELVE YEARS SINCE THE GERM of this book first surfaced and many people have helped me both directly and indirectly. Neil Macgregor, while editor of the *Burlington Magazine*, was the first to show enough confidence in my ideas to publish them and for that I will always be grateful. Marcus Binney, Jenny Greene and Clive Aslet, successive editors of *Country Life*, kindly allowed me to develop my ideas in that magazine, and Clive Aslet allowed me to reuse that material and to ransack *Country Life*'s incomparable photographic library – something that would not have been possible without the help of *Country Life*'s photographic librarian, Camilla Costello. My former colleagues John Cornforth and Michael Hall were the wall against which I constantly bounced ideas. Michael Hall read the text with perception and his constant enthusiasm has buoyed me up during the apparently endless task of writing and rewriting. Miss Joanna Watt must also be thanked for her forbearance.

Yale University Press's editorial team more than lived up to their excellent reputation. I shall always owe a strong debt of gratitude to my patient editor Gillian Malpass, who also designed the book, to Sheila Lee, who took on the burden of acquiring the foreign photographs, and to Celia Jones, who carefully copy-edited the text.

For John Newman, my erstwhile supervisor at the Courtauld Institute, I fear I have perhaps been more trouble as a post-post-graduate than I ever was as a student, but his sage advice has been invaluable, and certain key areas in the book owe much to seminars given to his post-graduate students. Dr Edward McParland introduced me to Dublin and kindly read the sections on Ireland, giving me confidence to write about an area that owes so much to his work. Innumerable other scholars, archivists, librarians and owners have helped. It is impossible to mention them all but they include in particular Andor Gomme, Eileen Harris, Richard Haslam, Richard Garnier, Richard Hewlings, Gordon Higgott, Gervase Jackson-Stops, John Martin Robinson and David Watkin. Special thanks must go to Ian Gow at the Royal Commission on Historical Monuments of Scotland; to Neil Bingham and Tim Knox at the Royal Institute of British Architects Drawings Collection; to the staffs of the Society of Antiquaries, the London Library, the National Register of Archives, the National Monuments Record and the British Library; and, collectively, to all those invaluable archivists in County Record Offices and historic houses.

More than anything else, the influence of two scholars lies over this book, both of whom read, commented upon and substantially improved a first draft of the text. No architectural student of this period can fail to be aware of the debt he owes to Howard Colvin's magisterial *Biographical Dictionary of British Architects*. This book could not have been written without it constantly to hand. Mr Colvin himself has been a constant source of inspiration and encouragement, while his astonishing accuracy provides the mark against which one constantly strives. (I only hope that where errors have crept in readers will let me know.)

An even greater debt is owed to John Harris who, eleven years ago, read the BA dissertation that was the germ for this book and by agreeing with it encouraged it to grow. His generosity in sharing ideas and information, his happiness to worry enigmas and suggest leads on a subject which he has made his own is quite astonishing. Even more so is his willingness to let me borrow extensively from his collection of photographs. This book would be for him, were it not that Thomas Worsley has, I think he will agree, a prior claim, for if it had not been for him this book could never have been written.

ANDREAS PALLADIVS VICENTINVS.

2 Imaginary portrait of Andrea Palladio, from Isaac Ware's edition of *The Four Books of Architecture* (1738).

PROLOGUE

Any attempt to impose some form of order on the architecture of previous centuries is problematic; but it is also necessary, for without order it is almost impossible to comprehend the significance of what we see. This book is my personal attempt to find a sense of order in seventeenth- and eighteenth-century British architecture and it arose from a growing dissatisfaction with the conventional view of the period as it has been accepted since the 1950s.

If one book crystallises that view it is Sir John Summerson's *Architecture in Britain, 1530–1830*, first published in 1953, most recently revised in 1991 and still the standard text today. It is a remarkable book, with a breadth and depth that would be hard to rival, but inevitably a different generation has an altered perspective. Perhaps the greatest difference between an architectural historian writing then and one writing now is the collapse of the consensus that surrounded modern architecture for much of the post-war period. Rather than see Modernism as the inevitable culmination of architectural development, the obvious rational style, as it was generally portrayed, it is seen as just one particular approach to building which happened to be extraordinarily influential during the middle decades of this century. These decades now appear as one of those rare periods in architectural history when a single style predominates. Today, in reaction, we live in an age of stylistic diversity – rather as the Palladian ascendancy of mid-eighteenth-century Britain was followed by the exotic range of architectural styles of the Regency.

This changed perspective on Modernism alters the way we look at architectural history. If there is an underlying philosophy behind this book it is that architecture cannot be seen as inevitably progressive. The teleological assumptions of architects and critics, whether Modernists or mid-nineteenth-century Goths, that architecture is leading towards a certain goal (the architecture of which they approve), have distorted our understanding of architectural history. Instead of seeing styles develop sequentially, one out of another, they should be seen as approaches to architecture, a number of which can co-exist at the same time, sometimes strong, sometimes weak.

This book concentrates on Palladianism because I believe that it was the dominant approach to architecture in Britain from about 1615 to the last decades of the eighteenth century. It takes as its primary source the buildings themselves and treats the published writings of architects, particularly those of Colen Campbell and Robert Adam, with caution. However, before setting out the standard view of British Palladianism and suggesting an alternative interpretation, it is necessary to consider exactly what is meant by Palladianism.

Andrea Palladio's own work is an amalgam of various different tendencies. As a sixteenth-century Vicentine architect he worked within the local tradition, particularly the tradition of the villa. His thinking was heavily influenced by the study of Vitruvius's *Ten Books of Architecture*, on an edition of which, published in 1556, he had worked with Daniele Barbaro, and by Leon Battista Alberti's *De re aedificatoria*, presented in manuscript to Pope Nicholas V in 1452 and first printed in 1485. In his reconstructions of Roman buildings, the work of Sebastiano Serlio and other architects and theorists who had made studies of Roman buildings was important. Finally, Palladio's trips to Rome in 1541, 1547 and 1554 were critical to him, not only because of the impact of Ancient Roman architecture, but also because of the influence on him of the preceding generation of Roman architects, particularly Bramante and Raphael, an influence that was further developed by the work of Raphael's assistant Giulio Romano in Mantua and Vicenza. The importance of these sources to Palladio meant that it was easy for subsequent interpreters to include earlier ideas, particularly those of Giulio Romano and Serlio, in the creation of a broader concept of Palladianism.

Palladio's stroke of genius, which ensured subsequent architects would build on his work, was to publish his *Quattro libri dell'architettura* in 1570. A lucid account of the orders of architecture is combined with theoretical reconstructions of Roman rooms and buildings as described by Vitruvius, reconstructions from surveys of remaining fragments of Roman temples and illustrations of his own work. This last divides principally into the churches, the palazzi and the villas. The churches were not published in the *Quattro libri* and were subsequently of little influence outside Italy, although San Giorgio Maggiore was published in William Kent's *The Designs of Inigo Jones* in 1727. The palazzi were significant principally in the Veneto, although they were not without their imitators elsewhere. It was the villas that proved to be Palladio's most influential designs. Here, his major innovation was to apply the Roman temple front systematically to domestic buildings, although he was not the first to do so, having been anticipated by Giuliano da Sangallo at the Villa Medici at Poggio a Caiano. In this way Palladio generally created tripartite façades (divided into three with the portico in the centre), often with wings or pavilions. The temple front was either expressed as a full portico, as an attached portico with columns or pilasters, or as an implied portico. Most of Palladio's villas are compact blocks, generally with a central hall. Another particular feature of Palladio's villas is the idea of a central block flanked by spreading, symmetrical wings or dependencies.

The *Quattro libri* allowed Palladio's work to be accessible to innumerable architects who never travelled to the Veneto, and meant that personal study of his buildings was often secondary to the study of the book. Palladio's last buildings were completed by his pupil Vincenzo Scamozzi who further developed Palladio's manner and published his own book, *Dell'idea dell'architettura universale*, in 1615. This was often studied by followers of Palladio as well as the *Quattro libri*.

Thus, there are a number of strands within Palladio's work which appealed to later architects in different ways at different times. As these followers were working within their own national contexts the consequent architectural interpretations often varied markedly. At the theoretical level, Palladio's first book on the orders was particularly influential and was studied by many architects and theorists who took no interest in what Palladio built; the resulting architecture cannot be described as Palladian. At a more basic level is the imitation of a number of motifs (which often have other derivations but came to be particularly associated with Palladio), particularly the portico, Serlian and Diocletian windows and rusticated arcading; when used in isolation, these show Palladian influence but cannot be described as evidence of a coherent Palladian style. More significant is the widespread use of the compact, tripartite villa that Palladio introduced; this can be described as simple Palladianism. Beyond this was the attempt to create a sophisticated architectural style based specifically on Palladio's work, partly on his plans but mainly on his elevations, which can be described as neo-Palladianism. This is seen most strongly in Britain and the Veneto in the eighteenth century, but should not be seen as a monolithic style as each architect's approach to neo-Palladianism differed, even at its core, where the extreme

theoretical rigour of Lord Burlington differs markedly from the more painterly manner of William Kent.

In Britain the influence of the early seventeenth-century buildings of Inigo Jones, based largely but not exclusively on the work of Palladio, proved important to later seventeenth- and early eighteenth-century architects and add a further level of complication to the study of Palladianism, for there was a strong element of Jonesian revival within English neo-Palladianism. In a similar manner, by the middle of the eighteenth century the work of English neo-Palladians of the first decades of the century, such as Lord Burlington, formed a further source of inspiration.

Finally, Palladio's interest in the reconstruction of Roman buildings from the writings of Vitruvius or from existing remains and his attempts to adapt them to contemporary use had its own specific influence. The significance of neo-Classicism in British, and indeed Continental, architecture has been much confused by the exclusive attachment of the phrase 'neo-Classicism' to the late eighteenth century, which is commonly described as the 'Age of neo-Classicism'. However, although the late eighteenth century was a particularly neo-Classical age, the architecture of that period was by no means exclusively neo-Classical, nor can neo-Classicism only to be found after 1750. Neo-Classicism is an approach to design in which architects turn directly to ancient buildings and writings as practical exemplars for their own age, ignoring the traditions of Classical architecture that have grown up since the Renaissance; it could almost be described as fundamentalist Classicism. This is an approach that can be found at different times in different countries, sometimes it is very strong, sometimes barely noticeable. It had an influence on English Palladians from Inigo Jones into the eighteenth century, a neo-Classical influence that needs to be distinguished from more conventional neo-Palladianism.

The standard view of Palladianism in Britain is that it was introduced by Inigo Jones in the second decade of the seventeenth century but failed to establish itself, the experiment being spoilt by the Civil War's destruction of the early Stuart court. An attempt by Jones's sole pupil, John Webb, to revive it after the Civil War also failed, and Palladianism is then seen as lying dormant until the second decade of the eighteenth century when, after a few experiments in Oxford, it was revived by Colen Campbell as a reaction to the Baroque style of Christopher Wren. Campbell's *Vitruvius Britannicus* of 1715 is considered to be the manifesto for this new style, subsequently picked up by Lord Burlington and given form as neo-Palladianism; only James Gibbs, of the major mid-eighteenth-century architects, maintaining his independence. Then, in the second half of the century, growing interest in neo-Classicism, inspired by archaeological discoveries in Italy and Greece, is believed to have led to neo-Palladianism being displaced by the neo-Classical work of architects such as Robert Adam, William Chambers and James 'Athenian' Stuart around 1760.

It can, however, be argued that Palladianism was a much more pervasive influence on British architecture; that Inigo Jones, far from failing to pass on a style, was profoundly influential in developing the type of regular, astylar house that became standard in the 1630s and formed the basis of domestic architecture after the Restoration; that the post-Restoration country house, typified by the work of Roger Pratt, grew out of this Jonesian foundation, despite being conventionally seen as an import from the Netherlands, but was given a strong, self-consciously Palladian approach, based on the villa, by Pratt. This compact villa-type house with a central pediment was to remain one of the fundamental architectural types until the early nineteenth century, altering only in detail and proportion, while its astylar architectural form with a regular, symmetrical grid of upright windows set in a bare wall and decorated with a limited amount of Classical detail, particularly around the doorcase, was to become one of the most pervasive of all British architectural styles, better known as 'Georgian'.

The early years of the eighteenth century did see new interest in the buildings and ideas of Palladio and Inigo Jones, but this was not introduced by Colen Campbell. It can be found in the work of William Talman, John Vanbrugh, Nicholas Hawksmoor and John James, as well as among such amateurs as Dean Aldrich and George Clarke, before Campbell arrived in London. It was this growing interest in Palladianism that encouraged Colen Campbell to recast *Vitruvius Britannicus* as a specifically Palladian work, but he himself was initially unable to suggest what form a British Palladianism should take. Instead, the most significant architectural development of the second decade of the eighteenth century was an increasing interest in austerity and the rise of the free-standing portico visible in the work of Vanbrugh, Hawksmoor and James as well as that of Campbell. Only in the early 1720s did a specifically neo-Palladian style, based primarily on the villa, emerge in the work of Campbell and Lord Burlington.

In the 1730s Burlingtonian neo-Palladianism developed into the country's dominant architectural style, receiving a second wind in the 1750s after the end of the War of the Austrian Succession in the work of such architects as James Paine, Robert Taylor and John Carr. It is to this second wind of neo-Palladianism that the work of Robert Adam and William Chambers belongs. Thereafter, the pre-eminence of Palladianism slowly declined. It remained an important element of the work of such architects as James Wyatt until the end of the century, but was challenged by other approaches to Classicism, particularly those of such architects as George Dance, James Gandon and Joseph Bonomi, as well as by the growing acceptance of asymmetry and the rise of the Greek Revival at the turn of the century. By 1815, with Gothic architecture accepted in certain circumstances as being as valid as Classical architecture, Palladianism was only one, increasingly unimportant, style among many.

Although Palladianism may have been the dominant style in England for the better part of two centuries, it was not the only style. Throughout these years a continuous strand of Gothic architecture can be identified. Baroque and Rococo architecture also make their appearances and it is important to consider the degree to which these clashed or co-existed with Palladianism. Nor was Palladianism an English aberration, as a study of the related cultures of Scotland, Ireland and the Americas makes clear. It is also important to realise that Palladianism was not a purely British phenomenon. Contemporary Palladian movements of varying degrees of strength can be found on the Continent throughout these years, with particular peaks coinciding with periods of more specific Palladian interest in Britain.

This book is not intended as a complete history of architecture in seventeenth- and eighteenth-century Britain. Inevitably, given that its subject is Classicism, there are large areas of contemporary building unexamined, particularly vernacular architecture and industrial buildings and the same is true of most urban architecture, although here a Classical framework does lie behind the Georgian town house. Questions of decoration have been addressed, but only as far as they concern architectural style. Completed in the depths of a recession after a long boom noted for its dramatic stylistic developments, particular attention has been paid to the economic context in which architecture is produced. In the seventeenth and eighteenth centuries war was the principal factor that determined the rate of building and the impact of sudden bursts and slumps in building on the development of architectural style is carefully examined. Finally, the way in which architectural taste can develop rapidly in a short number of years, so evident during the 1980s, has been taken into account when assessing the stylistic careers of architects whose work should not necessarily be seen as a unity but as a sequence of developments which may have led to very different types of buildings at different stages. This is particularly true of John Vanbrugh, Colen Campbell and James Gibbs.

NO LONELY GENIUS:
INIGO JONES AND HIS CONTEMPORARIES

THE ARRIVAL OF INIGO JONES, Britain's first truly Classical architect, comes as something of a shock in architectural history. One moment British architecture is confidently Jacobean, owing perhaps rather more to medieval Britain than to Classical Italy. The next, the Banqueting House – a building that would not have looked out of place in Vicenza or Rome – is rising in Whitehall (Fig. 6). Its appearance is rather like that of a comet bursting dramatically into view in the night sky; and it is as a comet that it is all too easy to view Jones, rising spectacularly above his contemporaries, but ultimately fading away, his pupil John Webb spluttering ineffectually in his tail, the prophet of a high Italianate Classicism which never became established in this country and was swiftly obscured by the rising sun of Christopher Wren.

There is, however, another possible interpretation of Jones; not as a member of a lonely, misunderstood Classical élite but as working hard, and with considerable success, among fellow architects and builders to achieve a broad-based Classical revolution, a revolution on which the architectural achievement of the second half of the century was built. Such an interpretation depends on placing Jones's different buildings in context, and, in particular, on seeing his architecture develop as he came to terms with the problems of introducing Classicism to Britain. Remarkable though it is, the Banqueting House should not be assumed to be representative of Jones's work as a whole.

The Banqueting House was, however, typical of Jones's early work, those buildings designed for the court between his return from Italy in 1614 and the cessation of royal building caused by the outbreak of war with Spain and France in 1624. These reveal a particular fascination with the Classical orders and the richness of Classical ornament. The Banqueting House, built in 1619, epitomises this, with a channelled surface supporting superimposed Ionic and Composite pilasters and attached columns, alternately segmental and triangular pediments over the first-floor windows, with balustraded balconies in the centre, swags in the upper entablature and the whole topped by a balustrade. Other contemporary designs, few of them executed, show a similar obsession with the orders, coupled with an understanding of the rules of propriety which govern their use. Thus, the extreme elaboration of the Banqueting House was appropriate for the building where the king displayed himself. Slightly less elaborate was the proposed Star Chamber (1617), the government's principal court of law, where the attached Corinthian portico announces the building's high royal status, its rusticated base and the rusticated architraves of the first-floor windows the stern justice to be found within (Fig. 3). Simpler again are the designs for the Queen's House at Greenwich (1616) and for the Prince's Lodgings at Newmarket (1618), both villas and neither intended for the king himself (Fig. 4).

These buildings are the immediate response to Jones's journey to Italy in 1613–14, where he was captivated by the remains of Roman antiquity and by the buildings of the great Vicentine architect, Andrea Palladio, who had died just over thirty years earlier. Jones was not alone among northern Europeans in the first decades of the seventeenth century in looking to Italy, specifically to the work of *cinquecento* architects, for a purer Classicism. The introduction to Peter Paul Rubens's *Palazzi di Genova*, published in Antwerp in 1622, declares that 'We see in these parts the mode of architecture which is called barbarian, and Gothic, is gradually falling out of use, and that some extremely fine minds are introducing the true symmetry which conforms to the rules of the ancient Greeks and Romans.'[1] Rubens set out to satisfy this new interest by publishing measured drawings of palazzi and villas in Genoa, principally those by Galeazzo Alessi, most of them built in the 1550s and 1560s.

Rubens was unusual in looking to Genoa, but there was considerable interest in the contemporary work of Palladio and Palladianism. Probably the first northern architect to sketch Palladio's buildings was Heinrich Schickhardt, who visited Vicenza in 1598–9, where he particularly admired the Teatro Olimpico and made drawings of the Palazzo Valmarana and the Palazzo

3   John Webb after Inigo
Jones, unexecuted design for
the Star Chamber, Whitehall,
London, 1617.

4 (below)   Inigo Jones,
unexecuted design for the
Prince's Lodgings at New-
market, Suffolk, 1618.

5 (bottom)   Vincenzo
Scamozzi, Palazzo Verlati,
Villa Verla, Italy, from
*Dell'idea dell'architettura
universale* (1615).

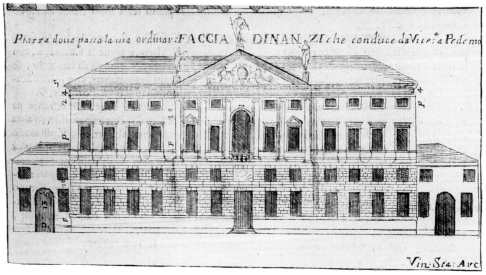

6   Inigo Jones, the Banqueting House, Whitehall, London, 1619 (Thomas Malton, watercolour, Victoria and Albert Museum).

Chiericati. However, this interest was not reflected in his architecture.[2] Further south, the leading architect in Augsburg was Elias Holl, who first visited the Veneto in 1600; in all he visited Venice about ten times although he never went to Rome. Many critics have seen Palladian influence in Holl's work, particularly Augsburg's Town Hall (1614), although that of Serlio is much more evident.[3] Further evidence of Palladian influence in Augsburg, a city that had strong economic links with Venice, can be seen in the remarkable model for a basilica, whose use of Serliana is based on the basilica at Vicenza, and which was made in 1607, possibly by Joseph Heintz and Mathias Kager.[4] In Heidelberg the purity of the Englischen Baues of the Castle (which looks to Serlio rather than Palladio) is such that this has traditionally been attributed to Inigo Jones, who visited the city in 1613.[5]

Whether anything as recognisably Palladian as the work of Jones would have emerged from these flickers of interest is impossible to tell. What survives shows an understanding of Palladio, but much transformed, rather than specifically Palladian buildings. The outbreak of the devastating Thirty Years' War in 1618, which brought almost all building in Germany to a halt, ended any

hope of an early seventeenth-century German Palladian movement.

Using Palladio's *Quattro libri dell'architettura* (1570) Jones systematically visited and studied Roman buildings and those of Palladio, noting his reactions in the margins. He also sought out Palladio's old pupil Vincenzo Scamozzi, quizzing him about Palladio's work – and jotting down his responses in the *Quattro libri* – as well as managing to acquire a collection of Palladio's drawings. But Jones found Scamozzi to be more than just a physical link with Palladio; he was also influenced by Scamozzi's own work, which developed Palladio's style. After his return to England he was to buy Scamozzi's *Dell'idea dell'architettura universale* within two years of its publication in 1615 and may have had access to Scamozzi's drawings, two chests of which were included in the sale of the collection of his travelling companion and patron, Thomas Howard, 2nd Earl of Arundel.[6] The influence of Scamozzi (Fig. 5) is particularly evident in Jones's designs for the Prince's Lodgings at Newmarket (Fig. 4) and in the west façade of the Chapel Royal at St James's, which is in essence the centrepiece of the second design for the Prince's Lodgings.

These early buildings, even the Banqueting House,

are all variations on the tripartite villa elevation. At the Banqueting House (Fig. 6) the superimposed orders and the balustrade give an immediate impression of an urban building, but the emphasis provided by the attached columns of the three central bays (contrasting with the pilasters of the end bays) and by the slight projection of the rustic shows that at heart this building has more in common with the villa. One almost expects the central three bays to be capped with a pediment – as they are in an early design. Moreover, contrary to appearance, the Banqueting House is not divided into two floors but is one double-height space (albeit with a first-floor gallery); nor does the central projection mark an internal division. Impressive though it is, the façade of the Banqueting House is ultimately another masque backdrop, but this time of stone. Thus, for all its control of the orders there is an ambivalence about the Banqueting House, with its confusion of urban and rural forms and a façade unrelated to the space behind. Perhaps George Gage's comment in May 1620 is not quite as presumptuous as it might seem: 'Frende, I have seen Inigo Jones his banqueting house which is a good lustie piece saving that it has some blemishes here and there . . . But though Architects may differ in opinion about ornaments, I am glad in substance to see good building begin to get into this island.'[7]

How influential were Jones's early buildings in introducing 'good building . . . into this island'? The time was certainly propitious, for increasingly sophisticated patrons were beginning to look to Italy for Classical designs, as can be seen at Danvers House in Chelsea, arguably England's first Italianate villa,[8] and the arcaded and pilastered west front of Castle Ashby, Northamptonshire, both dating from the early 1620s (Fig. 7).[9] At first, however, it was only the details of Jones's work that seem to have appealed to his contemporaries. Sir Roger Townshend, a keen amateur who owned 'many Italian and French books of architecture', made a detailed study of Jones's buildings in London and at Newmarket before he began to build his new house at Raynham Hall in Norfolk to his own designs in 1622 (Fig. 8).[10] The plan of Raynham was based on Palladio's Villa Poiana, but the elevation forms a collection of recognisable Jonesian quotations – the gables, for instance, from Sir Fulke Greville's house in Holborn, the centrepiece and use of coigning from Newmarket – arranged in a manner that is clearly not by Jones.

A similar process can be seen at Boston Manor, Middlesex, built in 1622 (Fig. 9). Here, the triple-gabled elevation looks back to Jacobean architecture but the sophisticated use of Classical ornament – moulded window-frames with triple keystones; triangular and seg-

7　Anon., Castle Ashby, Northamptonshire, 1624.

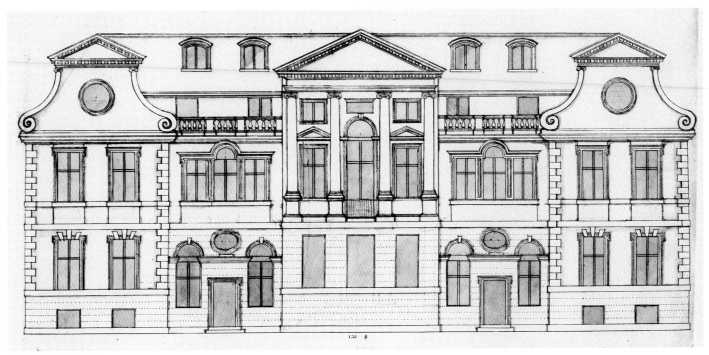

8   Roger Townshend, record drawing of Raynham Hall, Norfolk, 1622.

mental pediments over the ground-floor windows; a full
Ionic cornice above the first floor; round-headed niches
in the gables – does not.[11] The triple keystone in the
architrave of the ground- and first-floor windows was a
motif that Jones introduced on the ground floor of the
Prince's Lodgings at Newmarket in 1619 (Fig. 4), and
used shortly after on the extension to the Chapel Royal
at St James's Palace. Jones introduced segmental pediments – used on the ground-floor windows – for the first
time in the preliminary design for the Queen's House
and subsequently used them at the Banqueting House in
1619 (Fig. 6). The elaborate entablature has the accuracy
of those designed for the Prince's Lodgings or the early
design for the Queen's House. Certain solecisms, in
particular the running together of the architraves above
the pairs of second-floor windows, make it unlikely that
Jones was directly involved at Boston Manor, but the
architect must have been someone closely connected
with his work.

These borrowings show that contemporaries were
looking with attention at Jones's innovations, but no
pre-Civil War building by another architect matches the
sophisticated control of the orders shown on the Banqueting House. Indeed, only a handful of pre-Civil War
buildings – Sir Balthazar Gerbier's five-bay range at York
House in Whitehall for the Duke of Buckingham of
1624–5; Edward Carter's Castle Ashby screen of about
1630 (Fig. 10);[12] the gates to the Oxford Botanical Gardens, probably by Nicholas Stone, of 1632; the anonymous wings at Stoke Bruern, Northamptonshire, of
about 1630 – attempt a Classicism of equal richness, and
none attain the same degree of correctness. This has been

taken to show that Jones was an architecturally isolated
figure, but should not be, for there is more to his work
than the high Italianate Classicism of the Banqueting
House. For proof of this it is only necessary to look to
the period after 1630, when peace returned with the end
of the long and expensive war with Spain and France,
during which royal expenditure on building had collapsed and private and collegiate expenditure were
severely curtailed. While the 1620s had been disastrous
years, the 1630s seems to have been a decade of growing
prosperity. Population growth had at last begun to level
off and the resulting inflation to slow down. Better

9   Anon., Boston Manor, Middlesex, 1622.

10   Edward Carter, inner façade of the screen at Castle Ashby, Northamptonshire, 1630.

harvests also meant that the 1630 dearth was the last of the decade and one of the last of the century. Freed of war, the desperate state of government finances began to be sorted out, with income outstripping expenditure so that accumulated debts could begin to be paid off. Above all, for a decade England, alone among the great European powers, was not at war and trade with other countries flourished, in particular the important Spanish market was again open to English wool, and the country benefited from a booming re-export trade.[13]

The break in building work is so marked that for Jones the years after 1630 almost seem to be a second career, and he was not alone in finding the 1630s a much more prosperous decade than the 1620s. These years saw the Queen's House, which had been lying half-built since 1619, completed by Jones to a new design, and the building of a Classical lodge in Hyde Park (1634). In London, the development of Covent Garden from 1631 and Lincoln's Inn Fields were signs of rapid expansion; St Paul's Cathedral was recased and given a great west portico from 1633; a number of churches were built or rebuilt including St Katherine Cree (1631); St Michael-le-Querne, Cheapside (1638); the Broadway Chapel,

Westminster (1635); public buildings such as the Goldsmiths' Hall (1635) were rebuilt and substantial new houses such as that by Inigo Jones for Sir Peter Killigrew in Blackfriars (c.1630), Leicester House (1631) and Southampton House (c.1640) were erected. In the villages around London a series of suburban retreats arose, for example Forty Hall, Enfield (c.1629–36); the Dutch House at Kew (1631); Goring House, Westminster (1633); Cromwell House, Highgate (c.1637–8); Tart Hall, Westminster, and Swakeleys, Middlesex (both 1638). Both the universities were hives of building, with activity returning to the level of the 1610s after the barren years of the 1620s.[14] High points in Oxford included the Canterbury Quadrangle at St John's College, in 1632–6, an ornate south porch added to the Church of St Mary the Virgin and University College rebuilt from 1634 – although not to the elaborate Classical design initially suggested.[15] There was also a burst of building in the country, ranging from great palaces such as Bolsover Castle, Derbyshire (where work was resumed in about 1629 after being suspended for the better part of a decade) and Wilton, Wiltshire (1636), to new compact boxes like St Clere, Kent (c.1633), West

11 Inigo Jones, unexecuted design for the Strand façade of Somerset House, London, 1630s.

Woodhay Park, Berkshire (1635), and Balls Park, Hertfordshire (1638).

The outbreak of war with Scotland in 1639 and the subsequent slow slide into Civil War in 1642 largely brought this activity to a halt. Jones's last works for the Crown were alterations to Wimbledon House for the Queen in 1640–41. At Stoke Bruern Park, the new colonnaded wings were left unconnected when work on the house was abandoned. In Cambridge the south range of Clare College was built in 1640–42, but work on the west range, for which the foundations had also been laid, was suspended until 1662. The 1630s had been a busy decade in which the volume of building was matched by rapid stylistic advance, and a considerable amount of stylistic confusion. Conventionally, the decade is divided stylistically between the pure Palladianism of Jones and the Artisan Mannerism of his lesser contemporaries,[16] but the division between Jones and the others is by no means clear cut, while a widely diverging series of stylistic approaches are yoked together under the term 'Artisan Mannerism'.

Jones's architecture developed in three directions during the 1630s. For the proposed rebuilding of the royal palaces of Whitehall and Somerset House (Fig. 11), both of about 1638, he continued the rich Classical manner of his earlier period, but with his designs owing more to Scamozzi than to Palladio.[17] For the great ecclesiastical set-pieces of St Paul, Covent Garden (Fig. 54), and the west portico at St Paul's Cathedral (Fig. 56) he turned to a specifically neo-Classical manner which will be described in chapter three. For his domestic work he developed a restrained style which owes much to Serlio. At the Queen's House (Fig. 12), and at the extreme neo-Classical statements of St Paul, Covent Garden, and the portico of St Paul's Cathedral, we see the mature Jones

showing a confidence in his own ability to go beyond the work of his masters. Jones's work in the decade between 1614 and 1624 is essentially derivative; by the 1630s it is not. What particularly sets it apart is the growing tendency towards abstraction, to be found at all levels of his work. The restrained domestic style proved particularly influential among his contemporaries, and was to be Jones's most immediate legacy to British architecture.

The importance of Serlio, whom Jones had studied together with Palladio and Vitruvius when he first became interested in architecture,[18] has not gone without comment. John Summerson has shown that Serlio provided the model for the arcaded, pilastered houses round the Piazza at Covent Garden built in 1631–7.[19] John Newman has proved that Nicholas Stone's Goldsmiths' Hall in the City of London, built in 1635–8 with Jones's assistance, was a sophisticated attempt at a Serlian elevation (Fig. 13).[20] These were not alone, and a specifically

12 Inigo Jones, the Queen's House, Greenwich, 1630.

Serlian vocabulary is characteristic of many buildings of the 1630s and 1650s. One of the most distinctively Serlian features about the Goldsmiths' Hall is the pairing of *oeil-de-boeuf* and casement windows, an idea taken from Serlio's seventh book (Fig. 14). This was first used in England by Inigo Jones on the nave of the St Paul's Cathedral from 1633 (Fig. 16). At the same time as St Paul's Cathedral was being remodelled, the motif was being used on the renowned stables built for the Chancellor of the Exchequer, Lord Cottington, at Fonthill, Wiltshire.[21] Isaac de Caus used a similar combination of windows to flank the arcade on the nearby stables at Wilton (*c*.1639) and for the end bays of Wilton House (*c*.1636) (Fig. 15).

A variation of the motif, with the *oeil-de-boeuf* window above a door with a bracketed architrave, appears on the east and west fronts of St Paul, Covent Garden. This has its own source in Serlio's church designs and was later to be used at Forde Abbey, Dorset (*c*.1650). At St Paul, Covent Garden, this motif is flanked by two deep round-headed windows, consistent features of this style also found in the clerestory and east and west fronts of St Paul's Cathedral and on the Goldsmiths' Hall. This combination had already been used at Raynham Hall, Norfolk, and can also be found at Hale Church, Hampshire (1631), which is associated with Jones.

Serlian windows are another relatively common feature of early Stuart and Commonwealth architecture, appearing at least four times in Jones's work and eleven times in the work of others, whether in the form of a single window divided by columns or of three separate units divided by solid wall.[22] Although in England this window – disguised by its description as a Venetian window – is usually associated with Palladio, it only appears twice as an independent unit in the *Quattro libri*; it appears more frequently in Scamozzi's *Dell'idea dell'architettura universale* and repeatedly in Serlio.

Other Serlian motifs, alone or in combination, that occur regularly in early Stuart and Interregnum architecture include the round-headed window,[23] the *oeil-de-boeuf* window,[24] the rusticated door,[25] windows with key-stones[26] and quoining. They appear in Jones's early designs, especially at the Prince's Lodging in Newmarket, but become particularly persistent in his later work. A sheet of studies by Jones, dated 1618, after windows in Serlio show how he combed Serlio for ideas. Despite all the sophistication of Palladio's and Scamozzi's books, Serlio had more to offer in terms of architectural motif, particularly motifs that did not require the high standards of carving and proportion demanded by the orders. Jones's practice was followed by John Webb, whose drawings contain numerous studies of windows carefully annotated with their source in Serlio.[27] This is not, of course, to say that Jones used Serlio without refinement; as Gordon Higgott points out, 'while the general out-line of Jones's mature domestic designs may owe something to Serlio's domestic designs, the detail, in particular the coarse crowding of motifs, the crude proportioning and ugly moulding profiles are foreign to Jones's mature architectural manner'.

The similarities between St Paul, Covent Garden, and St Paul's Cathedral – aside from their porticos – with the Goldsmiths' Hall and de Caus's work at Wilton should be no surprise, as Jones's hand lay behind both the latter buildings. The Goldsmiths' Hall was rebuilt in a handsome Classical manner on the urging of Jones, and when discussing the design the records note that Stone 'gave this Courte to understand that in the doeinge thereof Mr Jones his Majestyes surveyor took especiall care and did advise and direct before the perfecting and finishinge of each piece according to the severall draughts now shewed'.[28] Jones's role was equally marked at Wilton, which was rebuilt on the urging of Charles I, who 'did love Wilton above all places'. The king

> intended to have it all designed by his own architect, Mr. Inigo Jones, who being at that time . . . engaged in his Majesties buildings at Greenwich, could not attend to it: but recommended it to an ingenious architect, Monsieur de Caus, who performed it very well; but not without the advice and approbation of Mr Jones.[29]

There are further connections between the two buildings, as Stone went from the Goldsmiths' Hall to carve a pediment for Lord Pembroke 'by order of Mr DeCaux'.[30] Indeed, both buildings follow the same basic module with a round-headed basement or rustic window, under a full-height window with an architrave, with a half-height window above.

Howard Colvin has pointed out similarities between the Goldsmiths' Hall and Balls Park (1638–40), which share similar rusticated basement windows and irregularly spaced cornice brackets,[31] The basic design of Balls Park, with its two storeys, broad cornice and wide single-bay central pediment also derives from a plate in Serlio's seventh book,[32] while the side bays, with a central round-headed window flanked by rectangular windows above three further windows, derive from the central feature of the north front at the Queen's House. Elements from this style can also be found in Stone's north range at Kirby Hall, Northamptonshire (1638).

The influence of this elaborate Serlian style was relatively limited. More significant was the part that Serlio's example played in Jones's development of a more austere, astylar manner for smaller houses, something that was to have a profound influence on British architecture (Fig. 17). This development can be seen in the design for Sir Peter Killigrew's house (*c*.1630) (Fig. 18), the two houses flanking St Paul, Covent Garden (1631) (Fig. 54), a design for a house for Lord Maltravers at Lothbury

FOSTER LANE

A

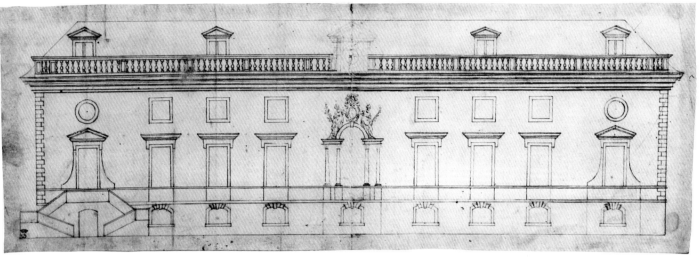

Scala Pedum

13 (top left)   Nicholas
Stone, elevation of the
Goldsmiths' Hall, City of
London, 1635 (demolished).

14 (top right)   Sebastiano
Serlio, design for a house,
from his seventh book of
architecture.

15 (above)   Isaac de Caus,
Wilton House, Wiltshire,
c.1636 (remodelled).

16 (left)   Inigo Jones, the
nave of St Paul's Cathedral,
City of London, 1633
(engraving after Wenceslaus
Hollar) (demolished).

17   Sebastiano Serlio, design for a small house, from his seventh book of architecture.

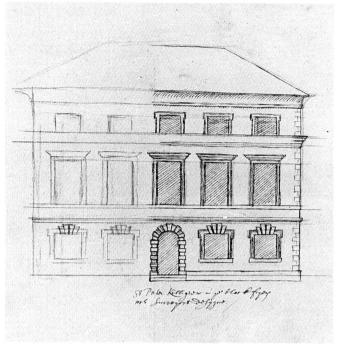

18   Inigo Jones, design for Sir Peter Killigrew's House, City of London, *c*.1630.

(1638) (Fig. 19), with its associated row of warehouses (Fig. 26), and an office-range of unknown date for Maltravers's father the Earl of Arundel at Arundel House, illustrated by Wenceslaus Hollar in 1646 (although there is no proof that this is by Jones).[33] To these should probably be added the lodge Jones built in Hyde Park in 1634. No illustration of this two-storey brick building with a coved eaves cornice and dormers sur-

19   Inigo Jones, design for Maltravers House, City of London, 1638.

vives, but the building accounts suggest that it had a first-floor 'terras' or portico-in-antis similar to that at the Queen's House; it is unlikely to have had a portico.[34] Probably the nearest comparison is the design for Hale Lodge, which John Webb produced in 1638, although this is not known to have been executed.

Slightly grander but following the same basic pattern was Southampton House in Bloomsbury, begun by the 4th Earl of Southampton before October 1640 (Fig. 20).[35] As befitted the town house of a great noble, Southampton House was more elaborately decorated than those so far mentioned, its thirteen–bay façade, with a rustic, *piano nobile* and half-height windows above in the manner of Jones's Prince's Lodgings at Newmarket, had a slightly projecting central seven-bay range; quoins; triangular pediments over the windows of the *piano nobile* with aprons below and a segmental pediment over the door; and channelled rustication on the rustic. It also had dormer windows, although these were removed and a balustrade added in the eighteenth century. The architect is unrecorded but it is hard to envisage such an assured scheme coming from anywhere apart from Jones's office in the 1630s, the most likely candidate being Webb.

These buildings mark a radical development both from Jones's earlier work, and an even more significant shift from Jacobean architecture.[36] They rely primarily on the relationship between window and wall, and eschew the orders. Unlike Jacobean houses where the roof is either hidden behind a balustrade or broken up by

20 Anon., Southampton House, London, 1640 (demolished).

gables, they have an obvious hipped roof, generally with dormer windows, a feature that had first been developed in England in one of his designs for the Prince's Lodgings at Newmarket. At Newmarket, however, the roof was still supported by a complete cornice, while in later buildings this is generally reduced to a block cornice of the Roman type.

There are problems with these designs and with showing that Jones intended them to have a wider influence, especially on country houses. In particular, while there is visual evidence for the houses flanking St Paul, Covent Garden, and the Arundel office range, Jones's exact part in their design is unclear, nor is it known whether the designs for Lord Maltravers were executed or whether Sir Peter Killigrew's house was built exactly as shown.[37] Moreover, all the designs are for relatively humble buildings in an urban context where display would have been unsuitable, a context very different to that of a country house. Nevertheless, it is unlikely to be coincidence that during the 1630s there was the sudden emergence in London and the country of a consistent style very similar to these designs. Leicester House in Leicester Square, begun for Robert Sidney, 2nd Earl of Leicester in 1631, was early proof of this. It was an astylar two-storey house with a basement, hipped roof and dormers, and a pergola over the first floor.[38] Leicester House was demolished in 1791, but a contemporary house that has survived, despite vicissitudes, is West Woodhay Park, dated 1635 (Fig. 21).[39] It was built for Sir Benjamin Rudyerd, a friend of the 8th Earl of Pembroke and of Sir Henry

Wotton, pioneering collector of Palladio's drawings and author of *The Elements of Architecture* (1624) which praises Palladio's architecture. West Woodhay's south front is particularly close to Jones's design for Lord Maltravers (Fig. 19). Both buildings are of five bays and two equal storeys with a plat band, hipped roofs and modillion cornices. West Woodhay has been attributed to Edward Carter, Chief Clerk of the King's Works and successor to

21 Anon., West Woodhay, Berkshire, 1635.

22   Anon., Forty Hall, Middlesex, c.1629.

23   Anon., Chevening House, Kent, c.1630 (remodelled).

Jones as Surveyor-General, who acted as surveyor at Covent Garden and was responsible for the elaborate screen at Castle Ashby. Similarities between West Woodhay and nearby Aldermaston Court of 1636 have led to suggestions that they are by the same hand. Aldermaston also shows the same relation of window to wall and use of hipped roof and bold cornice. Proof that Carter was capable of working in this fashion comes from a design in the Berkshire Record Office for Easthampstead Lodge, built for Sir William Trumbull.[40] The design is for a slightly larger building than West Woodhay, but follows the same pattern of two equal storeys with casement windows divided by a plat band and topped by a hipped roof with emphatic cornice and dormers. Trumbull bought the estate in 1626, but the date of the design is unknown.

Coupled with these two-storey houses is a series of astylar compact-block three-storey houses: Forty Hall, built between 1629 and 1636 for Sir Nicholas Raynton (Fig. 22); Chevening, Kent, said to have been built by the 13th Lord Dacre who died in 1630 (Fig. 23);[41] and St Clere, only a few miles from Chevening, built about 1633. All have been altered to some degree: at St Clere the orginal wooden cornice has been replaced by a later parapet;[42] Forty Hall has nineteenth-century windows lighting the staircase;[43] Chevening has been substantially remodelled, but its original state is known from an estate map of 1679. In their original state all three must have been very similar, with two full-height storeys and a half storey above – although St Clere has a pair of essentially Jacobean towers on the entrance front. All these houses are anonymous, but it is hard to believe there was no link with Jones, and it may be that he provided guidance for the architects of some of these houses as he did for Stone and de Caus.

Related to Jones's astylar manner is the series of terraces in London and houses outside the City which follow it in the use of hipped roofs and dormers, but with the added feature of giant pilasters. These include Baulms House, Hackney (c.1635); houses in Great Queen Street and Lincoln's Inn Fields (c.1636–41); Lees Court, Kent (c.1640) (Fig. 24); Syndale House, Kent (c.1652); and Bayhall, Kent, built for Richard Amherst who died in 1664. The origins of this variant also lie in Serlio, whose seventh book has several houses with giant pilasters, both examples with plinths that cut across the level of the window, as at Lees Court, and others where the plinths stop at the bottom of the window, as at Bayhall.[44] The influence of Jones, if any, on these houses has never been established, but the sophistication of Lees Court – which compares well with Wilton or the Goldsmiths' Hall – would have met with his approval.

Conventionally, these pilastered houses are described as 'Artisan Mannerist'.[45] This is really a blanket term used to describe a whole series of stylistic approaches which do not fit in with what is perceived as Jones's 'pure' Classicism. Thus, buildings such as Lees Court, the Goldsmiths' Hall and Swakeleys – which combined a traditional Tudor H-plan with exuberant North European Classical detail – and the Dutch House at Kew (1631) or Tart Hall, Westminster[46] – compact double-pile houses with a more restrained use of gables than Swakeleys but distinguished from the work of Jones and his followers by their elaborate brickwork and lack of a sense of austerity – are lumped together, although there is more that divides than unites them.

The concept of Artisan Mannerism has led to talk of a City style contrasting with, and indeed reacting against, a Court style, particularly during the Commonwealth. This view was most recently argued by A.A. Tait in his

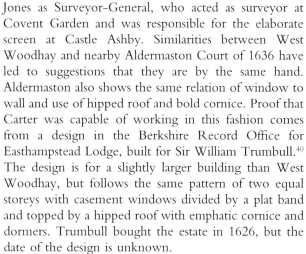

24   Anon., Lees Court, Kent, *c.*1640.

paper 'Post-Modernism in the 1650s', which argued that country houses built in the 1650s, epitomised by Thorpe Hall, Cambridgeshire (Fig. 27), were a conscious City-based rejection of the courtly work of Inigo Jones.[47] However, as has been shown above, much that is considered Artisan Mannerist was inspired by Jones. The stylistic dichotomy between 'pure' Jones and Artisan Mannerism only exists if Jones's buildings for the court of 1610 to 1624 are taken in isolation. Most of Inigo Jones's key Serlian or astylar buildings and designs – Sir Peter Killigrew's house, the Maltravers design in Lothbury, the Piazza at Covent Garden – were 'City' buildings, while the most important City building erected during the decade, the Goldsmiths' Hall, was heavily influenced by Jones. Furthermore, despite the precedent of the designs for the Prince's Lodgings at Newmarket with their pedimented centrepieces, the advanced country houses of the 1630s, for example West Woodhay, Chevening, Forty Hall, St Clere, built presumably under the influence of Jones, were urban types transported to the country, not Palladian villas. The exception is Stoke Bruerne, with its colonnaded wings, and it is significant that Sir Francis Crane was said to have 'brought the design from Italy'.[48]

It does seem that there were tensions between Jones and City artisans. This can be seen most clearly at St Michael-le-Querne where there was a direct confrontation with the City artisans who seem to have been unhappy with Jones's intervention – on the command of the Privy Council – in the church's design.[49] But, as seen above, the issue is by no means clear cut. Nor were the tensions only between the court and the City; they could also be found within the court. Howard Colvin has argued that in the frontispiece of the Canterbury Quadrangle at St John's College, Oxford (1631–6), Archbishop Laud, one of the country's most eminent courtiers, was responsible for promoting a very different Classicism to Jones's High Renaissance manner, based instead on the North European, specifically Flemish, Baroque. John Adamson has also pointed out that many of the great nobles who were the most important architectural patrons in London during the 1630s felt increasingly alienated from the court. Their number included the Earl of Southampton, whose Southampton House was the most distinguished example of the new Jonesian domestic Classicism built in London during the decade. Instead of dividing the 1630s into two camps, Jones and the rest, or into court and City, the 1630s should perhaps be seen as a period of stylistic diversity, with a number of different architectural approaches developing in parallel, although to a certain extent influenced by each other.[50]

By the late 1630s it is possible to identify a distinct new style, initiated by Jones but apparently taken up by others, a style of considerable sophistication, resting on a basic understanding of the principles of Classical propor-

tion. Its most important features are upright casement windows, set in a regular grid on bare brick walls; ground and first floors of equal height; hipped roofs, generally with dormers and emphatic wooden modillion cornices and quoining at the corners of the façades. Secondary characteristics are raised basements and plat bands, but these are not standard. Most of the houses whose ground-plans are known were compact double piles. The double pile, particularly when used in City houses, was not introduced by Jones. A significant number of Elizabethan examples can be found, particularly in John Thorpe's book of plans, and it seems to have been be increasingly common in the first decades of the seventeenth century; but with these houses it became a standard feature of medium-sized English houses.

The origins of this sort of house have yet to be properly analysed. In essence the compact two-storey double pile above a basement seems to have been an Italian rather than a North European idea, for example Giuliano da Sangallo's villa for Lorenzo de' Medici at Poggio a Caiano outside Florence begun about 1485, while this is the form of many of Palladio's simpler villas and innumerable examples can be found along the banks of the Brenta and elsewhere in Italy. However, Italian examples generally have shallow pitched roofs. The addition of steeper roofs with dormers seems to have been an adaptation to Northern European conditions, perhaps by Serlio, who worked in France in the mid-sixteenth century and whose seventh book, published posthumously in 1575 and owned by Jones in the Venice edition of 1619, includes a number of small astylar domestic buildings with windows set in a regular grid and hipped roofs with dormers and cornices.[51]

It is unclear what led Jones to introduce this novel style into England; it does not seem to have come from the Netherlands. He may have been led to it by his observations in Italy or he could have been taken it directly from Serlio – there is a particularly close source for the Maltravers design[52] – in the knowledge of its Italian origins. Alternatively, it may have specific origins in early seventeenth-century French architecture, but if so this source has yet to be identified. German examples may possibly have been significant; Elias Holl's St Anna Gymnasium in Augsburg (1612) anticipates much of what is later found in Jones.[53]

An austere domestic style did fit in with the understanding of architectural propriety which was always central to Jones's work.[54] Thus, in his mature architecture of the 1630s, temple-like porticos are reserved for religious buildings; royal buildings (the proposed Somerset House and Whitehall palaces) make elaborate use of the orders; and domestic buildings, even a royal villa such as the Queen's House, have their architectural ornament reduced to a minimum. Economy of material, where appropriate, no less than the correct use of the orders was one of the lessons Jones derived from Vitruvius.[55] However, Jones's system of decorum broke down when it came to designing the Lothbury warehouses, which are almost indistinguishable from his designs for houses despite their 'lower' status.

The extreme simplicity of Jones's domestic architecture probably also had a practical explanation. There can be no doubt that Jones wished to redirect the course of English building towards a more Classical manner; this can be seen in the support he gave to an architect such as de Caus and in the direct influence he exerted through his position as one of the Commissioners responsible for controlling new building in London. But Jones must have been aware of the problems of introducing Classicism when few craftsmen were skilled in its details. Where he was in charge of a building, Jones was able to enforce a sufficiently high standard of workmanship, as at the west portico at St Paul's Cathedral, but only through immense effort involving the use of full-scale models. To overcome this problem Jones would seem deliberately to have set about devising a Classical style that did not need highly trained craftsmen and was relatively cheap; Jones's Serlian and astylar manners are both marked by the absence of intricate Classical ornament.

Jones's great skill was his ability to work at two levels. In his most personal work he developed abstraction and neo-Classicism, but working with other less skilled architects and builders on more domestic projects he developed a practical, simple Classical style which did not require his depth of Classical knowledge. In this way he was not a solitary genius but a central figure in early Stuart architecture with a wide immediate impact.

Nor did Jones's influence cease with the Civil War. The war itself inevitably meant that new building ceased and, although fighting largely ended in 1645, little work apart from repairs was done before stability returned after 1649: in Dorset Captain Ryder repaired Cranborne Lodge for the Earl of Salisbury and added a new west wing from 1647; in Wiltshire de Caus's front at Wilton, which had been badly damaged by fire in 1647, was restored from 1648 by John Webb with the advice of Jones. From 1649 work seems to have picked up – Norgrove Court, Worcestershire, is dated 1649 on a bracket – and during the 1650s there was a wave of new country-house building, despite being a decade usually dismissed as of little architectural interest.[56] This new work was accompanied by the restoration or effective rebuilding of damaged houses, for example Belvoir Castle, Leicestershire, rebuilt by John Webb from 1655, and the series of Clifford castles rebuilt by Lady Anne Clifford in Yorkshire and Westmorland. Perhaps surprisingly, the decade was also one during which were erected or rebuilt a significant number of new churches: in London, St Matthias, Poplar (1654); in Berwick, Holy

Trinity (1652), and in Marlborough, St Mary's was given a new south arcade of Tuscan columns in 1653 after it was damaged by fire. Sir Robert Shirley rebuilt Staunton Harold Church, Leicestershire (1653), as a symbolic act of defiance to the regime, but the greatest church builder of them all was Lady Anne Clifford, who rebuilt no fewer than seven churches and chapels in Yorkshire and Westmorland.

Inevitably, building was dominated by those on the winning side – particularly in the first years of the decade, when Commonwealth confidence was at its peak following the final subjugation of Ireland and Scotland – and by those who accommodated themselves to the new regime. In Dorset, Sir Anthony Ashley-Cooper, who had led the Parliamentary forces in the county, rebuilt St Giles's House from 1651; Edmund Prideaux bought Forde Abbey in 1649, the year he was made Attorney-General, and substantially remodelled it; Sir Walter Erle, whose house at Charborough had been burnt, took his revenge by building a new one partly from material removed from Corfe Castle, owned by the Royalist Bankes family and scene of a bitter siege during the war. In Cambridgeshire, Chief Justice Oliver St John built Thorpe Hall (1653) and the Secretary of State, John Thurloe, built Wisbech Castle (1655). In Yorkshire, Lord Fairfax, former commander of the Parliamentarian armies, rebuilt or completed the rebuilding of Nun Appleton House; Colonel White extended Bishopthorpe Palace, formerly the property of the Archbishop of York, while Sir John Lewis, the East India Company's factor for nine years, profited from the fall of the Earl of Strafford by buying his partially rebuilt Ledston Hall in 1653 and completing it. Others include Chaloner Chute, subsequently Speaker of the House of Commons, at The Vyne, Hampshire (1654); Sir Henry Blount – who though a Royalist during the Civil War sided with the Commonwealth and sat on several of its commissions – at Tyttenhanger, Hertfordshire;[57] Sir John Maynard, sergeant-at-law in 1654 and Protector's sergeant in 1658, at Gunnersbury Park, Middlesex (c.1658); Sir George Pratt at Coleshill House, Berkshire;[58] Edmund Waller, a commissioner of trade from 1655, at Hall Barn, Buckinghamshire. There was even the odd Royalist such as Sir Justinian Isham at Lamport Hall, Northamptonshire (1654), or the Marquess of Hertford at Amesbury Abbey, Wiltshire, who could afford to build.[59]

Surveying these houses, it is the sense of continuity despite the hiatus of war and the change of regime that is most striking. As Timothy Mowl and Brian Earnshaw have reminded us, Jones's practice revived with the end of the war despite his great age (he died in 1652 aged seventy-eight).[60] He was not alone; his pupil Webb had a successful practice throughout the decade working for Parliamentarian and Royalist alike, while such men as Peter Mills, Edward Carter and John Jackson who had

25   Sir Roger Pratt, Coleshill House, Berkshire, c.1651 (demolished).

26   Inigo Jones, design for warehouses in Lothbury, City of London, 1638.

been practising before the war continued to do so under the Commonwealth.

The dominant style remained the compact double pile with hipped roof introduced by Jones. Generally, as at Charborough House, St Giles's House and Wisbech Castle, such houses were astylar, although some, such as Hall Barn and Welford Hall, Berkshire, had pilasters. Rather more ambitious were the houses of John Webb, but these were not alone in their architectural pretension. They would appear to have been rivalled by Chesterton House, Warwickshire (c.1655), which has been attributed to John Stone, the youngest son of Nicholas Stone. This is known only from a rather poor engraving which shows it to have been an impressively grand house based on Jones's Banqueting House with eleven bays, superimposed pilasters and a slightly empha-

27 Peter Mills, Thorpe Hall, Cambridgeshire, 1653.

sised frontispiece but no pediment.[61] Chesterton shows
how an intelligent architect such as Stone, who was
described as 'an excellent architect', was capable of developing a domestic style from Jones's early work for the
court. However, Stone was stricken with paralysis in
1660 and never recovered; he is not known to have built
any other houses and so Chesterton appears to be without issue. Instead, the two most significant houses of the
decade were Thorpe Hall (Fig. 27) and Coleshill House

(Fig. 25), both with intriguing links to Jones. The one
looks firmly back to the 1630s, the other forward into
the 1660s.

Thorpe Hall has been seen as a marked contrast with
the work of Jones, but it sits clearly in the tradition of the
three-storey compact country house of the 1630s, the
most direct parallel being with Chevening. There could
even be a direct link with Jones, for the façade closely
parallels Jones's unbuilt design for the Lothbury ware-

28   Peter Mills (attrib.), Wisbech Castle, Cambridgeshire, *c*.1658 (anon., oil).

houses (Fig. 26). Peter Mills may have learnt enough from studying Jones's work to design a house that coincidentally repeats one of his drawings, but there is a sophistication about the main elevations at Thorpe which is lacking in Mills's other works. It is known that Jones assisted other architects working after the Civil War in their designs, including John Webb at Wilton and probably Roger Pratt at Coleshill; the same could have happened at Thorpe. Mills would have known Jones before the Civil War when Jones was responsible for controlling new building in London and we know that Jones was not averse to working for Parliamentarians. It would have made sense for St John to consult the greatest architect of the day on his intended 'palace', about which he would probably have started thinking as soon as peace and his position was secure. Although the one building contract is dated 1654, planning could have begun before Jones's death in 1652. Without documen-

tary confirmation this remains speculation, but one cannot escape the close parallel between Thorpe and the Lothbury design.[62] What is certain is that Thorpe Hall shows how thoroughly the astylar manner had been established by the time of Jones's death.[63]

Coleshill House also sits firmly in Jones's astylar manner, but while Thorpe Hall continues the upright, essentially urban ideal of the 1630s Coleshill marks the development of a specifically rural style. The building history of Coleshill is extremely complicated.[64] Timothy Mowl and Brian Earnshaw have argued that Jones alone designed the house and that Roger Pratt only fitted up the interior after about 1656.[65] By contrast, Nigel Silcox-Crowe reckons that Jones had no part in the design of Coleshill and that the house was not begun until about 1657.[66] Certainly, fitting up continued into the early 1660s but this goes against the tradition of Jones's involvement which seems to be well founded. Sir Mark

Pleydell, who was born in 1693 and inherited Coleshill in 1728, recorded that John Buffin, 'Joyner to ye family for 50 years', who died an octogenarian in 1711, had told him that 'Sir G. Pratt began a seat in ye prest Cucumber Garden & raised it one storey when Pratt & Jones arriving caused it to be pulled down & rebuilt where it now stands. Pratt and Jones were frequently here & Jones was also consulted about ye ceilings.' Buffin, who would have been about twenty at the time, claimed that he 'often saw them both'.[67] If Buffin is to be believed, and was not confusing separate visits by the two architects, this would suggest that Jones gave his advice to a less experienced architect, as we have seen repeatedly happen elsewhere.

Much at Coleshill – the astylar elevations, the hipped roof, the quoins, plat bands and raised basement – is familiar from earlier works by Jones. In many ways the house is an extended version of the Maltravers design (Fig. 19), but it is Southampton House (Fig. 20) that provides the most important precedent for Coleshill, once it is realised that this dates from the late 1630s, not the late 1650s. Both have long and low elevations in contrast to the upright feel of most houses in the 1630s, and both try to control the width of their façades through subtle emphasis of the centre – the slight projection of Southampton House, the wider spacing of the windows at Coleshill. The most noticeable difference is that Coleshill has two full storeys over a rustic, not one and a half.

At Coleshill the arrangement of the façade creates a tripartite division that marks the internal organisation of the house. The only difference from Pratt's later houses is that this division is implied, not expressed through the use of a pediment. In plan the house has a highly complex and sophisticated arrangement of chambers, closets,

corridors and back stairs. There are elements of this at the Queen's House, particularly the double-height entrance hall and the use of chambers with pairs of closets, but the planning is more successful than at the Queen's House and the parallels are closer to Pratt's later houses. Finally, the form of the staircase appears to be based on that by Baldassare Longhena at San Giorgio Maggiore in Venice which Pratt could have seen but which Jones is unlikely to have known as it postdates his visit. It is true that extensive notes on Coleshill do not survive among Pratt's notebooks, but that does not of itself disprove his involvement, and if Jones was the sole original architect Sir George Pratt would certainly have needed somebody to control the erection of the house after his death in June 1652.

Coleshill, like other examples of the 1650s, was a transitional house. In the 1630s houses such as Chevening were characterised by their height, being five or seven bays wide and two and a half storeys high. Southampton House and Lees Court were exceptional in being markedly wider than they were tall. But while tall houses can still be found in the 1650s, particularly Hall Barn, Thorpe Hall, Tyttenhanger and Welford Hall, and many houses with only two storeys, such as Charborough, St Giles's House and Wisbech Castle (Fig. 28), are markedly compact, there is also a growing tendency to emphasise breadth rather than height. As well as at Coleshill, this can be seen at Highnam Court, Gloucestershire (c.1658) (Fig. 39), Syndale House and Yotes Court, Kent (1658). In the countryside there was less reason to build a tall but narrow house; a wide façade could appear more impressive. At Coleshill and elsewhere Jones's essentially urban domestic style of the 1630s began the change that would develop into Pratt's rural ideal of the 1660s.

POST-RESTORATION PALLADIANISM

JOHN WEBB THOUGHT HIS MOMENT had come with the Restoration of Charles II in 1660. He was much the most experienced architect in the country – as his petition to the king declared, he had been 'by the especiall command of yr Maties Royall Father of ever blessed memory, brought up by Inigo Jones Esqr, Yr Maties late Surveyor the Works in ye study of Architecture, for enabling him to do yor Royall Father and yr Matie service in ye said office'[1] – and he confidently expected to be made Surveyor-General of the Office of Works. The Interregnum had proved a hiatus in Webb's official career, but he had maintained a quietly prosperous private practice, remodelling Wilton, Wiltshire, in 1649, and Belvoir Castle, Leicestershire, from 1655, adding a sophisticated new range at Lamport Hall, Northampton-shire, in 1654 and building the first freestanding domestic portico to be seen in England at The Vyne, Hampshire, in 1654. When the Restoration occurred he was in the middle of erecting two impressive new houses, Gunnersbury House, Middlesex, and Amesbury Abbey, Wiltshire (Fig. 31). Not only did Webb believe that he had the best claim on the surveyorship, he could legitimately feel that with these houses he had developed an architectural style more advanced and Classically pure than anything any other British architect could offer. The time had at last come to place British architecture on a par with the Continent's most sophisticated buildings.

Webb was to be disappointed; the surveyorship went to Sir John Denham – 'a better poet than architect' according to John Evelyn[2] – and even the reversion of the post was denied him. But Webb's experience could not be ignored and he was given control of the monarchy's two most prestigious building projects, a new range at Somerset House, London, in 1661 for the Queen Mother (Fig. 29), and the new royal palace at Greenwich in 1664 (Fig. 30). Here at last Webb could show what he was capable of, designing an elaborate façade that looked back to Jones's early work for its inspiration, to the first confident flush of Stuart kingship – although at the same time developing Jones's ideas, particularly through the use of the giant order, a lesser but not unimportant feature of Palladio's work. Webb was using architectural

style to suggest that the Interregnum had been no more than a passing phase and to stress the continuing legitimacy of the Stuart line. But again Webb's hopes were not to be fulfilled; only one range of the palace was ever built and that was never fitted up. Inadequate finances were an important reason, but Charles II must have been aware of the political implications of his new palace and of Webb's use of an architectural style which for many of his subjects would have revived memories of absolutist monarchy. He must have realised that his position was not yet stable enough to make such a statement. It would not be until 1681 that the king, financially secure thanks to secret French subsidies, could afford to rule without Parliament and risk the absolutist statement of a new palace, at Winchester. This was begun in 1683 and was unfinished at the time of his death in 1685.

Denham died in 1669, but Webb was again passed over for the surveyorship in favour of an Oxford don, Dr Christopher Wren; disillusioned, he retired to Somerset, dying in 1672. His sophisticated style with its elaborate use of Classical detail and its complex system of proportion died with him. It was too much to hope that any private individual would emulate the lavishly expensive style of Greenwich Palace, but at Gunnersbury and Amesbury Webb had put forward models developed out of Jones's work for the increasingly fashionable compact villa-type houses, but neither seems to have exerted any significant influence. Nor did Somerset House, except at Badminton House, Gloucestershire, where it provided the model for the north front in the 1680s. Webb's problem, as Jones seems to have found before him, was that English architects and craftsmen were not ready for such sophisticated Classicism. Instead, the stylistic lead – and indeed Jones's mantle, assuming that they co-operated at Coleshill – passed to an apparently obscure Norfolk gentleman, Sir Roger Pratt, son of the younger son of a Norfolk squire.

Pratt is one of the more enigmatic figures of British architecture. Indeed, had it not been for the Civil War which forced him to spend six years among the Classical buildings of France and Italy he might never have become an architect at all. As it was, he practised for little more than a decade and is only known to have designed

29 John Webb, Somerset House, London, 1661 (Antonio Canaletto, oil, Yale Center for British Art, New Haven, Conn. (detail)) (demolished).

30 John Webb, Greenwich Palace, London, 1664, from *Vitruvius Britannicus* (1715).

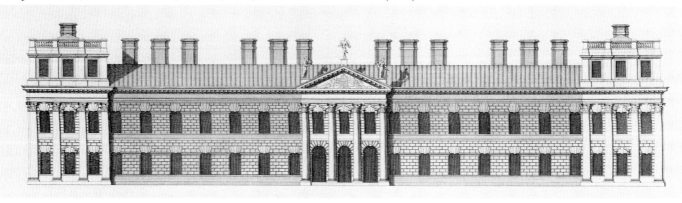

31 John Webb, Amesbury Abbey, Wiltshire, *c*.1660, from *Vitruvius Britannicus* (1725) (demolished).

32 Anon., Milton Manor, Berkshire, *c*.1660.

33 Sir Roger Pratt, design for Kingston Lacy, Dorset, 1663 (remodelled).

34 Sir Roger Pratt, Horseheath House, Cambridgeshire, 1663, from *Vitruvius Britannicus* (1725) (demolished).

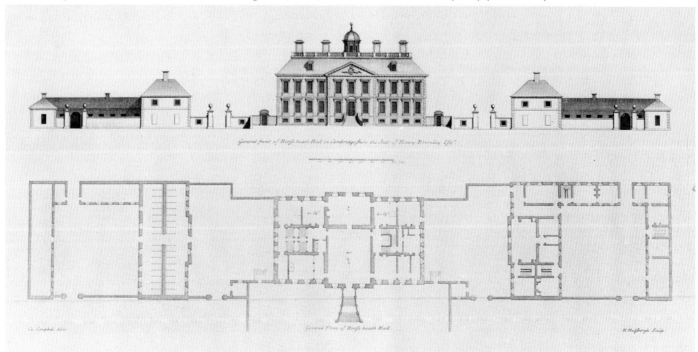

35   Sir Roger Pratt, Clarendon House, London, 1664 (demolished).

36   William Talman, Stanstead Park, Sussex, 1686, from *Britannia Illustrata* (1707).

37   Anon., Eagle House, Mitcham, Surrey, 1705.

four houses before he effectively gave up architecture when he succeeded to the family estate at Ryston on the death of his cousin in 1664. Thereafter, he designed only one more house, for himself in Norfolk, passing his time instead writing a treatise on architecture which was never published. Despite this brief career, it can be argued that Pratt was one of Britain's most influential architects.

Pratt's importance lies in the central role he played in the establishment of the classic Restoration house, epitomised by Kingston Lacy, the house he built in Dorset in 1663 (Fig. 33). Milton Manor, Oxfordshire, built about 1660–3, shows that the tall, compact, essentially urban type of house popular in the 1630s survived the Restoration, but it was one of the last of its kind (Fig. 32).[3] The type of house which took its place was a tripartite

double pile with a central pediment, of two storeys with a basement, dormers and cupola, generally of brick with quoins and a wooden modillion cornice, the prototype for which had been Coleshill House, Berkshire, built during the Interregnum (Fig. 25). In its more generous proportions, with breadth being emphasised rather than height, Coleshill shows how Pratt reinterpreted the city model of the 1630s to the country. In his later houses – Kingston Lacy (1663), Horseheath, Cambridgeshire (1663) (Fig. 34) and Clarendon House, Piccadilly (1664) (Fig. 35) – he added a pedimented centrepiece, partly because the length of the façade needed breaking to prevent it becoming monotonous (a problem which is evident at Lees Court, Kent (Fig. 24), and which Coleshill, despite its subtle fenestration, does not quite overcome); partly because the pediment provided the

38   Anon., Stedcombe House, Devon, *c.*1697.

39 Anon., Highnam Court, Gloucestershire, 1658.

40 Anon., Bell Hall, Naburn, Yorkshire, 1680.

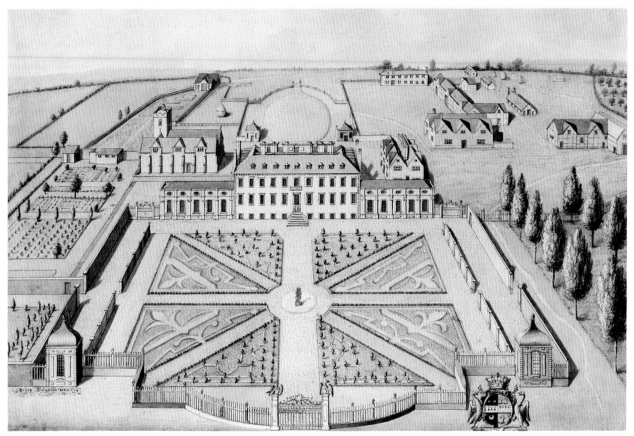

41   Anon., Croome Court, Worcestershire, c.1670 (demolished) (Henry Brighton, pen and wash, Society of Antiquaries, London).

mark of distinction which landowners thought suitable to their status; and partly because of the connotations of Italian sophistication which it carried.

As a model this was to be immensely influential, becoming the standard type of house for the greater gentry and lesser aristocracy for the rest of the century. The point is simply made by looking at *Britannia Illustrata*, published in 1707, where seven examples ranging from 1670 to 1692 make it easily the most characteristic type of new house (Fig. 36). It served equally well as a villa for the middle classes, as at Eagle House, Mitcham, built for Catherine of Braganza's physician, Fernandez Mendez, in 1705 (Fig. 37). These are only a small selection of the number that could have been chosen. Shorn of its wooden cornice, dormers and cupola, the basic ideal of the compact double-pile, tripartite house with a central pediment was to remain a dominant feature in British architecture throughout the eighteenth century.

At the same time, a simpler version, lacking a pediment and generally only five bays wide, quickly became the most common type of medium-sized urban and rural house, popular with lesser landowners, rich clergymen and merchants, such as Stedcombe House, built for Richard Hallett in about 1679 (Fig. 38). This derived

more directly from the smaller astylar houses of the 1630s, such as Jones's design for Lord Maltravers. Its diffusion into the provinces can be seen through houses such as Thorney Abbey, Cambridgeshire, a five-bay house built by the Peterborough mason John Lovin for the 5th Earl of Bedford in 1661, and Fairford Park, Gloucestershire, a seven-bay house only a few miles from Coleshill, built by the Taynton mason Valentine Strong in 1661–2. Rather grander was Croome Court, Worcestershire, built for the 3rd Lord Coventry, who succeeded in 1661 and died in 1681, which had an unbroken eleven-bay façade (Fig. 41).[4] Samuel Buck's sketches of Yorkshire houses, such as Bell Hall, Naburn (Fig. 40), made about 1720, reveal the prevalence of this model, illustrating more than twenty examples, which makes it much the most popular type of new house in the county.[5] The importance of metropolitan example in this spread can be seen at Lyndon Hall in Rutland, a seven-bay house planned in 1667 and built by John Sturges between 1672 and 1677. Here, Sir Abel Baker's notes on architecture are headed *Observacons concerning Architecture taken out of Palladio Gerbier and the Act for the rebuilding of the City of London* (that is, the 1667 Act following the Great Fire).[6]

Falling between these two types were houses which

42   Hugh May, Eltham Lodge, Kent, 1664.

43   Hugh May, Cornbury Park, Oxfordshire, 1666.

continued the traditional H-plan of the English manor house but clad in the astylar, hipped-roof and dormers manner and with the wings reduced to slight projections. West Woodhay Park, Berkshire (1635), and Aldermaston Court, Berkshire (1636), are early examples of this, and Commonwealth examples included Highnam Court, Gloucestershire (1658) (Fig. 39), and Yotes Court, Kent (1658). This model was taken up for some larger houses. Denham – subsequently Burlington – House, Piccadilly (1667) and Denham Place, Buckinghamshire (1688), are substantial examples of the type, but it was generally reserved for lesser houses, such as Whixley Hall, Yorkshire, which is illustrated in *Britannia Illustrata*.

This simple Classical style, based essentially on the relationship between a regular, symmetrical grid of upright windows and bare wall was to be immensely influential. With an overlay of Classical detail, particularly around the doorcase, it subsequently came to be described as 'Georgian' architecture, but, as already seen, its roots lie in the early seventeenth century, long before the first of the Georges came to the throne in 1715, and it continued to be one of the most characteristic ways to build in the countryside well after the death of the last George in 1830.

What are the sources for the Kingston Lacy type of house? The only astylar tripartite pedimented house that may have been built in England before the Restoration in 1660 was Inigo Jones's Prince's Lodgings at Newmarket of 1618–19 (Fig. 4), demolished about 1650, for which the drawing survives. Unfortunately, while the building accounts confirm many of the details in the drawing, they also make clear that the executed building was a severely reduced version of this scheme of five rather than seven bays, and make no mention of a pediment.[7] There is no evidence of any other astylar pedimented houses built in England until Pratt's Kingston Lacy and Horseheath House, both of 1663.

It is often claimed that the Restoration type of house was imported from the Netherlands after 1660, principally by Hugh May, and was based on the work there of Jacob van Campen and Pieter Post.[8] May, appointed Paymaster of the Works at the Restoration and Comptroller in 1668, designed three important houses in the 1660s: Eltham Lodge, Kent (1664) (Fig. 42), Berkeley House, Piccadilly (1665), and Cornbury Park, Oxfordshire (1666) (Fig. 43). He is known to have spent at least part of the Interregnum in the Netherlands, and there is an undoubtedly Dutch character about Eltham Lodge and Cornbury Park – particularly in their pilastered centrepieces and the Ionic capitals of Eltham – although the similarity is less with Jacob van Campen's Mauritshuis in The Hague (1633) (Fig. 44), to which they are generally compared, than with the Sebastiaansdoelen of Arent van 's Gravesande, also in The Hague (1636) (Fig. 45). But,

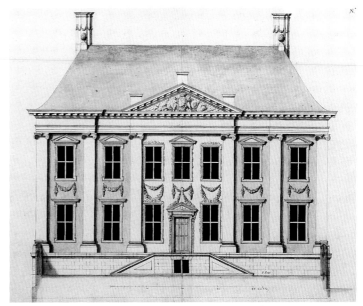

44 Jacob Van Campen, the Mauritshuis, The Hague, Netherlands, 1633.

45 Arent van 's Gravesande, Sebastiaansdoelen, The Hague, Netherlands, 1636.

as has been seen, much that is portrayed as being novel and therefore Dutch about Eltham – in particular the compact double pile, the basement offices, the astylar façades, the use of quoins and plat bands, the hipped roof, the cupola – had been current in England for thirty years, while Pratt had already perfected the idea of the tripartite pile before May built Eltham. Moreover, the elements which could be seen to be specifically Dutch about Eltham and Cornbury – the pilastered centrepieces and the Ionic capitals – seldom appear again in seventeenth-century English architecture, even in May's own work. One rare exception was Snitterfield House, Warwickshire, which was demolished in the nineteenth century but is known from a painting by John Wotton. This was probably built by Thomas Coventry, later Earl of Coventry, after he purchased Snitterfield in 1668. Its foreignness when compared with other Restoration houses shows how alien specifically Dutch imports appear in England.[9]

It is hard to see that the development of the Restoration country house would have differed in any way had May not built Eltham and Cornbury. It is possible (as will be argued below) that Dutch examples did have an influence on the Restoration house, but its essential origins lie in England, with Pratt taking the astylar house of the 1630s and recasting it in light of his own, specifically Palladian, ideas – not just the ideas of Andrea Palladio as revealed in his *Quattro libri dell'architettura* (1570) but also of his followers Vincenzo Scamozzi (whose *Dell'idea dell'architettura universale* was published in 1615), Inigo Jones and Roland Fréart (author of the *Parallèle de l'architecture antique et de la moderne* of 1650), together with elements of Palladio's predecessor Sebastiano Serlio, all being overlaid by respect for Vitruvius.

The influence of Jones's astylar manner is clear in Pratt's houses, but it is perhaps as important to point out that he borrowed with discretion, and that what he did not take from the Jonesian-led architecture of the 1630s is as significant as what he did. In particular no Serlian *oeil-de-boeuf* or round-headed windows are to be found in his buildings. Nor did he use columns, pilasters or rustication (except with great restraint at Coleshill). In this austerity he seems to have set a new direction for architecture, for while buildings erected during the Commonwealth reveal many of these features, they seldom appear after the Restoration. Althorp, Northamptonshire, built in 1665–8 for the Earl of Sunderland, stands out as a rare example of a house with pilasters, but it has few parallels. Thus, Pratt did not just take up where Jones left off, he made a specific selection from what was fashionable in the 1630s and 1650s and his architectural notebooks identify what lay behind that selection.

Pratt's notebooks reveal a close and critical study of buildings and books; a developed theoretical approach to architecture; and a firm grasp of constructional detail. 'No man', he declared, 'deserves the name of an Architect, who has not been very well versed both in those old ones of Rome, as likewise the more modern of Italy and France etc.'[10] Unfortunately, the thirteen critical pages in his history or 'complete body of architecture', which might have provided a concise summary of his architectural beliefs, are missing.[11] However, there are plenty of other references which make these easy to establish.

If the 'etc.' above refers to Dutch architecture, then it is the only reference to the buildings of that country in his notes. Pratt's architectural analysis concerns itself only with France and Italy. The notes show that he was well acquainted with French architecture, both domestic and religious. He distinguished French houses for 'the extent and cheerfulness of their courts; the multiplicity and curiosity of their ornaments and carvings; neatness and variety of their roofs; and delicacy of their whole composure' (all features noticeable by their absence in his buildings). But he considered that Italian houses far surpassed French houses 'in the greatness of their breadth, loftiness of their height; distinctness, regularity and judgment in all their ornament, and proportions; manliness of their strength and majesty of their aspect'.[12]

Pratt had spent time in Rome with John Evelyn, who described him as 'My old friend & fellow traveller (cohabitant & contemporarie at Rome)',[13] and knew Palladio's buildings at first hand: 'In Vicenza I have observed another order of work, in those houses designed by that excellent architect Palladio, whose country it was.'[14] He would have been able to examine these at greater length when he studied law at nearby Padua, which would have given him the chance to explore the villas of the surrounding countryside: 'I have besides these taken notice of other sorts of buildings in the country, called Villas, but in the Venetian Territory some whereof were of the design of the skilfull master aforesaid.'[15] This detailed knowledge of Italy gave Pratt the advantage over many of his contemporaries, and his cousin Edward Pratt was quite accurate to declare that 'they will get more secrets of your art brought from Rome, & so from Athens, then you from them' when congratulating him on his appointment to the commission to rebuild St Paul's Cathedral with May and Wren in 1666.[16]

Pratt identified three sorts of Italian architecture: 'Alla Romana, Venetiana, and Genoese.'[17] The general effect of Genoese architecture pleased him and he considered the view of Genoa from the sea 'one of the most ravishing sights that can well be imagined', but he was less impressed by its detail. Rubens's *Palazzi di Genova* (1622) was closely examined, but under the heading 'Faultes of these buildings', of which he specifically listed eleven, concluding that 'The contraryes to all which errors will easily give you the perfections of a building.'[18] On the other hand, Roman architecture is neither praised nor condemned, and Vignola is only referred to as a source of ornament.

There is no doubt of the architects whom Pratt considered to be fit models, above all 'that excellent architect Palladio': 'A man may receive some helps upon a most diligent study from those excellent, and most exact designs of Palladio, Fréart, Scamozzi and some few others.'[19] Again, when advising on the choice of architect he suggested chosing 'some ingenious gentleman who has seen much of that kind abroad and been somewhat versed in the best authors of Architecture: viz Palladio, Scamozzi, Serlio, etc.'[20]

This broad praise is consistently followed up by reference to these writers when faced by practical problems: 'Serlio hath supplied what yett seemed to be wanting, in exactly shewing us how a Portico may be made in Arco, without either Pilaster, or Columne, vide Serlio Lib: 4, Page 8 in foglio'; 'As to the ornament of them . . . *vide* Scamozzi in his books of Architecture'; 'As to the soffit the breadth of it is ascertained by Scamozzi . . .'; 'it is generally adorned with some single or double round Guiloche, or square one, whereof you may see divers examples both in Serlio and Fréart'; 'As concerning the depth of these seeming beams, I find only two dimensions set down by Scamozzi'; 'Cornices are either divided after the way of Scamozzi . . . Or, after the way of Palladio'; 'we proceed to divide the whole architrave, frieze and cornice as we find it set down in Palladio, Fréart, etc.'; 'The beams it's true here must be *Trabes Euerganeae*, whereof you will see examples in Vetruvius, Serlio etc.'; 'Mem. that a cornice is much easier drawn after the way of Scamozzi than of Palladio'.[21]

Pratt also had a profound, although not uncritical, admiration for Inigo Jones, particularly his use of antique and Palladian detail. His notebooks reveal close examination of Jones's work at St Paul's Cathedral ('recourse was therefore . . . had to the reliques of the most famous buildings of the Ancient Greeks and Romans, from which all things were borrowed . . . The first of these Cornishes was taken from that about the Court of Marte Vendicatore at Rome . . . The uppermost Cornish seems to be taken from that 2nd one of the Pantheon, *vide* Palladio Lib. 4. Pag: 78'); St James's Chapel; St Paul, Covent Garden; the Queen's House at Greenwich; the closet at Somerset House and the Banqueting House. He also makes it clear that he knew Wilton. In all cases his interest sprang from the problems of actual building, indeed, he sent his plasterer, Mr Grove, to measure the ceiling at the Banqueting House to help him at Coleshill.[22] The one building that is missing from this list of Jones's work is the Prince's House at Newmarket. It would be interesting to know if he ever saw this, but as it was demolished around the time that Pratt returned to England in 1649 and is not referred to in the notebooks it must be presumed he did not.

Pratt's Palladian philosophy influenced him in two principal areas: in the accurate use of Classical detail and in the general form of the building, particularly its simplicity of ornament. The range of Serlian details evident in buildings of the 1630s and 1650s is avoided, as is the complex Classical decoration found in John Webb's work and the multiplicity of ornament Pratt noted in French buildings.

Pratt prefered one plain, compact building under a single roof. 'They are generally but small, as from seven windows to nine, which are without ornament, and their height is sometimes one whole storey and two half

ones . . . and sometimes they are two whole ones' – his description of Palladio's villas could equally refer to his own houses. 'Distinctness, regularity and judgement in all their ornaments, and proportions', the best qualities of Italian architecture, were his own ideals.[23]

Pratt's description of Palladio's villas notes that 'their chief adornment is a portico with a frontispiece'.[24] None of his houses had porticos, unlike those of his contemporary, Webb. Pratt's reason was simple, the English climate made them impractical for country houses: 'by no means . . . proceede to a rash and foolish imitation without first maturely weighing the condition of the severall climes, the different manner of living etc.'.[25] In this Pratt was following a precept of Vitruvius's: 'If our designs for private houses are to be correct, we must at the outset take note of the countries and climates in which they are built . . . In the north, houses should be entirely roofed over and sheltered as much as possible.'[26] Secure in this knowledge Pratt severely criticised the hall and portico at John Webb's Gunnersbury as 'verry faulty', despite their Palladian precedents.[27] Not that Pratt was against the appropriate domestic use of porticos, that is on royal buildings, and his notes on a house for the prince, probably the Duke of York, include suggestions for a portico modelled on that of the Pantheon.[28]

Instead, Pratt kept the architectural accent and tripartite form provided by a central pediment, but placed it flat against the façade, rather than projecting it as a portico. Palladio provided precedents, some with pilasters, but others, such as the Villa Poiana and the Villa Saraceno, are astylar. Pratt was not concerned with the direct imitation of the plans of Palladio's villas, but his basic tripartite division, particularly at Kingston Lacy and Horseheath, where a deep entrance hall leads to a smaller parlour with lesser rooms on either side, derives from Palladio. In the absence of any corpus of drawings by Pratt, it is difficult to be certain about his attitude towards proportion, but this does not feature largely in his notes and does not appear to have held for him the significance it did for Webb. Thus, Pratt distilled the essence of the Palladian villa and applied it to current English architectural models to create the English version of the villa. It was this that made it such an ideal type for the country house.

Pratt was not working in isolation; his notebooks show how close links were between the handful of leading architects in London. It is clear that Pratt must have studied May's works closely (he refers to the detail of the brickwork at Eltham Lodge) and the two must also have exchanged technical information as he had a copy of the carpenter's agreement made by May for Berkeley House. Indeed, Pratt's notebooks show how aware contemporary architects were of each other's work: besides the references to May's houses he has detailed com-

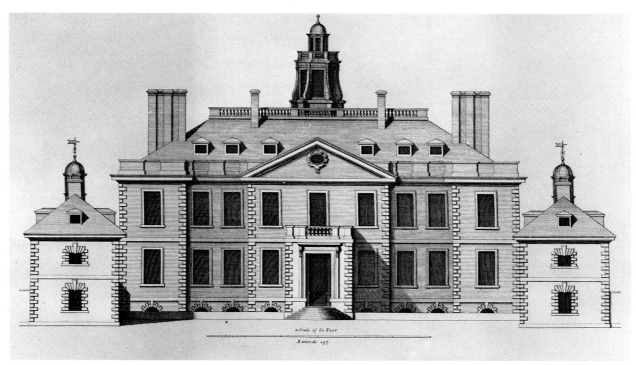

46   William Samwell, Eaton Hall, Cheshire, 1675, from *Vitruvius Britannicus* (1717) (demolished).

ments or information on John Webb's Gunnersbury
Park; Somerset House; Wisbech Castle, Cambridgeshire;
Wilde House and Mr Povey's house in Lincoln's Inn
Fields; Sir Charles Cotterell's house in Spring Gardens;
Belsize House in Hampstead; Sir John Denham's house
in Piccadilly and Southampton House in Bloomsbury.[29]
One architect whom Pratt does not mention is William
Samwell; of all the architects working in the 1660s and
1670s on the post-Restoration house, Samwell's plan-
ning was the most adventurous. Sadly, all his important
houses have been altered or demolished, but Eaton Hall,
Cheshire (1675), shows a sense of massing and a use of
rusticated window surrounds that sets Samwell apart
from his contemporaries (Fig. 46).[30]

This shared knowledge, and the close circle within
which the architects worked, helps explain how a new
style could be established so quickly. It also suggests that
it would be wrong to give Pratt sole credit for the
establishment of his Palladian style. He was certainly not
alone among his contemporaries in his respect for
Palladio and it would probably be fair to see his
Palladianism as, in part, the creation of a particular intellectual milieu.

The course had been set by Sir Henry Wotton's *The
Elements of Architecture* (1624), one of the few architectural books published in England before the Restoration,
and one of only two written in English – the other being
John Shute's very rare *First and Chief Groundes of Architecture* of 1563. Wotton's is a short book but it sets forward
a consistent theory of architecture: he saw the roots of

architecture as lying in Classical antiquity, and specifically Vitruvius – 'Our principall Master is Vitruvius', the
preface declares. 'Commoditie, Firmenes and Delight',
Wotton's paraphrase of Vitruvius's three maxims of
building, were to be its aim.[31] The book's practical base
lay in the more academic of the Italian Renaissance
writers and architects: Alberti, author of the strongly
theoretical *De re aedificatoria*, based on exhaustive study of
Vitruvius and Roman buildings, which was first published in 1485; Palladio – Wotton would have known
his work from his years as ambassador to Venice and
owned some of his drawings – whose *I quattro libri
dell'architettura* of 1570 included descriptions of the
orders, together with illustrations of his own works and
surveys of Roman remains; and his pupil Scamozzi
(whom Wotton could have met in Venice), author of
Dell'idea dell'architettura of 1615, which promoted a
purer, more academic Classicism.

It is unclear how much practical effect Wotton's book
had when it was first published, but by the Restoration
its influence was evident, being frequently cited, usually
in connection with Palladio or Scamozzi. Its most accessible version came in the condensed volume published in
1671 with *The Mirror of Architecture*, the English translation of Scamozzi's sixth book – a small book aimed as
craftsmen and builders. By 1750 the *Elements* had re-
appeared sixteen times in different forms.[32] The introduction to *The Mirror of Architecture* reveals the esteem in
which Wotton was then held: 'In this edition, that the
book may be the more complete, you have a Treatise

containing the ground rules of architecture being the substances of what was writ by the learned and judicious Sir Henry Wotton in his Elements of Architecture.' Significantly, it was to Wotton that Godfrey Richards appealed for justification in the preface of his 1663 translation of Palladio's first book: 'The subject of this translation, being architecture, doth in the opinion of Sr Hen Wotton need no commendation where there are noble men or noble minds.' Richards then goes on to praise the *Elements*:

> We have but few books which I can recommend to you, besides the excellent discourses of Sir H. Wotton and John Evelyn Esq, the former on the Elements of Architecture, and the latter in his accompt of Architecture and Architects (added to his elegant translation of the Parallel), where they comprised fully and clearly the weighty observations of the Art.

The 'Parallel' to which Richards refers was *A Parallel of the Antient Architecture with the Modern* (1664), a translation, with significant additions by John Evelyn, of Roland Fréart's *Parallèle de l'architecture antique et de la moderne* of 1650, and perhaps the most important of the handful of architectural books translated into English in the 1660s. In it Evelyn refers to Wotton in the same breath as the Classical and Renaissance masters when discussing the '*Matter and Form* of Buildings': study '*Vitruvius* l2 c3 ad 9. *Palladio* I c2. *Alberti* l.2.c45.46. *Dan Barbaro* lii. Sir H. Wotton in his concise and useful *Theorems*, etc. and in what shall be found most beneficial for our *Climat*.'[33]

Fréart's book was a powerfully argued polemic in favour of '*Andrea Palladio* and *Scamozzi*, two of the greatest *Masters* which we have of the *Profession*'.[34]

> The first of all is without any contest the famous *Andrea Palladio*, to whom we are oblig'd for a very rare Collection of antique *Plans* and *Profiles* of all sorts of Buildings, design'd after a most excellent manner, and measur'd with a diligence so exact, that there is nothing more in that particular left to us to desire: Besides the very advantageous opportunities which he has had at *Venice*, and in all the *Vincentine* his native country do leave us such markes as clearly shewd him not onely to have been a Spectator of these great *Masters* of *Antiquity*; but even a Competitor with them and emulous of their glory.[35]

In it, after several introductory chapters he describes each of the orders with comparative plates from Palladio and Scamozzi, Barbaro's commentary on Vitruvius and Cataneo, Alberti and Viola, de l'Orme and Bullant. His aim was to show that contemporary architects in France and Italy were licentious and that only a purer architecture based on Palladio and Classical antiquity should be followed:

the writings of the *Moderns* are but loose *Earth*, and ill bottom'd, upon which one can erect nothing that is substantial and solid . . . its now become as it were the *mode*, I should say an universal *madness*, to esteem nothing fine, but what is fill'd and surcharged with all sorts of *Ornaments*, without discretion or the least affinity to the *Work* or the *Subject* . . . In fine, one may truly say, that poor *Architecture* is very ill-treat'd amongst them: But it were not just to impute this great reproach to our *French* Work-men onely; The *Italians* themselves are now become more *licentious*.[36]

The solution was clear:

> I value nothing unless it be conformable to some famous and antient *Example*, or to the Precepts of *Vitruvius* that *Father* of *Architects*; so that (if possible) I may at last reestablish the *Art* on its genuine *Principles*, and original purity from whence those licentious *compositions* of our late *Workmen* have so exceedingly perverted it.[37]

However, Vitruvius remains 'grave and abstruse' even in Barbaro's commentary, 'the best of them all . . . without exception . . . as well for his excellent *Commentaries*, as for the exactitude, and cleanness of his *designs*'.[38] The answer was to follow Palladio and Scamozzi 'who having propos'd to themselves the imitation of the antient *Architects* by studying those admirable Monuments yet remaining in the City of *Rome*, have follow'd a *manner* infinitely more noble, and *proportions* more elegant than those of the School of Vitruvius.'[39] And of these two it is Palladio who is undoubtedly the greater, Scamozzi being 'a much inferiour workmen, and less delicate in his point of design . . . He is notwithstanding *this* the nearest that approaches him as to the regularity of his proportions, and the most worthy to be paralleld with *Palladio*'.[40] Thus, Fréart is a Palladian propagandist; it was not just because he was a convenient source of different versions of the orders that Evelyn translated him.

The *Parallel* was by no means the only book of a Palladian nature published in English during the decade. Other books sympathetic to the same programme include *The First Book of Architecture, by Andrea Palladio* (1663); Webb's *Vindication of Stone-Heng Restored* – an expanded edition of Jones's *Stone-Heng Restor'd* – (1665); Julien Mauclerc's *A New Treatise of Architecture, According to Vitruvius* (1669); and Scamozzi's sixth book as *The Mirror of Architecture* (1669).

Evelyn's diary reveals that his interest in Palladio, whom he describes as 'the great architect'[41] (in his addition to the *Parallel* he also refers to him as 'the incomparable Palladio',[42]) was based on first-hand experience of his work. He was full of admiration for Vicenza 'this swete towne [which] has more well built Palaces than any of its dimensions in all *Italy*';[43] although a desire to visit the Villa Rotunda was frustrated by his less architecturally-minded companions ordering the coach to leave before he was ready. He also praised San Giorgio Maggiore in Venice and (mistakenly) considered Santa Giustina in Padua (a building which Wotton also singled out) 'an incomparable piece of Architecture of *Andrea Paladios*'.[44] Nor was the translation of Fréart Evelyn's only contribution to architectural education; he was probably responsible for persuading Christopher Wase to translate Vitruvius into English, but although the text was completed by 1671 it was never published, perhaps because it was forestalled by Claude Perrault's French translation in 1673.[45]

It is Evelyn who provides evidence of May's interest in Palladio. When Evelyn noted that the porticos (by which he probably means the quadrants) at Berkeley House were taken from Palladio, the source was almost certainly May himself: 'my good friend Mr Hugh May, his lordship's architect, effected it'[46] (this reference is unusually precise documented proof of a Palladian design). Restoration houses often had wings containing stables and other offices flanking a courtyard, but May's use of quadrants at Berkeley House to link the house and its wings is unusual in the seventeenth century, although it had been anticipated before the Civil War at Stoke Bruern, Northamptonshire. Similar quadrants to those at Berkeley House, this time arcaded, were suggested in an anonymous plan for the outer courtyard at Lowther Castle, Cumbria, of about 1677. This must be the work of the unnamed 'Architect who came from London to survey the house at Lowther' in 1677. In the event, the quadrants were not built, but the suggested use of quadrants and the similarity of the stables to those at Cornbury Park, Oxfordshire, makes May a plausible candidate for their design.[47] Evelyn's comment that May

had chosen the worst model in Palladio's book only serves to emphasise his own close study of Palladio's work. Evelyn also reveals that May's interest in Palladio extended beyond using the Italian as a source of individual motifs to his wider principles: according to the preface to the *Parallel*, it was entirely at May's prompting that Evelyn finished its translation, even procuring a complete set of the plates from which Evelyn could work.

Evelyn and May's intention was to improve the taste of English workmen – who, when criticised, retorted that they were not prepared to be taught their trade – by overcoming the problem of the 'few assistances which our *Workmen* have of this nature'. Fréart was chosen, as Evelyn explained in the preface to his translation, because 'There is not in the whole *Catalogue* of *Authors* who have Written on this Subject a more safe, expedite and perfect guide than this Parallel . . . we might by the conversation of this *Author* alone, promise our *Country* and the *Age* to come, a miraculous improvement of their *Buildings* in a short time'. It was not without effect. Roger North later commented that

> Afterwards I procured some books of architecture, as Palladio and Scamozzi; but I found that the Parallel translated by Mr Evelyn gave me most clear instruction . . . hence I had a clear notion of the five orders, with their appendices: and besides the authors named, I procured Mr Desgodetz' *Survey of Antiquities*, which is a most exact and beautiful work. Vitruvius I had read over, as printed by Elzevir, with the notes of Danl Barbaro, but was more pleased with the French [presumably Perrault's edition] because of the great curiosity of the cuts, as the explanations and discourses annexed to the text.[48]

North's list is a straightforward enumeration of classic Palladian texts.

That reform was Evelyn's motivation is shown in the *Parallel*'s dedication, significantly to the Surveyor-General, Sir John Denham:

> all the mischiefs and absurdities in our modern *Structures* proceed chiefly from our busie and *Gotic* triflings in the *Composition* of the *Five Orders* . . . It is from the *asymmetrie* of our *Buildings*, want of *decorum* and proportion in our *Houses*, that the irregularity of our *humours* and affections may be shrewdly discern'd.

Reform was also Pratt's goal: 'Architecture here has not as yet received those advantages which it has in other parts, it continuing almost as rude here as it was at the very first.'[49] The plain simplicity of Palladio, together with accurate use of the orders, seemed to him the best way to achieve this. By reducing Classical design to its simplest elements Pratt introduced a style well suited to the architectural development of this country and its success is proof of the efficacy of his vision.

47   Sir Christopher Wren, Sheldonian Theatre, Oxford, 1664, from Daniel Loggan's *Oxonia Illustrata* (1675).

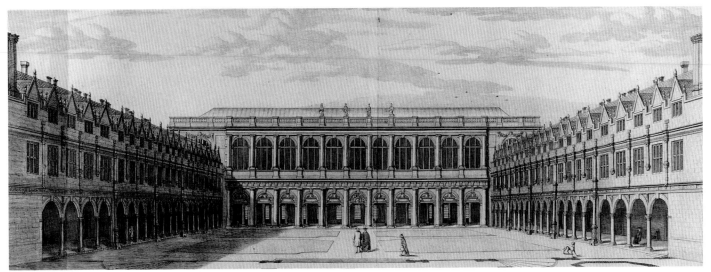

48   Sir Christopher Wren, Trinity College Library, Cambridge, 1676, from Daniel Loggan's *Cantabrigia Illustrata* (1688).

Another contemporary with an interest in Palladio was Christopher Wren, the sale catalogue of whose library includes three editions of the *Quattro libri*.[50] Wren must have known Pratt and May well as he was asked to give advice with them on repairs to St Paul's Cathedral in 1663, the three subsequently being appointed commissioners for rebuilding the City of London after the Great Fire in 1666. Palladio's influence can be seen clearly in the first half of Wren's career. The façade of the Sheldonian Theatre in Oxford (1664) (Fig. 47) with its interlocking pediments is probably based on Palladio's reconstruction of the Basilica of Maxentius, also probably the source for one of his early schemes for the west front of St Paul's. Wren's first design, of about 1676, for a new library at Trinity College, Cambridge, is a development of the idea of the Villa Rotunda. A single applied hexastyle Ionic portico leads into a circular reading room under a dome modelled on that of the Villa Rotunda but distorted by a slightly uncomfortable clerestory added to provide light.[51] As built (Fig. 48), the courtyard front of the library can be read as an interpretation of the cloister of the Convent of the Carità in Venice, illustrated in Palladio's second book, but without the attic storey (Fig. 49). Summerson notes that the portals on the river front are based on the attic doorway in Barbaro's edition of Vitruvius, which was illustrated by Palladio.[52]

Nor was Wren uninfluenced by the example of Jones and Webb. The Corinthian giant order of the portico on the Great Model of St Paul's followed in the tradition of Jones's portico. As built, the detail of the upper storey of St Paul's owes much to the Banqueting House. More directly, in his royal buildings Wren's followed the example of Webb at The Vyne and at Greenwich Palace in the use of attached and freestanding porticos. That initially intended for the east front of Hampton Court comes as no surprise after Greenwich,[53] while The Vyne

anticipated the freestanding porticos of Chelsea Hospital (1682) (Fig. 50). However, while there are Palladian influences in Wren's work his sources are too varied for him to be considered a Palladian, and in the second half of his career Palladian influence is hard to identify.

The second half of the seventeenth century is generally seen as a half century between the eras of Inigo Jones and Colen Campbell when Palladianism was dormant: 'During the years of Wren's Surveyorship up to about 1700 there is not one design that can be called Palladian, except perhaps in minor episodes or in certain room arrangements.'[54] It can, however, be argued that Palladianism, when understood as a respect for antiquity, Palladio, Scamozzi and Inigo Jones, was the dominant architectural movement of the decades that followed the Restoration. It can be seen in the buildings of Pratt, May

49   Andrea Palladio, detail of the elevation of the Conventa della Carita, Venice, from *The Four Books of Architecture* (1738).

50   Sir Christopher Wren, Chelsea Hospital, London, 1682.

and Wren and of those who picked up Pratt's style. Nor were the English alone in this mid-seventeenth-century interest in Palladianism, and here we need to look again at the Dutch connection.

Dutch mid-seventeenth-century Classicism has been analysed by both W. Kuyper in *Dutch Classicist Architecture* (1980) and H.J. Louw in his article 'Anglo-Netherlandish architectural interchange *c*.1600–*c*.1660', published in *Architectural History* in 1981. Both identify a sudden interest in Palladianism in the Netherlands from about 1625, reaching maturity in the 1630s, in marked contrast to the existing Flemish gabled style with its strong influence from Vredeman de Vries. The key figure in the development of this style is Jacob van Campen, of whom Kuyper writes that 'Palladio's classical manner adapted to a northern climate and way of life seems to have been his ideal'.[55] Van Campen probably visited Italy and owned a copy of Barbaro's edition of Vitruvius.[56] His Coymanshuis in Amsterdam of 1625 is the first significant example of this new style. It was followed in the 1630s by van Campen's Mauritshuis in The Hague of 1633 (Fig. 44); Constantine Huygens and van Campen's Huygenhuis of 1634–7; and 's Gravesande's Sebastiaansdoelen in The Hague of 1636 (Fig. 45). All are compact houses of two equal stories above a basement with a dominant pitched roof but no dormers or cupola, and the three examples of the 1630s have a pedimented, pilastered frontispiece. In the 1640s the style was spread by architects such as Philip

Vingboons, architect of the Joan Poppen House in Amsterdam of 1642, and Pieter Post, architect of Vredenburgh in Beemster of 1643, and it can still be seen in the 1670s in the work of an architect such as Willem van der Helm who was responsible for the Vierschaar in Leiden of 1671.[57] From the Netherlands this style spread to Sweden, the two countries being closely linked politically and economically. The pilastered, pedimented house which the Dutch banker and businessman Louis de Geer built in Stockholm in 1644, now the Dutch embassy, must have been designed by a Dutch architect who knew van Campen's work, but the most impressive of the Dutch Palladian buildings in Sweden was Justus Vingboons' Riddarhuset of about 1652, with its thirteen-bay pilastered façade and three-bay pedimented frontispiece.[58]

The parallel between what was going on in England and the Netherlands in the 1620s and 1630s is clear, and contrasts with contemporary developments in France, where François Mansart was at the height of his powers, and in Italy, where Bernini and Borromini were reaching theirs. Both Kuyper and Louw see the influence of Jones as being critical to the growth of Dutch Palladianism, with the Coymans House in particular taking the Banqueting House as its model.

Links between the Netherlands and England were close at the time. Sir Henry Wotton, who developed into a keen Palladian as we have seen, was ambassador to The Hague in 1614. In London the Dutch embassy was housed from 1625 to 1628 in the house Jones had altered for Sir Edward Cecil, while Sir Peter Killigrew's house (which Jones designed) was a centre for Anglo-Dutch intercourse. Constantine Huygens, considered by many to have been the intellectual force behind Dutch Classicism, is known to have visited England four times between 1618 and 1625 (he also visited Vicenza where he admired the Teatro Olimpico[59]). In 1622 he attended the opening ceremony of the Banqueting House, and in 1637 he promised to send prints of the house he designed for himself with van Campen to a friend in London so that he could show them to Jones and prove that 'the good Vitruvius is not altogether excluded from Holland'. In 1642 Huygens, van Campen and Johan van Brosterhuizen attempted to publish a Dutch treatise on architecture including Wotton's *Elements* and parts of Palladio's *Quattro libri*. They failed, but the *Elements* subsequently appeared in Joan de Laet's Latin edition of Vitruvius, behind which Huygens may have been the moving force.[60]

Huygens was not alone in the Netherlands in his interest in Jones: Abram Booth's journal of 1629–30 shows that he visited several of Inigo Jones's buildings both in London and at Newmarket and was so impressed that he claimed them to be the principal achievement of James I's reign. The close links between the Netherlands and England are epitomised by the intermarriage of the Stone and de Keyser families, two of the leading families of masons in the two capitals, who worked for Jones and van Campen respectively. Indeed, Willem de Keyser may have been working for Nicholas Stone when the latter was employed by Jones on the Banqueting House; letters show that the de Keysers were familiar with details of the Banqueting House.[61]

Nevertheless, although there are close parallels between English and Dutch architecture in the 1630s, the Dutch differed from the English in their concentration on tripartite façades with pedimented, pilastered frontispieces at a time when Jones's domestic architecture generally lacks a central emphasis. Is this because the Dutch were following Jones's earlier interest in tripartite elevations,[62] or does the use come directly from Palladio? A similar question could be asked about the importance of the Dutch precedent in Pratt and May's use of tripartite pedimented elevations after the Restoration. The answer in both cases is probably a complex mixture of the two, for just as it would be simplistic to say that Pratt copied the Dutch, so it would be to say that the Dutch copied Jones. Pratt's theoretical notes show that he was quite capable of working the idea out for himself, but he would have seen the work of van Campen and others as examples of the sort of Palladian architecture he was recommending and consequently been influenced by them. It is also important when considering Pratt and the Dutch, as when studying Pratt and Jones, to identify

what Pratt did not take as much as what he may have taken. Compared to van Campen with his pilasters and swags, Pratt is a much more austere architect.

English and Dutch Palladianism in the mid-seventeenth century should be seen as parallel movements, thriving on a shared intellectual background and gaining strength the one from the other. A contemporary movement can be identified in France which certainly influenced developments in England and which may in its turn have been affected by what was happening in that country and the Netherlands. Palladio's *Quattro libri* had had little impact in late sixteenth- and early seventeenth-century France. By the time it was published in 1570 a number of important Classical treatises had already appeared in France: Jean Martin and Jean Goujon's *Vitruvius* (1547); Martin's *Alberti* (1553); Philibert de l'Orme's *Nouvelles Inventions pour bien bastir et à petit frais* (1561) and his *Architecture* (1567); and Jean Bullant's *Reigle generalle d'architecture des cinq manières de colonnes* (1568), together with various volumes by Sebastiano Serlio. With these works to hand, the French had no need to study Palladio. In the late sixteenth century and the first half of the seventeenth century there were numerous references in contracts to Serlio and Vignola (even though Vignola was not translated into French until 1632, Salomon de Brosse for one submitted on many occasions to his authority) but Palladio was largely ignored.[63] This changed in the middle of the century with the publication in 1645 of Pierre le Muet's *Traité des cinq ordres d'architecture . . . d'après Palladio*, based on Palladio's first book with extra material of his own, and in 1650 of Fréart de Chambray's translation into French of the *Quattro libri* illustrated with the original woodcuts, including four previously unpublished.[64]

Le Muet was no Palladian apologist; what he valued in Palladio's book was his clear account of the orders, and the chapters which dealt with them were faithfully translated without commentary, but when it came to matters of distribution he was roundly critical of Palladio every time he went against French tradition. By contrast Fréart, as we have already seen, was a violent apologist for Palladio, publishing his *Parallèle* as well as his translation of the *Quattro libri*. In this he was the mouthpiece of a small group of 'Intelligents' gathered around Sublet de Noyers, Surintendant des Bâtiments from 1638 to 1643. Their goal was to purify French architecture after the excesses of Jacques du Cerceau and to protect it from the licence of the contemporary Roman Baroque. Their immediate goal was the rebuilding of the façade of the Louvre, as Fréart made clear at the beginning of the translation of the *Quattro libri*:

Vous savez . . . avec quelle affection [Monseigneur de Noyers] me charge de le [Palladio] rendre intelligible aux Français, quand il resolut d'achever le Louvre, dans la pensée qu'il avait de faire connaitre en meme temps, par la theorie et par la practique, les noblesses de l'architecture reguliers et de bannir cette capricieuse et monstreuse façon de bâtir que qualques modernes ont introduite comme une heresie dans l'art . . . Je dirai donc . . . avec le consentement universal des intelligents, que le Palladio est le premier entre ceux de sa profession et qu'on peut tenir ce livre comme le Palladium de la vraye architecture.

(You know . . . with what keenness [Monseigneur de Noyers] charged me translate it [Palladio] into French, for he is determined to complete the Louvre, and thus through the simultaneous combination of theory and practice reveal the nobleness of regular architecture and banish this capricious and monstrous method of building introduced like a heresy into the art by certain moderns . . . I will therefore say . . . with the universal consent of the knowledgeable, that Palladio is the first among those of his profession and that one can hold to this book as the touchstone of the true architecture.)

In this circle Palladio became the touchstone. André Félibien d'Avaux later wrote in his *Principes de l'architecture* (1676) of 'Palladio qui tient le premier rang entre les Modernes'. It was a circle that stretched as far as Rome, where Fréart's friend Nicholas Poussin made extensive, precise, borrowings from Palladio when trying to provide apparently accurate portrayals of antique buildings in his religious and Classical paintings. In this he differed from his contemporary, Claude Lorrain, who included just as many Classical buildings in his paintings but does not seem to have been so concerned about their architectural precision. Such archaeological speculation was encouraged by the group. Félibien was later to publish his reconstructions of Pliny's villas, while Jean Marot's reconstructions of the temples at Baalbek and Antoine Desgodetz's detailed surveys of Roman buildings stem from their ideals.

What interested the group was not the direct imitation of Palladio's forms but the purity of his architectural theory. Indeed, the Church of the Jesuits, begun by Étienne Martellange in 1630 and saluted by the 'Intelligents' as the ideal illustration of their aesthetic, is based on the Roman models of Vignola and Giacomo della Porta. Thus, it was Palladio's first book that appealed, not the details of the villas or the palazzi. In this the French differed markedly from Pratt and the Dutch, who lacked the French tradition of intellectual Classicism and saw Palladio as a practical model for their immediate building concerns. The intellectual aims of Fréart's *Parallèle* did not, however, stop Pratt finding it a valuable guide to practice.

Although disgraced after the death of Richelieu in 1642, the ideals of Sublet and the Fréarts remained astonishingly long lasting, because it was largely their ideas that were taken up by the Académie Royale d'Architecture on its foundation in 1671. The creation of an aesthetic with universal vocation was the grand preoccupation of French artists in the seventeenth century, and the creation of an architectural aesthetic was the aim of the Académie. Thus, again, the work of Palladio appealed less as a model to be imitated than as an exemplar which had to be analysed and reduced to its principles. The Académie devoted its first works to the critical examination of the *Quattro libri*, and the *Cours d'architecture* (1675) of François Blondel, the first director of the Académie, presents the most complete exposé of the French interpretation of Palladio.

While on the theory of the orders and on proportions, which remained the principal subject of the Académie, Palladio's Classicism was dominant, the Académie did not follow him unreservedly. C.A. Daviler's *Cours d'architecture* (1691) describes Palladio as 'mal executé' and praises Vignola instead; indeed Blondel proposed Vignola's orders to his student architects. When the young Gilles-Marie Oppendordt studying at the French Academy in Rome asked to go to the Veneto to study Palladian buildings, Villacerf answered that he did not think it would be much use to him.[65] And when it came to designing contemporary buildings it was found that the needs of seventeenth-century patrons differed too greatly from those of the sixteenth century for Palladio to provide a practical model. Moreover, when studying the remains of antiquity Desgodetz's *Les Édifices antiques de Rome*, published in 1682 for the Académie, revealed that not only were Palladio's measurements often wrong, he was often wrong in the number and forms of the antique elements he showed. Nevertheless, Palladio's name became synonymous with correct architecture, so that when Henri Sauval came to praise Jacques Lemercier, who with Martellange was the architect most closely associated with the 'Intelligents', he described him as 'prevoyant, judicieux, profond, solide, en un mot, le premier Architecte de notre siècle, et enfin s'il n'étoit pas le Vitruve de son temps, du moin[s] en étoit-il le Palladio'.[66]

Thus, the influence on French theory of Palladio's writings on the orders was pervasive, but the apparent disapproval or disregard of his buildings should not lead one to assume that there is no direct Palladian influence in late seventeenth-century French architecture. This is normally seen to be restricted to a number of limited borrowings: the garden front of the fifth design in Antoine Le Pautre's *Desseins de plusieurs palais* of 1652, with its central superimposed colonnades inspired by the Palazzo Chiericati; the gateway of the sixth design with its interlocking pediments derived from San Giorgio Maggiore[67] and Léonor Houdin's 1661 scheme for the façade of the Louvre which has so many Palladian

51   Louis le Vau, Hôtel Tambonneau, Paris, *c.*1639.

52   Jules Hardouin-Mansart, Château de Dampierre, Aube, France, 1675.

53   Anon., Château de Bouges, Berry, France, 1760s.

elements that Anthony Blunt suggested its author was an Italian operating under a French pseudonym.[68] Nevertheless, it can be argued that, despite the theorising of the Académie, Palladianism, perhaps thanks to Dutch and English example, did play a direct role in late seventeenth-century French architecture; this can be seen first in the introduction of the pedimented centrepiece to French domestic architecture, and then in the growing popularity of the compact villa with a tripartite, pedimented façade.

It was Palladio who first placed the abstracted temple front on a house, implied sometimes by a full portico but also by pilasters or by an astylar projection under a pediment. This is rarely found in French architecture of the first half of the seventeenth century, perhaps the earliest example being in the work of Louis Le Vau (who is not known to have travelled to Italy) at the Hôtel Tambonneau in Paris of about 1639 (Fig. 51). Its courtyard façade is of nine bays with a two-storey, three-bay pedimented, pilastered centrepiece. This feature became a regular motif in Le Vau's work and can be seen on the garden front of Vaux le Vicomte (1656). Le Vau also used a pedimented frontispiece, this time with French quoins rather than pilasters, on the façade of the Cour du Sphinx of the Louvre of 1661.[69] During the second half

of the decade, Le Vau's example meant that pedimented centrepieces began to creep into French architecture: Jean Marot used one on the Hôtel Pussort in Paris in 1672, as did François d'Orbay, probably following Le Vau's Cour du Sphinx, on the Comédie Française in 1688.[70] They became a regular feature of the work of Jules Hardouin-Mansart, the dominant architect of the period: at the Château de Dampierre (1675) (Fig. 52); the Château de Clagny (1676) (these two being astylar); the Palais des États, Dijon (1686); and the Place Vendôme (after 1687); in these two last cases the pediments were supported by attached columns and are used to marked Classical effect, particularly in the Place Vendôme which has pediments in the middle of the two main façades and in each of the four corners.

The growing use of the Palladian-inspired central pediment was paralled by interest in the Palladian villa model of a block-like house with a tripartite, pedimented façade. In the first half of the seventeenth century this was not a characteristic form in France. Instead, country houses were dominated by the work of François Mansart, epitomised by the Château de Maisons (1642) with its soaring roofs and distinctive massing of indi vidual pavilions. Houses built around courtyards re- mained a popular model both in the country and in towns. In the second half of the century an alternative compact approach crept in, based on the Palladian tripartite façade. Le Vau's Hôtel Tambonneau introduced the idea of the tripartite elevation, but this only forms one side of a courtyard. By contrast his last work, the Trianon de Porcelain at Versailles designed in 1668, the year of his death, has a straightforward Palladian plan. Although only single storey, it has a five-bay elevation with a three-bay pedimented centrepiece, and a courtyard flanked by two small pavilions.[71]

Again, Jules Hardouin-Mansart followed Le Vau's lead. His Château de Dampierre of 1675 has two storeys of equal height, a hipped roof with dormers and a three-bay pedimented centrepiece. (An important development of these years was the end of the French obsession with steep, dominant roofs so evident in the work of François Mansart but alien to Palladianism.) Compact villa-like houses can also be found in Hardouin-

Mansart's work in the King's Block at Marly (1679), which has a tripartite pedimented elevation and a plan which looks back to Palladio's Villa Rotunda, and the Château de Navarre (1686) which is square with a central cupola but no pediment. A similar compact Palladian plan with a corresponding tripartite elevation can be seen in Pierre Bullet's Château d'Issy near Paris of 1686 and later became common in France, a typical example being the anonymous Château de Bouges, near Valency, built in the 1760s (Fig. 53). Nor was this Palladian plan restricted to leading architects: the Château d'Ennery (c.1680) is a nine-bay, tripartite house with a central three-bay frontispiece, completely undecorated, in the manner of the English Restoration house.[72] It is unlikely to be coincidence that English and Dutch architects had been pioneering similar compact, tripartite pedimented houses in the middle decades of the century.

III

NEO-CLASSICISM FROM JONES TO HAWKSMOOR

THE STANDARD VIEW OF neo-Classicism in English (and indeed European) architecture is that it is a phenomenon of the second half of the eighteenth century. Traditional accounts usually start with Stuart and Revett's *Antiquities of Athens*, published in 1762, although it is generally accepted that this was anticipated by Lord Burlington's reconstruction of an Egyptian Hall for the Assembly Rooms at York in 1731–2. This view has most recently been expounded in Damie Stillman's monumental two-volume *English Neo-classical Architecture* (1988). But it can be argued that neo-Classicism in England has a much longer history of which late eighteenth-century neo-Classicism is only one part; that its origins can be traced back to Inigo Jones's St Paul, Covent Garden, to the theoretical reconstructions of his pupil John Webb and of members of the Royal Society in the seventeenth century and to the buildings of Nicholas Hawksmoor; and that its origins were essentially Roman, for lack of adequate Greek examples.

Neo-Classicism is often a dangerously imprecise term, but, at least in architecture, its true definition is simple: the conscious return to the Antique as a source for architectural example, ignoring the traditions of architectural style and theory that had grown up since the Renaissance. In Britain in the seventeenth and eighteenth centuries neo-Classicism co-existed with a more conventional approach to architecture which sought inspiration from the work of Renaissance and contemporary architects. Only a small number of buildings can be described as neo-Classical, but they are of particular interest for the insight they provide into attitudes towards antiquity and Classical architecture.

Four different approaches to neo-Classicism can be discerned: the Vitruvian, which tried to reconstruct ideal Classical buildings as described in Vitruvius's *Ten Books*; the literary, which took its source from contemporary descriptions of Classical buildings; the archaeological, which examined the surviving remains of Classical buildings; and the structural, which tried to deduce the true essence of Classical buildings from their constructional techniques. Different architects and theorists have often tried different approaches, or combined two or more of them in attempting a reconstruction, but the structural

approach does not seem to have influenced English neo-Classicists before the late eighteenth century.

Inigo Jones is correctly described as Britain's first true Classical architect, but he can also be seen as Britain's first neo-Classical architect. There is a clear contrast between the work of the first part of his career where the debt to Renaissance architecture, and in particular to Palladio and Scamozzi, is obvious, and the second part when in his monumental buildings he cast back beyond the Renaissance to ancient Rome to create architecture that is best described as neo-Classical.

Jones's three trips to France and Italy allowed him to make detailed studies of Classical remains as well as of Renaissance buildings. Annotations and sketches in his copy of *I quattro libri* and elsewhere show how closely he examined the works of Palladio; they also reveal that he devoted the same attention to the Antique, both in Italy and Provence. But the burst of activity that followed his appointment as Surveyor-General in 1615 shows that it was Renaissance buildings that had the most immediate effect on his designs. In his drawings and in his executed buildings, such as the Banqueting House, Jones proved himself to be a worthy successor to Palladio and Scamozzi, with a complete grasp of the principles and detail of their compositions. By the 1630s two new strands were apparent in Jones's work. In his domestic architecture (as seen in chapter one) he moved away from the Palladian and Scamozzian richness of articulation evident in his earlier designs to a more severe treatment of the wall surface, where windows sit isolated in plain stretches of wall. In his more monumental work, the church and piazza at Covent Garden of 1631–7 and the west portico of St Paul's Cathedral of 1633–42, he turned instead for inspiration to ancient Rome.

St Paul, Covent Garden, built as the centre of a new urban quarter for the Earl of Bedford, is an austere building, as Jones probably thought befitted a Protestant church, with a Tuscan portico and a great overhanging roof (Fig. 54). John Summerson pointed out that Jones's design was based on Palladio and Barbaro's reconstruction of Vitruvius's description of the Tuscan temple (Fig. 55).

The church is preceded by an arcaded forecourt,

54   Inigo Jones, St Paul's church, Covent Garden, 1631 (engraving after Wenceslaus Hollar).

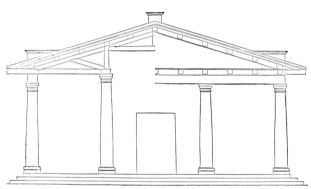

55   Reconstruction of the Tuscan temple from Daniele Barbaro's edition of Vitruvius's *Ten Books of Architecture* (1556).

the Piazza. Although there are plenty of late-antique, medieval and Renaissance examples of churches with arcaded atria that Jones would have known and might have taken as his source, this may again have been a specifically antique reference. It may be that he intended St Paul's, a recreation of a Roman temple, to have the sort of forecourt which Palladio illustrated in some of his reconstructions of Roman temples in the *Quattro libri*. In two of these cases the temple is at the far end of the court, as at Covent Garden. The third case (the mausoleum of the Emperor Maxentius which it is known Jones examined) places the temple in the centre of the court, but surrounds it with an arcade. Summerson suggested this may have inspired the arcades of the Covent Garden Piazza.[1]

As Gordon Higgott has shown, Jones's study of Vitruvius and Roman remains led him to realise that it was not necessary to imitate antique precedent slavishly:

'The architect should look to the antique for the best models but he is still free to vary from these models, provided he does so in a reasoned way.'[2] Annotating Palladio's fourth book Jones made his position clear: 'But in my opinion Palladio Immitates ye Best Bacmentes of thes antiquites as ye Tempels of Pola, of Nerua, of Fortune, of Scicci, but allwaes the libberty of composing wr reason is not taken awaye but who followes ye best of ye ansientes cannot much earr.'[3] Clearly, contemporary precedents for urban squares in Livorno and in Paris at the Place des Vosges must have been important to Jones in the planning of Covent Garden, as Serlio was for the elevations, but the detail of the planning and the form of the church suggests that Covent Garden is the first important example of neo-Classicism in England, an example that combines both Vitruvian and archaeological inspiration.

At St Paul's Cathedral Jones set to work on an even grander example of neo-Classicism (Fig. 56). Restoration of the cathedral began in 1633, and the following year the king agreed to finance work on the west front. At first sight no project could be a less promising subject for a neo-Classical treatment than the restoration of a great Gothic cathedral. Much of Jones's work was devoted to recasing, and there was little that anyone could do to alter the rhythm and structure of a medieval building. Royal generosity allowed him to be more ambitious at the west front. Nothing could disguise the basic shape of the medieval cathedral with its high nave and lower aisles, but on to this Jones grafted the largest portico to have been built north of the Alps. This is closely modelled on the similar, unpedimented, portico in Palladio's reconstruction of the temple of Venus at

56 (above)   Inigo Jones, St Paul's Cathedral, City of London, west front, 1633 (detail from an engraving after Wenceslaus Hollar) (demolished).

57   Inigo Jones, unexecuted design for a triumphal arch, City of London, 1636.

Rome. Both are Corinthian decastyle porticos topped by balustrades interrupted by statues. The most significant difference is at the ends, where Jones has a pair of columns, those on the outside being square, instead of the two attached columns separated by a niche of the original. Further neo-Classical elements at St Paul's appear in the rustication of the walls and in the eaves cornice of lions' heads alternating with triplets of drop motifs which John Harris has shown derive from Palladio's woodcuts of the Pantheon and from engravings by Hieronymous Cock of the Baths of Diocletian.[4]

The new portico of St Paul's was intended to be the climax to the royal ceremonial route by which the king entered the City of London. That route started at Temple Bar for which Jones designed a triumphal arch in 1636; a second design followed in 1638 but neither was executed (Fig. 57). The first of these designs was to be modelled principally on the Arch of Septimius Severus, particularly in its lower part, which was to be decorated with allegorical scenes, although the attic is closer to the Arch of Constantine.

After the overpowering mass of the portico of St Paul's and the proposed triumphal arch at Temple Bar, one small monument seems of little importance, but Jones's monument in St Giles-in-the-Fields to the poet George Chapman who died in 1634 is significant, for, based as it is on the form of a Roman altar, it differs markedly from the standard run of monuments and shows how Jones's mind was turning to Rome in small as well as in large things.[5] Finally, Jones's interest in

Stonehenge and his detailed, if erroneous, argument that it was a Roman temple should not be forgotten.

The outbreak of the Civil War in 1642 denied Jones any further chance to develop his neo-Classical leanings, but he passed his interest on to his pupil John Webb, among whose drawings at Worcester College, Oxford, is a series of reconstructions after Vitruvian descriptions of Classical buildings: reconstructions of the Roman house, the Greek house, various atria and halls, and of the different Vitruvian temple forms.

The purpose of these reconstructions is unclear, and it may be that they were intended for publication as part of an architectural treatise along the lines of Scamozzi's *Dell'idea dell'architettura universale* which combines theoretical reconstructions of Roman buildings with modern designs. Alternatively, they could have been practical exercises to assist Webb to establish appropriate Classical solutions to modern building types. Esther Eisenthal has suggested that the domestic reconstructions were intended to help him find a Classical form appropriate for designing great houses.[6] Certainly, his unexecuted second design for the Earl of Pembroke for Durham House, of about 1649, seems to be an adaptation of Scamozzi's interpretation of Vitruvius's Roman house, reduced to fit the restrictions of the site which lay between the Strand and the Thames. Another possibility is that Webb, like Jones at Covent Garden, hoped to recreate an antique building. His third design for Durham House, dated 1649 (Fig. 58), can be seen as a reconstruction of a Roman house based on Scamozzi (Fig. 59). Like

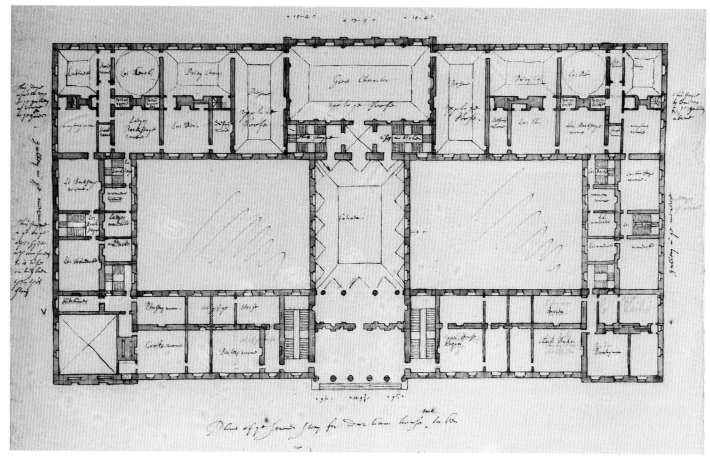

58   John Webb, unexecuted design for Durham House, London, 1649.

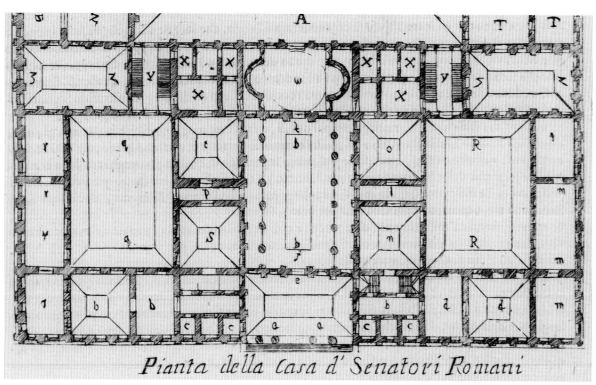

Pianta della Casa d' Senatori Romani

59   Vincenzo Scamozzi, detail from a design for the House of Ancients, from *Dell'idea del'Architettura Universale* (1615).

Scamozzi's reconstruction, this design is approached through a six-columned portico-in-antis leading into a large rectangular entrance hall or atrium, which is flanked on either side by enclosed courts. At the far end of the atrium is a cross-vaulted lobby in the place of the tablinum. Beyond this in a Roman house should be a courtyard or peristyle with a rectangular hall on the far side. The proximity of the Thames meant there was no room for this on the Durham House site, so Webb restricted his reconstruction to the first part of Scamozzi's house, while incorporating the hall into the body of the house as the Great Chamber. As John Bold has shown, the Durham House designs were not theoretical exercises but were worked out fully as a practical proposition, but how the Earl of Pembroke ever thought he would have been able to afford such a scheme is unclear.[7]

Durham House was not Webb's only attempt to reconstruct antique buildings and give them modern uses. One of his drawings, entitled *Exchanges or Merchants Piazzas*, is based on the Roman basilica and inscribed 'may serve for a Royal Exchange from a metropolis as London & ye like'.[8] Webb never had call to put this into practice, but he did have hopes that his most extensive neo-Classical design would be built, that for a new palace at Whitehall.

The project for a grand Classical palace at Whitehall was one that had concerned Inigo Jones in the 1630s, and with him Webb.[9] Of the various schemes, Webb is believed to have been largely or wholly responsible for three drawn up before the Restoration, those known by the letters 'K' (*c*.1637–9), 'E' (probably executed in the mid-1640s) and 'T'. This was probably the scheme which Charles I commissioned while a prisoner in Carisbrooke Castle on the Isle of Wight in 1647–8, making it contemporary with the Durham House plans. The first two schemes are very much in the manner of Inigo Jones and are strongly influenced by his scheme known as 'P'. The third is known from two similar plans that differ in detail, and was composed of three main elements, a large rectangular forecourt, a central section of vaulted and columned halls and courts, and a series of domestic ranges around a circular court (Fig. 60). The first and third elements can also be found in the 'K' scheme, but the central element has no precedent in English architecture.

The source lies again in antique architecture, but as Vitruvius does not discuss the design of palaces, Webb was forced to look to other building types for his model. An obvious source for a complex of halls and courts was the Roman baths, three of which, the Baths of Titus, Antony and Diocletian, Serlio illustrated in his third book (Fig. 61).[10] Webb's annotated copy of this, which his theoretical sketches show was thoroughly studied, is in Worcester College Library.[11] The Baths of Diocletian,

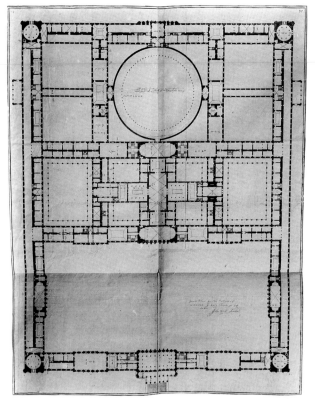

60 John Webb, unexecuted design for Whitehall Palace, London, 1647.

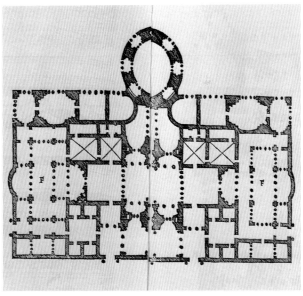

61 Ground-plan of the Baths of Diocletian, from Sebastiano Serlio's *The Five Books of Architecture* (1611).

with its series of symmetrically arranged columned, vaulted and apsidal halls and courts seem to have been Webb's model for the central section of the 'T' scheme. As in the baths, Webb's design is focused around a central rectangular hall with detached columns supporting a cross-vaulted roof, leading through columned screens into other halls and ending in a pair of rectangular colonnaded courts. This is clearest in the 'T2' scheme. Above and below the central hall in the 'T2' scheme are two identical halls with four pairs of columns with a small rectangle drawn in the centre. These can be read as Corinthian atria with their roofs open to the sky – not a model very practical in England. The 'T1' scheme is even more overtly neo-Classical. Here Webb has turned the central hall and Corinthian atria around on their axes, adding a tetrastyle atrium at each end of the central hall, approached through apsed vaulted halls. The result would have been a series of Classical spaces unparalleled since the fall of the Roman Empire.

Nothing came of the Whitehall schemes, and when Webb did design a palace after the Restoration at Greenwich there was nothing specifically neo-Classical about his plans. However, it may be that his plans for a grand exedra and portico set into the hill in the gardens at Greenwich were modelled on the Temple of Fortune at Palestrina with which Webb could have been familiar through J.M. Suarez's reconstructions in *Praenestes antiquae libri duo*, published in 1655.

Further attempts at Vitruvian reconstruction would have to wait eighty years, as the interest of the next generation of neo-Classicists, architects and antiquaries connected with the Royal Society, was more strictly theoretical. Their interest lay in trying to reconstruct famous buildings of antiquity, and their approach was primarily literary.

On 6 September 1675, Robert Hooke's diary recorded that he spent the evening 'with Sir Chr Wren. Long Discourse with him about the module of the Temple at Jerusalem.'[12] Wren and Hooke's interest was part of a long tradition in England of attempts at reconstructing the Temple of Jerusalem from descriptions in the Bible and from the account of the Jewish historian Josephus. Mark Girouard has argued that Robert Smythson's Wollaton Hall in Nottingham can be interpreted as such a reconstruction,[13] but as Eileen Harris has shown, English interest in reconstructing Solomon's Temple was to peak in the early 1720s. It had earlier been stimulated by the publication of Juan Bautista Villalpando's *In ezechielem explanationes* in 1604, with its influential plates of the reconstructed temple.[14] These were re-engraved for Bishop Walton's *Biblia polyglotta* in 1657, and again in John Ogilby's *Holy Bible* of 1660, and were also available on their own; Robert Hooke recorded that he bought a copy for 30s. in 1676.[15] Wren, however, once he had studied the matter, was somewhat dismissive of Villalpando:

> *Villalpandus* hath made a fine romantick Piece, after the *Corinthian* Order, which in that Age, was not used by any Nation . . . [an opinion he shared with Claude

Perrault who coincidentally must have been working on the same project at almost the same time, his reconstructions were published in 1678 in Louis de Veil's translation of the Code of Maimondes[16]] . . . if we run back to the Age of *Solomon*, we may with Reason believe they used the *Tyrian* Manner, as gross at least, if not more, than the *Dorick*, and that the *Corinthian* Manner of *Villalpandus* is mere Fancy.[17]

For Wren and Hooke there was nothing unique about the Temple at Jerusalem. It was only one in a number of antique buildings that they wished to reconstruct. On 4 October 1677, Hooke's diary records 'Discoursd of Porsennas tomb of which Sir Ch. Wren gave a description, but comparing it with the words it agreed not. I found the form of it quite otherwise and describd it'. Porsenna's tomb, a complex structure with three groups of pyramids one above the other, was described in detail by Pliny, quoting Varro, in his *Natural History*.[18] Wren and Hooke returned to it several times in the next few weeks: 'To Sir Chr Wrens. Discoursd with him long of Porcena's tomb which he had thus drawn . . . Discoursd also of hersepolis' (17 October 1677)[19]; 'drew a rationall porcena' (18 October 1677); 'discoursed with Sir Chr Wren . . . about Porsenas Tomb' (20 October 1677).[20] It was a building that particularly fascinated Wren: 'Now how these [that is, the layers of pyramids] could be born is worth the consideration of an Architect. I conceive it might be performed securely.' In his notes he apologises and explains the particular reason for his fascination: 'I have been the longer in this Description, because the Fabrick was in the Age of Pythagoras and his School, when the World began to be fond of Geometry and Arithmetick.' Speaking of his own time he elsewhere complained: 'It seems very unaccountable, that the Generality of our late Architects dwell so much upon this ornamental, and so slightly pass over the geometrical, which is the most essential Part of Architecture.'[21]

Tract IV of the appendix 'Of Architecture & observations on antique temples etc' appended to *Parentalia*, published in 1750, and the manuscript 'Discourse on Architecture by Sr CW' in the heirloom copy of *Parentalia* in the Royal Institute of British Architects reveal more of Wren's attempts at reconstruction. As it was published so long after Wren's death, and includes later emendations, *Parentalia* is a notoriously tricky source to use, but there is no reason to doubt the genuineness of the sections on antiquity or to suggest that they had been altered after Wren's death. It is, however, hard to establish their status, whether they were intended for publication and whether they were finished texts or provisional drafts. It is equally impossible to be certain of their date; Eileen Harris suggests the early 1680s as a likely *terminus post quem*, that being the publication period of Desgodetz's *Édifices antiques de*

Rome (1682), Perrault's *Ordonnance de cinq éspèces de colonnes* (1683), and the second, enlarged edition of his translation of Vitruvius (1684), three books with which Wren was certainly familiar.[22] However, from the references in Hooke's diary it is clear Wren was already addressing these issues in the mid-1670s. One also longs to know what influence Wren had on Johann Bernhard Fischer von Erlach. It is generally agreed that von Erlach came to London in 1704, when he would almost certainly have met Wren; on his return to Vienna the following year he set about researching his *Entwurf einer Historischen Architektur*, a comparative study of buildings of different cultures very much in the manner of Wren.[23]

As well as the three examples mentioned by Hooke, Wren analysed and attempted to reconstruct Noah's Ark, the Philistine Temple that Samson pulled down, the Sepulchre of Absalom, the Tower of Babel, the Temple of Diana at Ephesus, the Temple of Peace and Mars Ultor in Rome, and the sepulchre of Mausolus, King of Caria.[24] These attempts at reconstruction bear the stamp, so often found in the work of late seventeenth-century members of the Royal Society, of a logical mind trying to establish empirical laws from information of dubious veracity. Wren's reconstruction of the Philistine Temple is an ingenious example. Working from the single fact that the temple had been demolished at one pull, Wren decided that it must have been an oval amphitheatre with the *scaena* in the middle, with a vast roof of cedar beams resting on the walls, centred on one short architrave that united two cedar pillars in the middle.

Wren's researches were not carried out for reasons of idle curiosity, nor simply from a scientific desire to analyse how complex buildings like Porsenna's tomb could work structurally.[25] They were intended to provide him with facts to fight a contemporary stylistic battle. The criticism he faced over the design of St Paul's is well known, and he felt that such problems arose out of his critics' ignorance – 'I have found no little difficulty to bring Persons of otherwise a good Genius, to think anything in Architecture could be better than what they had heard commended by others, and what they had view'd themselves' – and narrow-mindedness:

> Modern Authors who have treated of Architecture, seem generally to have little more in view, but to set down the Proportions of Columns, Architraves, and Cornices, in the several Orders as they are distinguished into *Dorick*, *Ionick*, *Corinthian*, and *Composite*; and in those Proportions finding them in the antient Fabricks of the *Greeks* and *Romans*, (though more arbitrarily used than they care to acknowledge) they have reduced them into rules, too strict and pedantick, and so as not to be transgressed without the Crime of Barbarity.[26]

The problem, as he saw it, arose from the limited range of examples known to Renaissance architects and theorists:

> Those who first laboured in the Restitution of Architecture about three centuries ago studied principally what was found in Rome – ruins of theatres, baths, temples and triumphal arches for among the *Greeks* little was then remaining . . . in these there appeared great Differences; however, they criticised upon them, and endeavoured to reconcile them, as well as they could, with one another, and with what they could meet with in *Italian* cities.

Inevitably their sources were limited geographically and, in large part, to buildings that date from after the Age of Augustus; Wren hoped to correct these limitations, and, as he explained in the *Discourse*, 'to reform the Generality to a truer Taste in Architecture, by giving a larger Idea of the whole Art, beginning with the origin and progress of it from the most remote Antiquity'.[27]

Hence the need to collect examples of known antique buildings, from as many different styles as he could. Of the Sepulchre of Absalom, for instance, he wrote: 'It is to be wished, some skilful Artist would give us the exact Dimensions to Inches, by which we might have a true Idea of the ancient *Tyrian* Manner.'[28] The Tyrian manner was of particular interest because, as already seen, Wren believed it was the order of the Temple of Solomon.

Wren's particular aim was to show that Roman architecture was only one part, and not necessarily the most important part, of a longer tradition – 'The *Orders* are not only *Roman* and *Greek*, but *Phoenician*, *Hebrew*, and *Assyrian*'. Moreover, he sought to demonstrate that Roman architecture itself varied enormously, and that it was absurd to try and reconcile the great variety of Classical remains to the writings of one author, Vitruvius. Wren noted that even the Pantheon has scarcely two columns that are exactly the same, while Pliny, wanting to add a portico to an old temple on his estate, had ordered the architect to buy four marble columns of any sort he pleased:

> By this Method of purchasing, at any time, Columns of all Orders and Proportions, ready formed at the Quarries, as Goods in a Shop or Warehouse, the Ancients had an Advantage of erecting Porticoes (the stately Pride of the *Roman* Architecture) of any grandeur, or Extent, in a very short time, and without being over scrupulous in the Exactness of the Dimension.

He also recorded seeing a book of Pirro Ligorio's among Inigo Jones's collection, in which Ligorio seems to have made it his business to collect examples of Classical

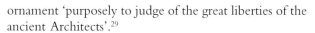

63 Sir Christopher Wren, Pembroke College Chapel, Cambridge, 1663, from Daniel Loggan's *Cantabrigiana Illustrata* (1688) (detail).

63 Reconstruction of a Roman temple at Tivoli, from Sebastiano Serlio's *The Five Books of Architecture* (1611).

ornament 'purposely to judge of the great liberties of the ancient Architects'.[29]

By demonstrating how architecture had changed over the millennia, Wren hoped to show that architecture of his own time should be allowed to develop further and should not be restricted by what he saw as arbitary rules. Thus, his researches, which seem largely to have been the product of his maturity, were intended to allow him to design as he saw fit, not to provide him with models on which to base his own buildings. Indeed, to reconstruct buildings, especially Roman buildings, would have run contrary to his basic philosophy of design. However, when he first took up architecture in the 1660s, while still a scientist and essentially an amateur architect, Wren had a very different attitude towards antique models. As Howard Colvin pointed out in discussing the Sheldonian Theatre in Oxford, it was natural for an academic with no experience of building, and for whom Latin was the language of learning, to turn first to the buildings of Rome for example.[30] The theatre (Fig. 47), begun in 1664, was an attempt to reconstruct a Classical theatre, although, as Summerson suggested, the interlocking pediments of the south façade are probably based on Palladio's reconstruction of the Basilica of Maxentius.[31] This attempt was given added veracity by Wren's technically impressive roof structure – perhaps partly inspired by a similar (but much smaller) one illustrated in Serlio[32]

– which allowed the roof to be spanned by comparatively small pieces of timber. Thus, the ceiling could be painted as if the building were open to the sky like a genuine Roman theatre. Robert Plot, author of *The Natural History of Oxfordshire*, in which he described Wren as the English Vitruvius, was particularly taken by this: 'The *Painting* of the *Cieling* of the *Theatre* is worth Examination; for in Imitation of the *theatres* of the ancient *Greeks* and *Romans*, which were too large to be covered with Lead or Tile, *this*, by the *Painting* of the *Flat-roof* within, is represented open.'[33]

Plot also noted the way ropes were painted onto the ceiling to give the impression that a giant awning could be unfurled at any moment to shelter the occupants.

The slightly curious way in which, in the building as executed, the attic appears to rest on the rustic without any intervening storeys could be said to undermine this comparison – John Summerson described the result as 'rather like a man with his trousers pulled up to his chin and his hat pulled over his nose'[34] – but Howard Colvin is surely right in arguing that Wren must have originally intended something more correctly Classical. This certainly seems to have been the impression of those who commented on the original model for the theatre when it was shown to the Royal Society in 1663. Abraham Hill, for instance, noted that it was to be 'more exactly accommodated to the Roman architecture than any now extant'[35]. As his son and biographer explains in *Parentalia*, Wren was forced to compromise his design for reasons of economy:

> This Theatre . . . [would have] been executed in a greater and better Style, with a View to the ancient *Roman* Grandeur discernible in the Theatre of *Marcellus* at *Rome*; but that he [that is Wren] was obliged to put a stop to the bolder Strokes of his Pencil, and confine the Expence within the Limits of a private Purse.[36]

The Sheldonian Theatre was not Wren's only reconstruction: a year earlier he had designed the chapel at Pembroke College, Cambridge, in the form of a temple, with a portico of applied pilasters probably based on Serlio's illustration of a temple at Tivoli (Figs. 62 and 63).

Wren's most ambitious use of antique prototypes appears in his proposals for rebuilding St Paul's Cathedral after the Great Fire of London in 1666. His plan for rebuilding the City of London after the Great Fire, drawn up in haste and presented to the king on 11 September, suggests a curious, almost keyhole-shaped plan for the cathedral. Two surviving drawings at All Souls show that this would have had a Pantheon-like rotunda and dome, with a three-bay nave almost certainly based on the Temple of Peace in Rome. The façade of the Temple of Peace, as reconstructed by Palladio, also formed the basis for an alternative contemporary design for St Paul's. Wren soon moved on from these visions of Rome, but he did build his version of the Temple of Peace. We know from *Parentalia* that this was the source for the plan of St Mary-le-Bow with its three-bay arcaded interior, begun in 1671. (This is the only one of the Wren churches for which an antique precedent is cited in *Parentalia*.) Wren may have considered such a source particularly appropriate as *Parentalia* notes that St Mary-le-Bow was built on the walls of a very ancient church which was considered to date from the early time of the Roman colony.[37] The west front of St Mary-le-Bow would appear to be an astylar version of Serlio's illustration of a Triumphal Arch. Elsewhere Serlio's Tivoli Temple, earlier used for Pembroke Chapel, was reused as the centrepiece of the west front of St Magnus, begun the same year. Even more direct in its derivation is the Monument, again begun in 1671, designed by Wren with Robert Hooke, his partner in the subsequent theoretical antique reconstructions mentioned above. As *Parentalia* shows – and as Hawksmoor deliberately emphasised in his engraving (Fig. 64) – the Monument was self-consciously modelled on the columns of Trajan and Antoninus.[38] The similarity would have been even more obvious if the intended colossal statue of Charles II had been placed on the top 'in the Manner of the *Roman* Pillars', as *Parentalia* puts it.[39]

Perhaps the last project where Wren shows such strong neo-Classical leanings was his abortive mausoleum for Charles I, of 1678. This small circular building does have broad precedents in sixteenth- and seventeenth-century royal mausolea on the Continent, in particular the Valois mausoleum at St Denis, which Wren would probably have known from engravings, but the scale and design have close parallels in Giovanni Battista Montano's reconstructions of small circular Roman mausolea published in his *Li Tempii e sepolcri antichi* of 1638. These are largely fantastic elaborations based on very little evidence, but Wren was not to know this. Montano's reconstruction of the tomb of Cecilia Metella, which has a round podium of chanelled masonry, a frieze of festoons, an upper storey punctuated by pairs of columns and a statue, is very close, although in Wren's design the dome is closer to such Renaissance examples as St Peter's in Rome.[40]

By the mid-1670s the Antique had largely lost its allure for Wren, as he became more versed in contempo-

64   Nicholas Hawksmoor after Sir Christopher Wren, the Monument, City of London, 1671.

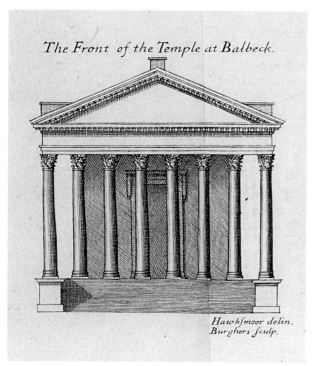

65 Nicholas Hawksmoor, recreation of the Temple of Bacchus at Baalbek from Henry Maundrell's *A Journey from Aleppo to Jerusalem* (1714).

rary Continental architecture and more aware of his own powers of invention. It was inevitable, given his enquiring, pioneering mind that reconstructions of antique buildings could never hold his interest for long. St Paul's as built owes little or nothing to direct neo-Classical quotation, and the same is true of his other later buildings. The one exception is the spire of St Bride, built in 1702–3, the diminishing octagonal *tempietti* of which may have been derived from the mistaken belief of early illustrators of Vitruvius that the octagonal Tower of the Winds at Athens had more than one storey. Reconstructions in Rusconi's and Martin's editions of Vitruvius or, indeed, in Serlio's sixth book show similar multi-storeyed towers.[41] However, as John Summerson pointed out, the idea for the spire is based on that of the Warrant design for St Paul's executed a quarter of a century earlier in the early 1670s.[42] Apart from this, Wren's mature attempts at neo-Classical reconstructions were confined to paper; the buildings for which he is most renowned owe little directly to antiquity.

Wren passed on this interest in reconstructions to his pupil Nicholas Hawksmoor. One of the drawings which illustrates the heirloom copy of *Parentalia* in the Royal Institute of British Architects' Library is an elevational reconstruction of the mausoleum at Halicarnassus, in Hawksmoor's hand, while the posthumous sale of his collection included twenty-eight drawings he had made of Porsenna's tomb.[43] He also reconstructed the Temple

of Bacchus at Baalbek (Fig. 65) to illustrate the 1714 edition of Henry Maundrell's *A Journey from Aleppo to Jerusalem* – these were added to plates of Daniel Marot's reconstruction of the Temple of Jupiter at Baalbek which had been included in the first edition published in 1703. But while, for Wren, practical reconstructions were a passing phase of his immaturity, for Hawksmoor they became a growing obsession.

At the most immediate level Hawksmoor's obsession with antiquity is hard to escape. His drawings are regularly annotated in Latin, as in his designs for remodelling Cambridge, where Market Hill becomes the *forum*, the King's Ditch a *vallum* and the castle was to have a *basilica*, or in his plan for Greenwich which was to have a *circus*, a *via regia*, a temple and a *pausilippo*. Despite this, Hawksmoor's dependence on antique sources has never really been taken seriously. John Summerson touched on it when he wrote that 'we must understand Hawksmoor's almost morbid passion for classical archaeology, his wide reading, his interest in reconstructions and in the less hackneyed specimens of Roman building',[44] but did not investigate the point in detail. Other writers such as Kerry Downes and S. Lang have noted occasional antique references or sources in Hawksmoor's work, but largely in passing. In part this is due to the assumption that neo-Classical reconstruction was a product of the later eighteenth century, but the main reason lies in the contrast between Hawksmoor's work and that of Lord Burlington, whose architecture *is* accepted as having neo-Classical leanings. Thus, Hawksmoor's use of Classical precedents to defend the Mausoleum at Castle Howard against Burlington's criticism is usually dismissed as wordy smoke-screen.[45] It should not, however, be forgotten that, according to George Vertue, Hawksmoor was 'bred a scholar, and knew as well the learned as the modern tongues'[46], that he had a vast library of books and engravings on antiquity and that he would have received a firm grounding of research into antique buildings from Wren, who must also have passed on to him his sceptical attitude towards architectural rules and contemporary Classical conventions.

Hawksmoor and Burlington were heirs to two very different approaches towards antiquity, of which Burlington's with its respect for the rules of Vitruvius and for the careful study of Classical remains, preferably through meticulous survey, could be said to represent the mainstream of Classical studies. It can be found in the work of such theorists as Alberti, Serlio, Palladio and Desgodetz; but Hawksmoor's unfettered approach to reconstructing Classical buildings, in which the imagination was as important as Vitruvius and literary descriptions as influential as physical remains, also followed a long tradition to be seen in the work of such men as Jacques Androuet du Cerceau, Palladio's contemporary Pirro Ligorio, Jacopo Lauro with his *Antiquae urbus*

66   Nicholas Hawksmoor, St George's church, Bloomsbury, London, 1716 (aquatint after Thomas Malton, from *Picturesque Tour through the Cities of London and Westminster* (1792))

splendor of 1612, Montano with his *Architettura con diversi ornamenti cavate dall'antico* of 1636 and his *Li Tempii e sepolcri antichi* of 1638, or Pietro Santi Bartoli with his *Gli antichi sepolchri* of 1697 and his *Romanae magnitudinis monumenta* of 1699.

Hawksmoor's first essay in the Antique still stands in the market square of Ripon in Yorkshire, where it was described in Daniel Defoe's *A Tour through the whole Island of Great Britain* in 1724: 'In the middle of it [the square] stands a curious column of stone, imitating the obelisks of the antients, tho' not so high'. Richard Hewlings has shown that this obelisk, the first in England since the Elizabethan obelisk at Nonsuch, was built for John Aislabie in 1702 by Hawksmoor, who wrote that it was designed 'according to the most exact antient symmetry'.

Thereafter, antique references and reconstructions ap-pear repeatedly in Hawksmoor's work. The reconstruction of the Mausoleum at Halicarnassus that illustrated *Parentalia* was the basis of one of his church designs, now at All Souls. In the event, this design was never built, but Hawksmoor used the upper half of his reconstruction for the steeple of St George, Bloomsbury (Fig. 66). William Stukeley recorded that the portico of St George was designed by Hawksmoor 'in imitation, and of the size, of that at Balbek' – not a surprising choice given that the church was begun in 1716, shortly after Hawksmoor had reconstructed the temple for Maundrell's book.[47] Across the City he turned to Perrault's edition of Vitruvius's *Ten Books on Architecture* (which he owned) for his initial designs for St Mary Woolnoth. The side elevation was to have been a reduced version of the end elevation of Vitruvius's Egyptian Hall. Perrault, with its scholarly illustrations of Vitruvius's obscure text, was a useful

67   Nicholas Hawksmoor, the Mausoleum at Castle Howard, Yorkshire, 1729.

source for Hawksmoor: the urn-like decoration in the spandrels of the arches of the garden front in his design for Worcester College, Oxford, was taken from the illustration of the Édifices des Tuteles at Bordeaux; the reconstruction of the Clepsydre of Ctesibius probably provides the source for the curious pedestals in the garden at Castle Howard (Figs 68 and 69). Nor should it be forgotten that Vitruvius talked extensively about fortifications; Hawksmoor may well have seen his fortifications at Castle Howard as Classical rather than Gothic.

Castle Howard, Yorkshire, and in particular its Mausoleum (Fig. 67), provides the best insight into Hawksmoor's attitude towards the Antique because of the clash he experienced there with Lord Burlington. From his first discussions with Lord Carlisle in September 1726, it is clear that Hawksmoor considered the Mausoleum to be a neo-Classical reconstruction:

> The most famous among the Greeks was that at Halicarnassus, which was call'd ye Mausoleum . . . That which was the most famous in Italy was the Monument of Porsenna . . . The manner, and form of either of these fabricks, may be imitated, in Little, as well as at a great Expence, and I will draw up a Scheme for your Lordship accordingly. There are many forms of this nature of fabrick, built to ye Memory of illustrious persons, the designs of which are published in ye Books of Antiquity, that your Lordship may see at pleasure.[48]

– a reference to Hawksmoor's extensive archaeological library.

In his design of the Mausoleum Hawksmoor aimed to 'stick close to ye imitation of the Antique',[49] a principle which he further explained when he wrote that 'I dont mean that one need to Coppy them, but to be upon ye Same principalls.'[50] This is a critical statement of Hawksmoor's neo-Classical beliefs; imbued with Wren's scepticism towards the rules of Classical architecture and aware of the enormous variety to be found in surviving remains, Hawksmoor felt no obligation to recreate pedantically one particular building. His approach combined the literary with the archaeological, with descriptions forming the basis of reconstructions that often depended as much on his personal, deeply romantic, view of antiquity as on surviving remains. Perhaps if he had been to Italy and surveyed Classical remains in person his attitude might have been different.

In the event, Hawksmoor's design for the Castle Howard Mausoleum followed neither the Mausoleum of Halicarnassus nor that of Porsenna, but is based on the standard Roman design for a mausoleum, a circular drum or colonnade set on a square base, epitomised by the Mausoleum of Hadrian in Rome. Howard Colvin has neatly demonstrated that Hawksmoor's source was

Bartoli's conjectural reconstruction of the mausoleum on the Via Appia, Rome, known as the 'Tomb of Gallienus', published in Domenico Rossi's *Romae magnitudinis monumenta* of 1699. The one major difference was that Hawksmoor changed the Corinthian of the original to the more forbidding Doric.[51]

Hawksmoor had already experimented with the concept of a Classical mausoleum a decade earlier at the Radcliffe Library, Oxford, in 1712. Hawksmoor's role in the design of the Radcliffe Library is well known – it was he who first suggested a freestanding circular library which Gibbs subsequently adapted – but Gibbs's most significant alteration is seldom commented upon. Hawksmoor planned the library as a circular colonnaded drum placed on a square base. In execution Gibbs pared down the base so that it was coterminous with the drum. Hawksmoor's design was not just for a library – for which it is a markedly expensive and impractical model – but for a symbolic mausoleum to the University's great benefactor. If it had been built as intended this would have been apparent to all Classically educated men. Could Hawksmoor have known of the tomb of Celsus Polemaeanus, set in a vault beneath the library he donated to the city of Ephesus?[52] There was no suggestion that such an example was literally followed in Oxford, but the parallel would have amused Hawksmoor.

The idea of such a mausoleum was obviously one that was preoccupying Hawksmoor, for his third design for the chapel for Greenwich Hospital, made the previous year, with a circular colonnaded drum on a square base, is another reconstruction of a mausoleum, presumably intended as a monument to the memory of Queen Anne. Had it been built, Hawksmoor would have created a building that rivalled Hadrian's mausoleum in scale and grandeur.

While the circular drum or colonnade on a square base was the standard form for the Roman mausoleum, there were other well-known examples; one of the most renowned of these was the tomb of Caius Cestius in Rome, a sharply rising pyramid with a column marking each of the four corners. This, rather than the Egyptian pyramids directly, is probably the inspiration for the pyramid tomb of Lord William Howard at Castle Howard, although Hawksmoor has replaced the columns at the corners by squatter piles. Hawksmoor even labelled one of his designs for a *belvidera* at Castle Howard, suggested for the site of Vanbrugh's Temple of the Winds in 1724, 'After the Antique. Vid Herodatus Pliny and M. Varo'. His second design for the same site, a circular building with concave walls, may have been based on the Temple of the Sun at Baalbek which he would have known from Maundrell's account, although he did not reconstruct it for that book.[53]

The Triumphal Arch at Blenheim, Oxfordshire, is

68   The Clepsydre of Ctesibius, from Claude Perrault's edition of Vitruvius's *Ten Books of Architecture* (1684).

69   Nicholas Hawksmoor, plinth for a statue at Castle Howard, Yorkshire (1720s).

another park building that should be seen as a neo-Classical reconstruction (Fig. 70). Professor Downes noted its apparent Classical feel, but states that there was no Roman prototype for a triumphal arch with an attic narrower than the structure and describes the building as a curious misrepresentation of the Arch of Titus.[54] However, in the eighteenth century the Arch of Titus was still immured in the walls of Rome and its exact form was unknown. Two published reconstructions, those of du Cerceau and of Serlio, both show the arch with the attic only the width of the inscription (Fig. 71). In Hawksmoor's eyes nothing could have been more appropriate as an approach to the palace of a victorious general than a triumphal arch.

Hawksmoor's university work, for a world dominated by the Classics, repays examination from a neo-Classical perspective. Much was never built, but he had ambitious plans for remodelling both cities on a Classical model, and his college designs reflect this. At the heart of the Oxford scheme was Radcliffe Square with the Radcliffe Camera already discussed. Facing this was All Souls, for which one design, dated 1720, features a screen facing Radcliffe Square inscribed 'The Cloister of All S. after

the Greek' (Fig. 73). This is not, as has been suggested, a recognition on Hawksmoor's part that the distinguishing feature of Greek architecture is the use of the column and lintel and the absence of the arch; instead it is inspired by one of Serlio's illustrations. As Serlio explained in his commentary, 'the Greekes were the principall founders and inventors of good Architecture . . . neverthelesse, by reason of their great warres, and their land so often overrun and spoyled by the enemies, a man can hardly finde any good worke standing in the whole of Grecia.'[55] This colonnade was one of the few Greek buildings illustrated by Serlio, and so was of particular interest to Hawksmoor. His only other annotation for a drawing as being after the Greek manner is for an earlier All Souls' drawing which also has a giant colonnade.[56]

A more extensive range of quotations would have been found if the Worcester College building of about 1718 had been carried out as Hawksmoor planned. His drawings are particularly fascinating as they list the sources for the various elements, most of them antique. Some are fairly straight-forward, such as the cornices of the chapel and the library modelled on those of the Pantheon and the Arch of Constantine, others, such as

70 Nicholas Hawksmoor, the Triumphal Arch at Blenheim Palace, Oxfordshire, 1722.

the quotation from Perrault already mentioned, the towers based on the Tower of Andromachus or Temple of the Winds at Athens as described by Vitruvius, or the triple Venetian window on the garden front taken from the Roman arch at Saintes in France, illustrated in Blondel's *Cours d'architecture* of 1698 (again owned by Hawksmoor), are more obscure. It has also been plausibly suggested that the tempietto with the statue of Queen Anne over the gateway at Queen's College, Oxford, is inspired by a similar tempietto in the Temple of Diana at Ephesus, one of the buildings reconstructed by Wren.

Thus, a desire to design buildings as he thought Romans would have built them was a central feature of Hawksmoor's work, but this is nowhere clearer than in the churches he designed for the Fifty New Church Commissioners in 1712–16. The Commissioners had been established under a High Church measure by the Tory government in 1711 to build an intended fifty new churches in the expanding suburbs of London. In the end only a dozen churches were built solely as a result of the Act, in large part because the churches they commissioned turned out to be extravagantly expensive. Hawksmoor's first attempts at church design – seen in his contemporary schemes for remodelling Oxford – revolve around adapting the standard Roman pedimented and columned temple.[57] In this he was not alone, for similar attempts to design a church in the form of a temple can be found in works of Colen Campbell,

71 Jacques Androuet du Cerceau, reconstruction of the Arch of Titus, from *Quoniam apud veteres*.

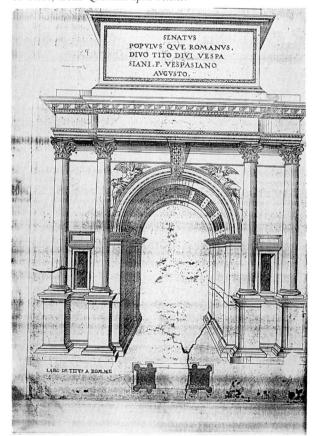

Alessandro Galilei and James Gibbs, also for the Fifty New Church Commissioners.[58] Of the ten models for churches submitted to the commissioners but unexecuted that were recorded by T.L. Donaldson in 1843, five were temple designs.[59] The plan of a standard peripteral temple was obviously impractical for use as a church, for if the 'cella' was to be large enough to hold a congregation the building would have to be enormously wide, while the cost of the colonnade would be exorbitant. So, for the design of St Alfege, Greenwich (Fig. 72), the first of the proposed Fifty New Churches, which was accepted in August 1712, Hawksmoor kept the idea of a temple-fronted single-gabled building but reduced the colonnade to pilasters. Despite the projecting north and south entrances – which John Summerson suggests may have been inspired by Vitruvius's description of the Basilica at Fano – the single gable makes this

the only one of the fifty new churches to be based on the classic Roman temple. By contrast, when Gibbs came to design St Martin-in-the-Fields he also used an applied order of pilasters, but the portico does not express the whole structure of the church as it would in a temple.

As Gibbs found, the difficulty with a straight temple derivation was deciding where to place the tower demanded by the Commissioners. Hawksmoor's solution at Greenwich was to create two separate but linked structures. His next three churches, St George-in-the-East, Wapping (Fig. 75), Christ Church, Spitalfields, and St Anne, Limehouse (Fig. 74), all begun in 1714, move away from the idea of the single-gable temple and incorporate their towers into the body of the church. No one has ever explained the inspiration behind these buildings, and they remain unique in European architecture. Their interiors, particularly that of Christ Church, Spitalfields,

72   Nicholas Hawksmoor, St Alfege's church, Greenwich, London, 1712.

73 Nicholas Hawksmoor, design for the Radcliffe Square front of All Souls College, Oxford, 1720.

are all strongly Classical, with columns, coffering and guilloche decorated beams, and it can be argued that their exteriors should be seen as antique reconstructions.

Among the publications of Androuet du Cerceau is one entitled *Quoniam apud veteres alio structurae genere templa fuerunt aedificata* which is a selection of reconstructions of Classical buildings including the Arch of Titus and Hadrian's Mausoleum. Included among these are a series of reconstructions of temples, mostly, but not all, unnamed (Figs 76 and 77). These differ markedly from the standard Classical temple with its pediment and columns and have none of the traditional Classical order and harmony of Palladio's reconstructions. Instead, they are dominated by towers (some topped with pyramids), have semi-circular apses, use giant porticos as entrances and make frequent use of columns. These are all features that distinguish Hawksmoor's churches, and while none of these directly copy any of the engravings, their similarity, given Hawksmoor's attitude towards Classical reconstruction, seems more than coincidence. We cannot be certain that Hawksmoor knew these engravings, but he was a voracious collector of such works. Furthermore, because some copies of du Cerceau's work lacked a frontispiece it may have escaped being specifically men-

tioned in the catalogue of the sale of his library but been included in such all-encompassing lots as 'miscellaneous collection of prints and palaces, views, ruins etc.', 'Collection of prints of Roman Antiquities', 'collection of prints and drawings related to ancient architecture', 'A Book of about 460 Prints & Drawings' or 'A Book of Prints and Drawings'.[60] While the du Cerceau illustrations were probably the inspiration behind Hawksmoor's designs, he may have looked to similar works for details. Howard Colvin has pointed out, for instance, that an engraving of a temple in Montano's *Scielta di varii tempietti antichi* has a circular vestibule that could have been the source for that at St Anne, Limehouse.

Thus, even where he appears to our eyes at his most outlandishly un-Classical, Hawksmoor was building what he thought were valid Roman structures. This is not to say that Hawksmoor's architecture can be explained solely by reference to the Antique. He was far too varied and inventive an architect to be constrained by one guiding inspiration. But an interest in neo-Classical reconstruction, however romantic that reconstruction might have been, was a central factor in his work. By contrast, Wren may have begun his career with a handful of neo-Classical reconstructions, but he had

74   Nicholas Hawksmoor, St Anne's church, Limehouse, London, 1714.

75 Nicholas Hawksmoor, St George-in-the-East, Wapping, London, 1714.

76 Jacques Androuet de Cerceau, reconstruction of a Roman Temple, from *Quoniam apud veteres*.

77 Jacques Androuet de Cerceau, reconstruction of a Roman Temple, from *Quoniam apud veteres*.

moved away from them by the time he was designing his mature work. Even when he was quoting directly from antiquity his approach was not the same as that of Hawksmoor, for his reconstructions rely fairly literally on the works of the two most reputable surveyors of antique buildings, Serlio and Palladio. He avoided the

more imaginative of their fellows and did not try to put his literary reconstructions into practice. Hawksmoor not only used Serlio and Palladio but was equally fascinated by the more imaginative reconstructions of du Cerceau and Montano. Literary reconstructions were as valid to him as those surveyed from extant remains.

IV

LATE SEVENTEENTH-CENTURY ARCHITECTURE
AND THE BAROQUE INTERLUDE

Roger Pratt's model for the country house, successful though it was, had its disadvantages and its critics. Roger North, writing about 1698, was particularly dismissive of what he believed was a style fit only for suburban villas, primarily because he believed the compact house was not suitable for an English gentleman:

> The country model, and that of a suburban villa, are different. The former partakes of the nature of a court, have great rooms to contein numbers, with fires suitable and other conveniences, according to his condition. A villa, is quasy a lodge, for the sake of a garden, to retire to injoy and sleep without pretence of enterteinement of many persons; and yet in this age, the humour takes after that, not the other . . . not onely in the cittys and townes, a compact model is used, but in all country seats of late built, the same method is practis't, to the abolishing of grandure and statlyness of that sort the former ages affected.[1]

Audley End was his ideal, but North was aware that things had changed: 'since the reigne of Charles II scarce any of that intention hath bin built'.[2] He was not happy with what was being designed instead, considering the 'pile' 'the corruption of building . . . It was an old fault to spread the housing too much, and a very commendable conduct to compose it more orderly together; that hath ledd to such compaction, that an house is lay'd on an heap like a wasps-nest, and much of greatness as well as conveniences lost by it.'[3] He cited Melton Constable, Norfolk, as an example: 'Now taking altogether the whole house, tho it be large, square and many windows, yet it looks small, and doth not humour the proposition of a large country family.'[4]

Much of his detailed criticism was pertinent. Cupolas almost inevitably leaked, and as the century wore on fewer houses were built with them, while, over subsequent centuries, many that were built have been removed. Other factors had their advantages as well as disadvantages – compactness led to economy of construction but could cause noise and smells to disseminate throughout the house; much depended on whether the kitchen was placed in the basement (which Pratt insisted upon) or in a detached building, something which remained a matter for debate.[5] But North's criticism was principally directed against the size of the compact house, the fact that it was not suited to entertaining large numbers and that it lacked the grandeur required by a great family. These were real problems, which meant that while the Pratt-type house was to remain popular into the eighteenth century it was increasingly superseded as the model for large houses.

Size and scale were still important factors in the impression presented by a nobleman's seat. It was not chance that led the Duke of Beaufort to keep the rambling nature of Badminton House, Gloucestershire, adding new façades where appropriate, rather than rebuild in a compact fashion (Fig. 80). Pratt acknowledged that courtyard houses were more appropriate than piles for great nobles, and the 1660s saw a series of such houses built or rebuilt: Hampstead Marshall, Berkshire (1662), for the Earl of Craven; Euston Hall, Suffolk, for Lord Arlington; Althorp, Northamptonshire (1665–8), for the Earl of Sunderland, and Syon House, Middlesex (before 1669), for the Earl of Northumberland. But the Pratt-type was so dominant as a model for country houses in the 1670s that even new or remodelled U-plan houses such as Holme Lacy, Herefordshire (1674), Hugh May's Cassiobury, Hertfordshire (1677), and William Winde's Combe Abbey, Warwickshire (1682–3) (Fig. 79), were given astylar pedimented façades. The problem was that these lacked the architectural strength to control such long, low buildings and did not express the plan as effectively as in a compact house. It is perhaps a sign of dissatisfaction that neither at Cassiobury nor at Combe Abbey was the remodelling completed.

One answer, as Pratt showed at Clarendon House (Fig. 35), was to add French-style pavilions to the corners of a compact pile. These were used at Ragley Hall, Warwickshire (c.1677) (Fig. 78), Kedleston Hall, Derbyshire (c.1700), and, on a smaller scale, at Hanbury Hall, Worcestershire (1701), and had the advantage that they

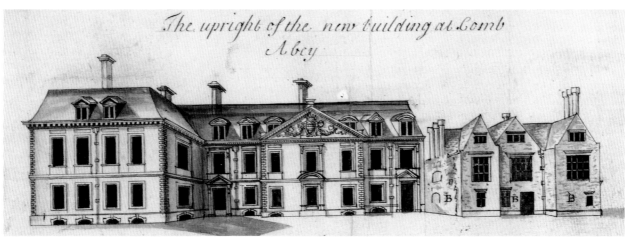

The upright of the new building at Comb Abey

78 (top) William Hurlbutt, Ragley Hall, Warwickshire, *c.*1677. The attic was added by James Wyatt in the 1780s.

79 (above) William Winde, Combe Abbey, Warwickshire, 1682 (partially demolished).

80 (left) Anon., Badminton House, Gloucestershire, *c.*1664, from *Britannia Illustrata* (1707) (detail).

81 (facing page top) William Winde, Belton House, Lincolnshire, 1685.

82 (facing page bottom left) Anon., Bourne Park, Kent, *c.*1700.

83 (facing page bottom right) Sir Christopher Wren, Winslow Hall, Buckinghamshire, 1699.

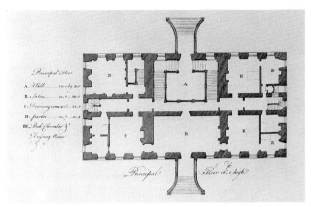

84   Sir Roger Pratt, plan of the principal floor of Coleshill
House, Berkshire, *c.*1651, from *Vitruvius Britannicus* (1771)
(demolished).

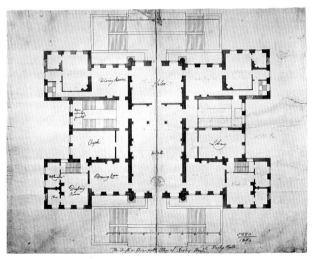

85   William Hurlbutt, plan of the principal floor of Ragley
Hall, Warwickshire, 1676.

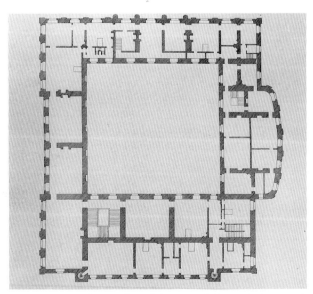

86   William Talman, plan of the second floor of Chatsworth
House, Derbyshire, 1687, from *Vitruvius Britannicus* (1715).

could neatly accommodate a chamber, closet and back
stairs. An alternative was to add wings to a compact
pile, as at Stow, Cornwall (1680), and Belton House,
Lincolnshire (1684) (Fig. 81). Neither solution could
escape a rather bloated feel, and both lacked the satisfying
logic of Pratt's compact piles. Other solutions were to
keep the tripartite division but expand the number of
bays – Bourne Park, Kent (1701) (Fig. 82), has a five bay
centrepiece flanked by four-bay ranges – or to add an
extra half storey, making the house two and a half stories
high, as Wren did at Winslow Hall, Buckinghamshire
(1699) (Fig. 83), and William Talman did at Kimberley
Hall, Norfolk (*c.*1700).

Particularly when extended by pavilions or wings, the
Pratt-type house could provide large numbers of rooms
and was well suited to the small apartment – a chamber,
a closet or two and perhaps a back stairs – which became
fashionable around the middle of the century. Coleshill
was the archetypal example of this and, like most of
Pratt's houses, was composed of a series of small apartments organised around the central reception rooms: the
hall, the great parlour and the great dining chamber on
the first floor (Fig. 84). However, changing fashions in
the use of rooms in aristocratic houses caused problems.
The disposition of the reception rooms at Coleshill was
based on the assumption that the grandest room was the
first-floor great dining chamber. During the second half
of the century such isolated reception rooms fell out of
fashion in large houses. Instead, the demand was for the
grandest room to be part of a state suite in enfilade with
at least an ante-room, withdrawing room, bedchamber
and closet.

The enfiladed state apartment was essentially a royal
concept, and it is not surprising that one of the earliest
non-royal English examples was at Wilton which was
rebuilt to accommodate Charles I. A similar motivation
may lie behind John Smythson's plan for the terrace
range at Bolsover Castle, Derbyshire, of about 1630.[6]
This was designed for the Earl (subsequently Duke) of
Newcastle and comprised a hall, great chamber, withdrawing chamber, bed chamber and closet, all in enfilade
with an adjacent gallery and chapel. The king visited
Newcastle at Bolsover in 1633 and was entertained at a
cost of £20,000, although he was not able to stay the
night as work was still in hand. In the event, Smythson's
plan was not followed, but the wing as built does
seem to have comprised a state apartment. So, it can be
argued, did the first-floor north range of Thorpe Hall,
Cambridgeshire, built in the 1650s.[7]

However, it was in the 1670s that the fashion for a
state apartment began to spread among the aristocracy,
with the Duke and Duchess of Lauderdale creating one
at Ham House, Surrey, in 1672–4 and the Duke of
Newcastle another at Nottingham Castle, begun in
1674. In both cases this was only possible because the

state apartment was made to double back on itself. Else-where, the Hurlbutt brothers created an enfilade for the 4th Lord Brooke at Warwick Castle between 1669 and 1678 and William Talman formed state apartments at Burghley House, Northamptonshire, in 1681–4 and at Chatsworth House, Derbyshire, in 1687–8 (Fig. 86). Warwick Castle had a sequence of four rooms between the hall and the closet; Burghley and Chatsworth had four from the top of the stairs to the closet – these can be identified as the great dining chamber, the ante-chamber, the withdrawing chamber and the bed-chamber. In these cases only a single state apartment was created, but the ideal was for a pair, as was achieved at Petworth House, Sussex (1688), Castle Howard, York-shire (1702), Blenheim Palace, Oxfordshire (1705), and Wanstead House, Essex (1714).

Increasing formality in planning was not restricted to the state apartment. At Ham the Lauderdales also created a pair of lesser apartments for themselves on the ground floor, comprising a central hall flanked on either side by a withdrawing room, bedchamber and closet. Such sym-metrical suites became increasingly common. On the grandest scale they are the dominant features of Montagu House, London (1687), Burley-on-the-Hill, Leicester-shire (1694), and Wentworth Castle, Yorkshire (1709), but they can even be found in houses as small as Hollin Hall, Yorkshire (c.1719).[8]

These two developments created great problems for the Pratt-type house. This could, with a certain diffi-culty, accommodate a pair of family apartments, particu-larly if it had pavilions, as at Ragley Hall, designed about 1676 for Lord Conway (Fig. 85). Here the withdrawing chambers were in the body of the house, flanking the hall and saloon, with bedchambers and closets in project-ing pavilions. But even these apartments went against the logic of the design, while the relatively small scale and essential symmetry around a central axis of the Pratt-type houses made a state apartment virtually impossible.

A common solution to the problem of the state apart-ment's position, particularly in a compact house, was to place it across an entire range, as at Chatsworth (Fig. 87), Boughton House, Northamptonshire (early 1690s), Dyrham Park, Gloucestershire (1698) (Fig. 105), or Beningborough Hall, Yorkshire (1716). This meant that there could be no central accent, as in the Prattian house, because the most important rooms were at each end.

87 William Talman, Chatsworth House, Derbyshire, 1687 (J. C. Buckler, watercolour, private collection (detail)).

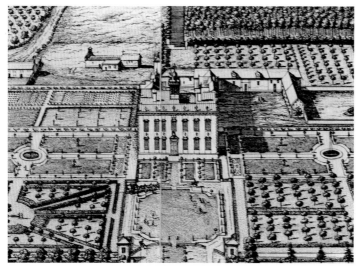

88 Anon., Acklam Hall, Yorkshire, 1683, from *Britannia Illustrata* (1707) (detail).

89 Anon., Antony House, Cornwall, 1710.

90 Anon., Boughton House, Northamptonshire, 1680s.

Instead, these rooms were often emphasised by projecting pavilions; but, even where the central accent was maintained by building a pair of apartments on either side of a frontispiece, the Prattian façade (particularly when astylar) lacked the vigour to dominate elevations on this scale.

Thus, the Pratt model was increasingly set aside for the design of larger houses towards the end of the century. However, it remained popular for medium-sized houses, although the latter decades of the century did see a move to replace the hipped roof and dormer windows that had been the dominant feature since the 1630s with a complete extra storey, often with half-height windows, topped by a balustrade and flat, or apparently flat, roof. This must partly have been caused by the desire to replace cramped dormer-lit attics with full-height rooms but aesthetics may have played their part. Acklam Hall, Yorkshire (1683) (Fig. 88), although only of two storeys, is an early example of the trend towards a flat roof; it was swiftly followed by other examples such as Thoresby House, Nottinghamshire (1685), Halswell Hall, Somerset (1689), and Lowther Castle, Westmorland (1692). This last example is particularly revealing because a drawing survives, attributed to Robert Hooke, showing that Sir John Lowther had considered building a house with hipped roof and dormers before settling for a flat roof.[9] Houses with hipped roofs and dormers continued to be designed into the eighteenth century, as can be seen at Ampthill Park, Bedfordshire (1704), and Antony House, Cornwall (1710) (Fig. 89), but they were exceptional. Instead, the dramatic potential of apparently flat-roofed houses was exploited with giant pilasters in a manner that is best described as Baroque.

The second half of the seventeenth century had seen the slow spread of a more ambitious Classicism, led by Christopher Wren but abetted by such amateurs and enthusiastic patrons as Robert Hooke and the 1st Duke of Montagu. The Netherlands were one source of ideas, particularly for such urban and commercial projects as Wren's Custom House (1672) or the façade of Robert Hooke's Royal College of Physicians (1672–8).[10] France was another; the circular vestibule which linked the courtyard of the Royal College of Physicians with Warwick Lane suggests that Hooke was aware of the latest Parisian architectural fashions, in particular Antoine le Pautre's Hôtel de Beauvais (1660).[11] Versailles was the model for Wren's plan of Winchester Palace, Hampshire (1683). France appealed to a section of the aristocracy: Euston Hall in the 1660s; Ribston Hall, Yorkshire, Arthington Hall, Yorkshire, Bethlehem Hospital, London, and Montagu House in the 1670s; Boughton House (Fig. 90) and Petworth House in the 1680s, are all sophisticated attempts at importing contemporary French ideas into England. But they remained isolated examples.

The culmination of this steady increase in Classical sophistication came at the end of the century, with the brief English flourishing of the most ambitious Classical style of all, the Baroque. A concise definition of the Baroque is almost impossible, partly because, like Palladianism, it encompasses a number of different strands. Put most simply, it is the reverse of the sense of Classical harmony found in Palladianism; an essential element is a sense of drama, almost of danger. At its most extreme the Baroque can involve subverting the rules that generally govern the orders, as when a giant broken pediment is placed on top of a building. Often it is expressed in a sense of movement in a façade as opposed to harmony, of contrasting planes, insistent skyline and varied sense of scale. Sometimes it can be seen in way the sculptural mass of a building is emphasised. Occasionally, in England at least, it may be no more than the application of borrowed Baroque details to an otherwise standard façade. English Baroque is seldom as full-blooded as Italian Baroque and it flowered for a much briefer period, but the beliefs that lie behind it are so much the reverse of conventional Palladian thought that no study of English Palladianism can be complete without some assessment of the success and coherence of the English Baroque, in particular of the way in which it differs from the Palladian norm, not least because it forms the background against which the dramatic rise of interest in Palladianism in the first two decades of the eighteenth century must be seen.

That English architects and craftsmen were capable of creating a native Baroque style by the end of the century is a tribute to the architectural programme adopted by Pratt, Evelyn and May at the Restoration. In 1660, skill in handling Classical proportions and ornament was weak among English craftsmen and they certainly lacked that complete control of the Classical vocabulary which the Baroque requires. Forty years on, the large number of architectural books published since the 1660s had helped educate a new, Classically literate body of workmen. It was a process given particular stimulus by the Great Fire of London in 1666 which sucked masons, carpenters, bricklayers and plasterers into the metropolis, exposed them (particularly those who worked under Christopher Wren at St Paul's Cathedral) to the highest standards of Classical architecture and then spat them out across the country. The Strong family, masons from the Cotswolds who became principal contractors for St Paul's and later helped to build Blenheim Palace, is only the most distinguished of many. Men like Edward Strong were capable of anything that Vanbrugh or his contemporaries asked of them.

Some commentators have traced the English Baroque back to John Webb's Greenwich Palace, with its giant pilasters, overbearing attics, emphatic keystones and spatially complex vestibule (Fig. 30). John Bold called

Webb the 'father of the English Baroque style'.[12] But the King Charles Building is not itself Baroque; it was inspired by Palladio's palazzi in Vicenza, for example the Loggia del Capitano and the Palazzo Valmarana, not by the Roman Baroque. Thirty years after it was built, the King Charles Building did have a certain influence on the English Baroque, but it was not itself responsible for the foundation of an English Baroque school.

The first and greatest English Baroque architect is usually held to be Christopher Wren, but it is questionable whether his work before the late 1690s deserves to be described as Baroque, and even then it is debatable whether the freedom that enters his architectural vocabulary should not be ascribed to the influence of Hawksmoor and Vanbrugh. As seen in the second chapter, Wren's first architectural essays were Palladian in inspiration and Palladianism remained an important element of his work into the 1670s and 1680s. Palladianism, however, has very little to do with his greatest work, St Paul's Cathedral (Fig. 91), which is often seen as a Baroque creation.

The building history of St Paul's is confused; Wren was already considering what should be done with St Paul's when it was destroyed in the Great Fire of London in 1666. Only fragmentary remains survive of Wren's first scheme for rebuilding, presented in 1670. Much more significant were the Greek Cross design, made early in 1672 and given royal approval in November, and the Great Model, a development of the same idea but with a freestanding portico and vestibule, which replaced it in September 1673. Clerical objections meant that this was rejected, and it was the compromise Warrant design that was given royal approval in May 1675. However, for Wren this was only a starting point and the church as built bore little relation to it. By the time the first building contracts were agreed that year, Wren had completely redesigned the cathedral and it was to this Definitive design that the body of the church was built. The form of the dome was left undecided until about 1697 – it was completed by 1708 – while the design of the west towers was not agreed until 1704.[13]

There is nothing Baroque about Wren's original intentions for St Paul's. The Greek Cross and Great Model designs show that what Wren wanted to build was a centrally planned domed church, one of the obsessions of the High Renaissance of which Bramante's design for St Peter's in Rome was the exemplar; an idea with which Webb had already toyed.[14] Nor is the church as built particularly Baroque. The compromise plan is essentially that of an English Gothic cathedral with a dome instead of a central crossing tower.[15] *Cinquecento* sources, and perhaps the influence of Inigo Jones's Banqueting House, rather than Baroque motifs also lie behind much of the detail of the executed elevations, particularly the use of columned, pedimented aedicules set in a rusticated field between pairs of pilasters. With the dome Wren wavered. The Definitive design owes something to the dome of the Val-de-Grace in Paris which had recently been completed when Wren saw it in 1665, but essentially looked back to the dome of St Peter's with its peristyle of paired columns (1586–93). During its final period of design the dome went through a bewildering series of proposals revealing a variety of sources, but the final proposal was chiefly influenced by Bramante. Serlio illustrated a design by Bramante for the dome of St Peter's with a continuous peristyle, but, as built, St Paul's owes rather more to the building which Serlio illustrated after St Peter's, Bramante's Tempietto – one of the few buildings of the Renaissance seen to rival antiquity. From this Wren probably took the form of the balustraded colonnade and attic above. Serlio's woodcut, which emphasises the niches on the drum of the Tempietto, may have given Wren the idea for interspersing the colonnade with solid piers decorated with niches. It was only with the west towers that St Paul's became genuinely Baroque.

Instead of seeking the dawn of the English Baroque at St Paul's it is necessary to look to a very different sort of architecture. The Baroque first appeared in England as a decorative style, a grand illusionistic manner for treating ceremonial interiors that had been familiar on the Continent, particularly in Italy and France, for half a century. One of the earliest, and certainly the most important, examples was at Windsor Castle, where Hugh May's state apartments, fitted up between 1674 and 1684 within the confines of a rather constricted structure, created a sequence of spaces which exploited variety of size and lighting in a way that had never been attempted in England.[16] This manipulation of space and light was further enhanced by the elaborate carvings of Grinling Gibbons and the illusionistic paintings of Antonio Verrio, who had probably arrived in England in 1672. In the chapel and St George's Hall (Fig. 92), decorated in 1682–4, their work reached a peak that was never rivalled and which led John Evelyn into raptures: 'then the Resurrection in the Chapel, where the figure of the Ascension is, in my opinion, comparable to any paintings of the most famous masters'. Evelyn's hyperbole is understandable, as Edward Croft-Murray rightly pointed out, 'the full-blooded exuberance of the Baroque had never before been let loose in this country'.[17]

The Baroque decoration of the state apartments at Windsor sparked off a series of comparable interiors, both in royal palaces and in the houses of great nobles. The Painted Hall and state apartments at Chatsworth (1687–96), designed by William Talman and decorated by Verrio and Louis Laguerre, are directly comparable to Windsor; at Burghley House (c.1688–98), again designed by Talman and decorated by Verrio and Laguerre, whose painting in the state apartment was not restricted

to the ceiling but covered the walls of the Heaven Room, where a host of gods cavort amidst an illusionary Corinthian colonnade; in the saloon at Blenheim Palace, Oxfordshire (1719), these were replaced by the rather more stately inhabitants of the Four Continents. Generally, it was staircases, with elaborate illusionistic architectural frameworks like that of the Heaven Room, that formed the most popular setting for Baroque painting, as at Hampton Court (1690); Petworth House (1692); Buckingham House, Middlesex (c.1705); Burley-on-the-Hill (c.1708); Powis Castle, Powys (1705); Hanbury Hall (after 1710) and Drayton House, Northamptonshire (c.1712).

In Sir James Thornhill the English produced a painter of Baroque interiors to rival the foreign imports, his masterpiece being the Painted Hall at Greenwich Hospital of 1707–14. But by the time Thornhill had finished the Painted Hall the doom of the Baroque painted interior had already been announced by the arrival in England of the Venetian Giovanni Pellegrini, who painted the entrance hall, staircase and High Saloon at Castle Howard in 1709, and the staircase at Kimbolton Castle, Huntingdonshire, in 1710. At Kimbolton, Pellegrini revolutionised the idea of the Baroque painted staircase, doing away with the grand architectural framework and replacing it with a lighter, more relaxed style, a style which Marco Ricci further developed in the staircase at Burlington House (c.1714). At first, Thornhill was unaffected, beating Pellegrini in the commission for the decoration of the dome of St Paul's in 1714 and starting on the Upper Hall at Greenwich in 1718. But at Blenheim he was dismissed after painting the hall in 1716; at Kensington Palace he was ignored in favour of William Kent in 1722 and at Moor Park, Hertfordshire, where he worked from 1720 to 1728, he suffered the humiliation of having his bill challenged and his work replaced by that of the Venetian Giacomo Amiconi. Thereafter, he had no more work, a victim partly of his own high prices and of Venetian skills, but more of changing tastes as the Baroque which he represented had passed away.

For all the lavish architectural framework of such paintings, these Baroque interiors received little or no external acknowledgement. At Windsor, Hugh May's castle style could hardly have been less Baroque, although in the Horn Court, which formed the approach to the king's apartment, he did devise a grandiose façade to the staircase, with giant Corinthian columns carrying a high panelled attic flanking an arch twenty-four feet high, lofty enough to open an unimpeded view through to the upper level of the King's Great Staircase.[18] At Burghley, Verrio's rooms were fitted into the Elizabethan shell. At Petworth, the Baroque decoration of the staircase was set in a peculiarly French house. The exteriors of Burley-on-the-Hill, Buckingham House,

91   Sir Christopher Wren, St Paul's Cathedral, City of London, 1675, (Antonio Joli, oil, Yale Center for British Art, New Haven, Conn.).

Wimpole Hall, Cambridgeshire, and Hanbury Hall give no hint of the glories within.

It is also noticeable that English painted Baroque decoration seems to have been treated as a cheap alternative to the expense and trouble of creating genuinely Baroque architectural interiors. There is nothing that compares with the genuinely Baroque staircases of Germany, particularly Bavaria. It is surprising that Vanbrugh, in particular, never made more of his staircases, particularly those at Castle Howard and Blenheim, hidden behind arcades and barely impinging on the visitor's consciousness. May's Windsor apartments are exceptional in their use of the Baroque tricks of light and space. At Hampton Court the magnificence of Verrio's staircase painting cannot disguise the blandly unimaginative box in which it stands, and this is true of most of the painted staircases mentioned. The one exception was Buckingham House, where the dramatic impact of the original staircase can be glimpsed from the views in W.H. Pyne's *The Royal Residences* (1819), although by the time this was published significant changes had already been carried out. Here, the way the visitor was led from the relatively low, dark entrance hall through a colonnade into the tall, immensely elaborately painted staircase with its ring of *trompe l'oeil* Composite columns and its ceiling, supported by caryatids, displaying a galaxy of the gods was a progression worthy of Windsor.

The spatial complexity of Buckingham House has led to suggestions that the mind behind it was that of William Talman. The idea of a relatively small vestibule leading through a screen to a great staircase, often an imperial staircase, was a regular feature of Talman's de-

92   Hugh May, St George's Hall, Windsor Castle, Berkshire, 1682, from W.H. Pyne's *The Royal Residences* (1819).

signs. Where there was space Talman liked to balance the staircase with a long hall on the other side of the vestibule, again approached through a screen, allowing a fluid interpenetration of spaces. This can be seen at its most developed in the plan for Kiveton House, Yorkshire (Fig. 93), where Talman planned an oval vestibule which opened on one side to a hall forty feet long and on the other to an imperial staircase, and then led under a colonnaded pergola into a garden hall where further columns would have flanked the two chimney-pieces. Slightly smaller, but no less carefully thought out, was the Trianon he designed for William III at Thames Ditton (*c*.1702). Here the approach would have been up two flights of external stairs, under a niched portico-in-antis, into an oval coffered vestibule from which an arcaded screen led into a large hall.[19] However, Talman, like May, seldom attempted the same Baroque complexity on his exteriors, and his more ambitious elevations are strongly influenced by the work of Palladio, Jones and Webb.

Sadly, Talman's spatial adventures remained largely on paper, but there is one house with an interior of com-

parable Baroque complexity, Nicholas Hawksmoor's Easton Neston, Northamptonshire (1702). In 1688 Hawksmoor had put forward a plan for Ingestre Hall, Staffordshire, very similar to those by Talman. This suggested a small central vestibule flanked by screens with the staircase on one side and the hall on the other, leading through to a long gallery with what appears to be a small dome in the centre, but it was never built.[20] Easton Neston was markedly more sophisticated. Here, the front door led into what appeared at first to be a narrow, single-storey vestibule with a vista through to the gardens. To the right, however, only a pair of columns separated the vestibule from the double-height hall, the vestibule being matched by a similar single-storey space at the end of the hall, creating a room of impressive spatial sophistication. Advancing from the vestibule into the centre of the house, the staircase then set off at right angles, slowly ascending to the first floor in a long, narrow dog-leg. At the top of the stairs the axis again turned ninety degrees, with a gallery running across the depth of the house from the entrance to the garden fronts. Without histrionic use of architectural

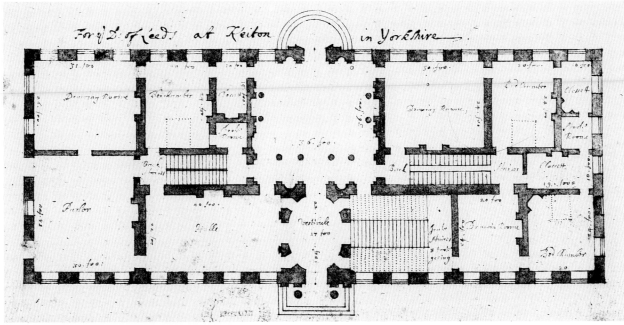

93 William Talman, unexecuted ground-plan for Kiveton House, Yorkshire, 1698.

forms, at Easton Neston Hawksmoor created a compact house of unparalleled spatial complexity.

Wren and Hawksmoor were responsible for a comparably impressive space in the Painted Hall at Greenwich (1698). Here, the visitor enters from the colonnade into the vestibule, a tall cylinder surrounded by giant Corinthian pilasters with overhanging entablatures opening up to the dome which is flooded by light. Then, climbing the stairs and passing between a pair of columns, the visitor enters the rectangular mass of the hall with windows on both sides separated by giant pilasters and Thornhill's elaborate allegory of William III and Queen Mary giving peace and liberty to Europe on the ceiling. At the end of this large, well-lit space is the high table, set in the Upper Hall, a more enclosed space approached up a few more steps, cut off by an arch from the Painted Hall.

At Greenwich, this spatial complexity must have been the work of Wren and Hawksmoor, for Vanbrugh was not appointed Comptroller of the Board of Works until 1702 and did not join the Board of Directors of Greenwich Hospital until 1703, by which time the Painted Hall had already been built. The only comparable domestic interior was the joint work of Vanbrugh and Hawksmoor – the hall at Castle Howard begun in 1702 (Fig. 95). Here, in a space worthy of the crossing of an Italian church rather than a country house in Yorkshire, Vanbrugh and Hawksmoor created the masterpiece of the English Baroque interior, with a great cupola supported on four arches, each opening through to a corridor or staircase, so that one is never quite sure of the depth of vision. Nothing built later would rival this *tour de force* which steals the thunder of both the Roman Catholic church and the English royal palace. By the

time the main block at Castle Howard had been completed, Vanbrugh and Hawksmoor's imaginations had already moved beyond the Baroque.

It is no coincidence that the high point of the English Baroque should have appeared in the years around the turn of the century. The five years between 1697 and 1702 were a welcome respite in a ferocious struggle with France that began in 1688 and would continue until the Peace of Utrecht in 1713. For the first time in a decade Englishmen were able to travel to France, Louis XIV's novel palace at Marly proving a particular draw, the gardener George London visiting it in 1699.[21] (A group of Scots nobles, led by the Earl of Mar, not to be outdone by the more proximate English, clubbed together to send Alexander Edward to France and the Low Countries in 1701 to 'view, observe and take draughts of the most curious and remarkable Houses, Edifices, Gardings, orchards, parks plantations, land improvements, coall works, mines, water works and other curiosities of nature or art'. A plan he made of Marly survives among the Gibbs drawings in Oxford.[22]) Contact with France encouraged stylistic innovation. William Talman proved particularly receptive, although there is no evidence that he travelled to France. His use of central projecting bows in his design for Castle Howard, Yorkshire, and for the Trianon at Thames Ditton,[23] suggests an awareness of contemporary work by Pierre Bullet at the Château de Champs, while French detail, especially French quoins and rustication, abound in his designs.

Peace also meant that there was time and money to devote to building. The war waged by William III had been extremely expensive, costing about £40 m. and leaving a debt of £14 m. which cost more to service

94 Anon., Petworth House, Sussex, *c.*1688.

than the whole ordinary permanent revenue granted to Charles II at the Restoration. To fund the fighting a land tax had had to be introduced, and as that proved insufficient the Bank of England was founded in 1694.[24] As a result, there had been little to spend on architecture in the 1690s, in contrast to the decade and a half of peace that followed the end of the Third Dutch War in 1674. These years had seen a marked building boom (although this seems to have slowed during the uncertain reign of James II from 1685 to 1688) including the remodelling of Windsor Castle and Whitehall, the abortive Winchester Palace, the Royal Hospital at Chelsea, the bulk of St Paul's Cathedral, most of the City churches and innumerable country houses. The 1690s are dull by comparison. Hampton Court was built for William and Mary, but, as an English rival to Versailles, it almost came under wartime expenditure and work was halted in 1694 on Queen Mary's death. The remodelling of Kensington Palace fulfilled the practical need for the asthmatic King to have a London palace where he would feel comfortable, and it was no larger than a reasonable-sized country house. Other public building was largely non-existent. Virtually all the City churches had been completed in the 1670s and 1680s, the only activity there being the completion of a couple of spires. Nor was country-house building particularly common, although there are exceptions (particularly where owners had done conspicuously well out of the Revolution of 1688) including Petworth (*c.*1688–90) (Fig. 94), Swallowfield House, Berkshire (1689–91), Boughton (*c.*1690–4), New Park,

Surrey (1692), Lowther Hall (1692–5), Kiveton (1694–1704) and Burley-on-the-Hill (1696–8).

With the return of peace, more ambitious schemes could be planned, in particular the completion of the dome of St Paul's. Whitehall, burnt down in 1697, was replanned on an extravagant colonnaded scale. That scheme was not executed, but at Greenwich Hospital, where a start had been made on the pair to the King Charles Building in 1696, a comparable project was executed with considerable speed, with the hall following in 1698, its dome being finished in 1704. At Kensington Palace the Orangery was begun in 1704. In the City nine spires and towers were completed between 1697 and 1704. At Warwick, St Mary's, burnt in 1694, was rebuilt from 1698. Elsewhere, Talman's Dyrham Park dates from 1698; Vanbrugh's Castle Howard, 1699; the north front of Chatsworth House and Vanbrugh's 'Goose-pie House' in Whitehall, 1700; Hawksmoor's extravagant rebuilding of Easton Neston, 1702; William Winde's Buckingham House, 1702. Other important houses begun or substantially altered during these years include Winslow Hall, Buckinghamshire; Herriard Park, Hampshire; Appuldurcombe House, Isle-of-Wight; Drayton House; Stanford Hall, Leicestershire; and Waldershare Park, Kent.

Thus, it was during this half decade of peace that the English Baroque flourished most freely, but, as can be seen in the work of Bernini and Borromini in Rome half a century earlier, two conflicting approaches to the Baroque can be perceived, one based on the ambiguity

95 Sir John Vanbrugh, the hall at Castle Howard, Yorkshire, 1702.

96   Sir Christopher Wren, Greenwich Hospital, London, (Antonio Canaletto, oil, National Maritime Museum, London).

of mass and architectural form, the other on the monumentality of the colonnade.

One of the two steeples added by Wren to City churches in the war years of the 1690s was that of St Vedast, the curving forms and contrasting concave and convex levels of which suggest knowledge of Borromini's buildings in Rome of the 1630s. It was a prescient work in a style that would be developed further with the return of peace. St Michael Crooked Lane (spire completed 1698), St Bride (1702), St Stephen Walbrook, St James Garlick Hill (1713) and St Michael Paternoster Royal (1713), together with the west towers

97   Sir Christopher Wren, King William Block, Greenwich Hospital, Kent, 1699.

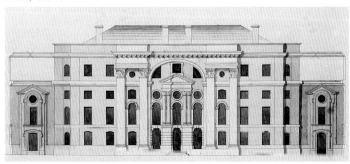

of St Paul's (1704), gave London's skyline an extraordinary array of Baroque ornaments unmatched in any other European city. Only in the twin towers of Hawksmoor's All Soul's College, Oxford, and at Vanbrugh and Hawksmoor's Blenheim Palace, in particular in the towers over the centre of the office ranges, is the spatial complexity of these London spires (and those of the later Fifty New Churches) matched. So alien do these appear after the restraint of Wren's earlier work that one cannot help but wonder at the role in their design of Wren's assistant Nicholas Hawksmoor, whose imagination was far wilder than that of his master.

The contrast seems even more marked when it is realised that at the time that these phantasms were appearing on London's skyline, Wren was developing the massive columnar manner already seen round the dome of St Paul's, in the unexecuted scheme for Whitehall Palace and then at Greenwich Hospital (Fig. 96). Bernini had developed the idea of using great rows of columns supporting a continuous entablature but serving no structural purpose in the wings of the Piazza of St Peter's (1657–67). Arranged in pairs, they form the key element in the east front of the Louvre in Paris (1667–8). At Whitehall, Wren planned to link the palace with the Houses of Parliament by a long covered colonnade,

98   Nicholas Hawksmoor, Easton Neston, Northamptonshire, 1702.

while a giant order would have run across the front of the palace. Nothing came of the Whitehall scheme, but at Greenwich Wren was able to transform Webb's giant order of pilasters into a paired colonnade running across the hall and chapel and then back towards the Queen's House. The horizontal drama of the colonnade is trans-

99 John Prince, Cound Hall, Shropshire, 1704.

formed vertically by the thrusting pair of cupolaed towers rising above the chapel and hall.

With the Greenwich colonnade, Wren introduced an almost academic Baroque to England, but its apparent serenity is broken by doorcases under the hall and chapel that thrust up among the pedestals of the colonnade. Their design gives the powerful impression that the visitor is being drawn down into the underworld, under a massive keystone, between heavy voussoires and architraves apparently distorted by pressure. This was the work of an artist who truly understood the dynamic potential of the Baroque. An even greater contrast comes in the courtyard of the King William Block, begun in 1699 and largely completed in 1703 (Fig. 97). Here, the east side is dominated by an arch rising the full height of the building, supported by pairs of giant Ionic pilasters, with the diminutive pairs of Corinthian columns beneath perched precariously on tall piers, supporting an out-of-scale broken pediment. On the west front, equally overscaled attached Doric columns and pilasters seem to crush any visitor who enters the doorway between them. The contrast between the academically

correct river front and the raw licence of the King William Block behind makes Greenwich Hospital seem almost schizophrenic.

The authorship of the King William Block remains uncertain, although the most probable candidate is Hawksmoor. At the same time he was also designing the façade of Easton Neston. Again, the giant pilaster is dominant, this time a string of Composite pilasters organised under a subtly differentiated entablature in which the end bays break forward slightly, the central five bays a little more and the central bay jumps out with a pair of attached columns. In the end elevations, where a pair of mezzanine floors break up the regular rhythm of the windows, the sense of disturbed order so apparent in the King William Block recurs.

At Easton Neston in 1702 (Fig. 98), the English exterior finally achieved a Baroque sophistication to match that found in internal spaces since May's work at Windsor. It was a sophistication sought for but not quite achieved by Vanbrugh and Hawksmoor in the contemporary but more ambitious façades of Castle Howard. At Blenheim Palace, where the foundation stone was laid in

100   Thomas Archer, Heythrop Hall, Oxfordshire, 1707.

1705, the pair succeeded on a monumental scale. If the hall of Castle Howard was the high point of the English Baroque interior, Blenheim was its external apogee.

The King William Block, Easton Neston, Castle Howard and Blenheim, all make repeated use of the giant pilaster. This had appeared at Lees Court, Kent, and a number of similar houses in the 1630s and 1650s, and again in Webb's Greenwich Palace in 1664, which Talman followed at Chatsworth in 1687. But it was Wren's use of the giant order in the pavilions of the wings at the Chelsea Hospital that provided the precedent for the King William Block. Only at the turn of the century did it enter regular architectural use. The idea soon spread beyond the circle of the Office of Works, appearing in London at Buckingham House in 1702; in Surrey at Addiscombe House in 1702; in Derbyshire at Calke Abbey in 1703; in Shropshire at John Prince's Cound Hall in 1704 (Fig. 99); in Buckinghamshire at Wotton House in 1704 and in Hampshire in 1703 at John James's Herriard Park.

As the dates of these last houses show, the impact of the renewal of war in 1702 was not immediate. A signifi-

101   Thomas Archer, Roehampton House, Surrey, 1710.

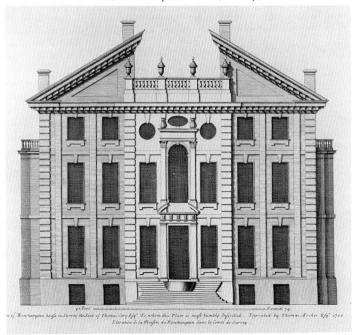

102　Thomas Archer, the Pavilion at Wrest Park, Bedfordshire, 1709.

cant number of houses was begun in 1704, with the greatest of the decade, Blenheim Palace, not being started until the following year. These two years saw the import of timber peak, a good determinant of the volume of speculative house building. Nor did new build-

ing cease entirely during the war: in Oxford, Henry Aldrich's Peckwater Quadrangle at Christ Church was begun in 1707; All Saint's Church and the south quadrangle of Queen's College in 1709; Heythrop House, Oxfordshire, and Kimbolton Castle were begun in 1707;

Marlborough House in London, Wentworth Castle, Yorkshire, and Vanbrugh's own house at Esher, in 1709; Roehampton House, Surrey, in 1710. But they were exceptions, funds grew progressively tighter. Financial crises in 1704, 1707 and 1710 saw a spate of bankruptcies, while 1709 was a year of near famine. Interest on government loans was so attractive that speculative building was starved of funds for, according to T.S. Ashton, 'there was little incentive to put one's money into bricks and mortar'. Work at Greenwich Hospital halted in 1708. By 1710 there had been a marked reduction in timber imports, with 1711 seeing the lowest level of building the century had seen.[25]

The wartime houses are less exciting than those built during the peace, and to a large extent their apparent novelty is decorative. Heythrop House (Fig. 100) and Wentworth Castle appear Baroque because of their lavish use of Italian detail, but both follow the standard five-part elevation already seen at Belton Hall with a three-bay centrepiece and two-bay wings. In both cases the detail is supplied by Domenico de Rossi's *Studio d'architettura civile* (1702), a pattern-book of Roman Baroque ornament which proved instantly popular in Engand. This is associated primarily with the work of Thomas Archer, but was also quickly picked up by such provincial master-builders as Francis Smith, William Thornton and the Bastards of Blandford.[26] De Rossi's detail was particularly influential in interiors. Wren's Marlborough House follows the same five-part elevation as Heythrop and Wentworth, but with French detailing, particularly French quoins.

The one architect who showed real imagination during the war years was Thomas Archer. Although he is credited with the Cascade House at Chatsworth of 1702, it is at Heythrop in 1707, the garden pavilion at Wrest Park, Bedfordshire (1709), Roehampton House (Fig. 101) and St Philip, Birmingham (1710), that he began to make his mark. The younger son of a country gentleman, Archer travelled abroad for four years between 1691 and 1695 after leaving Oxford, certainly visiting the Netherlands and Italy. Thanks to two lucrative sinecures, he did not need to earn his living from architecture, but he did attempt, unsuccessfully, to obtain the post of Comptroller of the Works in 1713. Despite being one of the commissioners for building Fifty New Churches under the Act of 1711, he always seems to lie outside the architectural mainstream. This is certainly true of his buildings, which show a much fuller understanding of the Continental Baroque than any other English architect, Vanbrugh and Hawksmoor's work being essentially insular.

While the pattern of the Heythrop elevation may have been standard, its plan (published in volume five of *Vitruvius Britannicus*, 1771) was innovative, with a complex apsed and niched vestibule connecting the hall and gallery. Archer was the first English architect to introduce details from de Rossi, arranging them, together with alternating pilasters and attached columns, to create an effect that belies the standard elements of the façade. With the giant broken pediment of Roehampton House, Chettle House, Dorset (after 1711), Russell House in Covent Garden (1716) and Monmouth House in Soho Square (*c.*1717) Archer challenged the rationality of the Classical vocabulary in a manner worthy of Borromini, whose work he must have known from Italy.

Archer was also fascinated by varied geometrical form. At the Cascade House at Chatsworth, the pavilion at Wrest Park (Fig. 102) and the Deptford Rectory[27] he combined circles, triangles and octagons to create centralised buildings of a sort more commonly associated with the Continental Baroque. This reached its apogee at St John, Smith Square, in 1713.

The War of the Spanish Succession slowly strangled the English Baroque and how it might have developed had building not been curtailed in the years after 1705 may only be imagined. By the time peace returned in 1713, architectural thought had moved on from the high Baroque of Blenheim, and tensions soon surfaced in the Commission for the Fifty New Churches. This, though set up in 1711 and beginning its first work, Hawksmoor's St Alphege Greenwich, in 1712, only really began to produce results in 1713 and 1714. For Archer at St Paul, Deptford, but above all at St John, Smith Square, the Fifty New Churches Commission at last presented the opportunity to build Baroque works on a grand scale. But the repeated attempts of other architects, such as Hawksmoor, Gibbs and Galilei, to design churches based strictly on the idea of the Roman temple showed how the tide was turning. As seen in the last chapter, Hawksmoor found his own idiosyncratic compromise for the Fifty New Churches, based on the neo-Classical musings of Androuet du Cerceau but imbued with a vigour and sense of architecture as sculptural mass that is archetypally Baroque. Hawksmoor's City churches were *sui generis*, and elsewhere he was already moving away from the Baroque towards Palladianism, along with most other leading English architects. Archer was increasingly isolated and his retirement to the comfortable life of a country gentleman was as much a mark of declining public interest in the Baroque as a statement of his own landed status.

V

REMOVING THE PALLADIAN STRAIGHT-JACKET

THE SECOND DECADE OF THE eighteenth century was one of the most exciting in English architectural history, but also one of the most confused. The standard account is dominated by the arrival of neo-Palladianism and by the publication of the first volume of Colen Campbell's *Vitruvius Britannicus* in 1715. This is portrayed as the successful manifesto of a new anti-Baroque style, a style that quickly established itself, based on the buildings of Palladio and Inigo Jones and having nothing in common with the current work of contemporary architects.

> How and among whom this Palladian taste became formed it will be our business presently to inquire. The first point to make is that it had nothing to do with Wren, Vanbrugh, Hawksmoor, or Archer except in so far as, by excluding the works of these architects from salvation, it was better able to distinguish its own particular sort of grace.[1]

This interpretation places a dangerously narrow stylistic straight-jacket on a complicated period of architectural flux. It assumes a complete division between Campbell and the 'Palladians', and Vanbrugh and the 'Baroque' architects. It also assumes that neo-Palladianism as it eventually emerged, was much the same as that which Campbell put forward in *Vitruvius Britannicus*. It can be argued, instead, that there was a growing interest in the work of Palladio and Inigo Jones before Campbell came to London, an interest visible among not only amateurs and dons but the country's leading architects. Many of the motifs which later became the common currency of neo-Palladianism can be found in the work of Campbell's contemporaries before he used them himself. It can also be argued that far from being a lone voice, Campbell's writings and buildings show that many of his stylistic concerns were those of his contemporaries: an increasing interest in the work of Palladio and related architects; a tendency towards a more austere use of the wall surface; and an interest in the portico. Indeed, an analysis of *Vitruvius Britannicus* suggests that at this date Campbell saw a similarity of intention between his work and the contemporary work of Vanbrugh. Finally, it

can be shown that the theoretical plates with which Campbell illustrated his book had little influence on his contemporaries. Neo-Palladianism as it has come to be known only emerged around 1720.

The signing of the Treaty of Utrecht in 1713 set off a building boom of unparalleled vigour, which peaked about 1725. In 1719 a pamphleteer calculated that the number of buildings erected in London between 1716 and 1718 amounted to 'a full fifth of the whole in 1695'.[2] The bursting of the South Sea Bubble in 1720 only temporarily checked the boom. Daniel Defoe writing in 1725 described 'an amazing scene of new Foundations, not of Houses only, but I might say of new Cities, new Towns, new Squares, and fine Buildings, the like of which no City, no Town, nay no Place in the World can shew'.[3] It was this boom that financed the extravagant churches of the Fifty New Churches Act and led to the development of the area around Hanover Square, the Conduit Mead estate centred on New Bond Street, the Burlington estate, the Cavendish-Harley estate and the Grosvenor estates in the West End, as well as the Wood-Michell and Tillard estates in Spitalfields.[4] With it came a wave of new country-house building that lasted into the mid-1730s but peaked in the early 1720s (a phenomenon first identified by Sir John Summerson[5]) which eclipsed that seen at the turn of the century. It was on this boom that the Palladian experiment was able to ride.

While both France and contemporary Italy were plundered for ideas and motifs, it is not surprising that architects should also have looked at the work of Palladio – which the *Quattro libri* made uniquely accessible – and of those architects associated with him, Scamozzi, Jones and Webb. The Prattian house was essentially Palladian but it purveyed a very restrained sort of Palladianism. There was much more, both individual motifs and broader ideas, that could be taken from Palladio. At the same time, the buildings of Inigo Jones and John Webb (whose work was often attributed to Jones) were now over half a century old and had the attraction of being examples of a sophisticated English Classicism for those patriots who sought refuge from

103   William Talman, unexecuted design for Haughton Hall, Nottinghamshire, 1703.

foreign styles, and particularly a style associated with the early Stuarts, for those whose loyalties lay with the House of Stuart.

Probably the first architect consciously to look back at the work of Jones and Webb as a source for ideas was William Talman, born in 1650 and therefore member of a new generation which had not been active in the years immediately following the Restoration, and for whom Palladio was also an important source of inspiration.[6] Talman's *oeuvre* is still a matter of debate. It was certainly eclectic: for lesser houses he was capable of designing in the Pratt manner, as at Stanstead Park, Sussex (1685) (Fig. 36); Holywell House, St Albans, Hertfordshire

104   Andrea Palladio, unexecuted design for the Palazzo Chiericati, Vicenza.

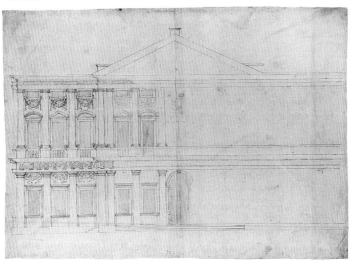

(1686); Uppark, Sussex (*c*.1690); Kimberley Hall, Norfolk (*c*.1700), and Fetcham Park, Surrey (1705); but for greater houses he turned out a fertile variety of schemes particularly marked by the ingenuity of their planning. In this he was aided by his extensive library which he claimed in 1713 was 'the most valuable Collection of Books, Prints, Drawings &c, as is in any one person's hands in Europe', and which included a large number of drawings by Palladio and Jones.

One of Talman's grandest designs was the unexecuted scheme he produced in about 1703 for the Duke of Newcastle at Haughton, Nottinghamshire (Fig. 103).[7] This has a pilastered ground floor supporting a heavy cornice, with a second pilastered order rising through one and a half storeys. Palladio's Palazzo Chiericati was probably the source – not the executed version with its colonnaded loggias illustrated in the *Quattro libri* but a preliminary version among the drawings Talman owned (Fig. 104). The Haughton plan is also probably the first English example of a house with a main block and four pavilions, a layout which derives from Palladio's Villa Mocenigo and was to be popular later in the century. Contemporary with the Haughton design is Talman's scheme for adding a screen to Witham Park, Somerset, which uses a columned arcade derived from the upper floor of the courtyard of the Palazzo Thiene in Vicenza.

None of Talman's specifically Palladian schemes was built, but his two most important houses were both inspired by buildings which Talman probably thought were by Jones. Chatsworth House, Derbyshire (1687), was the grandest commission of its day (Fig. 87). This had a complete state apartment, essentially a royal concept, running across its south front and for a suitable

105   William Talman, Dyrham Park, Gloucestershire, 1698.

model for this façade Talman seems to have turned to Webb's King Charles Building at Greenwich Palace, the most impressive of all the Stuart palace buildings (Fig. 30). Disregarding the centrepiece, for which there was no need at Chatsworth as the single apartment meant there was no central emphasis, and also the attics, which would have been overbearing on the south front, Talman repeated the three-bay pilastered pavilions at each end, the two equal stories and the heavy keystones over the windows. (Although giant pilasters were shortly to become commonplace in English architecture they do not seem to have been used between the King Charles Building and Chatsworth except by Wren at the Royal Hospital at Chelsea.)   It may be that the plainer wall surface and the more modest use of an Ionic rather than a Corinthian order was intended by Talman to present this building in a minor key, distinguishing it with appropriate propriety from the genuine royal palace.

At Dyrham Park, Gloucestershire (Fig. 105), Talman repeated the three-bay pavilions but took as his model for the elevation that of Thorpe Hall, Cambridgeshire, which he may have been under the misapprehension was by Jones (Fig. 27). (He would have known the house from his visits to Milton House, which is just over a mile away, in 1688.) The basic articulation, two and a half stories with windows linked vertically by aprons, with an emphatic plat band above the ground-floor windows and an alternating pattern of architrave and pediment above

the first-floor windows, is identical with that of Thorpe Hall. This is particularly clear if the three bays of the end pavilions of Dyrham are compared with the end three bays of Thorpe. At the same time the house was given a veneer of French and Genoese decoration with chanelled rustication on the ground floor and French-style quoins in place of the alternating quoins at Thorpe.

Talman was particularly interested in the idea of the villa. This occurs repeatedly in his sketches but was most extensively worked out in his designs for a Trianon for William III at Thames Ditton, Surrey, in about 1699. Elements of this can be seen as having specifically Palladian references, while the basic idea of a villa with a rustic, *piano nobile* and central portico-in-antis is clearly Palladian in inspiration. The Thames Ditton Trianon was never built, but less than a decade later a similar single-storey villa with a low rustic, hipped roof, cupola and tetrastyle portico was built in Wiltshire, Wilbury House. This was erected, according to Colen Campbell, about 1710 by William Benson to his own designs 'in the Stile of *Inigo Jones*'. The house, traditionally seen as a key forerunner of the Palladian revival of the second decade of the eighteenth century, has always been something of a mystery, as Benson showed no other signs of architectural ability. The debt to nearby Amesbury Abbey is clear, and the plan is based on Palladio's Villa Poiana, but it is hard to find a precedent for the basic format of the villa except in Talman's scheme. Could Benson have

106 Henry Aldrich, Peckwater Quadrangle, Christ Church, Oxford, 1706.

known of the Trianon? Could Talman have been an early adviser on the Wilbury project? He was the obvious architect for a strong Whig like Benson to consult. In the absence of documented links this must remain speculation.

Politically, Talman was prepared to adapt to the party in power, but as a leading court architect after the Revolution of 1688 his clients were mainly Whigs. Both the Duke of Devonshire at Chatsworth and William Blathwayt at Dyrham were key adherents to William III. Presumably, therefore, Talman's use of Jonesian precedent was stylistic and had no political connotations. This may not have been true at Oxford where Dean Aldrich and Dr George Clarke, who initiated a series of Jonesian schemes early in the eighteenth century, were Tories in a university where loyalty to the Stuarts was strong. There may well have been political overtones in

their harking back to the style of the early Stuarts at a time when the royal succession after the death of Queen Anne was uncertain and the return of the Stuart kings a real possibility.

Dean Aldrich's Peckwater Quadrangle, Christ Church, Oxford (1706–14) (Fig. 106), reveals an intelligent study of mid-seventeenth-century buildings then believed to be by Jones, and in particular of Lindsey House in Lincoln's Inn Fields. One may also see echoes of the first-floor, one-and-a-half storey hexastyle portico of Webb's Gunnersbury House – which lay just off the Oxford to London road – in the hexastyle frontispieces at the centre of each façade.

Across the High Street, the Fellows of All Souls College were also contemplating erecting a new quadrangle, and Aldrich presented them with a design in about 1705 (Fig. 107).[8] This lacks the specifically Jonesian references

107 Henry Aldrich, unexecuted design for the new building at All Souls College, Oxford, 1705.

of Peckwater Quadrangle, but depicts a giant hexastyle Corinthian portico in the centre of a new range flanked by a low colonnade of paired columns. It is an unusual design which may owe something to Palladio's reconstructions of the Temple of Antonine and Faustina. This again has a hexastyle Corinthian portico and a low forecourt lined with pairs of columns.[9] The idea of transforming a temple precinct into a college quadrangle by setting a domestic range behind the portico is rather incongruous and was never taken up. Dr George Clarke, a Fellow of All Souls and MP for the University of Oxford, who was closely associated with Aldrich, also submitted a design (Fig. 108). This parallels the Jonesian inspiration of the Peckwater Quadrangle, being based on a drawing in the Jones–Webb collection which Clarke had recently purchased.[10] The specific model was a design by Webb dated 1648 and inscribed as being for Cobham Hall (Fig. 109). Presumably Clarke believed it too was by Jones.

Clarke's purchase of the Jones–Webb drawings is evidence of the seriousness of his interest in Jones, but behind it lay a similar concern for Palladio. This was to come out strongly in his later collaboration with Hawksmoor. The same is true of Aldrich, a point neatly made by one of his surviving drawings which is a copy in his hand of one of Webb's drawings of Palladio's Teatro Olimpico at Vicenza. According to Charles Fairfax, Aldrich acknowledged Palladio as his professed master in architecture, and indeed it was Aldrich who persuaded Fairfax to translate Palladio's *Antichita di Roma*, which was published by the Clarendon Press in 1709.[11] Aldrich's debt to Palladio is made clear in his *Elementa architecturae*, of which only the first forty-four pages had been published at the time of his death in 1710. His 'overriding ambition was to discover the rational origins in antiquity of the elements of architecture', and in the *Elementa architecturae* Aldrich explained how, as Palladio came closest to the ancients, he decided to 'pass by other Writers and cheerfully follow his footsteps'. His other key source as an interpreter of antiquity was Claude Perrault. Aldrich subscribed to the translation of Perrault's *Ordonnance des cinq espèces de colonnes*, which sought 'not so much to correct the Antique as to re-establish it in its pristine Perfection', in 1708. 'As Mons. Perrault generally explains Vitruvius, and Palladio supplies the defects of M. Perrault' he laid both before the

108   George Clarke, unexecuted design for the new building at All Souls College, Oxford, 1705.

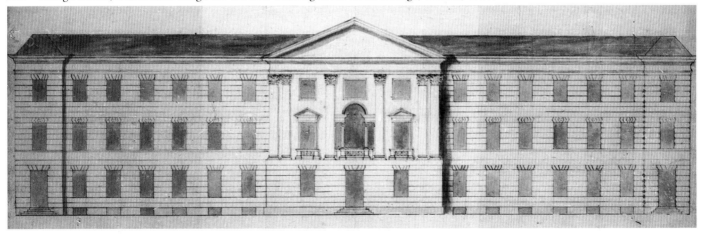

109   John Webb, unexecuted design for Cobham Hall, Kent, 1648.

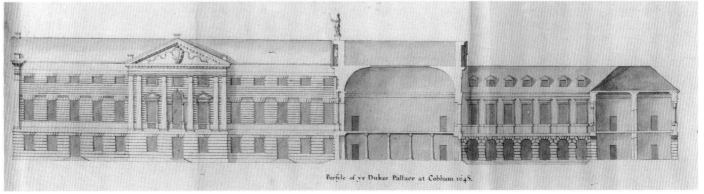

110   Nicholas Hawksmoor, Christ's Hospital Writing School, London, 1692 (demolished).

reader. The *Elementa* is divided into two books, much of the first of which was devoted to discovering the rational origins in antiquity of the elements of architecture. However, Aldrich's motives were not purely intellectual, in his second book he also included a selection of villas and palaces copied from Palladio and Pietro Ferrerio which he 'apprehended would suit best the English manners' and which young students 'may imitate with equal pleasure and advantage, either by varying them in some particulars, or copying from them in others'.[12] This suggests that he had a proseletising attitude towards Palladianism.

The translator of Perrault was John James, whose interest in Inigo Jones is revealed in a letter written in 1711 in which he told the Duke of Buckingham 'that the Beautys of Architecture may consist with the greatest plainness of the structure' something which 'has scarce ever been hit on by the Tramontani unless by our famous Mr. Inigo Jones'.[13] James may have been speaking from personal experience for it is likely that he worked for the Earl of Pembroke at Wilton House, Wiltshire, then believed to be by Jones. In 1705 the hall side of the quadrangle at Wilton was destroyed by fire and its plan as rebuilt is recorded in *Vitruvius Britannicus*. This shows that the entrance porch led into an intriguing apsed vestibule, with beyond it a double-height hall with a first-floor balcony that must have been modelled on Jones's Queen's House at Greenwich (James was appointed assistant Clerk of the Works at Greenwich in 1705). At the same time, the opportunity seems to have been taken to rebuild the north towers, giving them the same profile as those on the south. Both towers have a cavetto string course, probably of early eighteenth-century date, and the north-east tower still has its eighteenth-century roof timbers. Although the architect responsible is not recorded, James included the Earl of Pembroke in a list of names of those 'Persons of Quality'

who could vouch for his character, many of whom he had 'served in the business of their Buildings'.[14]

Another contemporary architect to show an interest in Palladianism was Nicholas Hawksmoor, who used a large number of motifs that were not common in Wren's work but would subsequently come to be considered Palladian. These were to form an essential element of his style throughout his career.[15] Typical of this was Hawksmoor's use of the Serlian window, in many ways the archetypal Palladian motif. Colen Campbell first experimented with a Serlian window in his design for a Vitruvian church published in 1717 in the second volume of *Vitruvius Britannicus*. He first used one in practice at Burlington House, London, in 1718. Hawksmoor anticipated him by four years at Christ Church, Spital-fields (the designs for which were accepted in April 1714), which has a Serlian east window. The thermal window was to be another classic Palladian motif, but while it was never used by Campbell it was included by Hawksmoor in his designs for the Clarendon Building, Oxford (1710), Queen's College, Oxford (1708–9) and Christ Church, Spitalfields. He also used it in his design for Worcester College, Oxford, of 1718 (Fig. 126).

One of Campbell's best-known designs was for Houghton Hall, Norfolk, where an unexecuted scheme dated 1722 uses pedimented pavilion towers modelled on those at Wilton. Hawksmoor anticipated this with

111   Nicholas Hawksmoor, unexecuted design for All Souls College, Oxford, 1708.

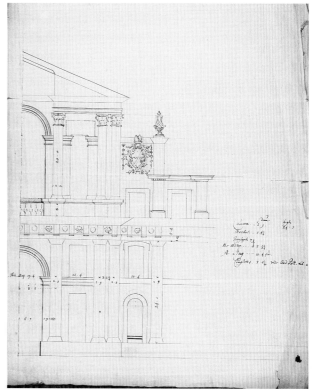

112   Sir John Vanbrugh, Castle Howard, Yorkshire, 1702.

the flanking ranges of the first Greenwich Hospital design, which may be seen as a paraphrase of Wilton.[16] Another Palladian motif frequently used by Hawksmoor but not by Campbell is the broken-based pediment. This appears in Palladio's *Quattro libri* on the Villa Poiana (Fig. 114) and his recreation of the Temple of the Sun and the Moon, and was first used by Hawksmoor at the Christ's Hospital Writing School of 1692 (Fig. 110).[17]

Hawksmoor's use of quotations from Palladio was not restricted to individual motifs. He also incorporated whole bay structures or elevations into his designs. A discarded drawing for All Souls, reused for one of the Queen's College drawings, shows that Hawksmoor's work for All Souls must date from about 1708–9. In both cases he worked in close cooperation with Dr Clarke. At first sight these designs seem to have little in common with Palladio, but a detailed design for the north lodging is annotated with a reference to page seven of book two of the *Quattro libri* (Fig. 111).[18] In the 1570 edition this illustrates a detailed drawing of the Palazzo Chiericati; like Hawksmoor's scheme, this is for a building with superimposed orders. Both have a full Doric order on a high base, but Hawksmoor replaces Palladio's Ionic with Corinthian. This annotation is probably the first documentary reference to Palladio as the authority for a specific eighteenth-century building. This chance survival raises the question whether there are other Palladian references in these designs which have been missed because Hawksmoor did not note them down.

A similar, though unnoted, contemporary use by Hawksmoor (and Vanbrugh) of Palladio's palazzi to provide one element of a larger design can be found in the ground-floor windows of the entrance front at Blenheim Palace, Oxfordshire, part of the building erected in 1705–6. These have no ordinary window-frames but are set between the baseless half pilasters under a heavy cornice separating ground and first floors, framed by a giant order. This unusual design is probably adapted from the street façade of the Palazzo Valmarana as illustrated in the *Quattro libri*.[19]

Hawksmoor's most extensive quotation was in the elevation of the side of the front quadrangle in Proposition 'A' for Queen's College. Like the other Queen's College designs, this must date from 1708–9. The ground-floor arcade is taken directly from the courtyard of Palladio's Palazzo Thiene in Vicenza as illustrated in the *Quattro libri*.[20] The upper storeys are a paraphrase of the same source. What singles out the Palazzo Thiene as the source for the Queen's College design is the use of lower, flat-headed openings at each end of the arcade. The upper storey of the Palazzo Thiene is formed by an open arcade. Hawksmoor wanted to fit two floors into the same space, so he placed a mezzanine lit by a lunette in the turn of the arch. He also simplified Palladio's design by replacing the columns between the arches with raised bands. However, he returned more closely to his model in the end bays, where he placed a square-headed opening at mezzanine level over a full-length window.

Hawksmoor's design provided the basis on which Clarke and William Townesend executed the quadrangle, but in the execution the specifically Palladian references were removed: the flat-headed end openings were not used, the rustication in the spandrels was channelled, the keystones were reduced in size and the mezzanine openings in the end bays above the first floor were lost.

Hawksmoor's colleague Vanbrugh shared his interest in Palladio; this should come as no surprise given that the *Quattro libri* is the only architectural treatise Vanbrugh is known to have possessed. He owned this in at least two versions, a French edition with plans, presumably Fréart's, which he asked Mr Tonson to buy for him in Amsterdam in 1703, and Leoni's edition of 1716 to which he subscribed. Clearly Vanbrugh made practical use of Palladio, for in 1711 when he mislaid his copy he thought that he might have left it at Blenheim.[21]

Vanbrugh's first house, Castle Howard, Yorkshire, reveals the use to which he put his study of Palladio (Fig. 112). It is seldom pointed out quite how remarkable Castle Howard is as a design. The idea of a house with a central two-storey block with single-storey wings and extensive service yards flanking the entrance front is unprecedented in English architecture and impossible to parallel in contemporary Baroque houses on the Continent. An examination of Palladio's *Quattro libri* suggests a source, Palladio's villas. The standard Palladio villa has a block-like pedimented core with single-storey wings running parallel, and extensive courtyards flanking the entrance front. In most cases the single-storey wings contain only a colonnaded walkway linking the house and the offices, but in the Villa Maser and the Villa Saraceno the wings house further apartments running *en suite* with the central block. The basic tripartite plan of the main block of Castle Howard can also be seen as coming from Palladio, as can the placing of identical staircases in secondary positions on either side of the hall,

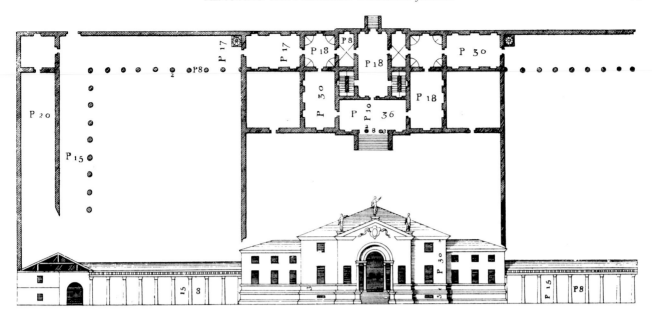

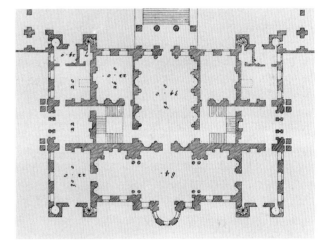

114 (above) Andrea Palladio, Villa Poiana, Italy, from *The Four Books of Architecture* (1738).

115 Sir John Vanbrugh, inverted detail from an unexecuted design for Eastbury, Dorset, 1716, from *Vitruvius Britannicus* (1717).

113 (facing page) Sir John Vanbrugh, Goose-pie House, Whitehall, London, 1700 (demolished) (Soane office, watercolour, Sir John Soane's Museum, London).

a feature found at the Villa Sarego, the Villa Thiene at Cicogna and the Villa Poiana. The placing and disposition of the offices wings, the curved links, the subtle drops in level, the extensive office courts can all be paralleled in Palladio.

Like that of Hawksmoor, Vanbrugh's work includes numerous broken-based pediments, Serlian windows and pavilion towers, often anticipating their use by Campbell.[22] Goose-pie House, Vanbrugh's own house in Whitehall, begun in 1700 and one of his very earliest works, has wings with Serlian windows under broken-based pediments that seem to be taken from the frontispiece of Palladio's Villa Poiana (Figs. 113 and 114). The unusual rusticated columns of the Villa Sarego appear on the office wing at Blenheim Palace; at Eastbury, Dorset (1718); Seaton Delaval, Northumberland (1721), and Grimsthorpe Castle, Lincolnshire (1723). The hexastyle portico with a paired pier and column at each end on the portico at Stowe (*c.*1720), attributed to Vanbrugh,

was used by Palladio at the Villa Trissini at Meledo. Vanbrugh also used the *Quattro libri* as a source for plans; this is clear in his first design for Eastbury (1716), in which a deep hall flanked by a pair of rooms and identical staircases gives onto a long saloon, with a further set of rooms on either side (Fig. 115). Palladio's Villa Poiana has an almost identical plan (Fig. 114), the only significant difference being that the flanking ranges have two, rather than three rooms. Seaton Delaval is a simplified version of the first Eastbury plan, and as at Eastbury the great arcaded courtyard owes much to Palladio.

Aldrich, Clarke, Benson, Talman, James, Hawksmoor and Vanbrugh, show that interest in Palladio and Inigo Jones was strong even before Campbell arrived in London, and that this interest grew during the first decade and a half of the eighteenth century. Nor was this interest restricted to England. The first decade and a half of the century also saw interest in Palladio increase markedly across the Continent.

116   Francesco Muttoni, Villa da Porto, Monticello di Fara, Italy, 1714.

The Veneto presents this revival in its purest and most obvious interpretation; unsurprisingly, given that architects could study Palladio's buildings at first hand. Palladio's influence can be found in the Veneto in the seventeenth century. It is particularly apparent in the work of Baldassare Longhena, as at Santa Maria della Salute in Venice (1633), and in villas such as the Villa Squarzi di Longara, begun in 1677 and attributed to Carlo Borella. It is, however, a muted influence, not a deliberate revival of Palladio's work. The years after 1700 saw the tenor of Venetan architecture alter, and for the first time Palladio's buildings were imitated in detail,

117   Germain de Boffrand, Château de Luneville, Meurthe et Moselle, 1702, from his *Livre d'Architecture* (1745).

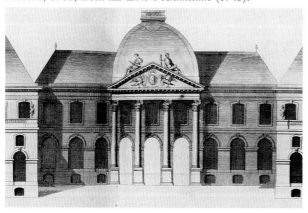

in particular churches, especially in Venice, and villas, where the revival was initially concentrated on the area of the Veneto immediately around Vicenza. In Venice Andrea Tirali's San Vidal of 1700 was a sophisticated combination of ideas from Palladio's San Giorgio Maggiore and Il Redentore; Domenico Rossi's façade of San Stae, begun in 1709, was more closely based on San Giorgio. On the *terra firma*, Antonio Piovene's church of San Filippo Neri in Vicenza was based on Il Redentore. Francesco Maria Preti and Giovanni Mazzi's Villa Spineda at Volpago del Montello (*c*.1700) shows the move towards Palladio, but, despite its portico-in-antis and its *piano nobile* over a rustic, this is not a building that could have been designed by Palladio. The unattributed Villa Negri (1709) could have been. Within a few years it was followed by Francesco Muttoni's Villa Piovene di Orgiano (1710) and Villa da Porto a Monticello di Fara (1714) (Fig. 116) and Cherrette's Villa da Porto (1712). These ushered in a growing interest in Palladio's villas which was to dominate Venetan architecture for the rest of the century.[23]

Less pure, but nevertheless strongly influenced by Palladio (although he never visited Italy) was the work of the French architect Germain de Boffrand working in Lorraine. Palladian influence is particularly marked in the repeated use of porticos on his domestic buildings: attached porticos as at Luneville (1702) (Fig. 117), Haroue (1712) and the Palace at Nancy (1717); and freestanding porticos as at Bouchefort (1705), which had a full Ionic portico on each of its four main façades.[24] In this, Boffrand was following in the footsteps of Le Vau and of his former master Hardouin-Mansart, whose Place Vendôme is particularly significant, but he developed the idea more consistently than either.

In Germany, the first two books of Palladio were translated into German and published in Nuremberg in 1698; joining translations of the third and fourth books of Scamozzi published there in 1678. In 1708 Nikolaus Goldmann's *Vollstandige Anweisung zu der Civil Bau-Kunst*, edited by L.C. Sturm and published in Leipzig, included illustrations of an Egyptian hall, of a house based on the Villa Rotonda, of an exchange derived from the Basilica at Vicenza and of an elevation of a Corinthian hall, together with text refering to Palladio. In Düsseldorf, the Venetian Matteo Alberti joined the court of the Elector Johann-Wilhelm of the Palatinate in 1695. Before settling at Düsseldorf Alberti had travelled through France, the Netherlands and England in the 1680s (where he stayed from 1682 to 1684 and admired Jones's Covent Garden). John Harris has described the wings of his Schloss Bensburg of 1700–10 as looking forward to Burlington's Westminster Dormitory, and suggested that his Neue Haus at Schloss Malbeg, Eiffel, of 1711 would not look out of place in *Vitruvius Scoticus*.[25] The garden front is a straight-forward, if large version of the Restoration house, astylar, nine bays, pedimented and tripartite, but with a marked rustic and an attic storey. The pilastered entrance-front with its flanking single-bay pavilions is rather less successfully handled but could be seen as a variation on the Villa Thiene at Cicogna. Düsseldorf was to prove an important stop on the road from Venice to London for such painters as Pellegrini and the Riccis and, perhaps more significantly, for the architect Giacomo Leoni who was at work there in 1708 on a manuscript treatise on the five orders based on Palladio.[26]

Palladian tendencies can also be identified in Austria in Fischer von Erlach's late works, the Böhmische Hofkanzlei (1708) and the Trautson Palace (1710), both in Vienna, and the Clam-Gallas Palace in Prague (*c*.1713). All have pedimented centrepieces, the tripartite form, if not the detail, of the Trautson Palace being clearly in the Palladian villa manner.

Except in the case of the Veneto, none of these examples developed into a fully-fledged neo-Palladian movement as in England, but it is unlikely to be coincidence that the first decade and a half of the eighteenth century, during which English architects investigated Palladio's work with growing but as yet undisciplined attention, produced parallel tendencies across the Continent.

So was *Vitruvius Britannicus* the radical manifesto for a new style that it is made out to be? Eileen Harris has shown how minor Campbell's role was in the genesis of *Vitruvius Britannicus*.[27] The book was initially planned as a broad survey of the best of recent British architecture and only took on a specifically Palladian slant with news of the imminent publication by Leoni of the first complete English translation of the *Quattro libri* accompanied by 'the several notes and observations made by Inigo Jones'. This threatened to make *Vitruvius Britannicus* seem old fashioned before it was even published. Consequently, the perspectives and garden plans intended for the book were taken out and replaced by a series of theoretical designs by Campbell. However, if these and Campbell's introduction are examined closely they are neither as original nor as influential as seems to have been assumed.

As Howard Colvin has shown,[28] five of Campbell's theoretical designs derive closely from drawings by James Smith based on Palladio, which he owned – as indeed did Shawfield House, Glasgow (1712), Campbell's only known commission before he moved to London. The remaining six, for which no Smith drawing survives, are fairly literal recastings of illustrations in the *Quattro libri*, specifically those of palazzi. The design for the Earl of Halifax, for instance, takes the arcaded courtyard of the Palazzo Thiene for its centre and flanks this with the street elevation shorn of its pilasters (Fig. 118). But the scale and architectural complexity of Campbell's designs, both those copied from Smith and his own schemes, found few imitators. In his own work, only the design for the Earl of Ilay bore fruit at Burlington House (for which, as a town house, a palazzo design would have been appropriate). Among his contemporaries, only Giacomo Leoni seems to have followed these designs. If the publication of the first volume of *Vitruvius Britannicus* in 1715 is supposed to herald a neo-Palladian dawn then it is not to be found in the supposedly Palladian style promoted by its plates.

Campbell's introduction was no more original. This time his source was not Smith but the seventeenth-century Palladian apologist Fréart de Chambray whose *Parallèle de l'architecture* had been translated by Evelyn in 1664. Evelyn's translation was reprinted in 1680 and again in 1707, just before Campbell's arrival in London. It was subsequently republished in 1722, 1723 and 1733, suggesting that it had a greater contemporary influence than has been remarked. Campbell's introduction says three things, that Palladio was the finest architect: 'the excellent *Architect* seems to have arrived to a *Ne plus ultra* of his Art'; that contemporary Italian architecture had lost its way:

> the *Italians* can no more relish the Antique Simplicity, but are entirely employed in capricious Ornaments, which must at last end in the *Gothick*. For Proof of this Assertion, I appeal to the Productions of the last *Century*: How affected and licentious are the Works of

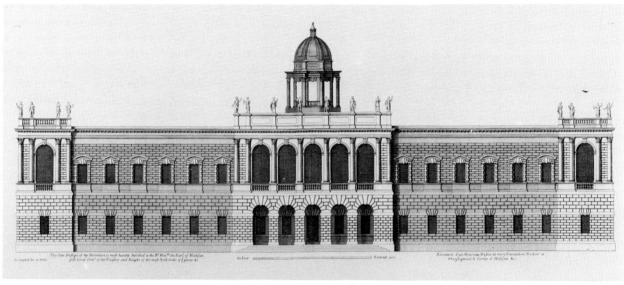

118   Colen Campbell, design dedicated to the Earl of Halifax, from *Vitruvius Britannicus* (1715).

Bernini and *Fontana?* How wildly Extravagant are the Designs of *Boromini*, who has endeavoured to debauch Mankind with his odd and chimerical Beauties, where the Parts are without Proportion, Solids without their true Bearing, Heaps of Materials without Strength, excessive Ornaments without Grace, and the Whole without Symmetry?

and that the way forward was through the work of Palladio and Inigo Jones.[29]

Except for the understandable lack of any reference to Jones all these sentiments can be found in Fréart. Fréart was fulsome in his praise of Palladio: 'The first of all is without any contest the famous *Andrea Palladio.*' He is crushing in his opinion of contemporary Italian architecture and also sees the problems of his day as arising from an obsession with ornament and a lack of concern with the Vitruvian proprieties:

> It is now become as it were the *mode*, I should say an universal *madness*, to esteem nothing fine, but what is fill'd and surcharged with all sorts of *Ornaments*, without choice, without discretion or the least affinity to the *Work* or the *Subject* . . . In fine, one may truly say, that poor *Architecture* is very ill-treated amongst them: But it were not just enough to impute this great reproach to our *French* Work-men only; The *Italians* themselves are now become more *licentious*, and shew us plainly that *Rome* has at present her *Moderns* as her *Antiques.*

Like Campbell Fréart hopes to reform architecture, 'so (if possible) I may at last reestablish the *Art* on its genuine *Principles*, and original purity from whence those licentious *Compositions* of our late *Workmen* have so exceedingly perverted it'. Like Campbell, the way forward is by

looking again at the work of Palladio. Campbell even seems to borrow from Evelyn's dedication where he speaks of 'All the mischiefs and absurdities in our modern *Structures* proceed chiefly from our busie and *Gotic* triflings in the *Compositions* of the *Five Orders.*' and 'It is from the *asymmetrie* of our *buildings*, want of decorum and proportion in our *Houses*, that the irregularity of our *humours* and *affections* may be shrewdly discern'd.'[30]

If, as Eileen Harris suggested, the revised edition of *Vitruvius Britannicus* had to be produced in a very short time, perhaps a fortnight, to counter the threat from the sudden announcement of Giacomo Leoni's translation of the *Quattro libri*, then it is not surprising that Campbell was reduced to reworking the drawings of Palladio and Smith and paraphrasing Fréart, but it suggests that his own stylistic theories were not yet mature.

While most of the theoretical plates follow Smith's grandiloquent interpretation of Palladio based on the palazzi, Campbell's own ideas for Wanstead House, Essex (Fig. 119), and his designs for a church in Lincoln's Inn Fields and for house for Lord Percival suggest that he was already turning to a more austere manner, and this is confirmed by analysis of the commentaries on the plates that Campbell put at the beginning of each volume. They are perhaps summed up by his statement that Jones's St Paul, Covent Garden, is 'the only Piece the Moderns have yet produced, that can admit of a just Comparison with the Works of the Antiquity, where a Majestick Simplicity commands the Approbation of the Judicious'.[31]

Of his design for a church in Lincoln's Inn Fields Campbell wrote, 'the whole is dress'd very plain, as most proper for the sulphurous Air of the City, and indeed, most conformable to the Simplicity of the Ancients', and

119 Colen Campbell, Wanstead House, Essex, *c.*1714 (Charles Catton, watercolour) (demolished).

of that for Lord Percival, 'I have left out all manner of Rusticks and other Ornaments generally practised, purely to shew the Harmony of Proportion in the greatest simplicity'. Similar comments are made about other theoretical designs such as that for Earl of Ilay, 'here I have omitted to continue the Rusticks, to entertain the Eye with some Repose'; that for the Duke of Argyll where the mezzanines were lit by low lanterns from the leads, 'whereby the Majesty of the Front is preserved from the ill Effect of crowded Apertures', and that for the Earl of Halifax, 'Here the windows are placed at due Distance, and free from that bad Effect we so frequently see when they are crowded, which destroys the Repose and Appearance of Strength, so necessary in Architecture.'[32]

Campbell repeats this comment several times when discussing the work of others. Of High Meadow, Gloucestershire, he says, 'the Windows are well dres'd, but the Piers are too narrow, and in the Wings the large Space from the Window to the Corner has a good Effect'; of the Covent Garden Piazza, 'It were to be

120 Colen Campbell, Sir John Hotham's House, Beverley, Yorkshire, 1716, from *Vitruvius Britannicus* (1717) (detail) (demolished).

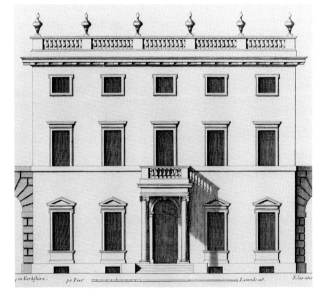

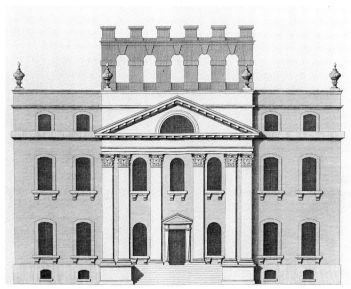

121   Sir John Vanbrugh, King's Weston House, Somerset, 1712, from *Vitruvius Britannicus* (1715).

wished our Artificers wou'd observe this just Proportion in Piers and Wi[n]dows, which wou'd prevent the Lanthorn way of Building, so much in Practice of late Years'; of Lindsey House, 'The Windows are well-proportion'd, gracefull dress'd, without Affectation . . . the whole is conducted with that Harmony that shines in all the Productions of this great Master who design'd it.'[33]

These sentiments, stressing above all the relationship between window and wall, fit in well with his designs for Wanstead (1714) and also for the two new commissions illustrated in volume two, that for Sir John Hotham at Beverley, Yorkshire (1716) (Fig. 120), and that for John Hedworth at Chester-le-Street, County Durham (1716). Campbell commented about Hotham's house that the windows are 'all regularly drest, and at proper distance, an Observation never to be neglected'. However, it is significant that Wanstead, Hotham's house and Hedworth's house owe nothing either to his own theoretical plates or to Palladio's *Quattro libri*. Wanstead is Campbell's response to Vanbrugh's Castle Howard, keeping the essential form of the garden front with its pedimented central block, dome (reduced to a cupola) and long, low wings set over a rustic, but re-expressing it in a much more austere language, stripped of all pilasters and ornament and with the addition of a portico. This can be seen particularly clearly when the preliminary designs are examined. Hotham and Hedworth's houses are modelled on Chevening House, Kent, which Campbell published on the preceding page as the work of Jones. The most significant difference is the replacement of a hipped roof with a balustrade. Unlike Chevening and the Hotham house, the Hedworth design is only two stories, but it does have quoins:

There being sufficient Space from the Windows to the Coines, I have drest them with large Rusticks of different Lengths, as most proper to express the true Office of those Stones, which is to cross-bind the Angles, and not as the *French* and some others have introduced them, of the same Extent in Place of Pilasters.

At this stage Campbell seems to have considered quoins important, perhaps because they had been used by Jones. In the description of Samwell's Eaton Hall, Cheshire, he pointed out that 'the Corners are dres'd with Rusticks of a good Tast'. There was the specific contrast of the French style of quoins to hand, and at Newbold Hall, Warwickshire, he specifically pointed out 'the Coines are rusticated after the *French* manner'. He could have made this point about Marlborough House and Dyrham in particular. At Hopetoun, West Lothian, he also mentions that 'the Facade is rusticated in the *French* Manner', presumably with disapproval.[34]

The other specific stylistic point Campbell made in the commentaries was in describing windows with segmental and triangular pediments as Palladian. In the design for the Duke of Argyll 'the windows are dress'd in the *Palladian* manner'. In the design for the Earl of Ilay 'the Windows are proportion'd and dress'd in the *Palladian* style'. Lack of Palladian windows was one of the things that distinguished the first design for Wanstead from that which was executed, and one of the reasons why the design was dropped.[35]

Campbell was extremely sparing about his praise for the work of other architects, although the work of dead architects, for example Webb, was sometimes criticised. Only one living architect had his work praised, Sir John Vanbrugh at King's Weston, Somerset, and in terms echoing Campbell's own work: 'the architecture is great, and Masculine; the windows at proper distance; and the whole design sufficiently demonstrates the great genius of the architect'. While this may at first be surprising, it is characteristic of a trend that runs right through *Vitruvius Britannicus*: whatever the book may be, it is not an attack on Vanbrugh; Campbell repeatedly praised Vanbrugh in words that go far beyond his usual polite thanks to architects. Of Blenheim in volume one he declared that:

I am at a loss how to express my obligations to this worthy gentleman for promoting my labours in most generously assisting me with his original drawings, and most carefully correcting all the plates as they advanced. All I can say falls infinitely short of what I owe . . .

and praised the house: 'The Manner is Grand, the Parts Noble, and the Air Majestick of this Palace, adapted to the Martial Genius of the Patron.' In volume two he speaks of the first Eastbury design, noticing the fine

Serlian window (of which there had been none in the first volume but which he specifically picked out in his notes on the Whitehall designs and on his Vitruvian church) as the work of 'the learned and ingenious Sir John Vanbrugh'. In volume three he called the Eastbury temple 'the most magnificent of its kind in *England*'. The admiration was not all one way: in 1721 Vanbrugh visited Campbell's Newby Park, Yorkshire, and expressed his approval.[36]

The amount of space given to Vanbrugh in volume three is remarkable. The book starts with the two grandest perspectives left over from the first two volumes, which are followed by three buildings thought to have been by Jones and Burlington's house for General Wade. Then there are eleven plates by Vanbrugh before any by Campbell. Moreover, the only other new architect to appear, apart from the mysterious amateur David Gansel, is Vanbrugh's associate William Wakefield, three of whose schemes are illustrated.

This is only surprising if Campbell and Vanbrugh's work is artificially divided as 'Palladian' and 'Baroque'. The two architects shared a similar approach to the relationship between window and wall, both were keen advocates of porticos, both used Serlian windows and rusticated basement windows, whose use by Vanbrugh went back to Blenheim. Presumably Campbell did not approve of Castle Howard. Despite his praise he probably had reservations about Blenheim, but these were houses begun a decade or more earlier. Since then Vanbrugh's style had moved on, and it is with his style around 1715 and later that Campbell's should be compared.

One stylistic declaration from Vanbrugh exists: 'Mr Van-Brugg's Proposals about Building ye New Churches', given to the Fifty New Churches Commissioners in 1711. Much of what he said could have been taken from *Vitruvius Britannicus*.[37] Like Campbell, Vanbrugh saw architecture as a patriotic vehicle, arguing

122 Nicholas Hawksmoor, the Clarendon Building, Oxford, 1712, (detail from an aquatint after Thomas Malton, from *Views of Oxford* (1802)).

that the churches 'shou'd not only serve for the Accommodation of the Inhabitants, in the Performance of their Publick Religious Dutys; but at the same time, remain Monuments to Posterity of Her Piety & Grandure And by consequence become Ornaments to the Towne, and a Credit to the Nation'. The first volume of *Vitruvius Britannicus*, published soon after the conclusion of the successful War of the Spanish Succession, makes repeated patriotic statements, for instance saying, of Jones's Whitehall palace designs, that: 'I hope *Britain* will still have the Glory to accomplish it, which will as far exceed all the Palaces of the Universe, as the Valour of our Troops and Conduct of our Generals have surpassed all others.'[38]

More significant are Vanbrugh's comments on style, making three specific points: about austerity of design, the churches

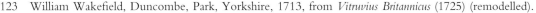

123 William Wakefield, Duncombe, Park, Yorkshire, 1713, from *Vitruvius Britannicus* (1725) (remodelled).

shou'd be made with the utmost Grace that Architecture can produce, for the Beauty of it: which Grace shou'd generally be express'd in a plain but Just and Noble Stile, without running into those many Divisions and Breaks which other buildings for Variety of uses may require; or such Gayety of Ornaments as may be proper to a Luxurious Palace;

about a low ratio of window to wall,

That for the Lights, there may be no more than what are necessary for meer use; many windows . . . take off very much, both from the Appearance & reality of strength in the Fabrick; giving it more the Air of a Gay Lanthorn to be set on the Top of a Temple, than the Reverend look of a Temple it self; which shou'd ever have the most Solemn and Awfull Appearance both without and within, that is possible

and about porticos, 'That they may be all Accommodated and Adorn'd with Portico's; no part in Publick Edifices being of greater use, nor no production in Architecture so solemnly Magnificent.'

Although Vanbrugh's remarks were specifically addressed to the question of church design, they fit in well with the trend of his own work away from the elaborate complexity of Castle Howard (Fig. 112) and Blenheim (Fig. 268) towards the austerity of King's Weston in 1712 (Fig. 121), articulated solely by an applied portico, and the first design for Eastbury in 1716, where Vanbrugh first experimented with a freestanding portico on a domestic building. This becomes even more apparent in his work at Greenwich, particularly at Vanbrugh Castle and at The Nunnery in 1718–20. Hawksmoor followed a similar pattern, moving away from the rich façade of Easton Neston of 1700 (Fig. 98) to the porticoed Clarendon Building of 1712 (Fig. 122) and the austere City churches (Figs. 74 and 75). A similar austerity can also be marked in the Vanbrugh-influenced Duncombe Park, Yorkshire, designed by William Wakefield in 1713, which again has a portico (Fig. 123). John James's statement in 1711 'that the Beautys of Architecture may consist with the greatest plainness of the structure', something which 'has scarce ever been hit on by the Tramontani unless by our famous Mr. Inigo Jones', expressed a similar concern.[39]

One further area which Campbell and Vanbrugh could have addressed but did not, was the question of colour in the modelling of façades. The black and white engravings of *Vitruvius Britannicus* disguise the way many of the most successful late seventeenth- and early eighteenth-century façades used different coloured brick and stone to create a sense of movement that can only be described as Baroque. Inigo Jones had achieved this at the Banqueting House through the use of different stones, and a similar effect can still be seen in the wings

at Stoke Bruern Park, Northamptonshire, but it was only later in the century that colour became an integral part of architectural design, good examples including the south front of Kensington Palace, Hampton Court and Archer's pavilion at Wrest Park, Bedfordshire. The Palladian drive for austerity included banishing this sense of polychromy, the simple whiteness of Marble Hill, Middlesex, or Chiswick House, Middlesex, being the effect that was sought.[40]

Not everyone shared Campbell and Vanbrugh's opinion. Such buildings as James Gibbs's south and east fronts of Cannons House, Middlesex (1716) (Fig. 143), James Thornhill's Moor Park, Hertfordshire (c.1720) (Fig. 124), and John Price's project for Chandos House, London (1720), which seethes with columns, pilasters and rustication as if they were suffering from a *horror vacui*, show that proponents of a busier style of architecture remained powerful into the 1720s, but they were steadily isolated by the broad trend to a more austere architecture; a trend picked up but not initiated by Campbell.

The third of Vanbrugh's recommendations was that churches should be built with porticos. Of all architectural motifs, none is more closely associated with Palladio than the portico. It was Palladio who first argued that the Romans built porticos on houses, and incorporated them into his domestic architecture on a wide scale. In most cases he used porticos-in-antis, but seven of the villas illustrated in the *Quattro libri* have freestanding porticos. Few Continental architects outside the Veneto followed him before the late eighteenth century. Freestanding porticos on public buildings also remained unusual on the Continent before the mid-eighteenth century. Porticos were generally expressed through pilasters and attached columns with pediments. Given this, the handful of seventeenth-century English examples is significant, although the portico never entered the mainstream of English seventeenth-century architecture. Jones designed two, at St Paul's Cathedral and St Paul, Covent Garden, but never experimented with one on a domestic building. Webb built domestic porticos at The Vyne, Hampshire, in 1654, and at Amesbury Abbey, Wiltshire, but, as with the rest of his Palladian style, these had no immediate successors. Wren, inspired by Jones, hoped to build a giant freestanding portico at St Paul's, but in the end compromised and built a two-storey portico-in-antis. His only executed freestanding portico was at the Royal Hospital, Chelsea, of 1682–9 (Fig. 50). The attached portico at Avington Park, Hampshire, may well be derived from Wren's work, but it is not clear whether this dates from the late seventeenth century or the early eighteenth century. More confidently dated is the portico added by Roger North to his own house at Rougham in Norfolk in 1690–91. This looks directly to Palladio, in particular

124   Sir James Thornhill, Moor Park, Hertfordshire, 1721.

to the Villa Thiene at Cicogna di Villafranca Padovana and the Villa Ragona.[41]

Campbell's Wanstead, for which the first design is dated 1713,[42] was 'adorned with a just Hexastyle, the first yet practised in this manner in the Kingdom'.[43] But although Campbell's may have been the first hexastyle portico it was not the first English portico to be built in the eighteenth century, nor even the first domestic portico. Precedence must be given to Oxford where a series of unbuilt schemes with porticos – by Dean Aldrich (Fig. 107), William Townesend and Hawksmoor at All Souls in 1705–8, and again by Hawksmoor at Queen's College in 1708–9 – culminated in the portico of Hawksmoor's Clarendon Building of 1712 (Fig. 122).[44] As all the surviving designs were in Dr Clarke's collection it is clear that, as at All Souls, he was closely involved in the project. Domestic precedence is shared between William Benson's Wilbury of 1710, with its single-storey portico, and Wakefield's Duncombe Park of 1713, which has the first giant domestic portico (Fig. 123). All are anticipated by the north front of Blenheim, although there the portico, slightly detached though it is from the body of the house, reads as a portico-in-antis, not as freestanding.

The next fifteen years saw a surge of freestanding porticos: Vanbrugh's first design for Eastbury (1716) (and as finally built in 1718); Hawksmoor at St George, Bloomsbury (1716) (Fig. 66); Vanbrugh at Seaton Delaval (1718); John James at St George, Hanover Square (1720); Vanbrugh at the north portico of Stowe, Buckinghamshire (c.1720); Hawksmoor's design for Brasenose College, Oxford (c.1720) (Fig. 128); Campbell's design for Stourhead, Wiltshire (c.1720–4) (Fig. 132)); Sir James Thornhill at Moor Park (1721) (Fig. 124); John James at Wricklemarsh, Kent (1721) (Fig. 139); Lord Burlington at Tottenham Park, Wiltshire (1721) (Fig. 158); James Gibbs at St Martin-in-the-Fields, London (1722) (Fig. 145); Campbell's Mereworth Castle, Kent (1722); Campbell's Houghton Hall (1722) (Fig. 134); Vanbrugh's design for the south front at Grimsthorpe Castle (1722); at Trumpeter's House, Richmond, where a portico was added in about 1722; Campbell's design for Goodwood, Sussex (1724); Lord Burlington at Chiswick (c.1726) (Fig. 137) and Vanbrugh at the Temple of the Four Winds at Castle Howard (1726). To these can be added several examples of porticos-in-antis: Hawksmoor at St Alfege, Greenwich (1712); Archer at St John, Smith's Square (1713); Gibbs's at Sudbrook House, Petersham (1715–19) (Fig.

142); Galilei's at Kimbolton Castle, Huntingdonshire (1718); Gibbs's design for Down Hall, Essex (1720); Campbell at Lord Herbert's house in Whitehall (c.1723–4); and Gibbs's designs for Whitton Place, Middlesex (1725).

The workings of the Fifty New Church Commissioners form a key part of this list, as they followed Vanbrugh's advice and included porticos as one of their requirements. The porticos of St George, Bloomsbury, St Martin in-the-Fields and St George, Hanover Square, are among the most impressive of their day. What is remarkable about this list is the way it crosses all conventional stylistic barriers.

It is interesting to note that these decades in which English portico-mania was at its height also saw a number of prominent Continental churches built with freestanding porticos. In Venice, Andrea Tirali's Chiesa dei Tolentini of 1706 has a hexastyle portico; on the edge of Turin, Filippo Juvarra's church of La Superga of 1715 has a tetrastyle Corinthian portico; in Vienna, Fischer von Erlach's Karlskirche of 1716 has a hexastyle Corinthian portico. The English example is the most extreme, but it was part of a European-wide interest in using freestanding porticos, whose emergence in a number of different countries within a few years is an intriguing phenomenon.

But what of Campbell's introduction to *Vitruvius Britannicus* which has traditionally been read as an attack on the architecture of Vanbrugh and Hawksmoor as well as that of Wren? This interpretation is largely the result of it being read in the light of Shaftesbury's attack on Wren – with whom Vanbrugh and Hawksmoor were closely associated – in 1712:

> Thro' several reigns we have patiently seen the noblest publick Buildings perish (if I may say so) under the Hand of one single Court-Architect; who, if he had been able to profit by Experience, wou'd long since, at our expence, have prove'd the greatest Master of the World. But I question how whether our Patience is like to hold much longer . . . Hardly . . . as the Publick now stands, shou'd we bear to see a *Whitehall* treated like a *Hampton-Court*, or even a new Cathedral like St Paul's.[45]

But, as has been seen, Campbell was fulsome in his praise of Vanbrugh and made not the slightest criticism of Hawksmoor; nor did he criticise Wren or even Thomas Archer, despite the extravagances of his Roehampton design.

The butt of Campbell's attack was undoubtedly James Gibbs, the ghost at *Vitruvius Britannicus*'s table, the only significant architect of the day not to be mentioned by name, whose design for Witham Park appears without credit. Gibbs was Campbell's most direct competition in those critical years when he was establishing himself as an

architect. A fellow Scot, he had the great advantage over Campbell, as a Classical architect, of having studied in Rome and of knowing the remains of Classical antiquity at first hand. Campbell would go to any lengths to do down his rival, even informing the authorities that Gibbs was a Roman Catholic in the hope that he would get his position as one of the two surveyors to the Fifty New Church Commissioners. Gibbs did lose his job, but was succeeded by John James not Campbell. Campbell was more successful at Burlington House, where he deposed Gibbs in mid-commission in about 1716.

The key to Campbell's attack on Gibbs comes in the commentary on his Vitruvian church in the second volume of *Vitruvius Britannicus* which can only be read as a savage assault on Gibbs's St Mary-le-Strand, begun in 1714 (Fig. 125). The commission for rebuilding St Mary-le-Strand must have been one which Campbell longed to have himself, set as it was at a key junction on London's principal highway, but his church designs had been rejected by the Fifty New Church Commissioners. Discussing the side elevation of the Vitruvian church Campbell noted that he had

> abstained from any Ornaments between the Columns, which would only serve to serve to enflame the Expence and clog the Building. In those admirable Pieces of Antiquity, we find none of the trifling, licentious, and insignificant Ornaments, so much affected by some of our Moderns. The ancients placed their chief beauties in the justness of the Intercolumniations, the precise Proportions of the Orders and the greatness of the Parts; nor have we one Precedent either from the *Greeks* or *Romans*, that they practised two Orders, one over another in the same Temple in the Outside, even in the most considerable, much less to divide it into little Parts; and whereas the Ancients were contented with one continued Pediment from the Portico to the Pastico, we now have no less than three in one Side where the Ancients never admitted any. This Practice must be imputed either to an entire ignorance of Antiquity, or a Vanity to expose their absurd Novelties, so contrary to those excellent Precepts in *Vitruvius*, and so repugnant to those admirable Remains the Ancients have left us.[46]

This is no less than a step-by-step criticism of St Mary-le-Strand, a criticism that is not just personal, for the church is completely contrary to all the precepts put forward by Vanbrugh; it lacks even a portico.

With this attack in mind, the significance of the key line in the introduction becomes clear: 'How affected and licentious are the Works of *Bernini* and *Fontana*?' Fontana was Gibbs's master in Rome and was himself Bernini's pupil. The introduction should not be seen as a wide-ranging attack on an English Baroque school, but as a specific attack on one potentially Baroque architect.

125 James Gibbs's, St Mary-le-Strand, London, 1714 (Thomas Malton, watercolour, Victoria and Albert Museum, London).

With hindsight, *Vitruvius Britannicus* achieved a ca-nonical position in the history of English Palladianism, but it is not a position that survives examination of the first two volumes. Campbell was only one among a whole series of architects and patrons in the first two decades of the eighteenth century who were advancing the cause of a more rigorous Classicism, specifically one inspired by Palladio. This can be seen in James's state-ment 'that the Beautys of Architecture may consist with the greatest plainness of the structure'. Lord Shaftesbury's rather conventional call in 1712 for an architecture 'founded in truth and nature' and 'independent of fancy' can also be seen in this light. (It is appropriate that in his portrait, now owned by the National Portrait Gallery, he should be shown beside a pure Grecian temple.) So can the work of 'the new Junta for Architecture', John Molesworth (envoy to the Tuscan court, 1710–14), his

father, Sir Thomas Hewett (Surveyor-General, 1719–26) and George Markham, who invited the Florentine architect Alessandro Galilei to England in 1714 to intro-duce a more Classical style into British architecture. The new edition of Fréart's *Parallel* of 1707, James's transla-tion of Perrault's *A Treatise of the Five Orders of Columns* of 1708, Dean Aldrich's *Elementa architecturae*, Charles Fairfax's translation of Palladio's *Antichita di Roma* of 1709 and Giacomo Leoni's 1715 scheme to translate Palladio's *Quattro libri* are all part of a similar urge which also spawned *Vitruvius Britannicus*. So is the work of Aldrich, James, Hawksmoor and Vanbrugh and of those architects who designed so many porticos. It is a move-ment that can be seen as moving towards neo-Palla-dianism, but this was a style that would only coalesce in the next decade.

VI

TOWARDS THE ESTABLISHMENT OF
A NEO-PALLADIAN STYLE

ELEMENTS FROM PALLADIO and Inigo Jones were a regular feature of Nicholas Hawksmoor's work from his earliest independent commission, but before 1715 such borrowings were unsystematic, the occasional motif, perhaps a whole façade, but no more. Two schemes drawn up between 1717 and 1720 for Oxford colleges, both associated with Dr George Clarke, show a rather different approach, an attempt to design complete buildings in a Palladian or Jonesian manner.[1]

The combined hall, chapel and library which Hawksmoor proposed for Worcester College in about 1717 is known from a series of drawings on which the sources for the various motifs used are meticulously annotated (Fig. 126).[2] These reveal a mixture of erudite quotations from antiquity, from *cinquecento* architects and from the work of Inigo Jones. The triple Serlian window on the west elevation comes from the Roman arch at Saintes in France, illustrated in Blondel's *Cours d'architecture* of 1698; the urn-like decoration in the spandrels of Serlian windows from the Édifice des Tuteles at Bordeaux, illustrated in Perrault's translation of Vitruvius of 1684; the cornice of the library from the Arch of Constantine and that of the chapel from the Pantheon. The towers of the façade are inspired by the Tower of Andromachus or Tower of the Winds, described by Vitruvius as a marble octagonal tower capped with a conical piece of marble.[3] The central superimposed Serlian motif on the east front probably comes from Serlio, while the round-headed pedimented windows on the west front are derived from Antonio da Sangallo's Palazzo Farnese in Rome. Hawksmoor also noted 'The Rusticks according to Mr Jones at St James Chapell'. Measured drawings at Worcester College show that Hawksmoor must have studied Jones's Queen's Chapel at St James's Palace before making the design, using this as a model for the Serlian windows of the hall and chapel and for the windows on the side elevations.[4]

Hawksmoor managed to combine these antique, Renaissance and Jonesian motifs in a design of Classical austerity which seems to anticipate the more neo-Classical works of Lord Burlington. Indeed, the idea of creating an entrance from superimposed Serlian motifs placed between single projecting bays and of placing a thermal window above a Serlian window – ideas which had no precedence in English architecture and are hard to find in Italian Renaissance architecture – recurs in Burlington's early work, specifically in the refacings of old Chiswick House, Middlesex (*c.*1723), and of Northwick Park, Gloucestershire (1730). It is tempting to wonder whether Burlington studied Hawksmoor's designs, perhaps visiting Oxford on his return from Italy late in 1719 fired with a love of Palladio and anxious to examine that half of the Jones drawings which Dr Clarke possessed.

The 1720 design for Brasenose College shows Hawksmoor taking a rather different approach. A birds-eye view of this was later published in Williams's *Oxonia depicta* in 1732–3 (Fig. 128), and a ground-plan survives, as does a variant drawing of the left half of the High Street elevation, dated 1720. Hawksmoor's scheme envisaged extending the college to the High Street, creating an arcaded front quadrangle and a High Street façade with a giant hexastyle Corinthian portico flanked by seven-bay five-storey ranges – or rather ranges with a basement, storey and mezzanine and a further storey and mezzanine separated by a plat band. These side ranges were to be divided by slightly projecting superimposed Serlian windows on a plain wall – lighting the staircases – the rest of the façade having channelled rustication[5].

Hawksmoor based his design on the series of drawings for palaces or large country houses, now known to be largely by Webb but then probably thought to be by Jones, among Dr Clarke's collection. The idea for a giant hexastyle Corinthian portico approached up steps flanked by a basement and surmounted storeys and mezzanines was taken from a 'Design for a great country house or palace' (Fig. 129). The use of channelled rustication across the entire façade was probably taken from Webb's designs for Cobham Hall, Kent (Fig. 109). Surmounted Venetian windows in the middle of a façade is an unusual motif which Hawksmoor took from a design by Webb for Somerset House.[6]

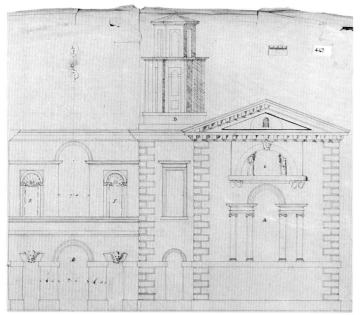

126   Nicholas Hawksmoor, unexecuted design for the east front of Worcester College, Oxford, 1717.

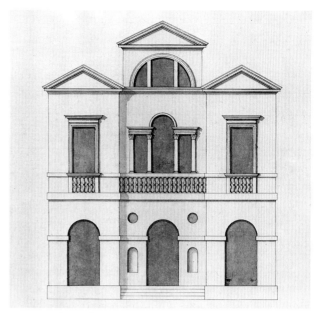

127   Lord Burlington, design for refacing Old Chiswick House, Middlesex, c.1723 (demolished).

Neither the Worcester College nor the Brasenose College schemes was built, but they show that for a brief period after 1715 Hawksmoor was trying to design buildings that were Palladian or Jonesian in ethos, not just in detail, neo-Palladian buildings. The influence of Dr Clarke must lie behind both schemes but does not explain why Hawksmoor was quite so thorough-going in his Palladianism. The two men had been associated for over a decade but before 1717 Hawksmoor had never attempted to design a completely Palladian building. Moreover, Dr Clarke was probably responsible for Worcester College as built, which follows the framework of Hawksmoor's scheme but much watered down and lacking most of the elements that gave it its specifically Palladian character.

The answer would seem to be that Hawksmoor was taken up by a growing architectural interest in Palladianism which becomes evident after the publication in 1715 of the first book of Leoni's edition of Palladio and the first volume of *Vitruvius Britannicus*. At Brasenose, in particular, he responded to Campbell's suggestion of a Palladianism based on palazzi-type designs, but this was an English Palladian style which was never to be. After Brasenose, Hawksmoor reverted to his usual free interpretation of sources and never again worked so closely from drawings which he must have thought to be by Jones, although he always remained sympathetic to Jones's work. As late as 1734 he sent Clarke revisions of Edward Holdsworth's designs for Magdalen College emphasising the corner pavilions and altering the proportions of the towers on either side of the library: 'In much the same manner, as Mr Inigo Jones

was used to do in like case'.[7] Meanwhile, Campbell was taking Palladianism in a direction that barely featured in the first two volumes of *Vitruvius Britannicus* – towards the villa.

Although they followed the general trend towards austerity of architecture, Campbell's commissioned designs of the 1710s do not seem to have been particularly influential. The only emulator of the palazzi designs was his own Burlington House, London (1717) (Fig. 130). His first great house, Wanstead House, Essex (c.1714) (Fig. 119), had no immediate progenitors, and it was not until the 1730s, twenty years later, that a series of houses was built that takes Wanstead as the model. Similarly, the Chevening style seen in the houses designed in 1716 for Sir John Hotham (Fig. 120) and John Hedworth, and the Rolls House in London of 1717 seems to have had limited national impact.

However, in the third volume of *Vitruvius Britannicus*, published in 1725, Campbell reveals a very different approach. A series of designs for villas, most of them executed, shows that he had been looking at Palladio's villas, a source in which before he seems to have shown minimal interest. The first of these is Ebberston Lodge, Yorkshire, which Campbell dates 1718. This is best described as a transitional design. The plan is a reduced version of Palladio's Villa Zeno at Cesalto, the colonnaded loggia of the north front must be derived from Jones's Queen's House at Greenwich and the central doorcase is in the spirit of Jones's gateways, such as those flanking St Paul, Covent Garden. On the other hand, the composition is quite un-Palladian, as are the emphatic keystones decorated with masks. Revealingly, when

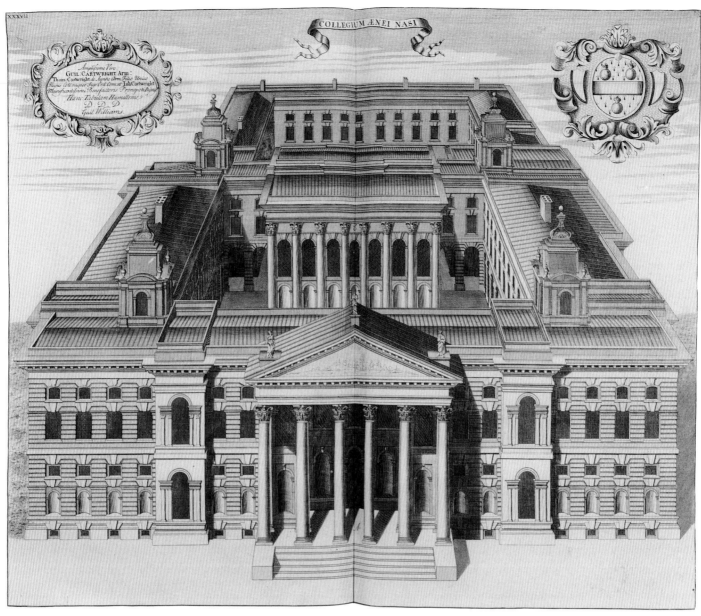

COLLEGIUM ÆNEI NASI

128   Nicholas Hawksmoor, unexecuted design for Brasenose College, Oxford, 1720 (from William Williams's *Oxonia Depicta* (1732)).

129   Anon., design for a great house.

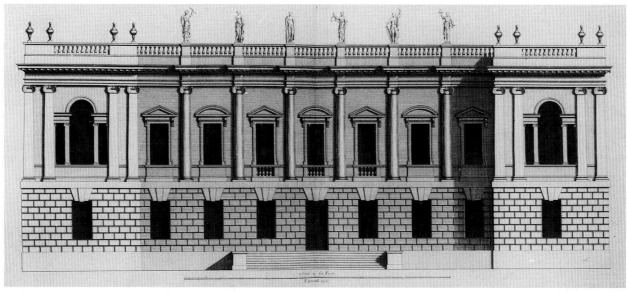

130   Colen Campbell, Burlington House, London, 1717, from *Vitruvius Britannicus* (1725) (remodelled).

Campbell came to illustrate Ebberston he altered the design so as to make it appear more Palladian.[8] In particular, he minimised the effect of the keystones, completely redesigned the cupola which in the original was much closer to that on the east wing at Castle Howard, replaced the six Baroque urns, which again paralleled those at Castle Howard, with four sober balls, and ignored the highly architectural plinth on which Ebberston Lodge sat, so that it appeared more of a villa.

At Newby Park, Yorkshire, which according to *Vitruvius Britannicus* was designed in 1720,[9] Campbell was much purer in his Palladian sources (Fig. 278). This has a plan taken from the Villa Emo at Fanzolo, with its two central rooms linked by a short passage between two small staircases, although the portico-in-antis has been replaced by an attached portico. The façade owes more to the Villa Ragona, although, as with a number of Palladio's villas, it has no basement and a balustrade hides the pitched roof.

Stourhead, Wiltshire (Fig. 132), which Campbell said was covered in 1722,[10] takes its plan, with a central staircase hall, from Palladio's Villa Ragona, the only difference being that it was planned to have a freestanding portico, not a portico-in-antis, and to have closets and service stairs on either side of the chapel (Fig. 131). Similarly, the basic disposition of the façade comes from the Villa Ragona, although the height of the basement has been reduced and again the pitched roof replaced by a balustrade.

Mereworth Castle, Kent, covered in 1723 according to Campbell,[11] is taken, with only minor changes of plan and elevation, from Palladio's Villa Rotunda. Pembroke House, London, built for Lord Herbert in 1724, is based,

with modifications, on a drawing for a villa by Jones then thought to be by Palladio.[12] The unexecuted design for Goodwood, Sussex (1724), is a variant on Mereworth, looking as much to Villa Mocenigo as to the Villa Rotunda.

The one exception to this run of villas in Campbell's work in the 1720s, apart from John Plumptre's house in Nottingham of 1724 which continues the Chevening tradition, is Houghton Hall, Norfolk (Fig. 134), which Campbell dated 1722 in his introduction and said was erected in 1723, three years after Thomas Ripley was appointed supervisor, two years after he began to look for materials and a year after the first stone was laid. John Harris has plausibly suggested that the initial design may have been by James Gibbs which was then executed, after some changes, by Campbell.[13] Could the repeated claim on each engraving 'Designed by Colen Campbell Esq' be hiding a guilty conscience? Neither the plan, which parallels that at Ditchley Park, Oxfordshire (1720),[14] nor the elevation derive from Palladio, but are attempts to dress up the standard large post-Restoration house epitomised by Belton Hall, Lincolnshire, with fashionable Palladian detail. Moreover, Houghton as illustrated in *Vitruvius Britannicus* differs markedly from Houghton as built (Fig. 133). In particular, the windows are much closer together; both the rustic and attic windows are three-quarter height, not half-height; the side-lights of the Serlian windows are blind and there never were pedimented pavilion towers. In illustrating Houghton, Campbell may have been carrying out a double deception, claiming the design of a house which was not really his and then making that house seem much more Palladian than it was.

The concept of the villa was well accepted in early

eighteenth-century England. Roger North had made the distinction about 1698 when he wrote that

> The country model and that of a suburb villa are different. The former partakes of the nature of a court, as a lord of a manor doth of regality, and should, like the court, have great rooms to contain numbers, with fires suitable and other conveniences, according to condition. A villa, is quasy a lodge, for the sake of a garden, to retire enjoy and sleep, without pretence of entertainment of many persons.[5]

But none of Campell's houses, although built in the manner of a villa, are the suburban resorts that North talks about nor are they the centres of farms that Palladio describes. Mereworth was a bachelor's house and Newby the country house of a former Lord Mayor of York, but Stourhead is positively deceitful, the entrance gives the impression of a small villa, but the side that of a large country house, and at Goodwood Campbell tried to fit what is really a ducal residence into a centralised villa. It is not surprising that the Duke of Richmond rejected the Goodwood design or that Sir Robert Walpole, who built Houghton specifically to impress his power and importance on friends and neighbours, insisted on a traditional great house.

One other thing stands out from the third volume of *Vitruvius Britannicus*, the repeated use of rusticated window- and door-frames. In the first two volumes

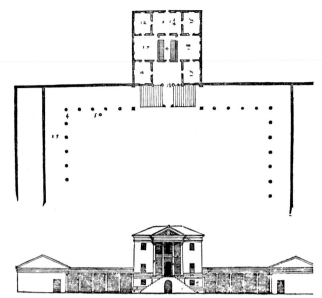

131 Andrea Palladio, Villa Ragona, Italy, from *The Four Books of Architecture* (1738).

Campbell favoured what he called Palladian windows, windows with alternating segmental and triangular pediments. The only exception is the design dedicated to Robert Walpole in the second volume, which has rusticated windows set on plain walls. Campbell did use these at Wanstead, but on the garden front which was not

132 Colen Campbell, Stourhead House, Wiltshire, 1722, from *Vitruvius Britannicus* (1725).

133   Colen Campbell, Houghton Hall, Norfolk, 1721.

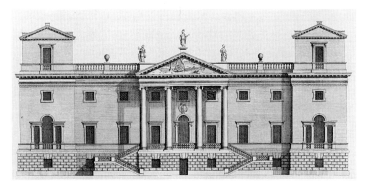

134   Colen Campbell, Houghton Hall, Norfolk, 1721, from *Vitruvius Britannicus* (1725).

illustrated in *Vitruvius Britannicus*. The source for such windows is Palladio's Palazzo Thiene, where they are set against heavily rusticated walls, and it was in this manner that Webb used them at Greenwich, a building illustrated by Campbell (Fig. 30). It is unclear why Campbell took so strongly to such windows, but as they were used by Webb at Greenwich to a design which he believed was by Jones and (against plain walls) by William

Samwell at Eaton Hall, Cheshire (Fig. 46), a design which he specifically praised; Campbell may have seen them as part of a specifically British Palladian tradition. Although generally (but only relatively recently) termed 'Gibbsian surrounds', Campbell was using such windows several years before Gibbs,[16] and in his designs of the 1720s used them far more consistently than Gibbs ever did.[17]

How can Campbell's sudden conversion to the idea of the villa be explained? Somehow it seems unlikely that Campbell made such a dramatic change in isolation. Although good at taking the ideas and designs of others and adapting them, he seems to have lacked the spark of genius necessary to make such a leap on his own. The one significant development that occurred between the first publication of *Vitruvius Britannicus* and the design of the villas was Campbell's involvement with the Earl of Burlington. Burlington visited Italy in 1714–15, returning when he came of age. He immediately set about rebuilding the wings at Burlington House in an essentially French style, linked by a colonnade which Terry Friedman has suggested was based on Hôtel de Souvre in Paris, using James Gibbs as his architect.[18] Work was

135 Lord Burlington, elevation of the Dormitory at Westminster School, London, 1722.

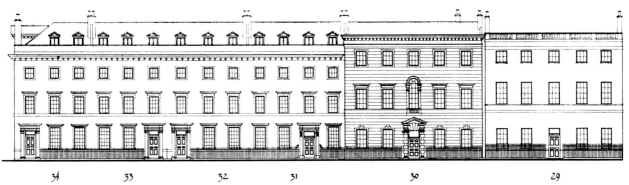

136 29–34 Old Burlington St, London, with 30 and 29 (General Wade's House), *c.*1721 and 1723 (demolished).

under way when he dismissed Gibbs and turned instead to Campbell, his eyes presumably being opened to the possibilities of Palladianism by the publication of *Vitruvius Britannicus*. Campbell later complained that at Burlington House he had to complete the designs of another, unnamed, architect. More significantly, Burlington commissioned Campbell to remodel Burlington House itself, following his palazzi style (Fig. 130). At this date Burlington's only design of his own was the gauche casina at Chiswick of 1717. In the summer of 1719 Burlington made a second trip to Italy, returning at the end of November, after making a detailed study of a number of Palladio's buildings and probably with a large collection of his drawings. In April 1721 these were joined by 'a Parcell of Architectonicall Designes and Drawings by Palladio', which he bought from John Talman, from whom he had already acquired 'a Book of Designes and Plans &c by Inigo Jones' in May 1720. Other Renaissance architects whose drawings could be found in Burlington's collection include Raphael, Giulio Romano and Peruzzi.[19]

Campbell's new approach to Palladio based on the villa coincided with Burlington's growing interest in

architecture and it was Burlington who was the probable catalyst. If so, the move to the villa was not sparked specifically by Burlington's acquisition of Palladio and Jones's drawings, as nearly everything that Campbell used in his key houses was already accessible in the *Quattro libri*. This would suggest Burlington's impact on Campbell predated his second trip to Italy in 1719, a suggestion that fits in with John Harris's belief that Campbell first put forward the idea of a house based on Palladio's Villa Rotunda to Burlington for Chiswick before the second Italian visit. A drawing always assumed to be for Mereworth in the Royal Institute of British Architects' Library cannot be for that site as it has a coronet in the pediment. Campbell's patron at Mereworth, the Hon. John Fane, did not acquire a title, and therefore the right to a coronet, until 1733.[20] But Burlington fell out with Campbell, and the first English Villa Rotunda had to wait until 1722.[21] Burlington's own architectural ideas were developing rapidly and he was presumably no longer satisfied with Campbell's derivative Palladianism. His views must have been reinforced by his close study of Palladio's buildings and by his purchase of the drawings, for his designs of the early

1720s veer sharply away from Campbell. Burlington's influence on Campbell was, in effect, posthumous, no buildings deriving from it were built until after they had separated, but it was profound and dominated Campbell's career until his death in 1729.

During the early 1720s Burlington began enthusiastically turning his architectural ideas into buildings. A villa for his brother-in-law Lord Bruce at Tottenham Park, Wiltshire, begun in 1721 (Fig. 158), was followed by a series of buildings in London, the Westminster School Dormitory of 1722 (Fig. 135), 30 Old Burlington Street (c.1721) and its next-door neighbour 29, General Wade's house (1723) (Fig. 136), and the gateway for Queensberry House (c.1723) (these last three all on his own estate behind Burlington House), and an abortive design for a school and almshouses at Sevenoaks in Kent (1724). At the same time Burlington was hard at work on his surburban estate in Chiswick, first refacing the old house in about 1723 and then, after the old house had been damaged by fire, building the new villa around 1726 (Fig. 137) and at the same time filling the garden with an array of smaller buildings.

The rapid development of Burlington's ideas in the first years of the 1720s was encapsulated in adjoining houses in Old Burlington Street. Number 30, built about 1721, could easily have been mistaken for a design by Campbell.[22] Number 29, built for General Wade in 1723–4, is markedly different, its street front being astonishingly austere, lacking any decoration, even window mouldings, while its garden front is a copy of one of the Palladio drawings that Burlington owned.[23] Such direct repetition of an entire façade (the only significant differences are the insertion of thermal windows on the ground floor and the vermiculation of ground-floor rustication) is unusual in Burlington's work, for although precedents for individual elements can often be traced, these are usually combined in a novel manner.

Nor are his sources restricted to the buildings of Palladio. It would be interesting to know more about what Lord Burlington saw in Palladio's contemporary Galeazzo Alessi, one of the very few architects Burlington is known to have studied on his Grand Tour. Kent, who described Alessi as 'Vitruvio', recorded that he was taken by Burlington to see two of his palazzi in Genoa in 1719 who ordered that they should be drawn.[24] The theories of Alberti were seen by Cinzia Sicca to lie behind Burlington's concentration on the structural use of the undecorated wall at the Westminster School Dormitory, the design for the Sevenoaks school (1724) and, subsequently, at the unexecuted Council House at Chichester, Sussex (1730), and the principal elevation of the York Assembly Rooms (1731).[25] She argued that these derive their form from Alberti's belief that the column can only support a horizontal architrave and that the arch must be supported on a pier, with or without engaged half-columns. Burlington certainly studied Alberti's *De re aedificatoria* (1485) carefully, underlining passages heavily in ink and making annotations in the margins. John Harris, however, felt that the source of the Westminster Dormitory is much closer to home and that it is an austere version of Jones's Covent Garden piazza (Fig. 54), while he traced the façade of the York Assembly Rooms to Palladio's drawings of the Roman baths.[26] It is also fair to point out that the Sevenoaks school, with its central pavilion and long, low arcaded wings, is taken from Palladian villa models, particularly the Villa Emo at Fanzolo, while its central pavilion has strong Scamozzian elements.

On the other hand, Richard Hewlings argued that very little at Chiswick can be ascribed directly to Palladio and that virtually all the individual elements should be seen as borrowed from antiquity.[27] Chiswick House (Fig. 137) will be discussed further in the next chapter, together with Tottenham Park, but it is fair to point out that it owes less to the Villa Rotunda than it does to Scamozzi's Rocca Pisani, itself a development of the Villa Rotunda. Like the Rocca Pisani, the Chiswick villa has only a single portico, no attic windows, a shallow octagonal dome with a pronounced drum, a five-bay side elevation with a central Serlian window and chimney-stacks disguised as obelisks. Whereas Campbell's mature work never moved far from Palladio, Burlington was more intellectual in his models and quarried a deeper seam of precedents. As his early works show, English neo-Palladianism was never restricted in its sources to the works of Palladio alone.

Note must also be taken of the suggestion that the Chiswick villa was built as a masonic temple in honour of the exiled Stuart monarch.[28] This makes particular significance of the fact that the central hall at Chiswick is octagonal (those of the Villa Rotunda and Rocca Pisani are round), with octagonal coffering, and of the spiral staircases at each corner of the dome. The use of octagonal coffering in the saloon at Holkham Hall, Norfolk, is seen as another example of masonic symbolism in a Palladian building, as is the use of sphinxes in gardens. However, it should be noted that the Odeo Cornaro and another design based on it, both published in Serlio's seventh book, had octagonal central halls, as does one of the Palladio drawings Burlington owned.[29] The same is true of Hardouin-Mansart's King's Building at Marly, which is a derivative of the Villa Rotunda. The second of the Serlio plans also has four spiral staircases in the corners of the dome. Octagonal coffering is an antique motif found at the Basilica of Maxentius and illustrated in Desgodetz's *Édifices antiques de Rome* (1682).

The search for masonic and Jacobite explanations behind Palladian architecture rapidly dissolves into a game of mirrors in which it is impossible to tell what is fact and what is disinformation. It is true that there were connections between English neo-Palladianism and freemasonry, which was formally organized in England in 1717 and reached a peak of popularity among the nobility and gentry and the crafts in the following decade. Both Lord Herbert and Sir Andrew Fountaine, later described by Roger Morris in *In Defence of Ancient Architecture* as the 'principal Practitioners and Preservers' of architecture along with Lord Burlington,[30] attended the installation of the Duke of Montagu as the first noble Grand Master in 1721. This connection can be seen most obviously in the books of Batty Langley,[31] but it has yet to be satisfactorily proved that the introduction of neo-Palladianism was in any way the result of masonic influence, and that freemasonry did not simply attach itself to the sympathetic language of a style that had already established itself. What can be said of the masonic claims is that all the elements that go to make up Chiswick have respectable Palladian precedents, and that it is not surprising to find them, even if there is a deeper masonic meaning lurking below.

Burlington never made use of Campbell again, but the two of them, together with Lord Herbert (later Earl of Pembroke) and Roger Morris – whose role progressed slowly from that of an executant architect, perhaps originally Campbell's assistant, to an independent architect – formed an interrelated circle of architects, the core neo-Palladians, sometimes working alone, sometimes together, into the next decade.

Pembroke House, built for Lord Herbert, who had studied at Christ Church under Dean Aldrich while the Peckwater Quadrangle was being erected and later developed into a keen amateur architect, appears in *Vitruvius Britannicus* ascribed to Colen Campbell; the drawing thought to be by Palladio on which it is based was owned by Burlington; an alternative design drawn by Morris survives among Herbert's papers at Wilton. Marble Hill, Middlesex (1724), another villa, has no architect ascribed to it in *Vitruvius Britannicus*, but an unsigned design, possibly by Campbell, survives at Wilton; the work was carried out by Morris, and payments were made through Herbert. A continuing link between Campbell and Morris is shown by a series of drawings corresponding to Campbell's Goodwood scheme, which are not in Campbell's hand and may be by Morris, and by the way that Morris acted for Campbell at Studley Royal, Yorkshire, in 1729.

Campbell died in 1729, but from that year there is a reference in building work at Castle Hill, Devon, that the entablature 'shall be as the Earl of Burlington and Lord Herbert shall direct . . . all other parts of the said cornice [shall be] according to the plan or drawing thereof signed by the said Roger Morris'.[32] Morris retained a close connection with Herbert, working with him at White Lodge, Richmond (1727), another villa (Fig. 138); the Column of Victory at Blenheim (1730–

1); Wimbledon House, Surrey (1730–5); the Palladian bridge at Wilton (1736–7), and probably at Westcombe House, Blackheath (*c*.1730) – yet another villa, this time for Herbert himself. Lord Herbert's specific contribution to the work of the group is hard to identify. No authenticated drawings by him survive and he worked so closely with Roger Morris that his own architectural identity is blurred. Nevertheless, it is clear from contemporary comments that he was more than just an enthusiastic patron. Between the two of them, Herbert and Morris developed an individual form of neo-Palladian villa, distinct from Burlington's work, characterised by its cubic shape and pyramidal roof which derive from Palladio's villas, particularly the Villa Pisani at Bagnolo and the Villa Emo at Fanzolo. What stands out from these houses is the tight-knit nature of the architects and the way that they are dominated by the villa. Other examples by the group include Campbell's Waverley Abbey, Surrey (*c*.1725), and Hackney House, Hackney (1727), and Roger Morris's Combe Bank, Kent (*c*.1725), and Whitton Place, Middlesex (*c*.1732–9) (Fig. 272). To these can be added the unexecuted Dalton Hall, Yorkshire (1737), probably by Roger Morris, and Rokeby Park, Yorkshire (1725), built by Sir Thomas Robinson for himself (Fig. 159). The only houses that are not villas are Castle Hill, which was an older house remodelled, and Wimbledon House, which was built for the architecturally outspoken Sarah, Duchess of Marlborough, who made it quite clear that she had no time for the follies of villa design and presumably insisted that her house, like Houghton, follow the traditional Restoration great-house plan.

Only Robinson was not a close member of the group, and in his case Lord Burlington's direct influence is clear. Robinson initially commissioned a villa design from William Wakefield in 1724, which was illustrated in the third volume of *Vitruvius Britannicus*, but then Burlington intervened as Robinson later noted in a letter: 'Lord Burlington persuaded me to build one [an Egyptian Hall] at Rokeby and told me he would give me a design'. In the event Robinson relied on his own abilities. He seems to have had access to Burlington's Palladio drawings but the basic form of the house corresponds to Herbert and Morris's contemporary cubic style. The reason for Wakefield's dismissal is clear in a letter of 1730 in which Robinson described him as a practical architect, but felt that his designs did not have 'so many Palladian strokes about them'. By 1731 Robinson was able to write that 'My house is now entirely fitted up . . . My chief expense has been in Palladian doors and windows which I am told have a very good effect.'[33]

Robinson's remarks show that by 1730 the idea of a specifically Palladian style was becoming understood, and they can be paralleled in the comments of others

137   Lord Burlington, Chiswick House, Middlesex, c.1726 (Jacques Rigaud, watercolour, Chatsworth).

who were not so sympathetic to the idea. In 1726 John Molesworth had written to Alessandro Galilei:

I must give you one piece of necessary advice which is in the meantime take the first possible opportunity of engaggeing some of our travellers to carry you with them in Lombardy, particularly in Venice and Vicenza; for here the reigning taste is Palladio's style of building and a man is an Heretick that should talk of Michel Angelo or any other modern architect. You must diligently copy all the noted fabricks of Palladio for those very drafts would introduce you here, and without them you may dispair of success . . .[34]

Lord Hervey writing to the Prince of Wales in 1731 talked of 'the technical jargon of a true follower of

Palladio and Vertruvius', of 'Palladian votaries' and of his desire not to be 'put into the Burlington-inquisition for want of implicit faith'.[35] Subsequently, Horace Walpole would describe Mereworth Castle, in 1752 as being 'perfect in the Palladian taste',[36] but in *English Architecture* in 1752 architects were warned against slavish dependency on Palladio's book which 'being considered by the generality as the sole model of truth and perfection, stops the progress of the science and gives a dull sameness to all our buildings'[37] while Allan Ramsay in his *A Dialogue of Taste* of 1762 described how 'An Artist may, by a Palladian receipt done, without any taste, form a very elegant Corinthian pillar'.[38] A common jibe against the Palladians was their insistence on low window to wall ratios, as Lord Chesterfield make clear in a letter written in 1728 to Mrs Howard (for whom Marble Hill was built) describing a room he proposed to build at The Hague: 'Whether these are the right proportions or no, I must submit to you and Lord Herbert . . . It will, I am sure, have five great faults, which are five great windows, each of them big enough to admit intolerable light.'[39] This obsession was a source of particular irritation to Sarah, Duchess of Marlborough, who complained of 'our present architects' that 'I observe one aversion they have, which is light, and that is the reverse of my inclination. My Lord Herbert particularly seems to dislike extremely windows in a room.'[40]

The erection of a series of similar designs for one building type by a small group of architects does not mean that the style they projected was necessarily the dominant one. Other architects working in the 1720s show that while Campbell and Burlington's ideas were influential they were by no means universal, but that a pervasive interest in Palladio, Jones and the villa was shared by architects who were not members of the immediate neo-Palladian clique.

James, or Giacomo, Leoni is an interesting case. Leoni was a Venetian who had come to England via the court of the Elector Palatine where he must have come into contact with the Matteo d'Alberti, whose architecture seems to reveal a debt to Inigo Jones.[41] It was the announcement of Leoni's anticipated translation of Palladio's *Quattro libri* that had led to the remodelling of *Vitruvius Britannicus* at such a late stage. Despite his publication, Leoni's first significant commission did not come until 1721, when he designed 7 Burlington Gardens for Lord Clifton, who sold the unfinished house to the Duke of Queensbury. This commission must have been gained at Burlington's recommendation as the house was the largest and most lavish of those on Burlington's Picadilly estate, looking out over Burlington's garden to Burlington House. As Leoni was keen to show, Burlington approved the design and himself designed the courtyard entrance on Old Burlington Street.

This suggests some connection with Burlington's circle, and, indeed, four of Leoni's patrons were related to Burlington. The connection was also stylistic and Richard Hewlings has shown the substantial debt Leoni's architecture owed to Campbell. As Hewlings has pointed out, the irony of Leoni's career is that 'Apparently a Venetian architect could come to a country where anything Venetian was greatly in demand, fail to exert any apparent influence on native practitioners who were more than ready to learn, and instead produce a corpus of design almost exclusively of native type.'[42] But Leoni's debt is to Campbell's palazzi designs and, it would appear, to his unpublished drawings for great houses, not to the later villas. As a result, his architecture developed in a markedly different direction to that of Campbell and Burlington. Whereas their country houses

after 1720 are largely based on Palladio's villas, Leoni tried to adapt the ideas of Palladio to the English great house. His most elaborate schemes, for Carshalton Park, Surrey (1723), Lyme Park, Cheshire (1725), his designs for Cliveden House, Buckinghamshire (1727), Bold Hall, Merseyside (1731) (Fig. 140), Lathom House, Lancashire (c.1740), and Wortley Hall, Yorkshire (1743), show that he was not without success in his attempt, although his influence on others was limited.

Of the nine architects praised by name in the introduction to *Vitruvius Britannicus*, Hawksmoor and Vanbrugh have already been discussed, Bruce was dead, Wren, Archer, Winde and Talman were effectively retired, and Christopher Wren (son of the surveyor) was never a serious architect. That leaves John James. Chiefly renowned as a reliable surveyor, James was not a designer of particular genius, but his position at the heart of the architectural establishment makes his reactions to the stylistic developments of the 1710s and 1720s of interest, particularly in view of his praise for Inigo Jones in 1711 and his possible work at Wilton around 1705. James's most substantial commission was Wricklemarsh, Kent (1723–4) (Fig. 139), a house that sits ambiguously in relation to Houghton (Fig. 133). It shares the same basic disposition, nine bays wide divided 1 + 2 + 3 + 2 + 1 with a central three-bay portico (although Houghton was designed and published with a freestanding portico it was reduced in execution to an applied portico) and one and a half storeys over a rusticated rustic. However, Wricklemarsh also differs significantly. It has no Serlian windows in the end bays; the windows are closer together than those at Houghton, both as built and as illustrated; the portico has no pediment and the rustic has continuous 'French' rustication. It may be that the absence of a pediment was inspired by Jones's nearby Queen's House at Greenwich whose portico-in-antis has no pediment. James, who was Clerk of the Works at Greenwich, also used a form of Serlian window found on the side elevations of John Webb's King Charles Block at Greenwich. John Brushe has suggested that Wricklemarsh should be given precedence over Houghton, perhaps even being the source for that design.[43] This is unlikely; instead, it would seem that Wricklemarsh shows that James was aware of the Palladian tide but felt no need to follow the stylistic 'purity' of Campbell's design.

Wricklemarsh was James's largest house. His smallest, the house he built for himself at Warbrooks, Hampshire, in 1724, is no less interesting, for it reveals a similar concern with the villa to that shown by Campbell. Warbrooks is only three bays wide but set under a giant pediment with the orders reduced to strips (perhaps as much because of cost as for reasons of style). The giant pediment was a feature Palladio had used at the Villa Angarano and the Villa Maser and which Campbell had

138 Roger Morris, White Lodge, Richmond, 1727.

included in his design for Robert Walpole in the second volume of *Vitruvius Britannicus*. Iver Grove, Buckinghamshire (Fig. 141), built in 1722 and plausibly attributed to James, shows a similar examination of the possibilities of the villa. In its use of coloured brick and its segmental-headed ground-floor windows, Iver Grove seems to look back to the architecture of Queen Anne, but the house has a bold applied portico, a Diocletian window (something still rare in 1722), and the 1.3.1 disposition of a classic Palladian villa. The source for Iver Grove would appear to be Palladio's Villa Ragona with the basement removed. A similar approach can be found at Lee Place, Charlbury, Oxfordshire, which was refaced about 1725 with a five-bay front, a central three-bay Doric pilastered centrepiece and a Diocletian window in the pediment; but the architect of Lee Place is unknown.

A close parallel to the way that James was interested in the villa while differing from Burlington and Campbell stylistically can be found in James Gibbs's work at Sudbrook House, Petersham (1715) (Fig. 142), whose

plan is based on Palladio's Villa Thiene at Cicogna. Like Vanbrugh in his contemporary borrowings of Palladio's plans, the elevation owes nothing to Palladio, sharing the same segmental windows as Iver Grove, although the balustraded, pedimentless portico-in-antis probably shows an awareness of Jones's Queen's House at Greenwich. When Gibbs published Sudbrook in his *Book of Architecture* (1728) he tidied up the elevation, removing the segmental-headed windows and replacing the French quoins with English quoins, a change that is aptly characteristic of the way he had adapted his style in response to Campbell and Burlington's success. Indeed, of all the architects working around 1720 it is James Gibbs who provides the most interesting barometer of stylistic change.

Gibbs did not find it easy to establish himself as an architect on his arrival in England in 1709, despite his Continental training and the patronage of Lord Harley. Four years later in 1713 he was 'in a starving way', in debt and without employment.[44] His position as a

139   John James, Wricklemarsh, Kent, 1723, from *Vitruvius Britannicus* (1767) (demolished).

Roman Catholic definitely stood against him and, in the light of Vanbrugh and Campbell's calls for a patriotic architecture based on an austere but noble style, his Italianate St Mary-le-Strand (1714) (Fig. 125) must have seemed dangerously exposed, especially after Campbell's vicious attack in *Vitruvius Britannicus*. Thus, it comes as no surprise to discover that Gibbs had adapted his style to fit in with the demands of the Fifty New Church Commissioners by the time he put forward his design for St George, Bloomsbury, and St Martin-in-the-Fields, in 1720 (Fig. 145).[45] It is also interesting to see Gibbs picking up specifically Jonesian details – such as the lower window-frames with a triple keystone from Jones's Chapel Royal, St James's Palace, in the rectangular design for St Martin's or the rusticated front door of

Webb's Gunnersbury (illustrated by Campbell) used as the model for the windows of the approved St Martin's design – as if trying to assert his own patriotic credentials.

A similar development can be seen in his domestic architecture. In his design of about 1716 for the south front at Cannons House, Middlesex (Fig. 143), Gibbs proposed a façade that equalled St Mary-le-Strand in its Italianate complexity, with giant pilasters and round-headed windows leaving virtually no wall at all. Nothing could have contrasted more strongly with Campbell's message in *Vitruvius Britannicus*, and it would be interesting to know whether Gibbs's dismissal from Cannons in 1719 was influenced by this, as was undoubtedly the case at Burlington House. The executed design by John Price, while perhaps retaining elements of Gibbs – the

140   James Leoni, Bold Hall, Lancashire, 1731 (demolished).

141   Anon., Iver Grove, Buckinghamshire, 1722.

142   James Gibbs, Sudbrook Park, Surrey, 1715.

central round-headed windows recall those of St Mary-le-Strand – follows Campbell's strictures on the spacing of windows and may look to John Webb's Greenwich Palace for the side ranges.[46] Gibbs did get his way with a version of the Cannons design at the Senate House, Cambridge, but only after enormous difficulties and at the cost of a reduced scheme. Significantly, whereas the original scheme of 1721 had called for a rusticated wall surface as at Cannons, the Syndics insisted on this being replaced by a more austere plain wall surface.[47] Gibbs was equally frustrated with an Anglo-French style in the office wings and colonnade at Burlington House (1716). Although these were built he was replaced by Campbell in mid-commission.

After these difficulties it is not surprising to find Gibbs adapting his style to a more restrained English idiom at Ditchley Park (Fig. 144) in 1720, a reworking of the post-Restoration great house with quoins, plain walls and a rusticated, pedimented door, as recommended by Campbell. If the evidence of Gibbs's *Book of Architecture* of 1728 is to be believed, this year also saw a series of remarkably early neo-Palladian villa designs, which would mean that Gibbs anticipated all of Burlington's and nearly all Campbell's villas. One of these an octagonal central hall that seems to look forward to Chiswick; another has a double-height central Venetian window; while the façade of the third seems to anticipate Pembroke House and has a plan modelled on Palladio's Villa Thiene at Cicogna.[48]

This evidence must be treated with caution, given Gibbs's propensity, as at Sudbrook Park, to doctor the evidence in the book to stress his Palladian credentials. The third of these schemes is described as being for Matthew Prior at Down Hall, Essex, where nothing was built because of Prior's death in 1721. However, Gibbs did produce a plain version of the Prattian villa with extra end bays for Prior, and it is this design, not the villa, that is shown in Charles Bridgeman's plan of the gardens intended for Prior at Down Hall. The original simple design could have been within Prior's means but it is hard to see how he could have expected to afford the much more elaborate second design which would have been better suited to be a peer's villa. Gibbs is known to have produced a subsequent scheme for Down Hall for

143   James Gibbs, unexecuted design for Cannons, Middlesex, 1719.

144   James Gibbs, Ditchley Park, Oxfordshire, 1720.

Lord Harley and it is quite possible that the published design for Down Hall is Lord Harley's subsequent scheme given an earlier date. When compared with the carefully dated designs by his bitter enemy Colen Campbell in *Vitruvius Britannicus*, this would have allowed Gibbs to claim that he was the earlier, better Palladian and to be the pioneer of villa design.[49]

Two other facts support this hypothesis: when discuss-

145　James Gibbs, St Martin-in-the-Fields, London, 1720 (aquatint after Thomas Malton, from *Picturesque Tour through the Cities of London and Westminister* (1792)).

146   James Gibbs, Kelmarsh Hall, Northamptonshire, 1728.

147   Thomas Ripley, Wolterton Hall, Norfolk, 1727.

ing domestic architecture, 1720 is the only date Gibbs used in his book, otherwise he did not generally date his schemes. The year 1720 was very significant in the development of neo-Palladianism, something of which contemporaries would almost certainly have been aware, particularly as it was the date Campbell gave in *Vitruvius Britannicus* for Newby Park, his first neo-Palladian villa design. More tellingly, Gibbs was unable to produce a single executed neo-Palladian scheme that is this early; The first firm date for a neo-Palladian villa scheme from Gibbs is 1725 at Whitton Place, Middlesex, where he was in direct competition with Burlington's circle, and produced two Palladian villa designs, one with a portico-in-antis based on the Villa Emo, the other with a Diocletian window above a single-storey portico, a

motif based on the Villa Pisani. Both were rejected in favour of a villa by Roger Morris.[50]

If the evidence of the *Book of Architecture* is to be believed, Gibbs was developing the idea of the neo-Palladian villa at exactly the same time as Campbell and Burlington. This is possible, but does not fit in with what is known of Gibbs's earlier stylistic development. Even if Gibbs did design these unexecuted neo-Palladian villas when he claimed, their importance is limited as only he – and clients he might have shown them to – would have known of them. They are not enough to show that Gibbs was a significant figure in the spread of the neo-Palladian villa.

Despite these setbacks, Gibbs stuck close to the stylistic example of Campbell and Burlington – he used the rusticated door and window reintroduced by Campbell so frequently that it has been given his name – but taking up neither their sense of proportion nor their obsession with the villa. At King's College, Cambridge (1724), Gibbs Palladianised Hawksmoor's scheme, giving it a rusticated base and balustrade and replacing Hawksmoor's triumphal arch with a pedimented centrepiece above a portico and Diocletian window such as he tried at Whitton Place. His unexecuted designs for Milton House, Northamptonshire (1726), and Lowther Castle, Cumbria (after 1728), were attempts to dress the Ditchley-type house with appropriate neo-Palladian detail: rusticated basements, free-standing porticos, balustrades. His unexecuted design for Kedleston Hall, Derbyshire (1726), is a reduction of Campbell's first Wanstead design. His first design for the Radcliffe Library, Oxford (1737), is a neo-Palladianisation of Wren's library at Trinity College, Cambridge, with a rusticated base and Diocletian windows in the arches.

Gibbs's detail does differ in significant ways from that of Campbell and Burlington. His windows invariably rest on bracketed sills rather than string courses, although this is a detail he could have taken directly from Palladio. In the *Quattro libri*, windows are nearly always set flush into the wall, but at the one exception, the Villa Valmarana, the ground-floor windows have cornices and rest on brackets very similar to those used by Gibbs. Similarly, he nearly always used quoins on the corners of his elevations, instead of leaving them plain, but such quoins had been reintroduced by Campbell.[51]

After the failures of the 1710s Gibbs's concern was not with the style in which he built, but simply to build. The competition he had to overcome was that of the neo-Palladians, and, as it was their elevations that were fashionable and liable to attract custom, he quarried them for his designs, particularly for the great house, but without Leoni's ability to adapt the style with imagination. By 1728 when he came to publish *A Book of Architecture*, his counter-blast to Campbell's third volume

148   Anon., Aldby Park, Yorkshire, 1726.

of *Vitruvius Britannicus* of 1725 and William Kent's *The Designs of Inigo Jones* of 1727, he was well enough aware of the way the stylistic tide had flowed to skate over his early Baroque manner. Palladio was described as 'the great Restorer of Architecture' and Gibbs shamelessly redrew early designs, such as Sudbrook and Ditchley, so that they appeared more Palladian than they were in reality. The aggravation he felt at being outmanoeuvred comes out in the introduction, where his view on those, such as Burlington and Campbell, who pretended to know about Roman architecture but had spent less time in Italy than he had, is apparent in the comment that 'a cursory View of those August Remains can no more qualify the Spectator, or Admirer, than the Air of the Country can inspire him with the knowledge of Architecture'.[52]

Underlying Gibbs's work, and that of other contemporary architects, is the older Prattian tradition of the tripartite pedimented house derived from Palladio's villas which had been erased neither by the flowering of the Baroque nor by the rise of neo-Palladianism. His Kelmarsh Hall, Northamptonshire (1728–32) (Fig. 146), makes an interesting comparison with Thomas Ripley's Wolterton Hall, Norfolk (1727) (Fig. 147), and Henry Flitcroft's Boreham House, Essex (1728). Ripley acted as executant architect at Houghton. Flitcroft had been trained up as a draughtsman by Burlington, and Boreham was his first independent commission. All three buildings reveal the influence of Campbell and Burlington – Wolterton's rustic, the relationship between window and wall, the detail of the window-surrounds – but lacking the purity of Campbell and Burlington's designs none of them could be mistaken for their work. In this way the new ideas of neo-Palladianism were grafted onto the older, Prattian Palladian stock.

Although by 1730 contemporaries were beginning to accept the concept of a neo-Palladian style of architecture, its active promotion was still restricted to a narrow group of architects, and it was still primarily concerned with the villa. Many architects and buildings of the 1720s show no trace of Campbell's or Burlington's influence. In Yorkshire this is true of Wentworth Woodhouse (1725) and Aldby Park (1726) (Fig. 148). In the Midlands Smith of Warwick had a highly successful practice with his own distinctive style seen at Davenport House, Shropshire (1726), Wingerworth Hall, Derbyshire (1726), and Mawley Hall, Shropshire (1730). The same could be said in the West Country of Nathaniel Ireson, an apprentice of Smith's, with houses such as Ven House, Somerset (c.1725), and Crowcombe Court, Somerset (1734). Even John James at Standlynch House, Wiltshire (1731), took no more from Campbell than the idea of rusticated window surrounds.

During the 1730s, however, the Burlingtonian style began to gain pre-eminence, despite Campbell's death in 1729. This had much to do with the way Burlington packed the Office of Works, easily the most important source of architectural patronage and the nearest England had to a school of architecture, with his protégés. Thomas Ripley – as executant architect at Houghton he was really a protégé of Sir Robert Walpole rather than Burlington – was first made Master Carpenter in 1721 and then Comptroller in 1726. His post as Master Carpenter was taken by William Kent – Burlington's particular associate – who became Master Mason and Deputy Surveyor in 1735. Henry Flitcroft – 'Burlington Harry' – was made Clerk of the Works at Whitehall, Westminster and St James's in 1726, to which he added Clerkship of the Works at Kew and Richmond in about 1728; he progressed to be Master Carpenter in 1746, Master Mason and Deputy Surveyor in 1748 and Comptroller in 1758. Isaac Ware, moved successively from Clerk of the Works at Windsor (1729), to Clerk of the Works at Greenwich (1733) and, finally, Secretary to the Board (1736). John Vardy held a succession of clerkships from 1736. Roger Morris was made Clerk of the Works at Richmond New Park Lodge in 1727 (and was Master Carpenter to the Office of Ordnance from 1734. His Labourer in Trust at Richmond was Daniel Garrett – of whom Sir Thomas Robinson wrote 'My Ld Burlington has a much better opinion of Mr Garret's knowledge and judgement than of Mr Flitcroft's or any person whatever, except Mr Kent'[53] – until his dismissal for inattendance in 1737.

The developing style was also backed by a programme of Burlingtonian-sponsored architectural publication, starting with William Kent's *The Designs of Inigo Jones,*

with some Additional Designs in 1727. Robert Castell's 1728 plans for a translation of Vitruvius backed by Burlington proved abortive, but his *Villas of the Ancients* was published the following year. Burlington's own *Fabbriche antiche* should have appeared in 1730 but may not have been published until 1740.[54] Neither of these two works would have been of much practical value to architects, but Isaac Ware's three books *Designs of Inigo Jones and Others* (c.1733), *The Plans, Elevations and Sections of Houghton in Norfolk* (1735) and his translation of Palladio's *Quattro libri* (1738), would have been. So would John Vardy's *Some Designs of Mr Inigo Jones and Mr William Kent* (1744) and Isaac Ware's comprehensive *A Complete Body of Architecture* (1756), although the latter did not always follow Burlington's ideas.

Rather different were the works of Robert Morris, principally *An Essay in defence of Ancient Architecture* (1728). Morris was the only serious English architectural theorist to publish in the first half of the eighteenth century, and might appear at first sight to be a neo-Palladian propagandist. However, he was not a member of Burlington's circle and while he praises Palladio above other architects he points out his blemishes; he does not allow Jones to eclipse Wren; and Kent, for encouraging Gothic Architecture, is considered contemptible. Morris sought to improve harmonious composition through genius guided by Nature, rules founded on reason and the example of the Antique. The writings of Vitruvius, Alberti and Palladio all had their influence on him, but were of far less importance than the works of Shaftesbury, Addison and Pope. Morris's influence was probably limited, as his theoretical essays were seldom quoted and then only by his friends.[55]

Until about 1730 the Burlingtonian style was essentially a villa (and to a lesser extent town-house) style, despite Burlington's majestic Dormitory at Westminster School, but with the erection of the Assembly Rooms at York in 1731–2 (Fig. 153) a new phase opens. It was specifically this building to which Robinson was referring when he made his comment about 'Palladian strokes'. York was only a provincial city, and it was upon London that Burlington had his eye. In 1733 St George's Hospital was founded at Hyde Park Corner, the western gateway to London, the existing Lanesborough House being remodelled by Isaac Ware into an austere Palladian design complete with Serlian and Diocletian windows and broken-based pediments. The year before, work had begun on a building for the Bank of England in the centre of the City. The Bank rejected Theodore Jacobsen's design, the ground-plan of which, with a four-columned vaulted entrance hall and colonnaded courtyard behind, could have been lifted from Palladio's plans of his Vicenza palazzi in the *Quattro libri*,[56] in favour of George Sampson's more ambitious elevation. Although Burlington is not known to have had any

149 William Halfpenny, Prince's Street Assembly Rooms, Bristol, 1754.

150 Francis Smith, Davenport Hall, Shropshire, 1726.

involvement in Sampson's design, it shares a similar tetrastyle Ionic triumphal-arch centrepiece (whose originality suggests a common source) with Roger Morris's Chichester Council House begun in 1731.[57] Jacobsen was more successful with his Foundling Hospital, London, in 1742, unlike the Burlingtonians in the competition for the new Mansion House of 1739 facing the Bank. Isaac Ware's entry was rejected in favour of George Dance's confused – to Palladian eyes – design. Although this has many of the obvious attributes of Palladian architecture, in particular a freestanding hexastyle portico, a rusticated perron and an Egyptian hall, the Mansion House is an overcrowded *mélange* of Classical motifs lacking the intellectual integrity of Palladian thought. In this it represents a confident commercial attitude towards Palladianism characteristic of the City of London, but particularly evident in provincial cities such as Liverpool and Bristol. In Bristol buildings such as Frenchay Manor (1736), William Halfpenny's Cooper's Hall (1743) and Prince's Street Assembly Rooms (1754) (Fig. 149) epitomise the way merchants welcomed the rich effect of Classical detail, particularly columns and pilasters, but were unconcerned by neo-Palladian notions of Classical correctness.

Interestingly, the one building type which remained almost entirely immune to Palladian influence was the church, despite the example of Palladio's Venetian churches, Il Redentore and San Giorgio Maggiore. Probably the only British example of a church deliberately modelled on one of Palladio's buildings was John Smith's St Thomas, Marlborough Street, in Dublin (1758), a fairly literal rendering of Il Redentore. This is despite the fact that in Venice and the Veneto eighteenth-century neo-Palladian churches are commonplace. One obvious reason for this must be that Palladio did not include any of his churches in the *Quattro libri*, although San Giorgio Maggiore was published in Kent's *Designs of Inigo Jones* (1727). Also significant must be the fact that under Wren the English had developed a native tradition of Classical church building which owed nothing to Palladio and little to Jones, and was formalised and extensively illustrated in Gibbs's *Book of Architecture* (1728). It was this that formed the model for English church building for much of the eighteenth century.

With the Office of Works packed, the way was open for the Palladians to remodel the seat of government, Whitehall. Philip Ayres considered the concluding verse-paragraph of Alexander Pope's *Epistle to Burlington*, published in 1731, a call for a programme of 'Imperial Works' in which Burlington would hold the position that Vitruvius had during Augustus's rebuilding of Rome when he found it brick but left it marble.[58] If Burlington had had his way the effect on Whitehall would have been as dramatic. First came the Royal Mews, rebuilt in

151   William Kent and others, Holkham Hall, Norfolk, 1734.

1731 to Kent's design, then the Treasury in 1733. That year the *Gentleman's Magazine* reported that 'The Earl of Burlington has projected a Plan for building two new Houses of Parliament [for which numerous drawings by Kent survive], and a public Library between them.'[59] There were also hopes of a new Law Courts and ultimately a royal palace. Kent got as far as a wooden model for a new palace at Richmond, but the project came to nothing, although John Vardy reused the idea of a hexastyle applied Doric portico at Spencer House, London, in 1756.

Kent had come back to England in Burlington's train in 1719 after spending ten years in Italy, principally Rome. Burlington's initial hopes for him were as a painter. According to Vertue, Burlington 'promoted him on all occasions to everything in his power, to the King, to the Court works, & Courtiers declared him the best History painter – & the first that was a native of this Kingdom'.[60] It was as a painter that Kent first appeared at Kensington Palace in 1722, where his role slowly changed into that of a creator of architectural interiors, a role he developed further at Houghton Hall from 1725 and at Chiswick House from about 1726. Kent was to remain supreme as an interior designer, as he showed at 22 Arlington Street and 44 Berkeley Square in the 1740s. As an architect, however, he was surprisingly slow to mature and played no part in the development of the first phase of neo-Palladianism, despite his presence in Burlington's household. It was only after 1730 that Kent came into his own as an architect, particularly of garden buildings.

Kent's output of new houses was limited – Kew House, Surrey, Holkham Hall, Norfolk (where he was by no means the dominant force), Devonshire House, London, and Wakefield Lodge, Northamptonshire – and

it is with his grand public schemes for Whitehall that his architectural character was fully developed. As Cinzia Sicca has shown, Kent's years in Italy, where he had taken a particular interest in the work of Raphael and Giulio Romano, meant that he brought a new vigour to neo-Palladianism, marked particularly by his fascination for rustication.[61] However, Kent's Roman sources were only one more layer added to an already complex Palladian mix: Palladio's buildings and his drawings of Roman remains, Inigo Jones's works and Burlington's earlier designs all play their part in Kent's public architecture.

Intriguingly, as Kent developed as an architect, Burlington seemed to retire. In the 1720s he had been as busy as any professional but, with the completion of the York Assembly Rooms, the link building at Chiswick and Petersham Lodge in 1732–3, he faded away, designing only a couple of garden buildings and the wings at Tottenham Park for his brother-in-law before working on Kirby Hall, Yorkshire, of 1747, where Roger Morris was probably the dominant force. There can be no suggestion that Burlington had run out of inspiration as an architect. In many ways the early 1730s show him at his most creative. At the York Assembly Rooms, as will be seen in the next chapter, he reached the perfection of his neo-Classical manner. In the link building at Chiswick he introduced an architectonic style, described by John Harris as 'a staccato sequence of parts, each of a unity, but joined by walls slightly recessed'[62] that was developed in collaboration with others at Holkham Hall from about 1734 (Fig. 151) and in the wings added to Tottenham Park shortly afterwards. In the hands of such architects as James Paine, Henry Keene, Robert Taylor and Robert Adam this was to have a profound influence on the architecture of the 1750s.

152   Henry Flitcroft, Wentworth Woodhouse, Yorkshire, 1733.

Had the gibes of those who considered that he demeaned himself by acting as an architect finally persuaded Burlington to pack up his pencils? Was he tired of running what was effectively a professional office? Or does some deeper psychological trauma lie behind both his abandonment of large-scale architectural practice and of political office in 1733? It is certainly remarkable that he should have bowed out of designing just when the prize that had eluded architects for so long, the rebuilding of Whitehall, seemed in his grasp. It may be that he felt that in Kent he had a worthy successor who could carry on the fight. Or was Wittkower right when he suggested that 'Burlington regarded the [York] Assembly Rooms as an achievement beyond which it was impossible to go?'[63]

If Burlington's ambitions at Whitehall had been realised Vicenza would have been recreated on the Thames, but in the event all except the Mews and Treasury – which was never finished on the scale intended – were scuppered by the outbreak of war in 1739, and only the idea of a new Horseguards was saved, to be started once peace was declared in 1748, although by then Kent was dead.

Ambitious plans in London in the 1730s were paralleled in the country, where the Burlingtonians turned their hands to devising a suitable model for a great house. This had not been a problem in the 1720s, for not only were most neo-Palladian houses built to a villa plan, but the majority of them were suburban villas, designed for heirs, such as Lord Pembroke at Westcombe; younger sons, such as the Earl of Ilay at Whitton; merchants, such as Stamp Brooksbank at Hackney; and royal mistresses, such as Henrietta Howard at Marble Hill. The demands of a family seat were very different from those of a suburban villa, even one built for an aristocrat like Lord

Burlington at Chiswick. One solution (as had been found at Houghton) in adapting the style to the great house was to keep the accepted H-plan great house but apply the lessons of austerity learnt from Palladio's villas, reducing decoration to an absolute minimum with a high ratio of wall to window, as Kent did at Devonshire House in London (1734). Perhaps inevitably, architects also looked back to Wanstead, by now nearly twenty years old, for a model. Wentworth Woodhouse (Fig. 152), begun about 1733, was a close copy of Wanstead as built (Fig. 119). Prior Park, Bath, begun about 1735 by John Wood the elder who was not one of the Burlingtonian circle, was consciously modelled on the first Wanstead design. Nostell Priory, Yorkshire, begun about 1737 by the Yorkshire amateur and friend of Burlington, James Moyser, could also be seen as a reduced version of Wanstead I with the balustrade replaced by a hipped roof, although the design may relate to another drawing of Campbell's which Moyser may have seen. Another contemporary block-like house with a portico was Garendon Park, Leicestershire, built by the amateur Ambrose Phillipps on his return from Italy in about 1734.[64] A less successful approach was tried by John Sanderson at Stratton Park, Hampshire, built for Lord John Russell in 1731, which flanks a three-bay temple front with long, low wings. The most ambitious attempt at creating a Palladian model for a great house was in Norfolk where, at Holkham in about 1734, (Fig. 151) Burlington and Kent, together with the Earl of Leicester and Matthew Brettingham, set out to build one of the most remarkable of Palladian houses; but there they turned to a rather different source for inspiration – ancient Rome (as will be shown in the next chapter).

Thus, by the late 1730s a recognisable neo-Palladian style, led essentially by Lord Burlington, seemed at last to be achieving dominance. The Office of Works had been captured and the greatest sequence of royal works since Hampton Court begun. Neo-Palladianism had moved beyond the confines of the villa to be considered suitable for every type of country house. It had no serious stylistic rivals, and only a handful of provincial architects were still working in alternative styles. Even Francis Smith had produced a recognisably Palladian design in one of his last designs, Wynnstay, Denbighshire, begun in 1736. In one of architectural history's ironies, the diffusion of a Palladian style to provincial architects such as Smith probably owed more to Gibbs than it did directly to Burlington.

Gibbs's *Book of Architecture* of 1728, the first book by a British architect to consist entirely of his own designs, was not a revolutionary book in terms of style. By the time it was published Gibbs was working in a loosely neo-Palladian manner derived from Campbell and Burlington but still heavily influenced by the older Prattian tradition and without the intellectual rigour of Burlington. Nevertheless, its influence was profound, perhaps because it did not attempt the same architectural pretension as Burlington. While such leading architects as Paine and Adam maintained Burlingtonian purity and can be considered neo-Palladians, for the mass of provincial builders Gibbs was the model. This is particularly true of interiors, where few professionals, even one such as Henry Flitcroft who had been schooled by Burlington, were prepared to follow antique austerity – although amateurs were more likely to follow the Burlington line. By taking Palladian detail and ideas learnt from Lord Burlington's circle and grafting them onto the older Prattian tradition, Gibbs became the catalyst for the 'Georgian' style of building, the common currency of every local builder in the eighteenth and much of the nineteenth century.

Gibbs specifically intended his book to be a pattern-book 'of use to such gentlemen as might be concerned in Building, especially in the remote parts of the Country, where little or no assistance for Designs can be procured'. Everything that an aspiring builder could want was provided: plans and elevations of houses of every size, as well as models for churches; details of doorcases and window architraves; models for chimney-pieces and staircases. But it is not just through the book itself that Gibbs's influence percolated. Aimed, as the introduction shows, at gentlemen, it was far too expensive at four guineas in sheets, or even at a reduced three guineas for the second edition of 1739, for ordinary builders. The treasury of designs that he presented was, however, swiftly plundered by the opportunistic authors and publishers of such competitively priced pattern books as those by William Halfpenny, Edward Hoppus, Batty Langley and William Salmon, which are such a phenomenon of British architecture from the 1720s. In 1731, for instance, 'artists' could buy for one shilling a suite of *Thirty-Three Shields & Compartments* engraved by J. Clark 'from the designs of that curious architect Mr. James Gibbs'. As Eileen Harris pointed out, 'It was largely through such second-hand versions that 'Gibbs' motifs entered the vocabulary of Georgian architecture.'[65]

It is true that the pattern-book publishers also drew on the Burlingtonian publications, and, indeed, other sources. Hoppus's *The Gentleman's and Builder's Repository* of 1737 has eighty-six plates copied from Gibbs, Campbell's edition of Palladio, Price's *British Carpenter* (1732), Gaetano Brunetti's *Sixty Different Sorts of Ornaments* (1731) and other publications.[66] The Langley brothers had an extraordinarily large collection of prints, including not only all the familiar items from England, France, the Netherlands and Italy but also such rarities as Roger Kaseman's *Seilen Bochg* (1616) of Mannerist designs for orders.[67] But the influence of Gibbs was pervasive.

Nor was it only as a source of motifs that Gibbs helped spread the Palladian style. In 1732 he published *The Rules for Drawing the Several Parts of Architecture, In a More exact and easy manner than has been heretofore practised, by which all Fractions, in dividing the principal Members and their Parts, are avoided*. For those who were unskilled in architecture any attempt to copy Palladio's orders from Campbell's edition or any other was fraught with great difficulty, with modules, minutes and fractions of minutes which could not be divided by compasses into small parts. In Gibbs's method the diameter of the column has no function in the arithmetical system of proportioning the orders, instead, the height of the column and its diameter were determined by a series of simple divisions, starting with the height of the proposed order.[68]

Gibbs's system made calculating correct Classical proportions much easier and, despite his attempt to protect his idea by copyright, it was swiftly copied by Batty Langley in his *Ancient Masonry* (1733–4), Edward Hoppus in the *Gentleman and Builder's Repository* (1737), in the second edition of William Salmon's *Palladio Londoniensis* (1738) and was repeated by Langley in the *Builders Compleat Assistant*. Salmon's introduction, for instance, announces that it contains

> plain and easy Directions for the Construction of the Five Orders of Architecture, with their several Pedestals, Columns and Entablatures, accurately described; and a Parallel drawn between this and Mr Gibbs's Method, and that of the Builder's Respository . . . Also how to calculate the Diameter of the Orders, according to the Proportions laid down by Mr Gibbs.[69]

It is in the pattern-books that one must look to find the dissemination of a Palladian style to the mass of builders, and, just as the comments of such men as Sir

Thomas Robinson and Lord Hervey demonstrate that a Palladian style was recognised among patrons, so the title-pages of innumerable pattern-books show that builders were well aware of the roots of the style in which they built. Examples include Halfpenny's *Practical Architecture . . . with their several Doors & Windows taken from Inigo Jones & other Celebrated Architects . . .* (1724); Langley's *The Builder's Chest-Book . . . consider'd and explain'd with respect to the Practice of Palladio . . .* (1727) and Salmon's *Palladio Londoniensis* (1734).

Not that pattern-book publishers necessarily accepted the dictates of high architectural fashion without murmur. Langley savaged the works of Jones, Burlington and Kent in his review of James Ralph's *Critical Review of the Publick Buildings, Statues and Ornaments in and about London and Westminster* (1733), principally out of a patriotic desire to defend the work and prospects of English craftsmen (especially freemasons) against the import of foreign artists and the blind worship of foreign styles.[70] Halfpenny's *Andrea Palladio's First Book of Architecture* (1751) was intended to reveal Palladio's mistakes and correct them with what is 'most suitable to British Taste'.[71] But, filtered though it may have been through the works of Gibbs and the pattern-books, crude and distasteful though it appeared to Burlington and his friends, including Alexander Pope,

> You show us, Rome was glorious, not profuse,
> And pompous Buildings once were things of use.
> Just as they are, yet shall your noble Rules,
> Fill half the land with Imitating Fools;
> Who random Drawings from your Sheets shall take,
> And of one Beauty many Blunders make[72]

in the 1730s a form of Palladianism began to spread across the country into the work of every level of builder. Yet the real triumph of the neo-Palladian style had to wait nearly another decade as the War of the Austrian Succession blighted the building world.

VII

PALLADIAN NEO-CLASSICISM

O N 25 AUGUST 1732, Nicholas Hawksmoor wrote to the Earl of Carlisle regretting that his health would not allow him to attend the opening of the 'Egyptian Sal' at York (Fig. 153).[1] His comments had he done so would have been fascinating, for the 'Egyptian Sal' was the new Assembly Room designed by Lord Burlington on the model of Vitruvius's description of an Egyptian hall (Fig. 154); a model that Hawksmoor himself had considered using two decades earlier at St Mary Woolnoth in the City.[2] But shared sources mask very different approaches towards neo-Classicism: Hawksmoor was essentially romantic, more concerned with the essence of antiquity than with literal reconstruction. Burlington believed in a strict adherence to the rules of Classical architecture as laid down by Vitruvius and interpreted by Palladio. Two months later the opposing approaches were to clash over the design of the Mausoleum at Castle Howard (Fig. 67), a design by Hawksmoor based on Classical precedent, but too free in its interpretation for Burlington. Pragmatism meant that Hawksmoor won, but elsewhere a new, self-consciously accurate approach to neo-Classicism, epitomised by the York Assembly Rooms, was gaining strength.

Despite the theorising of Wren and Hooke, there was only limited interest in the direct study of antiquity in late seventeenth-century England. This was to change markedly during the first half of the eighteenth century. Burlington's library, as recorded at Chiswick in 1742, makes clear how important the archaeological study of antiquity was to him, his fine collection of architectural treatises being complemented by an equally impressive collection on Roman remains.[3] In this he was not alone, and many of those who will be discussed in this chapter – including the Earl of Leicester, Thomas Worsley and Sir Francis Dashwood – owned important collections of archaeological books.[4] Nor did Burlington restrict his researches to published material. He also sought out drawings of Roman remains, both by Palladio and by other draughtsmen. These included a volume of drawings of antiquities then believed to be by the sixteenth-century architect and antiquarian Pirro Ligorio, who had a great influence on Palladio's studies, although they are now attributed to Giovanni Battista Montano.[5]

These drawings formed the material for Burlington's most important publishing projects. Although he was responsible for a number of architectural books devoted to Palladio, Inigo Jones and the work of his own circle, the only book published under his name was the *Fabbriche antiche disegnata da Andrea Palladio Vicentino e date in luce da Riccardo Conte di Burlington*, Palladio's reconstructions of the Baths of ancient Rome. This is dated 1730, but may not have been printed until as late as 1740.[6] Burlington also hoped to see his Palladio drawings after Vitruvius, together with others from the Pirro Ligorio album, used to illustrate the first translation of Vitruvius into English. The untimely death of its author, Robert Castell, in the Fleet Prison in December 1728 cut short this plan which had been announced only six months earlier. However, Castell had already prepared another work, initially without Burlington's assistance, *Villas of the Ancients*, which was published after his death in 1729.[7] This was an attempt to work out what Roman domestic architecture looked like through an analysis of contemporary literary descriptions. Its core was the reconstruction of Pliny's two villas at Laurentinum and Tuscum, from the descriptions in his letters, to which was added (apparently at Burlington's suggestion) an account of the 'villa rustica' as referred to by Varro and Columella.

Burlington was not alone in seeking out drawings of antique buildings and decoration. John Talman, son of the architect William Talman, spent the years between 1709 and 1716 in Italy, where he employed five draughtsmen to make illustrations for an intended book on Italian antiquities.[8] Among those he employed was Francesco Bartoli, who had succeeded his father Pietro Santi Bartoli as Antiquary to the Pope. Talman's companion in Rome was William Kent who, in 1716, assisted Thomas Coke, later Earl of Leicester, to acquire a sketch-book attributed to Raphael largely devoted to studies of capitals, bases and entablatures as well as drawings of Classical buildings. In 1718 Kent was instrumental in commissioning a series of 158 studies after antique paintings from Francesco Bartoli for Coke.[9]

Bartoli's work was the product of a revived interest in Roman antiquity in the mid- to late seventeenth century

153   Lord Burlington, interior of the Assembly Rooms, York, 1731.

centred around the artist Nicolas Poussin. One of the sponsors of this revival was Cardinal Massimi, for whom Pietro Santi Bartoli made many drawings after antique paintings – including painted ceilings – which were currently being unearthed, principally during the construction of new roads and buildings (Figs. 168, 172 and 176).

Bartoli's intention was to produce a complete corpus of all Roman paintings known at the time, in conjunction with the theorist Giovanni Pietro Bellori. Together they published *Le pitture antiche del sepolchro de Nasonii* in 1680, which was followed after Bellori's death by *Gli antichi sepolchri* in 1697. Francesco Bartoli maintained this interest after his father's death, republishing the Nasonii tomb and other paintings in *Le pitture antiche delle grotte di Roma e del sepolchro de Nasonii* in 1706, as well as making his own drawings of new discoveries.[10]

Drawings by Bartoli were highly prized by English collectors in the early eighteenth century. Francesco Bartoli also supplied drawings for Richard Topham who devoted most of his income to forming a library devoted to antiquity, which by his death in 1730 totalled about four thousand books, many on architectural and archaeological subjects, together with nearly three thousand drawings and engravings, particularly of sculpture and antique decoration. Many of these were specially commissioned from Italian artists such as Bartoli, but the collection included one drawing done in Rome by William Kent. Topham had corresponded with Kent's companion in Rome, John Talman, in 1714, and Talman was almost certainly a guiding influence behind the initial formation of the collection.[11] Topham later acquired some of Talman's drawings when that collection was dispersed in 1727.[12] After his death in 1730 his

154 Andrea Palladio, the Egyptian Hall, from *The Four Books of Architecture* (1738).

collection was bequeathed to Eton College, where a copy of the *Fabbriche antiche*, given in 1740, pays tribute to Burlington's friendship with Topham. Indeed, some drawings after the antique in the Topham Library appear to have a Burlington provenance.[13]

Another admirer of the Bartolis' work was Topham's executor Richard Mead, a wealthy doctor and passionate collector, as a letter written by Andrew Hay to Sir John Clerk in 1738 reveals: 'Dr Mead is being impatient for Mr Ramsay's arrival expecting by him those drawing of Pietro Santi Bartoli from the ancient paintings in the Sepulchrum Nasonii etc which belonged to Prince Massimo at Rome, for which the doctor is to pay £200 sterling.'[14] Whilst in Rome these drawings had been considered one of the greatest curiosities in the city.[15] Dr Mead also managed to purchase some original paintings from the Massimi collection, many of which were reproduced in George Turnbull's *A Curious Collection of Ancient Paintings, accurately engraved from excellent drawings, lately done after the originals* (1741).

Mead was at the centre of a wide circle of aquaintance which included Burlington, as is shown by a letter Kent wrote to Burlington in 1745:

I met Dr Mead he enquired much how you all doe he has sent me a book wrote by Monsr Bianchini to look over, its account of what was found in year twenty in the Firnese Garden on Monte Palatine with Plans of ye rooms etc but they have imagined uprights alla Romanesco – as Politicks are not my Genius, it diverts

me much now at nights to look & read of these fine remaines of Antiquity.[16]

Mead was subsequently sent the first two volumes of Bajardi's *Antiquities of Herculaneum* by the King of Naples.

The product of this interest in Roman antiquity among early eighteenth-century gentlemen and scholars was a series of studies of Roman life which made full use of both archaeological and literary evidence, of which Castell's *Villas of the Ancients* was only one example. In 1722 Jonathan Richardson published *An Account of some of the Statues, Bas-reliefs, Drawings and Pictures in Italy* – the first modern study to give due emphasis to the significance of antique sculpture that had been lost. A similar work was *Polymetis: or, an Enquiry concerning the agreement between the works of the Roman Poets and the remains of the antient Artists* published by Joseph Spence in 1747, another member of the Mead circle who subsequently communicated an 'Account of some Antiquities at Herculaneum' to the Royal Society in 1757. The same approach was also applied to agriculture and gardening by Richard Bradley in *A Survey of the Ancient Husbandry and Gardening, Collected from Cato, Varo, Columella, Virgil and others the most eminent Writers among the Greeks and Romans* (1725) and, indeed, by Dr Mead to medicine, his Harveian Oration in 1723 being on the position of the physician in the ancient world.[17] It is also possible that James Deacon's strange Classical landscapes of around 1743 were attempts to recreate the sort of Roman landscapes illustrated by Bartoli.[18] Unfortunately, Deacon died young of a fever caught at the Old Bailey and, apart from a couple of watercolours, very little is known about his art.

This combination of literary and archaeological studies of Roman antiquity was not restricted to Italy, for eighteenth-century antiquarians were acutely conscious that Britain had once been a Roman colony. Francis Drake, for instance, in his dedication to Lord Burlington in *Eboracum: The History and Antiquities of the City of York* (1736) made much of the fact that the city's greatest days had been under the Romans, when it had been briefly the capital of the Empire, with two emperors dying and possibly a third born within its walls. Drake conjured up 'that *Praetorian* palace, once in old EBORACUM' and specifically compared it to Burlington's new Assembly Rooms: '[it] must, if now standing, have given place to your *Egyptian* hall in our present *York*'. Burlington even suggested to Drake that York's Micklegate Bar was of Roman origin.[19] In this he was mistaken, but genuine Roman remains were discovered in York and the surrounding countryside. A hypocaust and a mosaic from a Roman villa, for instance, were found at Hovingham, eighteen miles north of York, in 1745. Lord Burlington paid for these to be engraved by George Vertue.

Burlington also paid for engravings of excavations of the Roman road found on his estate at Londesbrough in the East Riding. Another site in Yorkshire that excited interest was Aldborough, near Boroughbridge, where the discovery of a mosaic in 1757 prompted the antiquary William Stukeley to declare in a letter: 'How commendable would be our boasted taste, did we imitate this Roman elegance!'[20] Stukeley was a keen investigator of Roman remains, and a sketch which he made of a Roman hypocaust discovered in Lincoln survives among the papers of Sir Francis Dashwood at West Wycombe Park, Buckinghamshire.

The discovery of Roman mosaics, tombs and altars was a relatively common occurrence in eighteenth-century Britain. This was reflected in a series of publications on Roman Britain, which was particularly marked between 1710 and 1730, and was probably stimulated by Edward Gibson's greatly enlarged, annotated 1695 edition of Camden's *Britannia* (first published in 1586). Chief among these was Alexander Gordon's study of Roman ruins in Scotland and the North of England, *Itinerarium septentrionale* (1726) and John Horsley's remarkable *Britannia Romana* (1732), which as late as 1907 was described as 'till quite recently the best and most scholarly account of any Roman province that had been written anywhere in Europe'.[21]

Typical of these antiquaries was William Stukeley, who studied medicine under Dr Mead and later commented that it was thanks to the constant dinners he had with Mead 'where we drank nothing but French wine' that he subsequently suffered appallingly from gout. Stukeley made long tours searching out antiquities which he subsequently published, as in the pamphlet *Of the Roman Amphitheatre at Dorchester* of 1723, while he persuaded the mason Andrews Jelfe, who had been sent by the Board of Ordnance to Scotland to repair forts, to make measured drawings of the country's finest Roman remains, the mausoleum known as 'Arthur's O'on' (Oven), which Stukeley published with a commentary in 1720. ('Arthur's O'on' was demolished in 1734.) Stukeley's dedication to the study of Roman Britain was shown by his creation in 1723 of the (shortlived) Society of Roman Knights whose aim was 'to adorn and preserve the truly noble monuments of the Romans in Britain . . . The business of this Society is to search for and illustrate the Roman monuments in the Britannic Isles.'[22]

As Francis Drake's comments make clear, eighteenth-century scholars and gentlemen felt a close affinity with Roman Britain, and it was a combination of this affinity and studies emanating from Rome that spurred some of them on to try and recreate Roman buildings themselves. It is noticeable how many of these reconstructions can be found within a short distance of Roman remains.

There was good precedent for such an approach in

155   Andrea Palladio, the Doric order, from *The Four Books of Architecture* (1738).

Palladio's *Quattro libri*. The *Quattro libri* is a curious hybrid combining a standard account of the Classical orders, a description of Palladio's own buildings, illustrations of Classical remains as surveyed by Palladio and Palladio's reconstructions of the antique buildings described by Vitruvius. This meant that Palladio's influence varied, depending on which aspect of the book subsequent generations studied. Most neo-Palladian architects concentrated on Palladio's own designs, particularly his villas, but Burlington and a number of others were equally concerned with Palladio's Vitruvian reconstructions. Their treatment of one of the fundamental elements of Classical architecture, the Doric order, is evidence of how much these architects were prepared to ignore post-Renaissance architectural tradition and turn instead to the Roman original.[23]

Vitruvius's description of the Doric order was confused, and while he did not say that the order should be baseless he did not specify a base as he did for the Tuscan, Ionic and Corinthian orders. Because of this, and because most surviving Roman Doric columns were baseless – including that most frequently cited as a model for the order, the Theatre of Marcellus in Rome – it was accepted by all Renaissance architectural writers that the Doric order should not in theory have a base; but they went on to add that the order was much more attractive if an Attic base was added, and this was standard practice in post-Renaissance architecture. Palladio was ambivalent, declaring that an Attic base added greatly to the beauty of the Doric column, but illustrating his theoretical chapter on the Doric order with baseless examples (Fig. 155). Most of his executed buildings use Doric

156 Anon., Temple of Piety, Studley Royal, Yorkshire, c.1736.

columns with bases, although the Villa Pisani at Montagnana has baseless Doric columns.

The first architectural theorist who positively declared that Doric columns should be baseless was the Palladian apologist Fréart de Chambray in his *Parallèle de l'architecture* of 1650, but his attack was either ignored or vehemently condemned by other writers, until Robert Castell included a cryptoporticus or colonnade with baseless Doric columns in his reconstruction of the villa at Laurentinum in his *Villas of the Ancients* of 1729.

At least nine examples of English buildings with baseless Doric columns can be found during the middle years of the eighteenth century, a radical departure from Renaissance norms.[24] Four are relatively small structures, the earliest of them being the mausoleum at Elmore, Gloucestershire (c.1732),[25] the other three garden buildings: the Temple of Piety at Studley Royal, Yorkshire

(c.1736) (Fig. 156); the now-demolished Doric colonnade in the park at Shugborough, Staffordshire (c.1745–50), and the Doric Rotunda incorrectly known as the Tuscan Temple at the Rievaulx Terraces, Yorkshire (c.1749–57). One is a church, St Lawrence, Mereworth, Kent (1744–6) (Fig. 157). Four are country houses: the east portico, now demolished, of the west wing of Castle Howard, Yorkshire (1753–9); the portico on the south front of West Wycombe Park, Buckinghamshire (1750s); the portico at Rokeby Park, Yorkshire (c.1753) (Fig. 159), and several different places at Hovingham Hall, Yorkshire (c.1752–74) (Fig. 164).

The direct return to Vitruvian precedent encapsulated by the use of the baseless Doric column was taken to its logical end with Burlington's York Assembly Rooms of 1731–2. This is a literal copy of Palladio's reconstruction of the Egyptian hall, the grandest of the interiors which

Vitruvius describes, but as an attempt to reconstruct a Vitruvian building it was not unique. In 1744–6 John Fane, 7th Earl of Westmorland, built the church of St Lawrence, Mereworth, probably using Roger Morris as his architect. For a church, its interior was unprecedentedly neo-Classical with a wide barrel-vaulted and coffered nave, narrow coffered aisles decorated with Classical motifs and baseless Doric columns supporting a heavy entablature rather than arches (Fig. 157). It should probably be seen as a reconstruction of a Roman basilica, modelled on that in Barbaro's edition of Vitruvius, the only edition to use baseless Doric columns.[26] A contemporary, but unexecuted, neo-Classical scheme which would have eclipsed these was that of about 1734 by Robert Trevor, subsequently Viscount Hampden, for the Radcliffe Library, Oxford, modelled on the Pantheon in Rome.[27]

Public buildings – churches, libraries and assembly rooms – which were essentially comprised of a single large room were relatively easy to design on Roman models. It was less easy to apply the same criteria to domestic architecture, for most Classical remains were of public buildings. As Allan Ramsay wrote in 'Dialogue on Taste' in *The Investigator*:

> The present taste of architecture was formed, not upon the palaces and dwelling houses of the antient Greeks and Romans, of which there where no vestiges at the revival of the arts, but upon their temples and other public buildings, from which the ornamental part has been borrowed and applied to domestic use, in a manner abundantly absurd, for the most part; and which, nevertheless, custom has rendered agreeable to the sight.[28]

Little survived of Roman domestic architecture, and that which had been excavated was both too grand and too fragmentary to be of much practical value – although it was possible to recover the decorative schemes. Serlio, for instance, published a plan of 'the ruines of a most costly Pallace' on Mount Caballo in Rome, but it is hard to interpret and would have been even harder to adapt to use. Pirro Ligorio published the results of sixteenth-century excavations at Hadrian's villa at Tivoli, but its scale and sprawling nature made this an unsatisfactory domestic model. Systematic excavation was resumed in 1724 but attention was largely focused on the statues that were recovered.

In the absence of physical remains, Renaissance theorists were forced to rely on literary sources. Vitruvius had descriptions of the Roman house and villa and of the Greek house, but, as Palladio admitted, this section of Vitruvius is more than usually obscure. As a result, every theorist who tried to reconstruct his descriptions made a different design. There are also frequent references to villas in the theoretical works of such agricultural writers

as Cato, Varro, Columella and Palladius, and in the letters of Cicero. However, the theoretical writers concentrate mainly on the situation of the villa, and letters only make passing references – although these sometimes give a glimpse of a house's decoration. The same is true of a writer such as Petronius, with his description in the *Satyricon* of Trimalchio's house, with its four dining rooms, twenty bedrooms, two marble colonnades and a guest apartment that slept one hundred; or Tacitus whose life of Nero includes a description of the Golden House, with its vestibule large enough to contain a statue of the emperor 120 feet high and so extensive that it had a triple colonnade a mile long, dining rooms with fretted ceilings of ivory whose panels could open up to shower flowers or sprinkle perfume, and a circular dining-room with a roof that revolved with the heavens.

The exceptions are Pliny's two letters describing his two villas, the Laurentinum villa on the coast near Rome and the Tuscum villa in the Apennines. It was these descriptions, together with Vitruvius's accounts, that provided the basis for architectural theorists to try to reconstruct the Roman house. Even the discovery of Herculaneum, and later Pompeii, gave eighteenth-century theorists little advantage over their predecessors, despite the publication of various accounts in the 1750s, in particular Bellicard's *Observations upon the Antiquities of the town of Herculaneum*, published in London in 1753, and the Neapolitan Academy's *Le pitture antiche d'Erculano e contorni*, published in six volumes between 1757 and 1771. As Bellicard observed:

> Scarce any thing is to be seen of the private houses, the greatest part of which have been buried again by the earth which was thrown into them, to make room for digging in other places. [Herculaneum, which had been buried in mud, was tunnelled, not excavated in the conventional modern fashion.] I could examine but a very small number of them, and the few columns I saw, were overthrown, and very much defaced.[29]

The two most influential editions of Vitruvius in England were Barbaro's Italian edition illustrated by Palladio, published in Venice in the 1560s, and Perrault's French edition of 1684. Barbaro's edition, perhaps because of Palladio's involvement, is the one that seems to have been most influential among eighteenth-century English amateurs. Palladio discussed Vitruvius's account in greater detail and with more illustrations in his *Quattro libri*. His conclusions followed those of Barbaro in general but differ in detail. He also gave his interpretation of the Roman villa and the Greek house, and tried to put his interpretation of the Roman house into practice in his design for the Convent of the Carità in Venice. Palladio was aware of Pliny's descriptions, but deliberately restricted his text to an analysis of Vitruvius. His follower Scamozzi devoted several rather longer chapters

157 Roger Morris, St Lawrence's church, Mereworth, Kent, 1744.

158   Lord Burlington, Tottenham Park, Wiltshire, 1721 (John Buckler, watercolour) (remodelled).

to the subject. As well as publishing reconstructions of
the Roman house and villa and the Greek house, he also
made a reconstruction of Pliny's Laurentinum villa (Figs.
59 and 163). Then, in 1699, Jean-François Félibien
d'Avaux published his reconstruction of Pliny's two villas, *Les Plans et les descriptions de deux des plus belles maisons
de campagne de Pline le Consul*. In its cheap duodecimo
edition this seems to have been quite common in England, where it was published in 1707. Castell's sump-
tuous folio, *Villas of the Ancients* (1729), was a much
more lavish attempt at reconstruction.

The first house Burlington designed was Tottenham
Park, Wiltshire (Fig. 158), for his brother-in-law Lord
Bruce in 1721, probably before he purchased the
Palladio and Jones drawings. This was an unusual compact, square villa with four pyramidal turrets, one at each
corner, something without precedent in England and
with no obvious source in Palladio's *Quattro libri*.
Burlington seems to have taken Scamozzi's recreation of
the Roman *villa rustica* as his model (Fig. 163), but
reduced Scamozzi's reconstruction to its key element,
the four towers.[30]

A similar, but rather more sophisticated process may
have taken place at Chiswick House, Middlesex, built
about 1726 (Fig. 137). Richard Hewlings has argued that
this should be seen less as an imitation of a Palladian villa

than as an attempt to create a Roman villa. As he has
pointed out, the building owes little exclusively to
Palladio except the triple Serlian-windowed garden
façade; Burlington may have believed that the Palladio
drawing from which this was taken was intended as a
reconstruction of an antique building. Dr Hewlings has
linked many of the identifiable sources to known antique
precedents, often mediated through the work of
cinquecento Italian architects, and has suggested that other
innovations may be from the same source.[31]

A third compact villa, probably begun before
Chiswick, was Rokeby Park, built by Sir Thomas
Robinson, an associate of Burlington's, for himself between 1725 and the early 1730s (Fig. 159). Robinson
was a noted collector of local Roman remains and
had been given the Earl of Carlisle's collection from
Naworth Castle, Cumberland, close to the Roman Wall.
Greta Bridge on the edge of his park was the site of a
much-noted Roman fort, guarding the Roman road
over the Pennines, which Robinson marked on a survey
as 'The Great Roman Road', and some commentators
even suggested that the bridge itself was Roman.
Rokeby Park's twin towers appear to be unique in
English neo-Palladian architecture, and were almost
certainly a deliberate reference to Pliny's Tuscum villa,
one of whose key features was its twin towers. An this

159   Sir Thomas Robinson, Rokeby Park, Yorkshire, 1725 (George Cuitt (attrib.), oil, private collection).

attempt to recreate a Roman villa would explain other unusual features about the house. Robinson added a baseless Doric portico during alterations in the 1750s, and Mr Donald Findlay has suggested that the unusual north–south orientation of the church Robinson built at Rokeby was to allow it to appear like a Roman mausoleum on the Via Appia when viewed from the Roman road. The church had extensive vaults for tombs.[32]

Certainly, informed contemporaries could pick up direct antique quotations. In 1727 Pope complimented Lady Howard on a room at Marble Hill, Middlesex, that was modelled on Palladio's interpretation of a Roman atrium.[33] This must have been the hall, the first example of what was to become a relatively common type of neo-Palladian room, the four-columned hall in the rustic, based on Palladio's Corinthian atrium.

Tottenham, Chiswick and Rokeby were all attempts to recreate small villas, for which insufficient evidence of Roman originals survived for the architects to be sure of a plan. Instead, their Roman credentials are proclaimed through the use of specific motifs. At Holkham Hall, Norfolk (Fig. 151), begun in 1734 and unfinished at his death in 1759, the Earl of Leicester attempted a more thorough-going recreation, but in the absence of a detailed description of a villa in Vitruvius he turned to the Roman town house as his model. Holkham's authorship

has always been unclear, but it probably owes its inspiration to the Earls of Leicester and Burlington, with William Kent and Matthew Brettingham acting as executant architects and designing interiors.

Holkham's plan, with its columned hall, internal unused courts and circuit of rooms is highly unusual and has no English precedent (Fig. 160). Wittkower suggested Palladio's Egyptian hall as interpreted by Burlington at York as a model for the hall, but a more direct source for this room, and indeed for the whole house, can be found in Barbaro's interpretation of Vitruvius's Roman house (Fig. 161).[34] If the range on the far side of Barbaro's peristyle is removed and the wings bent back on themselves, we have the ground plan of Holkham. The hall should be seen as an atrium; this is even clearer in Kent's detailed drawing. Like Barbaro's atrium, the hall is essentially a square with six columns along each side, set out slightly from the wall (in a Roman house the spaces between the columns and the wall are known as alae), and has a coffered ceiling. The blank area in the middle of Kent's ceiling is probably meant to represent the roof open to the sky in Barbaro's atrium. The one major difference was caused by the need for the hall to raise the visitor from ground to first floor level, which was achieved through a staircase set in an apse. It is probably this that Brettingham referred to when he stated that the

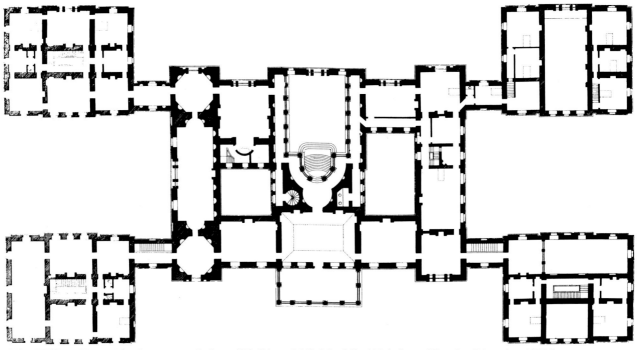

160 William Kent and others, ground-plan of Holkham Hall, Norfolk, 1734, from *Vitruvius Britannicus* (1771).

161 Reconstruction of the plan of the Roman House from Daniele Barbaro's edition of Vitruvius's *Ten Books of Architecture* (1556).

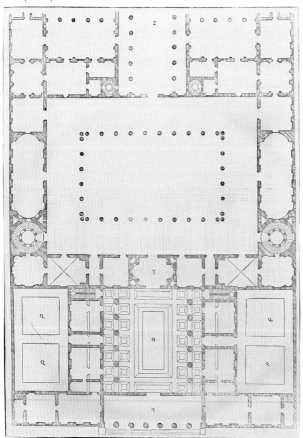

idea of the great hall was suggested by the Earl of Leicester himself from Palladio's example of a basilica depicted in Barbaro's translation of Vitruvius.[35] Even the heating of the hall was inspired by Roman principles, with underfloor heating based on the idea of a Roman hypocaust.

Moving on from the hall, the saloon takes the place of the tablinum in the Roman house, the two drawing-rooms those of the two rectangular rooms that flanked the tablinum. The gallery is modelled closely on the wing to the right of the peristyle in the Roman house, with a rectangular apsed room in the centre, and square niched rooms at either end. Even the brick with which the house was built was seen to support the antique link – Brettingham noted that Vitruvius said the Romans prefered brick even to marble for durability and that the Holkham brick made a very good comparison with Roman brick, of which an example had arrived in a packing case.[36]

Barbaro's reconstruction provided a workable ground-plan but no elevation. The early designs for Holkham in the British Library show how Coke arrived at the present elevations (Fig. 162).[37] He originally considered compressing the whole house into one block, with a chamber floor along the south front. The source for his design was again Scamozzi's Roman *villa rustica* which also has a basement, *piano nobile*, chamber floor, four corner towers and central portico (Fig. 163). In the end it must have been decided that the difficulty of actually living in a Roman house was too great, and, as

162 William Kent and others, first design for the elevation of Holkham Hall, Norfolk, 1734.

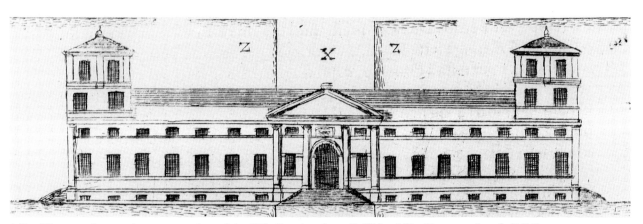

163 Vincenzo Scamozzi, reconstruction of the Villa Rustica, from *Dell'idea dell'architettura universale* (1615).

built, all the domestic parts of the house, the family's living-rooms, the guest rooms and the kitchen were placed in wings, the idea of a second floor being abandoned.

At Hovingham Hall, where a Roman villa had been discovered in 1745, the model chosen by Thomas Worsley in the house he built for himself between 1751 and 1776 was Palladio's reconstruction of the Roman house in the *Quattro libri*.[38] Worsley included no fewer than five examples of baseless Doric columns in his designs. Like the Roman house, Hovingham was based around two courts. It was approached through the riding school or atrium (Fig. 164) – in this case the roofed *atria testudinate* appropriate to a northern climate – off which, as in the Roman house, were the stables and offices. Beyond this, through the square Samson Hall or tablinum (frontispiece), was the peristyle, flanked by family rooms. On either side of the Samson Hall were two further vaulted rooms, rectangular as in Palladio's

design, which led to staircases in the corners of the house. The one major concession to practicality at Hovingham was that the 'peristyle' was not closed, allowing a view of the park from the main rooms. The clarity of Worsley's reconstruction was somewhat spoilt by the failure to build the south wing.

The impracticality of a wholescale reconstruction of a Roman house as at Holkham and Hovingham must have been very obvious, and Sir Francis Dashwood took a different line at West Wycombe House, which he slowly rebuilt between about 1748 and 1771. Here the effect was concentrated instead on recreating individual neo-Classical elements rather than a complete house. The most obvious of these is the west front of 1771, a reconstruction by Nicholas Revett of the Temple of Bacchus at Teos (Fig. 165). Equally remarkable is the south front which was probably built in the late 1750s. Here the surmounted colonnades (the lower one being baseless Doric) which stretch the entire length of the

164   Thomas Worsley, the Riding School, Hovingham Hall, Yorkshire, 1768.

façade have no precedent in English architecture, or indeed probably in post-Restoration architecture. However, Palladio used such a double colonnade for the peristyle of his reconstruction of Vitruvius's Roman house, and this was probably Dashwood's model.[39]

Even more self-consciously 'Roman' was the house the amateur architect and astronomer Thomas Wright built for himself from 1756 at Byer's Green in County Durham. Wright's description of his house drew particular attention to the proximity of the former Roman fort of Vinovium and of a Roman circus two miles in compass. He even suggested that the annual village games were relics of Roman games. Unfortunately, Byer's Green has been demolished but its neo-Classical nature comes out in his description which referred to it as a *villula*. Adjacent to the house were two courts or *suggestia*, with between them a small *praetorium* adjoining the house. Within the house he refers to the *triclinium*, the *sedes heatorum* and *cubicula*.[40]

One of the more enigmatic lost eighteenth-century houses, Holland House at Kingsgate on the Isle of Thanet in Kent, only fifty yards from the sea shore, built by the amateur Thomas Wynn for Henry Fox from 1764 to 1771, may have been another Roman reconstruction, this time of Pliny's Laurentinum villa. Attention is drawn to the house by a contemporary reference that the architect intended the house 'to resemble an Italian villa; but more particularly that of Tully's Formian villa on the coast of Baiae, near the city of Pozzuolo, one of the most celebated in the Roman state, upon the eve of the Augustan age, when all the polite arts were at the zenith of their glory'. 'Tully' is Marcus Tullius Cicero: little is known of Cicero's villa at Baiae, except for the occasional reference in his letters to Atticus, and although a site was identified for it near Pozzuoli, little remained. The specific comparison with the Baiae villa must therefore be a literary comparison. Cicero had retired to the country having lost his office after the Civil War. Per-

165　Nicholas Revett, the west portico, West Wycombe Park, Buckinghamshire, 1771.

haps Fox, who was was forced to resign his post as Paymaster-General because of corruption, identified himself with Cicero.

Contemporary descriptions which note that the house was built 'on a very different plan from any other house in the country' suggest that it was a different Roman coastal villa that Wynn intended Kingsgate to resemble, Pliny's Laurentinum villa. The house has been largely demolished and no plan survives, but the statement that 'The back front consists of several buildings which exactly answer to each other on the opposite sides of the garden' suggests that the rooms behind the façade were arranged round a courtyard. Only eight major rooms are mentioned, suggesting that the courtyard was not as wide as the wings of the façade, as in both Félibien and Castell's reconstructions of the Laurentinum villa. It was almost certainly an antique villa that Holland referred to when he wrote to his wife in June 1767 that 'The Back part of the House looks now just like such a Villa as I

meant.'[41] By the time Kingsgate was finished the idea of reconstructing Roman villas was sufficiently mainstream for Edward Stevens, one of William Chambers's pupils, to exhibit his model of a Roman villa at the Royal Academy in 1771; a copy of his drawing survives in the Soane Museum, London.

Palladio and Vitruvius made it relatively easy – if rather curious – to recreate the layout of a Roman house. It was more difficult to know how to decorate it. As Vitruvius spoke of rooms having cornices, the initial consensus was to take this to mean that rooms should be decorated with full Classical cornices. This is the case at Chiswick, Holkham (Fig. 166) and Hovingham, where the source can usually be identified. Other decoration is kept to a minimum; there are no dados and no decorative plasterwork.

Painted decoration was more problematic. According to Vitruvius the ancients decorated their rooms with 'realistic paintings of real things', but he was dismissive of

166   Matthew Brettingham, detail of the cornice of the drawing-room, Holkham Hall, Norfolk, 1734, showing motifs taken from Antoine Desgodetz's *Edifices antiques de Rome* (1682).

the wall paintings of his day, declaring that 'these subjects which were copied from actual realities are scorned in these days of bad taste. We now have fresco paintings of monstrosities, rather than truthful representations of definite things.'[42] All too often it was these that were discovered in excavations. Even the wall paintings published at length in *Le pitture antiche d'Erculano* seem to confirm Vitruvius's complaint and inspired Bellicard to write that

> There is a very considerable number of these paintings of architecture or ruins; but they scarce deserve no-tice: for, they are altogether out of the proportion of Grecian architecture . . . the profil of the mouldings of the cornishes, the chapiters and bases, is of a wretched Gothic taste; and most of the Arabic mixture in the architecture, is as ridiculous as any Chinese designs.[43]

However, Vitruvius did mention that some rooms were decorated in a grand style, with figures of gods or detailed mythological episodes. At Hovingham, Thomas Worsley acquired a number of large grisailles of classical sacrifices by Sebastiano Ricci and Andrea Courlandaio, which he hung in his dining room, commissioning a further canvas from Cipriani in 1772 to make up a set. In the absence of antique sources to copy, one solution was to turn to the mythological scenes of Raphael and the Carracci whom connoisseurs considered, with reason, to have most closely emulated the Ancients. This Dashwood did in the Yellow Drawing Room, the Blue Drawing Room and the Music Room at West Wycombe. These rooms were painted by Giovanni Borgnis, who was responsible for a similar painted scheme in the Ionic temple on the Rievaulx Terraces.

The alternative was to accept the *grottesche* which were being regularly discovered in Rome, even if Vitruvius condemned them. There was an English precedent for this, Jones's ceiling for the Queen's Presence Chamber in the Queen's House at Greenwich uses *grottesche* mo-tifs, but this is based on Renaissance interpretations not on antique originals. It was William Kent who took up the idea most energetically. In Rome he studied under the painter Giuseppe Chiari who held Raphael in the greatest respect and would have been made, among other tasks, to study the decoration of the Villa Madama. But it was his companion John Talman who suggested that Kent himself design *grottesche*, as Kent revealed in a letter written from Rome in 1717 about a ceiling he proposed to paint for his patron Burrell Massingberd: 'Mr Talman was here this morning and would have me done this ceiling after the grotesk manner . . . I believe you may remember this sort of painting as what the Ancients used.'[44]

Kent returned to London two years later, working initially as a painter, his most important commission being the decoration of the state rooms at Kensington Palace. He was first introduced in 1722 to add a painted coffered ceiling to the Cupola Room which had already been fitted up by Sir Thomas Hewett in 1720 'in the fine Grecian taste' (Fig. 167).[45] Hewett's austere use of giant Ionic pilasters was novel for its day and he undoubtedly saw it as a recreation of a Roman room, probably a *tablinum*, although the feel of the room seems to owe more to French academicism, perhaps to Perrault's 1684 edition of Vitruvius, than Palladio.[46] In 1725, Kent somewhat modified Hewett's austerity when he added painted decoration to the walls. Among Kent's work at Kensington was the ceiling of the Presence Chamber, done in 1724. This was commented upon by George Vertue, who noted Kent's source for this correctly but was dismissive of the result: 'The ceiling in imitation of the antient Roman subterraean ornaments . . . poor stuff.'[47] Vertue's comment is the first sign of a prejudice against a style based on antique *grottesche*, which probably derives from Vitruvius.

Kent executed three other *grottesche* ceilings at Kensington Palace and one in the parlour at Rousham House, Oxfordshire, of 1738, for General Dormer, whose intimate status is revealed by the fact that Burlington gave him a copy of the *Fabbriche antiche*. These were not his only ventures in imitation of anti-quity. At Houghton Hall, Norfolk, between 1725 and 1731,[48] and possibly at Stowe House, Buckinghamshire, and Mereworth Castle, Kent, in the 1730s, he designed ceilings with decoration strongly based on antique pre-cedent. The sources for these were probably record drawings made by Pietro Santi Bartoli and his son Francesco of recently discovered Roman tomb decora-tions. Kent would have known these drawings both

167   Thomas Hewett and William Kent, the Cupola Room, Kensington Palace, London, 1720, from W.H. Pyne's *The Royal Residences* (1819).

through originals owned by such friends and acquaintances as Francis Topham, Dr Mead and the Earl of Leicester (for whom he was acted in the purchase of a set of Bartoli drawings), and through engravings made from them and illustrated in a work such as Francesco Bartoli's *Le pitture antiche delle grotte di Roma e del sepulchro de Nasonii* (1706). The ceiling of the White Drawing Room at Houghton (Fig. 169) is particularly close to one of the drawings in the Topham collection (Fig. 168), while the distorted lines of the Cabinet Room ceiling suggest that it is based on a drawing of a vaulted ceiling adapted to a flat surface.

Kent made the most regular use of antique sources in his decoration, but he was not alone. None of the decorative ceilings in the villa at Chiswick seems to have specifically antique sources, although they do have painted decoration comparable to Houghton, the model

for the design seems to be Inigo Jones rather than antiquity. But on the first floor of the link building of 1732–3, which has a screen of columns at each end, Lord Burlington installed a plaster ceiling copied from a drawing in his collection of an antique ceiling at Pozzuoli (Figs. 170 and 171).[49] Although this room seems today to be tucked away, when Burlington was living at Chiswick it would have been in constant use as the link between the old house and the new, and John Harris has also suggested that it may have been used as a dining-room. Its importance is shown by its central position on the main axis of the garden, looking down the avenue to the *patte d'oie*. The timing is interesting. While it is possible that Burlington had only recently acquired this drawing, he would certainly have known Bartoli's drawings of antique ceilings, and yet before this date he had not used any antique ceilings in the villa itself, which although

168   Francesco Bartoli, record drawing of an ancient Roman ceiling.

comprised of antique motifs takes the basic form of a *cinquecento* villa, not an antique building. In 1732 Burlington was completing the York Assembly Room, closely based on Vitruvius's Egyptian hall. From 1734 he was heavily involved in the design of Holkham Hall, a literal attempt at recreating a Roman house. This suggests that in the early 1730s Burlington developed into a more rigorous neo-Classicist.

Burlington's friend Sir Andrew Fountaine was another contemporary who designed ceilings based on antique tomb decoration. At Narford Hall, Norfolk, Fountaine, decorated the ceiling of his library closet with a brightly coloured design based on a Bartoli engraving. The vignettes set into the ceiling are a curious mixture of Jewish and Roman motifs, including the Temple of Solomon, the Sanctuary of the Temple and Jewish temple vessels, together with the Arch of Titus, the Amphitheatre of Vespasian and reliefs taken from the Arch of Titus. Ingrid Roscoe suggested that this complex iconography celebrates 'Roman' Fountaine's appointment as Warden of the Mint in 1727 in succession to Sir Isaac Newton, whose *Chronology of the Ancients*, published posthumously in 1728, centred on a long, visionary description of the Temple of Solomon.[50] The date of this ceiling is uncertain. Sir Matthew Decker referred to the newly created library on his visit in 1728, but his account is quite detailed and does not mention the closet ceiling, suggesting that it was probably done subsequently, probably in the 1730s and certainly before Fountaine's death in 1753. Fountaine, who had a particularly distinguished library of architectural and archaeological books, was

coupled with Burlington and Herbert as one of the 'principal Practitioners and Preservers' of architecture and as 'great Protectors of Antiquity'. He was friends of both. His copy of the *Fabbriche antiche* is still in the house, while Vertue, who notes that Fountaine was friends with both the 8th and 9th Earls of Pembroke, records that he was responsible for the published catalogue of the collection of sculpture at Wilton.[51]

Another example that probably dates from these years can be found in Yorkshire, at Studley Royal, where we have already seen the pioneering use of the baseless Doric order at the Temple of Piety. Here, the decoration of the twin apses of the Banqueting House is taken directly from an engraving in Bartoli's *Gli antichi sepolchri* of a 'shell' ceiling apse (Figs. 172 and 173).[52] It also seems probable that the apsed niches installed at either end of the Great Hall in the Bishop's Palace at Hereford by Bishop Bisse between 1713 and 1721 are inspired by the same engraving, although simplified; their fan-like design is certainly not neo-Palladian.[53]

It was Sir Francis Dashwood at West Wycombe who tried hardest to find a suitable antique interior. Decorative paintings of scenes of the gods, following Vitruvius's description, after Raphael and the Carracci, seen in the eighteenth century as the most Classical of all *cinquecento* artists, was one answer. Another, which he tried in the Tapestry Room and the Red Drawing Room (Fig. 175), was to copy a Bartoli drawing of an antique ceiling from the Topham collection, setting into the latter a panel taken from a Roman painting in Dr Mead's collection (Fig. 176). Dashwood's final solution, used in the entrance hall (which has an underfloor central-heating system based on the hypocaust excavated at Lincoln noted by Dr Stukeley) in the inner hall and in the church, came from a new source, the ceilings published in Robert Wood's *Ruins of Palmyra* in 1753, the first in a wave of archaeological books published by Englishmen which was to change the nature of neo-Classicism.[54]

It was not only houses which were seen with neo-Classical eyes, the idea spread to gardens as well. It was not by chance that William Kent referred to Robert Castell as 'the author of Pliny's Gardens',[55] and his book, which included reconstructions of those gardens, certainly had more influence on garden design than it did on architecture (Fig. 174). Given a desire to recreate antique houses it is not surprising that there should have been a parallel desire to recreate antique gardens. Here, Vitruvius was of no value but Pliny's detailed descriptions, which contrasted the formality of the immediate setting of the house with the semi-wild landscape beyond, lent themselves to recreations. The house was placed in a hippodrome, a broad lawn in front of the house bounded on either side by plane trees, closed at the far end by a semi-circle or exedra, but with a gap left through to an eye-catcher. Beyond the symmetrical

169   William Kent, the White Drawing Room, Houghton Hall, Norfolk, *c.*1725.

170   Anon., drawing after an antique ceiling from Pozzuoli.

171   Anon., the ceiling of the Link Room, Chiswick House, Middlesex, 1732.

172   Engraving of an ancient Roman apse from Pietro Santi Bartoli, *Gli Sepolchri Antichi* (1704).

173   Anon., apse of the Banqueting House at Studley Royal, Yorkshire, *c.*1739.

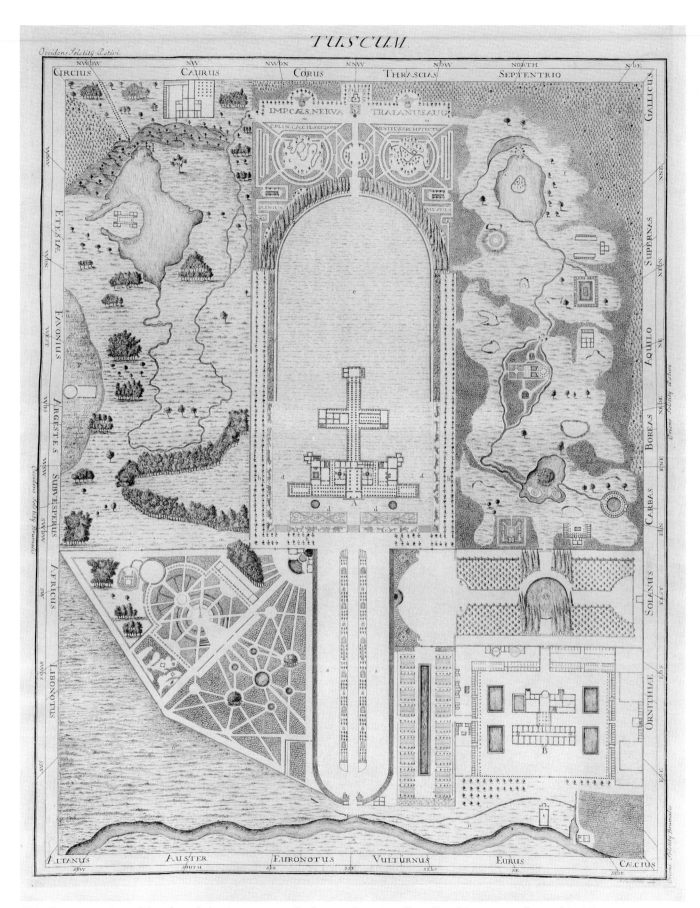

174   Reconstruction of the plan of Pliny's Tuscum Villa from Robert Castell's *Villas of the Ancients Illustrated* (1728).

175 Anon., ceiling of the Red Drawing Room, West Wycombe Park, Buckinghamshire, *c*.1750.

lines of trees was much rougher ground. Similar layouts could be found at Chiswick, Holkham, Rokeby and Tottenham.

It is no coincidence that virtually all the names mentioned in this chapter are of scholars, amateur architects or dominant patrons who were largely responsible for the intellectual cast of the buildings they erected. The one exception is William Kent, whose romantic attitude towards neo-Classicism, particularly evident in his garden buildings but also apparent in his designs for the Houses of Parliament, stands in contrast to the careful precedent-seeking of the amateurs; indeed, his approach has a surprising amount in common with that of Nicholas Hawksmoor. Setting Kent aside, the Palladian neo-Classical tradition was very much a movement of amateurs, a movement that would have gained confidence from Vitruvius's statement that:

> I can find nothing but praise for those householders who, in the confidence of learning, are emboldened to build for themselves. Their judgement is that, if they must trust to inexperienced persons, it is more becoming to them to use up a good round sum at their own pleasure than that of a professional.[56]

The literalness of the Palladian neo-Classical approach was condemned by professional architects. The baseless Doric column provided a touchstone: apart from Gibbs's *Book of Architecture* there were three important books on

176 Francesco Bartoli, record drawing of an ancient Roman ceiling.

the theory of architecture published in the eighteenth century, all condemn the use of the baseless Doric column. The first was Robert Morris's *An Essay in defence of Ancient Architecture; or, a Parallel of the Ancient Buildings with the Modern*, published in 1728. He specifically disagreed with Fréart:

> I cannot agree with Monsieur *Fréart*, the aforemention'd Author of *the Parallel*, in not introducing Bases to the Columns of this Order; for there is as seeming a Necessity that they should be executed in this as the other; the first and principal Member, the Base, being always practis'd by almost all who have writ upon this Subject and Order: Nothwithstanding whatever maybe alledged from the most antient Example.[57]

Morris was unable to break from the dominance of Renaissance architectural tradition and trust surviving evidence. Instead, he was forced to argue that Doric bases, being covered by soil, might have decayed so much that could have been missed by excavators or that they might have found it too troublesome to dig them out. Isaac Ware, although intimately involved with the Burlington circle, followed the general line in his *A Complete Body of Architecture* (1756) that, while the Doric order was originally baseless, it looked better with a base.[58] Finally, William Chambers in his *A Treatise on Civil Architecture*, published in 1759, had no time for

Fréart 'whose blind attachment to the Antique is, on many occasions, too evident', and quoted Le Clerc's comments on Fréart's defence of the baseless Doric columns at length, as 'they are very judicious and as they will serve to destroy a notion, which is too prevalent among us'. He concluded with Le Clerc's statement that 'if columns without bases are now set aside, it is a mark of the wisdom of our architects, rather than their being governed by prejudice, as some adorers of antiquity would insinuate'.[59]

In all this there is a clear difference in the attitude of amateurs and professional architects to antique architecture. Many amateurs, gentlemen bred on the Classics, wanted to recreate the Ancient World in eighteenth-century England. Architects saw antique architecture as a source from which to create a new architecture. The difference in education between the professional and the amateur is perhaps not sufficiently emphasised. Professional architects nearly always rose through apprenticeship, whether as a craftsman or as an architect's assistant. Their approach was therefore essentially practical – it had to be or they would have no more clients – and their architectural style tended to reflect that of other architects. Amateurs, however, were gentlemen, and as they were paying for the execution of their designs they could sacrifice practicality to pedantry should they so wish. They stayed at school until their late teens, might go to university and almost certainly went on a Grand Tour. In all this, Classical antiquity was constantly forced upon them. At school they had an almost unadulterated diet of the Classics; university was unlikely to be very different; on the Grand Tour it was above all the Classical remains that they studied. Thus, Classical Rome – and to a lesser extent Greece, but education largely concentrated on Rome and only a handful of gentlemen had the chance to visit Greece – dominated the intellectual consciousness of the amateur architect in a way that is hard to envisage today. Nor should it be assumed that, because to modern eyes Latin was 'forced down their throats', that their acceptance of the Classics was in some way grudging. Classical texts predominated in most gentlemen's libraries and many writers expressed a genuine love for the Classics. It was this empathy with Rome that led them to ignore the conventions of contemporary house design and try to recreate Rome in England.[60] The difference between neo-Classicism in the first and the second halves of the eighteenth century is that in the first half it is confined largely to amateurs. In the second half many architects were equally taken by the idea of directly imitating the ancients.

VIII

PALLADIANISM ON THE PERIPHERIES:
SCOTLAND, IRELAND AND THE AMERICAS
BEFORE 1748

No study of Palladianism that ignored its influence in Scotland, Ireland and America would be complete, although such a study can only shed partial light on the architectural history of those countries which encompasses many other factors, light that is, to a certain extent, inevitably Anglocentric. All three countries (if a region as diverse as the English colonies in the Americas can be called a country) shared the same monarch and were ultimately governed from Whitehall. In each case England was the dominant cultural influence. But the three had very different histories and cultures and responded to English architectural fashions, particularly Palladianism, in markedly different ways.

Scotland

To write about Scottish architectural history is to enter a minefield of nationalist passions, both contemporary and modern. Scotland before the Act of Union was, in a sense, more European and less insular than England. As an independent country it had a Classical tradition quite separate from that in England and had its own direct links with the Continent, particularly with the Low Countries, which need to be borne in mind when considering the relationship between English and Scottish architecture in the seventeenth and eighteenth centuries. However, that relationship should be seen as one of synergy, of growing interdependence and shared strengths, not of cultural competition. Without such Scottish architects as Colen Campbell, James Gibbs, Robert Adam and Robert Mylne – not to mention those of Scottish descent, for example James Stuart and William Chambers – English architecture would have been very different. At the same time it can be argued that it was English architectural fashions, led by Palladianism, that came to dominate Scottish architecture from 1660.[1]

Despite the Union of the Crowns of England and Scotland in 1603, English influence on Scottish architecture before the Restoration of 1660 was limited. The Dean of the English cathedral of Rochester, George Balcanquhall, may have produced a 'paterne' in 1627 for George Heriot's Hospital in Edinburgh, the most ambitious building begun in Scotland during the first half of the seventeenth century, but by birth he was a Scot and his model was a plate from Serlio's *Seventh Book of Architecture*, not a specific English building.[2] An Englishman would have found Scottish country-house architecture in the first half of the seventeenth century, dominated as it was by L-plan and Z-plan tower houses, very alien. By 1707, the year of the Act of Union which merged the two kingdoms into one, he would have felt much more at home, thanks, above all, to the work of the two leading Scottish architects, Sir William Bruce and James Smith.

Bruce was the younger son of a minor laird for whom architecture was only one part of a successful political career – at least until he was dismissed from office following the death of Charles II – which included being appointed Surveyor-general and Overseer of the King's Buildings in Scotland in 1671. Nothing is known of his architectural education, although he did travel abroad, but he also visited England on several occasions and it is there rather than France or Italy that the roots of his architectural style should he sought.

During the seventeenth century Scottish architecture was at a disadvantage compared to that in England, for to the country's relative poverty (and that of its aristocracy and gentry) must be added the absence of the court from 1603. Restoration Scotland was weary from decades of religious and civil strife which had culminated in occupation by an English army from 1650 to 1660. Heavy fines imposed by the occupiers on most of the aristocracy and gentry had, according to one contemporary authority, left half of them bankrupt and few of the others worth more than £500 a year.[3] It was only slowly that the confidence and resources to build emerged, and in

177   James Smith, Drumlanrig Castle, Dumfriess-shire, 1675.

particular the confidence to build from scratch rather than alter and extend existing buildings. Panmure House, Angus (1666), designed by the Edinburgh mason John Mylne, was a new house, but remodellings were more common – as at Leslie House, Fife (1667); Balcaskie House, Fife (c.1668); Glamis Castle, Angus (1670); Thirlestane House, Berwickshire (1670); Holyrood Palace, Edinburgh (1671); Brunstane House, Midlothian (1672), and Drumlanrig Castle, Dumfriess-shire (1675). All, apart from Balcaskie and the royal palace at Holyrood, were substantial houses for leading aristocrats, able to build thanks to their positions at court. Bruce was involved at Thirlestane, Holyrood and Brunstane, while Balcaskie was his own house. None of these buildings reveals any desire to emulate the contemporary English architectural advances which had begun in the 1630s and crystallised after the Restoration. The constraints of economy and existing fabric are partly responsible for this, but, equally, the Classical tradition had grown weak in Scotland, while the tower was still seen to symbolise power and lineage, as at Glamis and Drumlanrig (Fig. 177).[4] This is particularly evident at Holyrood where Bruce designed a Classical courtyard but also added a

south-west tower to match the existing early sixteenth-century tower.

It was only in 1676 that Bruce was able to design a completely new house, Dunkeld House, Perthshire, a winter house for the Marquess of Atholl. This was followed by Moncrieffe House, Perthshire (Fig. 179), for Thomas Moncrieffe of that Ilk, which was finished by 1679. Compact, square, two-and-a-half storey hipped-roofed houses raised above basements, Dunkeld and Moncrieffe are the first examples in Scotland of the classic Jonesian astylar house of the 1630s. In English terms these houses were not especially advanced, particularly for patrons as distinguished as the Marquess of Atholl or Thomas Moncrieffe of that Ilk, although in their greater width, and in the careful use of window spacing for architectural effect at Moncreiffe House, they seem to show an awareness of post-Restoration architectural developments, and, perhaps, of Sir Roger Pratt's Coleshill House, Wiltshire (Fig. 25). Given the tight-knit circle of architectural enthusiasts in London after the Restoration, it is quite possible that Bruce met Pratt on his visits to London in the 1660s. These houses introduced a building type that was to remain popular in

178   Sir William Bruce, Kinross House, Kinross-shire, 1686.

Scotland well into the eighteenth century, as at Blairdrummond, Perthshire (1715), Brucefield, Clackmannanshire (1724), Pollok House, Glasgow (1747), Newtown, Aberdeenshire, and William Adam's Banff Castle, Banffshire (1750).

Much more exceptional was Bruce's own house at Kinross, Kinross-shire, begun in 1686, and without doubt the most considered Classical house to have been built in Scotland. This is a classic double-pile house set on a low rustic of the type popularised by Pratt, and indeed the plan would seem to be based on his principles, and in particular on Coleshill. As at Coleshill, the reception rooms lie in the centre with a first-floor great room taking up the whole of one side, while the three end bays encompass pairs of bedchambers each with two closets and back stairs linked by short corridors. However, the need to provide a state apartment at Kinross breaks the symmetry of Coleshill. But while Coleshill has an unbroken astylar façade, Kinross has pavilions marked by giant pilasters. Apart from John Webb's Greenwich Palace, no giant pilasters were used in England (except on porticos) from the Restoration until the south front at Chatsworth was begun the year after Kinross. The

Kinross pilasters, which form pairs flanking each of the pavilions, differ markedly from the groups of four pilasters on the pavilions at Greenwich. Bruce's model was probably Bernini's famous design for the Louvre, as

179   Sir William Bruce, reconstruction drawing of Moncreiffe House, Perthshire, 1679 (demolished).

180   Sir William Bruce, Hopetoun House, West Lothian, 1698.

published in the *Grand Marot*, in particular the front towards the Tuileries which has three-bay pavilions of two storeys above a rustic with an emphatic entablature flanked by Corinthian pilasters. This source is a reminder that the Continent must always be borne in mind when analysing Scottish architecture at this date.

The sophistication of Kinross House seems to have had no successors and, despite its plan, would have felt alien in England, but with his last houses, Hopetoun House, West Lothian (1698) (Fig. 180), and Mertoun House, Berwickshire (1703), Bruce was treading on more familiar ground. Both are tripartite, two-storey villas with cupolas and basements of the type popularised in England nearly forty years earlier by Pratt. In both cases the detail is essentially Jonesian – the use of quoins, the aprons under the windows – but with a contempo-

181   James Smith, Newhailes, Midlothian, *c*.1690.

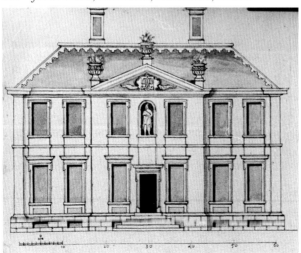

rary French gloss (such as might also have been found in England at the same time) thanks to the use of channelled rustication at Hopetoun, and the channelled rustication of the basement and the French-style quoins of the centrepiece of Mertoun. Hopetoun's plan with its central octagon is also unusual and may be based on Marly, but the use of three-bay corner pavilions seems to point back to Pratt's Clarendon House.

With Hopetoun and Mertoun, Bruce's architecture joins the English mainstream – either could have appeared without comment in *Britannia Illustrata* (1707). However, in the introduction of the Prattian villa, Bruce had been anticipated by James Smith, a mason rather than an amateur, at Newhailes, Midlothian (*c*.1690) (Fig. 181), Strathleven House, Dumbartonshire (*c*.1690), Raith House, Fife (1694), and Yester House, East Lothian (1710). Each of these houses is of seven bays (nine bays at Yester) with a three-bay pedimented centrepiece and a raised basement. Newhailes and Strathleven both have quoins, while Raith House has windows linked vertically by aprons, such as Pratt had used at Horseheath, Cambridgeshire, Kingston Lacy, Dorset, and Clarendon House (Figs. 33, 34 and 35). However, although these houses follow Pratt in their elevations this is not true of their plans, which are adapted to the demands of the Scottish great apartment. In England state apartments were restricted to the grandest houses and were preferably placed in enfilade. In Scotland they can be found in houses which to English eyes would appear very modest, but only in the largest houses were they placed in enfilade.[5]

Not all Smith's houses were compact villas: his most important work was the remodelling of Hamilton Palace, Lanarkshire, for the Duke of Hamilton in 1693 (Fig. 182). This was built around three sides of a courtyard and has been criticised for having an old-fashioned plan. However, as Pratt noted, the courtyard was still considered the most appropriate model for such very grand houses and indeed, Daniel Defoe noted of Hamilton Palace that 'The Apartments are very noble, and fit rather for the Court of a Prince than the Palace or House of a Subject.'[6] A courtyard plan also allowed an enfiladed apartment to be placed in each of the wings, joined across the centre by a long gallery. Again, the sources of the elevation can be traced to England, in particular the use of quoins and of windows with aprons. The tetrastyle Corinthian portico is more exceptional and Palladio's San Giorgio Maggiore has been cited as a possible source.[7] Smith did visit Italy and his theoretical drawings reveal a particular interest in Palladio.[8] However, instead of adapting one of the Italian's ecclesiastical motifs, Smith is more likely to have been influenced by Christopher Wren's contemporary palaces in England. The Duke of Hamilton is known to have consulted Wren about Hamilton Palace, while Smith certainly

182　James Smith, Hamilton Palace, Lanarkshire, 1693 (demolished).

visited Hampton Court.[9] Smith may well have had Wren's Winchester Palace, with its deep courtyard leading to a portico, in mind when he planned Hamilton Palace. The design of the portico, formed of attached columns set on pedestals the height of the ground floor, follows Wren at Hampton Court, although the portico rises through two storeys, not one as at Hampton Court. Smith's niches in the end wings may be based on those used by Wren at Tring Manor House, Hertfordshire (c.1670). The influence of Winchester can perhaps also be seen at Smith's Dalkeith House, Midlothian (1702), where there is a similar sense of recession leading to a central portico.

The importance of English architectural fashion in the work of Bruce and Smith is not surprising. It was to the court in London that Scottish aristocrats looked for political advancement, and this was inevitably the dominant cultural influence upon them. Government posts were a common feature (indeed perhaps a necessity) among those who could afford to build, and many of the leading aristocrats for whom Bruce and Smith worked were familiar with the English court. Often, as in the case of Lauderdale, they resided there. The Earl of Rothes, who rebuilt Leslie House, directed operations from London; for Lauderdale, who fashionably remodelled his London villa, Ham House, London, was the touchstone of taste, one room at Brunstane, for instance, was described as being 'as broad as the galleries at Whitehall'.[10] It is important to note that none of the designs by Smith

(now in the Royal Institute of British Architects) in which he directly imitated Palladio, were executed. They may never have been intended as more than ideal schemes.

Bruce died in 1710, and Smith had little significant work after that year. Their place was taken by William Adam, who dominated Scottish architecture from the 1720s until his death in 1748. William Adam has always proved something of a conundrum to architectural historians. After the austere Prattian Palladianism of Bruce and Smith, Adam is much more ambitious in his use of Classical decoration. In this he parallels a similar development in England where post-Restoration austerity gave way to a much more exuberant Classicism in the first two decades of the eighteenth century. But should Adam he be described as a Baroque or a neo-Palladian architect? Elements of both styles can be found in his work. Was he essentially a ham-fisted provincial incapable of understanding the rigour of neo-Palladianism or a gifted architect who took the dry motifs of the neo-Palladians and recast them in a fresh and exciting manner?

Adam's first commission, Floors Castle, Roxburghshire, begun in 1721, is a case in point. On a first reading its use of a *piano nobile* above a low rustic, its unbroken run of windows, its pavilion towers crowned by pediments could be read as a paraphrase of Wilton House, Wiltshire. Indeed, it seems to anticipate Campbell's use of pedimented pavilion towers at Houghton in Norfolk

183   William Adam, Chatelherault, Lanarkshire, 1733.

where work began in 1722, and Campbell's (unexecuted) design was not published until 1725. However,
the proportions are all wrong, the central range is too
wide and the house has too many storeys. Similarly, the
dog kennels at Chatelherault, Lanarkshire, of 1733 (Fig.
183), have pedimented pavilion towers with Serlian
windows and walls topped with ball machiolation, but
combined in a manner which is completely un-
Palladian, using French-style channelled rustication.

   Adam's unexecuted design for Newliston, West
Lothian, of about 1723 (Fig. 184), has been described
as an example of 'strict Palladianism',[11] but although
the elements are Palladian – the projecting portico, the
channelled rustic, the perron, the alternating segmental

and triangular pedimented windows and the attic – the
composition would have been dismissed with disdain
by any English neo-Palladian as overfussy and inept. It,
and Adam's other ambitious schemes, could almost
have been the target of Pope's later tribute to Lord
Burlington:

> . . . yet shall your noble Rules
> Fill half the Land with Imitating Fools,
> Who random Drawings from your Sheets shall take,
> And of one Beauty many Blunders make.[12]

A study of *Vitruvius Britannicus* – of which Adam is
known to have owned the first two volumes by at least
1726[13] – reveals that he was indebted to it for many of

184   William Adam, unexecuted design for Newliston, West Lothian, *c.*1723, from *Vitruvius Scoticus* (1812).

his motifs, but his sources are not necessarily Palladian buildings. Hopetoun House, where Adam began remodelling the south front in 1723 was his greatest house. Its central section is a straight paraphrase of Powis House, London, illustrated in volume one, although without the channelled rustication, the emphatic keystones or the breaks in the entablature at each end.[14] Duff House, Banffshire (1735), returns to the same source, again without the channelled rustication and with different window surrounds, but this time keeping the breaks in the entablature, incorporating from Castle Howard, Yorkshire, the idea of a pilastered, pedimented centrepiece with round-headed windows. The shape of the roof and platform of Mavisbank House, Midlothian (1723), may be taken from Campbell's house 'in the style of Inigo Jones' illustrated in the first volume of *Vitruvius Britannicus*.[15]

Adam was a practical builder who seems to have shown no considered interest in neo-Palladian ideals nor in the principles that lay behind Baroque architecture. Nevertheless, like his sons, he was aware of the value of being up with the latest architectural fashion. For him *Vitruvius Britannicus* was useful not as a supposed Palladian manifesto but because it provided a valuable stock of fashionable architectural motifs; and he was always eager to keep up to date. In 1726, when he already owned an incomplete edition of Palladio's *Quattro libri* and the first two volumes of *Vitruvius*

Britannicus, he was anxious to acquire illustrations of Inigo Jones's work.[16] Nor did Adam look only to England in his desire to be abreast of architectural fashion; as a leading businessman as well as architect he seems to have had direct links with the Low Countries and, if the early books listed in the library at Blair Adam in about 1785 can be assumed to have been bought by William Adam and not by his son John, owned a wide selection of Continental works – including copies of Le Pautre and Marot, Pietro Ferrerio's *Palazzi di Roma*, Guarino Guarini's *Architettura civile* and Paul Decker's *Architectura civilis* – which would have meant he was well informed about the European Baroque.[17] These works were probably plundered for individual details in much the same way that *Vitruvius Britannicus* certainly was.

William Adam should not be seen as a failed neo-Palladian, nor as a Baroque architect out of his time. Instead, the best stylistic comparison that can be drawn is not with the intellectual refinement of Burlington and court-based architecture but with the vigorous, loose Classicism of the English commercial classes, epitomised by George Dance the elder's Mansion House in London. In Adam and Scotland's case the appropriate comparison is with those mason-architects working in stubbornly independent provincial cities such as Bristol and Liverpool where the latest fashionable motifs and ideas were quickly picked up but the essentially austere message of neo-Palladianism fell on deaf ears.

Ireland

Ireland remained a separate kingdom throughout the seventeenth and eighteenth centuries, ruled by a lord-lieutenant or viceroy who was generally absent for most of the year. Like Scotland its architectural history during these years can only be understood in parallel with English architecture, but while Scottish architecture before 1748 remained essentially provincial, Ireland had at least one architect who could stand comparison with any English architect.

Before the 1660s, Classicism had only a tenuous hold on Ireland. Unlike Scotland, Ireland had never had a strong Renaissance Classical tradition, and before the Restoration defence, not architectural expression, was the primary consideration of most country houses. Despite the presence of Charles I's favourite the Earl of Strafford as Viceroy from 1636 to 1639, Caroline Classicism, in particular the astylar double-pile house sponsored by Inigo Jones, was not introduced in the 1630s. Indeed, Jigginstown, County Kildare, Strafford's own house, was chiefly remarkable for its great length rather than its Classical innovation.

All this changed after the devastating rebellion of 1641 and subsequent wars that lasted until 1650. Their violence did much to disrupt the existing Plantation and caused the widescale destruction of many of those semi-fortified houses which had already been built. It also led to extensive confiscations of land which was then regranted to English and Scottish settlers. The situation in Ireland in the second half of the seventeenth century was thus very different to that in Scotland. Instead of an impoverished native aristocracy proud of their ancestral tower houses, Ireland saw a new class of owners with no option but to build, owing no loyalty to earlier building forms and happy to make a statement of their power and their English origins in the houses they built. When the Earl of Orrery repaired the castle at Castlemartyr, County Cork, he made it 'English like', while a lease for a house in Belfast stipulated that it should be a 'good handsome Englishlike house'.[18] It is not surprising to find that the Prattian revolution appeared sooner in Ireland than it did in Scotland (which it seems to have reached in the 1690s), aided by the fact that the 1670s and 1680s were years of marked economic growth in Ireland. A significant increase in building was one result. Whereas in 1670 a traveller noted that there were few houses in the country, the Earl of Clarendon, lord-lieutenant from 1685 to 1686, could report that 'there were many buildings raised for beauty, as well as use, orderly and regular plantations of trees and fences and enclosures throughout the kingdom'.[19]

The introduction of English architectural models was helped by the fact that most of the new landowners were English, many of the greater Irish landowners having houses in London and estates in England where they sometimes experimented with architecture. These men were often closely interconnected. Thus, the 1st Earl of Conway, who built Ragley Hall, Warwickshire, in 1679–83 to a plan of William Hurlbutt's (extensively revised by Robert Hooke), had earlier employed Hurlbutt to design and build his great stable at Portmore, County Antrim. This was closely modelled on Hugh May's important early Classical stable at Cornbury Park, Oxfordshire (1663).[20] Conway was advised at Ragley and at Newmarket by Lord Ranelagh, a keen amateur architect who designed his own house in Chelsea and was subsequently made 'sur-intendant generall of our Buildings & of our works in our parks' by William III.[21] Ranelagh owned extensive estates in Ireland and was Chancellor of the Irish Exchequer from 1668 although it is not known what if any building work he carried out there. However, he was appointed one of the commissioners for the building of the Royal Hospital at Kilmainham in Dublin in 1680, the architect of which, the Surveyor-General William Robinson, became a close friend. Robert Hooke is known to have had 'much Discourse about his buildings' with Ranelagh.[22] He was also employed in London by Sir Robert Southwell, owner of estates in England and Ireland, who encouraged Hooke to advise his nephew and former ward, Sir John Perceval, in the building of Burton House, County Cork, in 1681. Subsequently, Charles Fairfax, a protégé of Dean Aldrich at Christ Church, Oxford, and translator of the *Antichita di Roma*, was appointed Dean of Down and placed in charge of building the school erected there by the Southwells which was begun about 1721. The way in which contemporary English fashions were imported into Ireland can be seen in a letter from Perceval to Thomas Smith, his builder at Burton, suggesting alterations: 'because upon inquiery here in·London I find ye fasion to have ye Doores of Roomes as much as may be in ye Corners of ye Roomes . . .'[23] Nor should it be forgotten that one of the few native Irish to flourish in these years, Daniel O'Neill, built Belsize House, a large post-Restoration house, on the edge of London.

The lord-lieutenant also served as an important conduit: When the Earl of Essex, lord-lieutenant from 1672 to 1677, repaired Dublin Castle it is possible that his kinsman Hugh May provided designs, as he did when Essex subsequently remodelled Cassiobury Park, Herts. May is also known to have been consulted about the Duke of Ormonde's Kilkenny Castle, County Kilkenny, in 1681.[24] Similarly, the designs of important royal buildings were often sent for comment to the court in London. Thus, in 1661 John Westley travelled to London to show the Duke of Ormonde, the lord-lieutenant, plans for additions to Phoenix House, County Dublin, while in 1679 William Robinson, the surveyor-general, was sent to England with plans, probably those for the Royal Hospital at Kilmainham.[25]

It was not only landowners who settled in Ireland in these years. Whereas in Scotland ideas might be sought from England but those who executed them were Scots, many of those who acted as architects in Ireland were immigrants, such as John Westley, John Webb's son-in-law, who arrived about 1656 to practise as a lawyer but also served as an architect.[26] A significant number of craftsmen also emigrated. Rolf Loeber mentions twenty-three glaziers, carpenters, masons, bricklayers and plasterers who arrived between 1664 and 1673, bringing with them the skills necessary for building large Classical buildings.[27] These included the bricklayer Richard Mills, who contracted to erect Sir Hierome Alexander's buildings at Trinity College in Dublin (1672) and was subsequently Assistant to the Master of the City Works.

Although there seems to have been a certain amount of country-house building during the Cromwellian period, little is known about the results, and it is only with the Restoration that a clearer picture emerges. Defence as a primary consideration was abandoned, and with it projecting towers and defensible roofs. To a certain extent, as at Burton House, these were replaced by turreted, walled enclosures, but, apart from the corner turrets, these were only marginally different from the walled enclosures common in England at the time. By 1687 this fortification had been reduced to mere decoration when Carton House, County Kildare, was built (Fig. 185).

Disappointingly little evidence survives about the appearance of houses in the years that immediately followed the Restoration, nearly all having been demolished. What is known shows that the models chosen closely followed those in England with the astylar Pratt-type house (Figs. 33, 34 and 35) quickly being established, as at Eyrecourt Castle, County Galway (Fig. 186), a double-pile house built in the 1660s with a central three-bay pediment in a seven-bay front, hipped roof, wooden eaves and dormers. Other examples include Carton House (1687) (Fig. 185); Kilmacurragh, County Wicklow (1697); Santry Court, County Dublin (c.1703); Castle Coole, County Fermanagh (1709); Molyneux House, Dublin (1711); Crom, County Fermanagh (c.1716);[28] Adare House, County Limerick, of the 1720s; Red House, Youghal, County Cork, and Stackallen, County Meath, and Beechwood, County Tipperary, these last two being seven bays wide but two and a half storeys high. Thomas Burgh's Dublin Custom House of 1707 followed the same pattern but blown up to an enormous scale, fifteen bays wide and three storeys high, with an arcaded ground floor.

An alternative to the pediment was a recessed three-bay centrepiece and slightly projecting two-bay wings, of the type pioneered in England at West Woodhay

185   Anon., Carton House, Co. Kildare (William van de Hagen (attrib.), oil, private collection (detail)) (remodelled).

186   Anon., Eyrecourt Castle, Co. Galway, 1660s (demolished).

Park, Berkshire. Late seventeenth- or early eighteenth-century houses of this type included Ardfert Abbey, County Kerry; Rathaspick, County Wexford, and Kilcreene House, County Kilkenny. It has been suggested that Beaulieu, County Louth (Fig. 187), dates from the 1660s, but John Curle is known to have carried out a great deal of work there in the 1720s and similarities with his work at Castle Coole suggest that the house is essentially of this date.[29] The grandest of this group of houses were Blessington, County Wicklow, with an arcaded five-bay centre and three-bay pavilions, built for the Archbishop of Armagh who was granted the manor in 1669, and Kenmare House, County Kerry (c.1726), with a seven-bay centre and three-bay pavilions.

The third type of post-Restoration-type house followed the Coleshill model in having no central em-

187   Anon., Beaulieu, Co. Louth, 1660s.

phasis. Examples include Burton House, a seven-bay house of 1671; Stillorgan House, County Dublin (1695); Shannongrove, County Limerick (1709); Kiltullagh, County Galway; and Ullard, County Kilkenny.[30]

As in England, the austere simplicity of Prattian Palladianism was well-suited to the undeveloped architectural situation in Ireland in the 1660s. However, whereas in England the last decades of the century saw marked advances in architectural skills which led to a much more confident use of Classicism in the early years of the eighteenth century, in Ireland this did not happen. The bitter struggles of the Williamite wars of 1689–91 led to much destruction, (including the burning of Burton House), and subsequent reconstruction might have been expected to lead to new directions in architecture, but it did not. As Loeber makes clear, although rebuilding after the war was widespread, there were few innovative designs and the wide-hipped Restoration style of house remained common into the 1720s.[31] Economic circumstances must largely be to blame. Ireland, being a much poorer country than England, had not been able to build up a comparable body of architects and craftsmen, nor had it benefited from the rise in architectural standards that the rebuilding of the City of London after the Great Fire of 1666 encouraged. More-

over, despite a brief recovery in the 1690s, the years between 1689 and 1730, especially after 1702, were not prosperous ones for Ireland, with the first decade of the century being particularly poor and the 1720s a decade of economic crisis. The economical Pratt manner remained dominant in Ireland far longer than it did in England.[32]

Thus, it is not surprising that nothing came of Sir John Perceval's bold 1707 scheme to rebuild Burton House to plans sought in Italy, perhaps from James Gibbs.[33] The Classical gatehouse at Kilkenny Castle, of about 1709 was exceptional in its architectural ambition and only a handful of houses built in the first two decades of the eighteenth century suggest a growing interest in the Classical orders. There are, however, a few examples of the contemporary English fashion for giant pilasters. Castle Durrow, County Leix (1716–18) a nine-bay, hipped-roof and dormered house of the Coleshill type, was distinguished by four giant Doric pilasters supporting an entablature and carrying urns.[34] Thomas Burgh's strange Oldtown, County Kildare (1709), and Castle Bernard, County Cork (1715), also had giant pilasters. But the most ambitious example was the east front of Drumcondra House, County Dublin, now All Hallows College, which is likely to predate Edward Lovett Pearce's front of 1727. This has a five-bay pilastered

188   Anon., Castletown, Co. Kildare, 1722.

centrepiece with giant Corinthian pilasters supporting a balustraded entablature, niches and elaborate architraves round the niches. Although this façade is a slightly clumsy composition, Drumcondra shows Classical ambition unusual for its time.

Thus, Speaker Conolly's great thirteen-bay, two-and-a-half storey, flat-balustraded house at Castletown, County Kildare (Fig. 188), begun about 1722, forms a much greater contrast with other country houses than it would have done in England. The origins of this design are still a matter of debate: there is no doubt that the Italian architect Alessandro Galilei provided Conolly with a plan, following his trip to Ireland in 1718, and the following June Robert Molesworth wrote to Galilei that 'Mr Conolly is going on with his designs and no doubt will be glad of your advice now and then', but there is no certainty that the house was built to this plan. Galilei returned to Italy by 1719 and when building work began in 1722 it sounds as if there was some confusion over the design, for it is reported that the cellars were arched before the elevation was agreed.[35] Moreover, it is questionable whether there is anything about Castletown, whose elevation is not particularly sophisticated, which calls for the intervention of an Italian architect. It is certainly very different from Galilei's impressive portico

at Kimbolton Castle, Huntingdonshire (1718), or the markedly Baroque unexecuted designs for English buildings that survive in the Uffizi, Florence.[36]

Castletown's plan, with its spinal corridors and its arrangement of rooms into suites with pairs of closets, would appear to be modelled on that of Pratt's Coleshill House, Wiltshire. The elevation owes much to the series of two-and-a-half and three-storey flat-roofed, balustraded houses in the first two volumes of *Vitruvius Britannicus*, particularly, perhaps, to Cliveden House, Buckinghamshire. Cliveden may also have been the source for Castletown's much-commented-upon wings, with their Ionic colonnades, although there are a significant number of other examples of such colonnades in *Vitruvius Britannicus*. Nor was the scale or design of the house quite as novel in Ireland as might be thought: ten years earlier work had begun on the new library at Trinity College, Dublin, built to the designs of Thomas Burgh, Surveyor-General from 1709 and architect of a series of substantial buildings in Dublin and elsewhere, including the vast Royal Barracks in Dublin of 1701. Trinity College Library is as tall as Castletown, has its windows equally close together, has a balustraded roof and, at twenty-five bays, was considerably wider than Castletown. Interestingly, both the library and the barracks have ground-floor rusticated arcades on the model of Palladio's Palazzo Thiene, which were to become a common feature of English Palladianism but which have no parallel in England at this date.

Castletown is a difficult house to assess and, except in its colonnaded wings, hardly deserves the epithet Palladian which is often bestowed upon it. Even the wings are probably based on the example of *Vitruvius Britannicus* rather than on Palladio directly. It is as a response to innovations in English architecture in the first decade and a half of the eighteenth century, encapsulated in that book, that Castletown should be judged, not as a specifically Palladian work. Nor was Castletown as influential as is sometimes made out; the main block found few if any imitators, and although the idea of colonnaded wings was to prove important, that was principally thanks to the architect who was responsible for executing them, Sir Edward Lovett Pearce.

After the long depression of the first three decades of the eighteenth century, the Irish economy finally began to take off in the 1730s, years which mark the beginning of a period of rapid growth in Irish foreign trade. Although economic circumstances continued to fluctuate, being particularly dependent on the state of the harvest, the general trend was upwards and this was reflected by

a new wave of country-house building which Maurice Craig noted was particularly concentrated in the mid- to late 1730s.[37] Accompanying this were significant stylistic advances.

If Castletown can be seen as a response to the publication of *Vitruvius Britannicus*, the same can probably be said of Mount Ievers, County Clare, built about 1731 (Fig. 189). This is a fairly literal transcription of the illustration of Chevening House, Kent, copying in particular the high, hipped roof and the stone cornice with pulvinated frieze, but with the windows grouped much closer together. Mount Ievers can be seen as an attempt to follow English Palladian fashion but with the proportions misunderstood. A similar but later instance of Palladian borrowing from *Vitruvius Britannicus* is provided by the centrepiece of Upper Castle Yard in Dublin Castle, based on Lord Pembroke's House in Whitehall, illustrated in the third volume.

Just when Irish architecture might have been vulnerable to the growing dominance of neo-Palladianism in England, an architect appeared who was to ensure that Ireland followed its own Palladian path, Edward Lovett Pearce. Pearce remains something of an enigma: he established himself in Dublin by 1726, became an Irish Member of Parliament in 1727 and succeeded Thomas

189   Anon., Mount Ievers, Co. Clare, *c.*1731.

190 Sir Edward Lovett Pearce, Bellamont Forest, Co. Cavan, 1729.

Burgh as surveyor-general in 1730 when he was only thirty-one, only to die three years later. Yet, during his brief life Irish architecture developed dramatically, for the first time competing with English architecture on its own terms.[38]

Pearce's architectural style is strongly imbued with contemporary Palladianism but there is no sign that he ever met Lord Burlington. Similarly, it bears the influence of Vanbrugh, his father's first cousin, but it is unclear whether Pearce ever studied or worked under him, although he did inherit the architect's drawings and one of his clerks. Evidence from his Grand Tour, which included Nîmes and Florence in 1723 and Venice, Vicenza, Bologna and Geneva in 1724, shows that Pearce studied widely. In Nîmes he drew the first century BC Maison Carrée; in Florence the *cinquecento* Palazzo Pandolfini. He vigorously annotated his copy of Palladio's *Quattro libri* with comments made at the villas and was in contact with Galilei.[39] It would seem that Pearce was an architect alive to the fashion of his times but capable of working out his own coherent interpretation of Palladianism. In this he cuts a rather different figure to the contemporary Scottish work of William Adam.

Pearce's tragically brief life meant that he had time to design only a limited number of buildings. Inevitably, the villa was of particular interest to him, as numerous schemes among his drawings show. These culminated in Bellamont Forest, County Cavan (Fig. 190), a single-storey, five-bay villa with a hexastyle Doric portico. Initial plans show this was to have had a Doric portico-in-antis with a single great room behind, flanked by lesser ranges. In the event, the portico-in-antis became a full portico, but one cannot help wondering whether Pearce was influenced by a design among his drawings by William Talman for a similar single-storey villa with a Doric portico-in-antis, low basement, quoins on the ground floor and windowed, quoin-less attic.[40] Interestingly, Bellamont's details are not pure Palladian, again showing Pearce's free spirit; the brackets supporting the windows look back to Rossi.

Bellamont shows Pearce at his most Palladian. If Desart Court, County Kilkenny (c.1733), is by Pearce then one can also see him being Jonesian. Here the model is the Queen's House at Greenwich, illustrated in *Vitruvius Britannicus*, although the elaborate window surrounds do not follow the austerity of Jones's original. At Stillorgan House, County Dublin, a seven-bay Coleshill-type house of 1695, he suggested keeping the existing house but Palladianising it by adding a portico-in-antis and rusticated arcaded wings.[41] Cashel Palace, County Tipperary (c.1730), takes the standard tripartite Pratt-type house, but varies it by removing the central pediment and adding Serlian windows in the side ranges, rusticating these and the central door and its flanking windows. At Drumcondra House (Fig. 191) Pearce placed superimposed Serlian motifs in the centre of an otherwise undifferentiated two-and-a-half-storey elevation, a motif that he may have developed from an unexecuted design by Vanbrugh for the Belvedere at King's Weston, Gloucestershire,[42] and which was to be widely used in Ireland in the following decades.

Rather than look for the specific influence of Burlington in Pearce's work, one should perhaps instead study the illustrations of Colen Campbell's buildings published in *Vitruvius Britannicus*, particularly in the third volume of 1725. Pearce's use of a low ratio of window to wall, his interest in rustication, particularly of Serlian windows and his use of single round-headed windows in the centre of a façade, all find precedents in Campbell's work. The elevation for the unexecuted royal palace at Richmond of about 1727 takes its essence from Campbell's north front of Houghton Hall, Norfolk, al-

though the paired rusticated columns flanking the entrance probably come from the designs for Whitehall published in Kent's *The Designs of Inigo Jones* (1727).[43] On the side elevation of Stourhead, Wiltshire, Campbell anticipated Pearce's use of a rusticated Serlian motif as a doorcase,[44] something that was quickly picked up by other architects at Brianstown, County Longford (1731), and Bonnetstown, County Kilkenny (1737). 9 Henrietta Street, Dublin, shows the influence of Campbell's Plumtre House in Nottingham, although Burlington's unpublished 30 Old Burlington Street is an alternative source.

If Campbell rather than Burlington was the more influential of the English neo-Palladians on Pearce, Pearce was able to transcend the original, thanks to his own architectural studies and the influence of Vanbrugh. His well-thought-out scheme for a royal palace at Richmond[45] bears comparison with anything his English neo-Palladian contemporaries might have designed, but his masterpiece is the Parliament Building in Dublin, begun in 1729 (Fig. 192). This was a building which Burlington would have been proud to include in his projected rebuilding of Whitehall. The House of Lords, for instance, is based on Palladio's reconstruction of the Temple of Venus and Rome, and in his memorandum explaining the design Pearce paraded his use of antique sources, a reference to 'those who have studied Antiquities' clearly meaning himself.[46] However, the use of a giant colonnade and continuous entablature is not something that the English neo-Palladians had suggested before this date, although it had appeared in works designed or executed by Nicholas Hawksmoor: the colonnades at Greenwich Hospital, the wings at Blenheim Palace and in unexecuted designs for All Souls College, Oxford, of 1720. At All Souls, Hawksmoor had described his use of such as colonnade as being 'after the Greek', and would appear to have based it on an engraving of a Greek building in Serlio.[47] Pearce, in his memorandum explaining the design for the Parliament House, describes the colonnade as being 'in the Manner of a Grecian Peristyle as described by Vetruvius'.[48] The two architects were clearly trying to achieve the same effect. What is not obvious is whether Pearce was aware of Hawksmoor's earlier attempts to build 'after the Greek'. It would be interesting to know whether Pearce ever saw Hawksmoor's designs for rebuilding the Houses of Parliament in London. With its giant colonnade, its domed, colonnaded octagonal House of Commons, its coffered, barrel-vaulted House of Lords, and its careful use of Palladian geometry, the Parliament building speaks of a sophisticated synthesis of Classical and Palladian sources which contemporary English architects would have found hard to match.

Pearce's early death cut short what would have been an extraordinary architectural career, but his work served

191   Sir Edward Lovett Pearce, Drumcondra House, Dublin, c.1730.

192 Sir Edward Lovett Pearce, the Parliament House, Dublin, 1729 (Thomas Malton, watercolour, National Gallery of Ireland, Dublin).

to send Irish architecture in a different direction, partly because he was assisted by the German Richard Cassels (or Castle), who was to be Ireland's dominant architect until he died in 1751. Pearce's influence is clear in Castle's work. Russborough, County Wicklow (*c*.1741) (Fig. 194), is based on Bellamont but with colonnaded wings similar to those Pearce had built at Castletown. Bellinter, County Meath, and Tudenham, County Westmeath, take the superimposed Serlian motifs of Drumcondra and use them as the main architectural feature in otherwise plain two-and-a-half-storey elevations. The garden front of Leinster House in Dublin is close to the side elevation of Pearce's Richmond Lodge. One feature which Castle introduced that was to prove fruitful in Ireland in the second half of the century was the semi-circular bow, seen on the garden front of Ballyhaise, County Cavan (*c*.1733), the side elevations of Belvedere, County Westmeath (*c*.1740), and Leinster House in Dublin (1745). Castle may also have been responsible for the diminutive canted bays on the en-

trance front of Carton (1739) which he remodelled. These were the years in which the canted bay was becoming popular in England, and while Castle and his clients may have been aware of this, it must be significant that, apart from Carton, Castle seems to have used only semi-circular bows. Pearce had considered using a pair of semi-circular bows in one of his villa schemes, but this had got no further than a sketch.[49] His inspiration would almost certainly have been Vanbrugh, who made extensive use of semi-circular bows, numerous examples of which survive among the drawings of his which Pearce owned. This suggests that the Irish use of the semi-circular bow, which became popular at a time when it was relatively rare in England, should be seen as a Vanbrugh derivative.

Although Castle designed the printing house at Trinity College, Dublin, in the form of a Doric temple in 1734, his work never attained Pearce's Classical purity. Nor, despite the Egyptian Hall at Powerscourt, County Wicklow (1731–40), which exactly repeated the width

193 Richard Castle, the Egyptian Hall, Powerscourt, Co. Wicklow, 1731 (destroyed by fire).

194   Richard Castle, Russborough, Co. Wicklow, *c*.1741.

and height of Palladio's model but not its length (Fig. 193), did he aspire to the correctness of the English neo-Palladians. The elevation of Powerscourt, with its mix of window surrounds, its three central round-headed windows and the busts set in niches above, would have been severely criticised by Burlington. Like the contemporary work of William Adam it has the raw exuberance of City Classicism. Indeed, it is remarkable how little influence strict neo-Palladianism had on Ireland before 1748, with porticos being especially scarce. Nevertheless, Pearce and Castle established a particular interpretation of Palladianism in Ireland, with such characteristic marks as the Serlian motif in the centre of a façade and the semi-circular bow. Its distinctive feature was the extended spread of wings and courts – introduced at Castletown but epitomised at Russborough – which give many Irish houses an extraordinary grandeur. Often these have vaulted stables, but their particularly Irish feature is the fact that they frequently include farm buildings. In this Irish Palladianism followed Palladio's example more faithfully than the English themselves.

The Americas

Architecture in the Americas before 1748 present strong contrasts with Scotland and Ireland, but also interesting parallels. One of the most marked contrasts is the diversity of the Americas. Whereas both Scotland and Ireland, each with their recognised capital, present a strong unity, the Americas were little more than a series of independent economic communities spread out along the same

side of the Atlantic: New England and Atlantic Canada; the Middle Colonies concentrated around New York and Philadelphia; the Upper South, Virginia and Maryland; the Lower South, North Carolina, South Carolina and Georgia, and the West Indies.

Each area had been settled independently and at different times, and each had a very different economy. Virginia had been established in 1607 and was dominated by tobacco plantations. The West Indies and New England were settled in the 1630s, the former dominated by sugar plantations, the latter by small farms. New York, which had been founded by the Dutch, was taken over by the English in 1664, with Pennsylvania and its capital Philadelphia founded in 1682. These were more diverse in their economies, but with the trade of their ports being very important. Finally, Carolina was founded in 1670 and was dominated by rice. Nor was there a single dominant town or city, although in the half century between 1690 and 1740 Boston, New York and Philadelphia blossomed into commercial centres rivalling such English provincial ports as Hull, Bristol and Glasgow.[50] The other main towns, also ports, were Newport, Rhode Island, and Charles Town, South Carolina (known as Charleston after 1780).

Despite this diversity, the architectural history of the Americas before 1748 follows a fairly standard path. Inevitably, the rigours of early immigration meant that building on a substantial scale was slow to occur. First off the mark were the West Indies where substantial fortunes were made from sugar in Barbados from the 1630s. Although the West Indies have suffered particularly severely from the devastations of hurricanes making the study of their architectural history difficult, one impor-

195   Anon., Bacon's Castle, Virginia, 1665.

tant house survives from the 1650s, Drax Hall on Barbados. This is built as if it were an English Jacobean manor, with thick brick walls and plenty of chimneys despite the hot climate. More ambitious architecturally but still clearly Jacobean in style is St Nicholas Abbey, with its main façade decorated with three elegantly curved gables, built after 1660.[51] The same approach can be seen on the mainland at Bacon's Castle, Virginia (1665) (Fig. 195), where the dominant diamond-shaped chimney-stacks, curved gables and projecting two-storey porch and staircase turrets show a similar Jacobean influence.[52] On Jamaica, Colonel John Colbeck's Colbeck Castle, dating from the late seventeenth century, with four great corner towers and a two-storey central arcaded loggia, also seems to look back to Jacobean architecture.[53]

Slowly, the Jacobean manner was displaced by the Jonesian hipped-roof astylar manner of the Maltravers design; but not without difficulty. In 1665 the Maryland Colonial Assembly employed William Smith to build a State House at St Mary's in the up-to-date Restoration manner, a forty-foot-square, two-and-a-half-storey house with hipped roof and cellar. He proved unable to fulfil his contract and was dismissed. When the assembly tried again in 1674 they were less ambitious and hired John Quigley to build a two-storey cruciform building, presumably along the lines of Bacon's Castle.[54] The anachronistic two-storey projecting porch proved hard to abandon. In South Carolina even some of the grandest houses of the early eighteenth century, for instance Ashley Hall (c.1704) and Middleton Place (built after 1704) maintained this essentially Jacobean feature.[55] It also took time for the single pile to be replaced by a

double pile. In 1687 Durand de Dauphine noted in Virginia that 'Whatever their rank they build only two rooms with some closets on the ground floor and two rooms in the attic above.'[56]

Fairfield, Virginia, of about 1695 – a reduced version of the Maltravers-type house, only one storey and three bays wide and retaining the diamond-shaped chimney-stacks associated with Jacobean buildings, but with a wooden modillion cornice and pedimented dormers – shows the colonists still struggling to come to terms with English architecture of the mid-seventeenth century, but with growing prosperity around the turn of the century came greater architectural confidence.[57] Critical to this were the series of ambitious government buildings in Williamsburg, the capital of Virginia. The main building of the College of William and Mary was laid out in 1695 on a grand thirteen-bay scale, with two stories and a hipped-roof with dormers over a basement, crowned by a cupola. This was joined in 1701 by the Capitol and in 1705 by the Governor's House, a five-bay, two-storey, hipped-roofed, dormered house with a cupola (Fig. 196). With this display the ideals of Restoration architecture, or rather of Jones's domestic work of the 1630s, common in England for the better part of a century, finally arrived in America.

The Governor's House, astylar, hipped-roofed and generally of five or seven bays, was to form the standard type (although without the cupola) for the substantial early colonial American house. It proved particularly popular in Virginia, where examples include the President's House of the College of William and Mary (1723), Westover (1730) (Fig. 197), Ampthill (c.1732), Shirley (1735) and Sabine Hall (1733).[58] Examples in South Carolina include the Brick House on Edisto Island (c.1725) and Fenwick Hall (1730).[59] Nor was the model restricted to houses in the countryside: a 1739 view of Charles Town (which had doubled in size and tripled in population since 1700) shows a large number of Maltravers-type houses.[60]

Growing wealth and sophistication among plantation owners meant that not all were prepared to accept a design that in England was already old fashioned. Archdale Hall, South Carolina (c.1706) (Fig. 199), would not have looked out of place if built in the suburban villages of London.[61] A two-storey, five-bay house, with a raised basement, it was framed by giant pilasters, had a single-bay pedimented frontispiece and brickwork in the latest fashion with glazed headers. Rosewell, Virginia (c.1722) (Fig. 198), a solid three-storey, five-bay house with keystoned segmental-headed windows and elaborate brickwork, looked more suited to Hanover Square than a tobacco plantation. Equally remarkable is Stratford Hall, Virginia (1738), the great house of the Lee family. This represents an attempt to create a great house suited to American needs, although to English eyes the effect

196 Anon., Governor's Palace, Williamsburg, Virginia, 1705 (rebuilt)

197 Anon., Westover, Virginia, 1730.

would have appeared rather old fashioned. A single storey, in effect a *piano nobile*, is placed over a rustic, with a square hall in the centre allowing cool draughts to blow through during the summer, flanked by corner pavilions of the type introduced into England at Clarendon House in 1664 and popular among large English houses during the second half of the seventeenth century. But these houses remained the exceptions.

Thus, by 1748 substantial, well-proportioned houses were not uncommon in the Americas, but attempts to match English architectural fashion were rare. Tripartite houses with pedimented centrepieces in the Prattian manner are noticeably absent. Most plantation owners were satisfied by the Maltravers model, which was given an air of sophistication it no longer held in England by its use at the Governor's Palace at Williamsburg. Not that owners were unaware of English architectural fashion; the doorcase at Westover was taken directly from a plate in William Salmon's *Palladio Londoniensis* published in 1734.[62] Even among the richest plantation owners, the Maltravers model remained common into the 1750s and beyond, as in Virginia at Cleve (*c.*1750), Carter's Grove (*c.*1750), Wilton (1750) and Hillsborough (*c.*1755).[63] However, it is noticeable that even where such houses were only five bays wide the scale on which they were built was much more substantial than equivalent houses

198   Anon., Rosewell, Virginia, *c.*1722 (demolished).

199   Anon.,   Archdale   Hall,   South   Carolina,   *c.*1706
(demolished).

in England. Nor was the model immutable. The later
houses show a move away from the use of dormers and
the introduction of a much shallower pitch for roofs.

Attempts at a more Classically sophisticated architecture tended to be restricted to churches, such as St Philip,
Charles Town (1711), and Christ Church, Philadelphia
(1727). English neo-Palladianism had had little impact.
The one exception was in Barbados where Sir Thomas
Robinson, an amateur Palladian architect, arrived as
Governor in 1742. Unable to repress his architectural
obsession, he soon ordered extensive alterations to his
official residence and undertook to build an armoury and
arsenal. As he did this without consulting the colonial
assembly there was uproar and Robinson finally left in
1747, but traces of neo-Palladianism on the island, such
as the rusticated, balustraded arcade of Clifton Hall,
suggest that his architectural influence may have been
significant.[64]

However, on the mainland things were beginning to

200   Anon., Drayton Hall, South Carolina, c.1738.

201   Anon., Charles Pinckney House, Charleston, South Carolina, 1746 (demolished).

stir. In South Carolina Drayton Hall (Fig. 200), built about 1738, reveals a serious attempt to create a Palladian villa with a tripartite ground-plan and central two-storey portico. Although uncomfortably proportioned and clearly not the work of a professional architect, Drayton Hall shows that the colonists were beginning to interest themselves in neo-Palladianism. The Charles Pinckney House in Charles Town of 1746 (Fig. 201) was an even more correctly Palladian design with a central three-bay pilastered centrepiece flanked by single bays.[65] In the early 1740s in Annapolis, the capital of Maryland, the Governor, Thomas Bladen, began building a substantial nine-bay house, astylar with a three-bay pedimented centrepiece, a basement and quoins.[66] It was a house that Sir Roger Pratt could have designed eighty years earlier, but for America it represented a major step forward. These three buildings were straws in the wind of architectural change which blew over the Americas in the next couple of decades.

THE CONTINUING GOTHIC TRADITION

WHILE CLASSICISM, AND in particular Palladianism, dominated British architecture in the seventeenth and eighteenth centuries it was not the only stylistic approach to be found during those years. A parallel strand of Gothic, sometimes called the Gothic Revival, can also be identified which, given Classicism's claims to be all-embracing, deserves some form of explanation. It is a subject in which Horace Walpole has always loomed large; this is not perhaps surprising, for Walpole had the gall to establish himself as the self-appointed guardian of the style and he has been taken on his own estimation ever since. His uniquely well-illustrated creation, Strawberry Hill in Twickenham, survives, and so, perhaps more importantly, do vast numbers of his eminently quotable letters. But to see Horace Walpole, or his circle, as the driving force in the formation of a new style, indeed to talk of eighteenth-century Gothic as 'Strawberry Hill Gothic', is to misunderstand the nature of Gothic architecture in the seventeenth and eighteenth centuries.

The incidence of Gothic architecture in England in this period has generally been marginalised by architectural historians. Examples in the seventeenth century are usually seen as 'Gothic Survival', the assumption being that the designer knew no better, while the standard account of the Gothic Revival in the eighteenth century commonly starts with Walpole – with perhaps a nod at William Kent's Gothic designs. The Gothic work of Christopher Wren and the Office of Works is acknowledged but seen to be without issue.[1] It can be argued, however, that instead of being a brief, rather frivolous episode of the 1750s, Gothic should be seen as a continuous undercurrent in English architecture from the sixteenth century, a document of antiquarian ideals and aspirations, not a stylistic footnote. Indeed, the assumption that the eighteenth century saw a Gothic Revival is debatable. Instead, we should perhaps be talking of the continuing Gothic tradition, although it is a tradition whose intellectual roots require further examination. It would be interesting to know how strongly Gothic architecture was associated with England's traditional parliamentary freedoms, and again the degree to which High Church principles should be associated with

Gothic design. To put the 'Gothic Revival' of the eighteenth century in context it is necessary to retrace our steps to the sixteenth century.

During the middle years of the sixteenth century English builders and patrons began to demonstrate a firm grasp of Classical architecture at such places as Lacock Abbey, Wiltshire (1540), Somerset House, London (1547), Kirby Hall, Northamptonshire (1570), and Longleat House, Wiltshire (1573), but this incipient Renaissance appears to have petered out in the 1570s leading John Aubrey to complain a century later that 'Under Elizabeth architecture made no progress but rather went backwards.'[2] This relatively pure Classicism was superseded by a style inspired more by late-Perpendicular buildings, particularly those associated with the court of Henry VII and the young Henry VIII. But, as Mark Girouard suggested in an important early article,[3] this should not be seen as a case of ignorant regression but as a deliberate stylistic choice. Three examples illustrate the point, Burghley House, Northamptonshire, Snape Castle, Yorkshire, and Wardour Castle, Wiltshire.

William Cecil, who began rebuilding Burghley House in 1556, would have been quite capable of obtaining a Classical scheme had he wanted one. Created Lord Burghley in 1571 and Lord High Treasurer in 1572, he was the most powerful man in Elizabethan England. However, the general form of the house, especially the west front of 1577 with its great central gatehouse (Fig. 204), deliberately harks back to pre-Classical, early Tudor and even medieval buildings. This is particularly clear in the impressively large, hammer-beamed Great Hall (Fig. 202) and in the vaulted kitchen. At the same time, much of the detail – of the windows, the mouldings, the chimney-pieces – and many important elements such as the staircase, perhaps modelled on that in the Hôtel de Ville in Paris, shows a firm grasp on advanced Classicism. Thus, Burghley House presents an overall impression of venerable antiquity coupled with evidence of the latest fashions in Classical detail.[4]

It was not only through architecture that Lord Burghley tried to present an image of respectable antiquity. An elaborate but optimistic pedigree, commissioned by Burghley from the heralds, survives at Hatfield

202   Anon., the Great Hall, Burghley House, Northampton-shire, c.1577.

House 'proving' that his ancestry stretched back into the mists of time. Illustrating this is a scene of two armoured knights fighting, one a putative Cecil ancestor. As if linking himself with that ancestor, Burghley's lavish tomb in the Church of St Martin, Stamford, depicts him clad in full armour. In fact, Burghley's origins probably lie in the minor Welsh gentry, a fact of which he remained sensitive, despite holding the highest offices of state. Thus, the Earl of Northumberland's suggestion that Burghley's line would benefit if it 'were planted in some stocke of honour' fell on receptive ears, and Burghley quickly agreed to a proposed marriage between his eldest son Thomas and Northumberland's sister-in-law Dorothy Neville. The marriage took place in 1564, and in 1577 the young couple inherited the manor house at Snape in Yorkshire. As if to stress this link with one of England's oldest families, Thomas Cecil transformed the substantial but unfortified manor house into a sham castle, complete with crenellations and towers (Fig. 203), although surviving fragments show that the internal decoration, as at Burghley, was carried out in an advanced Classical manner.[5]

Cecil's remodelling of Snape Castle makes an interesting comparison with Robert Smythson's luxurious remodelling of fourteenth-century Wardour Castle for Sir Matthew Arundell in the 1570s. Smythson would have had no difficulty working in a pure Classical manner. Longleat House was being erected to his designs at the

203   Anon., Snape Castle, Yorkshire, c.1577.

204   Anon., the west front of Burghley House, Northamptonshire, 1577.

same time, while many of the details at Wardour such as the door-cases are accurately Classical. However, when he came to refenestrate the castle Smythson deliberately kept the two-storey Gothic windows lighting the Great Hall, and used arched lights separated by mullions only for the new windows – a Gothic form which contrasted with the fashion of the 1570s for square-headed mullion and transom openings.[6] Arundell's medievalising attitude towards Wardour can probably be explained by his parentage. His father had risen to considerable wealth from a humble gentry background before being attainted on the disgrace of the Duke of Somerset in 1554, while he himself had so increased his fortune that by 1588 he was one of twelve knights listed as being of 'great possessions' and rich enough to support a peerage. Such a dizzy rise inevitably brought accusations that he was an upstart, and it is not surprising that Arundell wanted to associate himself with the Middle Ages.

As Dr Girouard has shown, this Gothic Revival in architecture was part of a wider revival of interest in the Middle Ages to be found among courtiers in the latter part of Queen Elizabeth's reign. This expressed itself in such medieval obsessions as heraldry, pedigrees, elaborate tournaments, fireworks[7] and a chivalric cult concentrated on the queen. It was a fascination that spilled over into the next reign where it can be seen in the Jacobean sham castles of Lulworth, Dorset (1608), Bolsover, Derbyshire (1612), and Ruperra, Glamorgan (1626). Bolsover, in particular, which was built on the site of a genuine castle and makes extensive use of vaulting, has a decidedly medieval feel (Fig. 205).

Although Elizabethan architecture is marked by a deliberate move away from Classicism, in form if not necessarily in detail, and a return to earlier, essentially Gothic styles, the clash between Classical and Gothic is less marked than it was to be in the seventeenth and eighteenth centuries. Such houses as Longleat show that

Classicism had been understood in England, even if it was still a long way from the purity to be found in Italy, but as the Gothic tradition was still very recent it was not difficult to revive it during Elizabeth's reign. Indeed, it could be seen as a natural continuation of an earlier style. The firm establishment of a Classical tradition by Inigo Jones in the years leading up to the Civil War changed this perspective. Classicism became accepted as the 'correct' style, the only style in which it was respectable to build, while Gothic architecture was dismissed, in John Evelyn's words, as 'Heavy, Dark, Melancholy and *Monkish Piles*, without any just Proportion, Use or Beauty, compar'd with the truly *Antient*'.[8] For the rest of the seventeenth century and for nearly all the eighteenth century the undisputed preeminance of Classical architecture was accepted by all educated men. During these years anyone who chose to use Gothic designs did so as a deliberate reaction against Classicism.

Inigo Jones had no time for Gothic architecture, and no qualms about encasing the nave of St Paul's Cathedral in Classical dress (Fig. 16). His contemporary Palladian enthusiast Sir Henry Wotton was outspoken in his contempt, arguing that pointed arches 'both for the natural imbecility of the sharp angle itself, and likewise for their very uncomeliness, ought to be exiled from judicious eyes, and left to their first inventors, the Goths or Lombards, amongst other relics of that barbarous age'.[9] This did not prevent the fellows of Oxford and Cambridge colleges deliberately commissioning buildings incorporating Gothic elements. During the first half of the seventeenth century, and particularly during the 1630s, a whole sequence of Gothic buildings was built in Oxford, including the chapel windows and hammerbeam roof of the hall at Wadham (1608–10), the purely Perpendicular chapel of Lincoln (1629–31), the chapel windows of Jesus (1621 and 1636) and the hall and chapel of St Mary Hall (1637–42).[10] It has been questioned whether this was the result of Gothic Survival – that Gothic was the only style understood by the fellows and their craftsmen – or Revival – that the fellows deliberately chose Gothic rather than Classical. It seems clear that the latter is the case. Members of the university were certainly aware of alternative styles, as can be seen from a proposed plan for University College of about 1634 which would have produced a Classical quadrangle with three projecting porticos, but which was rejected in favour of the executed scheme which is essentially Gothic in inspiration.[11] But, as Nikolaus Pevsner pointed out, it is the example of St John's College, Cambridge, that proves the point. Here, the new library (Fig. 206), built in 1624, was deliberately given traceried Gothic windows on the grounds that 'men of judgement like the best the old fashion of church window, holding it the most meet for such a building'. The statement was made by Bishop Valentine Cary of Exeter, the 'medium [of

205   Robert Smythson, the Little Castle, Bolsover, Derbyshire, 1612.

206   Anon., the Library, St John's College, Cambridge, 1624.

Bishop Williams] in his benefaction to St John's College'[12] who was doubtless expressing the latter's views. Williams also paid for the pure Perpendicular chapel of Lincoln College. The strength of the Gothic tradition in Oxford and Cambridge probably arises from antiquarian and ecclesiastical leanings – all the dons were clerics and many of the students were intended for the church – but also from dislike of radical change.

The case of Sir Richard Wynne is further evidence that knowledge and association with the new Classical style did not necessarily mean that it was used in all circumstances. Wynne, as Treasurer to Queen Henrietta Maria, must have had frequent dealings with Inigo Jones, who appears often in his accounts, but this did not stop him building a Gothic funerary chapel at Llanwrst in North Wales in 1633. As Howard Colvin pointed out, 'some seventeenth-century English funerary chapels were more convincingly Gothic than those of the Elizabethan period, perhaps suggesting that what in the sixteenth century had been unconscious conservatism, could in the seventeenth be a deliberate stylistic choice on the part of the patron'.[13]

This was definitely the case with Lady Anne Clifford. Few people could have been as exposed to Jonesian Classicism as the wife of the 4th Earl of Pembroke, the builder of Wilton, the greatest of the Caroline Classical

houses; and yet, when she retired on his death in 1650 to her ancestral Clifford estates in Yorkshire and Westmorland she deliberately put that Classicism behind her. In a positive orgy of building intended to reassert Clifford influence in the area, Lady Anne set about restoring the family castles of Skipton, Brough, Appleby and Barden Tower, at the same time rebuilding or repairing the associated churches of St Lawrence and St Michael, Appleby; Outhgill, Mallerstang; St Ninian, near Penrith; St Michael, Brough; and St Wilfred, Brougham. New work on both the castles and the churches was in a style sympathetic to the original. At Skipton Castle, for instance, she restored the towers, which had been slighted at the end of the Civil War, to their original height (Fig. 207). All the churches were executed in an, admittedly not particularly ambitious Gothic manner, without a trace of the Classicism which she would have been quite capable in some degree of imposing on her workmen had she so wanted.[14] Instead, she wished to stress the antiquity of the Clifford line and its connections with the great families of medieval England, the Lucys, Berkeleys, Nevilles and Percys, something which she did through an obsessive use of heraldry: there are seventeen shields of arms on her father's tomb, twenty-four on her own. This could best be done by using the Gothic style and ignoring Classicism.

An equally overt statement was made by Sir Robert Shirley when he built an almost pure Perpendicular church at Staunton Harold, Leicestershire, from 1653 (Fig. 208). Shirley succeeded to the baronetcy and his estate on the death of his brother in 1646 when he was only seventeen, and shortly afterwards inherited substantial sums on the death of his uncle the Earl of Essex. He soon proved himself a devoted Royalist who continued to conspire even after the king's execution. The result was a succession of spells in the Tower of London where he died in 1656.[15] Shirley's motivation in building such

207   Anon., the gatehouse, Skipton Castle, Yorkshire, c.1650.

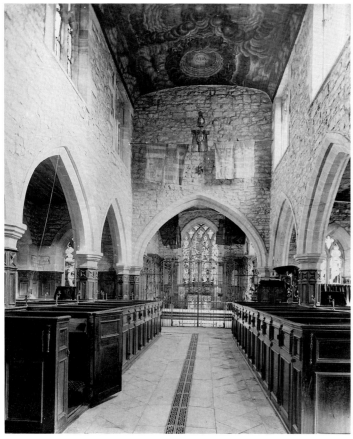

208   Anon., interior of Staunton Harold church, Leicestershire, 1653.

209   Anon., the chapel, Auckland Castle, Bishop Auckland, Co. Durham, 1661.

a church is made clear on an inscription over the west entrance:

> In the yeare: 1653 when all things sacred were throughout ye nation Either demolisht or profaned Sr Richard Shirley Barronet Founded this Church whose singular praise it is to have done the best of things in ye worst times And hoped them in the most callamitous. The Righteous shall be had in everlasting remembrance.

For a Royalist to build a church during these years was clearly an act of defiance, but that defiance was made even more overt by the choice of Gothic, inevitably making a link with the traditions of the Church of England, when it would have been possible to find craftsmen who could have built the church in a manner that was at least superficially Classical, as happened at the contemporary church at Berwick-upon-Tweed.

It is not surprising that Shirley should have chosen a church as his symbol of defiance, for under the Commonwealth the Church of England suffered severely, and this was particularly true of the bishops, whose offices were abolished and estates and palaces sold. Those returning at the Restoration often found their palaces badly neglected or partly demolished, and, as a result, the bishops were among the most active builders in the early 1660s. The most noteworthy example of this was the rebuilding of the Great Hall at Lambeth Palace, the Archbishop of Canterbury's London seat, by Archbishop Juxon in 1660–3 (Fig. 211). The use of Gothic traceried windows and a hammer-beam roof has led some commentators to assume that Juxon was unable to find an architect capable of designing a pure Classical building.[16] But contemporary work in a similar vein by other bishops suggests that Juxon deliberately chose this style. At Durham Cathedral, Bishop Cosin installed new woodwork in 1663–5 that is Gothic in form with some Renaissance detail, the finest surviving example being the great font.[17] In the castle at Durham, Cosin restored the Great Hall in 1662–3 and specifically ordered that the windows of his new staircase tower should match those of the tower at the other end of the north front with their pre-Classical hood-moulds, mullions and arched lights.[18] At his other palace of Bishop Auckland, County Durham, Cosin had to make good the damage done by Sir Arthur Haselrigg, including the demolition of the chapel. Cosin converted the twelfth-century hall into a chapel, refacing the exterior, adding the clerestory and commissioning new woodwork, all in a markedly Gothic manner (Fig. 209). He also turned the Presence Chamber into his Great Hall.[19] At Bishopthorpe Palace, Yorkshire, the Archbishop of York, Accepted Frewen, found the thirteenth-century Great Hall and chapel in ruins. He could have abandoned them and lived in the

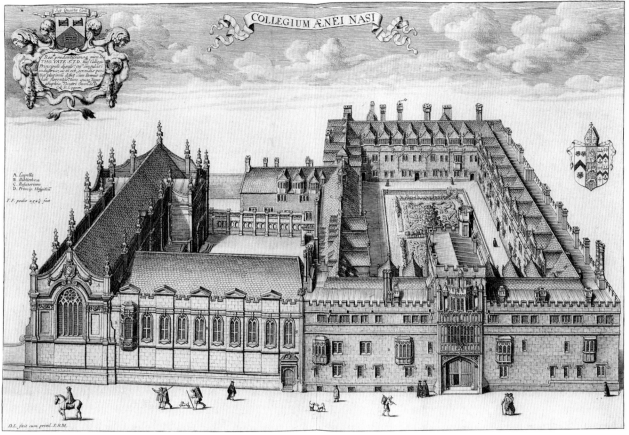

210   Anon., Brasenose College, Oxford, 1656, from Daniel Loggan's *Oxonia Illustrata* (1675).

211   Anon., the Great Hall, Lambeth Palace, London, 1660.

extensive north wing or rebuilt the palace to a Classical plan. Instead, like Cosin, he maintained the archaic medieval plan, restored the chapel and rebuilt the Great Hall.[20] Similarly, the cathedral at Lichfield, Staffordshire, had been extensively damaged during the Civil War, losing its spire and much of its roof. Between 1662 and 1669 it was restored by Bishop Hacket in a Gothic manner, with even the spire being rebuilt.[21]

Had these bishops wanted to build in a Classical manner there would have been no shortage of craftsmen capable of doing so, for knowledge of Classicism was widely distributed by the 1660s, even if the understanding may have been limited. Indeed, the combination of Gothic forms with quite pure Classical elements, which had been anticipated in the Chapel and Library at Brasenose College, Oxford, built in 1656–66 (Fig. 210), makes it clear that this mixed style was deliberate. The bishops must have chosen to use Gothic forms and maintain medieval models, in particular the great hall which secular peers were abandoning, to emphasise the antiquity of their buildings and so reassert episcopal continuity after the unfortunate break forced by the Commonwealth.[22] By the time the new Bishop's Palace at Lichfield was built in 1685–9 this sensitivity had worn off, and the design is unambiguously Classical.

212   Anon., Hoghton Tower, Lancashire, 1692.

For the rest of the seventeenth century and into the early eighteenth century the Gothic stream runs low but does not dry up. These decades saw the final triumph of Classicism as it spread to all levels of building across the whole country, but Gothic work continued in two branches, in domestic architecture where the antiquarian interests of a number of aristocrats were expressed in medievalising references, and in public buildings, especially churches, where respect for existing fabric meant that alterations were carried out in a sympathetic style. A surprising number of examples of the former have been identified and others may remain to be discovered, masquerading as earlier work.[23]

Sometimes, as at Skipton Castle, these came about as the result of restoring Civil War damage. Chirk Castle, Clwyd, was seriously damaged in 1659 when two towers and the curtain wall between them were demolished and other parts of the castle fired. The devastation was such that the family lived elsewhere for at least a decade and it must have seemed probable that Chirk, like many other castles after the Civil War, was to be abandoned. Sir Thomas Myddelton chose to return and rebuilt the demolished east front between 1672 and 1678, repeating the original appearance of the castle, rather than rebuilding it in a more fashionable style.[24] Hoghton Tower, Lancashire, was also severely damaged during the Civil War and this may explain why it was extensively remo-

213   Anon., Beaulieu Abbey, Hampshire, *c.*1714 (anon., pen and ink, private collection).

214   Anon., Shirburn Castle, Oxfordshire, 1716.

delled by Sir Charles Hoghton between 1692 and 1702. Hoghton's traditional leanings can be seen from the fact that he restored the Great Hall, but he also created a new axial approach centred on a new towered, castellated gatehouse range (Fig. 212).[25]

With some owners, antiquarian tendencies are clear. Henry Mordaunt, 2nd Earl of Peterborough, was fascinated by his ancestors, and in 1685 published *Succinct Genealogies*, a genealogical study of them, under the pseudonym 'Robert Halstead'. This included a series of plates of horsemen in armour which were repeated as overdoors at Drayton House, Peterborough's medieval Northamptonshire seat to which he refers several times in *Succinct Genealogies* as 'the old castle at Drayton'. It was, in fact, a fortified manor house, but Peterborough emphasised its castle air by adding a new castellated gatehouse between 1660 and 1676.[26] A similar antiquarian impulse, but on a much more massive scale, lay behind Hugh May's remodelling of Windsor Castle for

Charles II from 1675 to 1684. This is chiefly famed for its elaborate Baroque interiors which contrasted markedly with May's gaunt exteriors. There was no stylistic or financial reason – £200,000 was spent on Windsor – why May should not have also have designed elaborate Baroque façades, at least to the Upper Ward.[27] Instead, he chose to emphasise the castle-like feel by designing round-headed windows with a deliberately neo-Norman feel. There was probably more to this than respect for the antiquity of the castle. Windsor's particular significance was that it was the seat of the Order of the Garter, the oldest of the Europe's chivalric orders. Charles II's remodelling was intended to stress this, as can be seen from the fact that the largest and most lavish of the interiors was St George's Hall, scene of the annual festivities of the Order. On the outside the one decorative feature of May's work was the monumental gilt Garter star on the north front. May's medieval air was intended to emphasise this chivalric association.

215   Sir Christopher Wren, Tom Tower, Christ Church, Oxford, 1681 (John Buckler, watercolour, private collection (detail)).

On a smaller scale, Hampton Court, Herefordshire, was given a symmetrical castellated north front between 1706 and 1717 by Lord Coningsby, who was similarly obsessed with the Middle Ages and his forebears.[28] This can be compared with the 1st Earl of Macclesfield's rebuilding of Shirburn Castle, Oxfordshire, between 1716 and 1725 (Fig. 214). A symmetrical moated castle with four corner turrets, Shirburn preserves its medieval form, but most of one tower and all of two others, together with the walls that link them, are Macclesfield's work.[29] At St Michael's Mount, Cornwall, between 1731 and 1736, Sir John St Aubyn, under the influence of the celebrated local antiquarian William Borlase, re-modelled what had become an almost derelict building into an occasional retreat, emphasising its castle-like air. His son, working in the 1770s, chose to play up its ecclesiastical tradition when he Gothicised the chapel.[30] All of these examples are based on earlier work, unlike Clearwell Castle, Gloucestershire, which was designed in a similar vein for Thomas Wyndham in 1728 but on a virgin site.[31]

Perhaps the most interesting of all these early Goths was the 2nd Duke of Montagu, to whom Batty Langley was to dedicate his *Ancient Architecture Restored* in 1742. Montagu, later a friend of the antiquary William Stukeley, had a fascination for heraldry and genealogy and was first Grand Master of the newly revived Order of the Bath. A large collection of his Gothic designs survives at Boughton, one, an elevation for a symmetrical castle-style house, must predate 1718. Others show him adapting medieval structures to the demands of eighteenth-century country-house life. Most of these schemes seem to have been hypothetical, but Montagu was responsible for designing the steward's house in Clitheroe Castle, Lancashire (1740), in a deliberately spare style without plinth, cornice, architraves or other ornaments and with 'plane comon iron casements' rather than sash windows. Tantalising references to Ditton, his favourite country house near Windsor, in 1733 refer to 'that enchanted Island, fortification, tents, Cabins, draw bridge'. Montagu considered rebuilding Weekly Hall Farm on his Boughton estate in Northamptonshire as an irregular castellated structure. However, his most substantial work was at Beaulieu Abbey, Hampshire, where in about 1714 Montagu turned the monastic gatehouse into a castle-style house in the manner of his drawings, complete with moat, drawbridges, walls and corner towers (Fig. 213). When the duke died in 1749 Stukeley noted sadly:

> We had exactly the same taste for old family concerns, genealogy, pictures, furniture, coats of arms, the old way of building and gardening . . . [also] in a general imitation of pure nature in the Gothic architecture, in painted glass, in the open-hearted, candid designing and free manner of conversation.[32]

The other Gothic strand was dominated by the Office of Works. Christopher Wren was the first English Classical architect to argue that Gothic buildings should be completed or repaired in a manner sympathetic to the original. The Sheldonian Theatre in Oxford, built in 1663–9, is one of Wren's earliest works. It is designed in a firm Classical manner, but opposite it is a doorway surmounted by a Gothic ogee inserted into the fifteenth-century Divinity Schools in 1669, almost certainly by Wren (Fig. 216). This is the first sign of a principle which Wren was later to enunciate when asked to complete Tom Tower at Christ Church, Oxford, in 1681, that it 'ought to be Gothick to agree with the Founders worke' (Fig. 215).[33]

The Divinity School door was the first in a long series of Gothic works, often of remarkable ambition, carried out by Wren and his colleagues at the Office of Works, Nicholas Hawksmoor and William Dickinson, together with John James who, while never holding an Office of Works position, was closely connected with both Wren

216   Sir Christopher Wren, doorcase (right) inserted in the Divinity School, Oxford, 1669, from Daniel Loggan's *Oxonia Illustrata* (1675).

and Hawksmoor. Unfortunately, the architect of the earliest and most ambitious of this group of churches, St Mary Aldermary in the City of London (1681) (Fig. 217), with its shallow plaster domes intended to look like fan vaulting, is unknown.[34] This was followed by St Alban, Wood Street, City of London (1682); designs for rebuilding St Mary, Warwick, after the fire of 1694 (these were not executed, but the church as rebuilt by Sir William Wilson, was Gothic); St Dunstan-in-the-East, City of London, which was 'new beautified' with windows and steeple 'of modern Gothic' in 1698; extensive repairs, including rebuilding the front of the north transept, at Westminster Abbey from 1698–1722; the tower of St Christopher-le-Stocks, City of London (1712); the tower of St Michael, Cornhill, City of London, begun by Wren in 1715 but completed by Hawksmoor in 1718–22; Hawksmoor's north quadrangle of All Souls

College, Oxford, 1716–35; the west towers at Westminster Abbey begun by Hawksmoor in 1735 and completed by James in 1745 (Fig. 218), and the repair, recasing and raising of the tower of St Margaret, Westminster, by James in 1735.

Like most architects throughout the eighteenth century, neither Wren nor his colleagues had any doubts about the superiority of Classical architecture. Indeed, it was Wren's Classical belief in the need for a building to be uniform that lay behind his acceptance of Gothic, as he explained when putting forward plans for the restoration of Westminster Abbey in 1713:

I have made a design which will not be very expensive, but light, and still in the Gothic form, and of a style with the rest of the structure, which I would strictly adhere to throughout the whole intention: to

217   Anon., interior of St Mary Aldermary, City of London, 1681.

deviate from the whole form would be to run into a disagreeable mixture, which no person of good taste could relish . . . for all these Additions I have prepared perfect Draughts & Models, such as I conceive may agree with the original Scheme of the old Architect, without any modern Mixtures to show my own Inventions.[35]

John James's comments at Lincoln Cathedral show a similar desire to remain in keeping. Called in at the same time as James Gibbs in 1726 he suggested 'making the heads of all the apertures . . . with the pointed angular arch . . . after the Gothick manner in which the whole Church is built [rather] than the semicircular arch as drawn by Mr Gibbs, and consequently the ornaments about them of the same style'. For structural reasons, both James and Gibbs suggested removing the spires on the west towers, but James thought that Gibbs's proposed cupolas would not 'add any beauty, [and] may do great mischief', suggesting instead 'thin peramidal acroteria [in the corners], after the Gothick manner'.[36]

However, when Wren stated that Tom Tower should be Gothic 'to agree with the Founder's work'[37] he was revealing a secondary motivation on top of the Classical idea of congruity, which fits closely with the antiquarian attitude discussed above, a historical respect for the founder of the college. Hawksmoor repeated the point in his explanation of the designs for All Souls in 1715:

I must ask Leave to Say Somthing in favour of ye Old Quadrangle, built by your most Revd founder, for altho this may have Some faults yet it is not without its virtues. This building is Strong and durable much more firm than any of Your New buildings, because they have not ye Substance nor Workmanship, and I am Confident that much Conveniency and beauty, may be added to it, wheras utterly destroying or barbarously altering or mangleing it, wou'd be useing ye founder Cruelly, and a Loss to ye present possessours.[38]

In an age when respect for an institution or a family was significantly enhanced by its antiquity, it is not surprising that the importance of preserving and enhancing buildings which demonstrated that antiquity was to be an important element in the use of Gothic architecture in the eighteenth century, as it seems to have been in the seventeenth century.

This Office of Works Gothic tradition is often seen as a self-contained episode,[39] but William Kent's early Gothic work needs to be placed firmly within it. Although Kent's use of Gothic detail may differ from that of Wren, Hawksmoor, Dickinson and James – as they do from each other – the spirit remains the same. Kent, who returned to England in 1719 and joined the Office of Works that year, would have known the extensive Gothic work, particularly in Westminster, of Hawksmoor and James in the 1720s and 1730s. His own Gothic work – a gateway in the Clock Court at Hampton Court (1732), a screen enclosing the Courts of Chancery and the King's Bench in Westminster Hall in (1739), a pulpit and choir furniture in York Minster (1741), a choir screen in Gloucester Cathedral (1741) – shows a similar pattern of alterations in a sympathetic manner to ancient royal or ecclesiastical buildings. Indeed Juliet Allan's account of Kent's work at Hampton Court stressed his debt to Wren's Tom Tower and suggests that Hawksmoor's influence may also have been significant.[40]

While Kent's role in the mid-eighteenth-century Gothic Revival has never been doubted, Hawksmoor's Gothic has always been seen to be too idiosyncratic to have had much impact, partly because his towers at Westminster Abbey mix Classical with Gothic details. Interestingly, this was not Hawksmoor's original intention. As recently discovered drawings show, his first designs made around 1724 were pure Gothic, and it was only the final design of 1735 that included Classical details, in particular emphatic cornices intended to throw off the water.[41] Kent's influence was in the main direct, through the effect of his work on followers like Daniel Garrett, John Vardy and James Paine, but was partly based on the publication of a number of his Gothic schemes in Vardy's *Some Designs of Mr Inigo Jones and Mr*

218   Nicholas Hawksmoor, west towers of Westminster Abbey, London, 1735 (Antonio Joli, oil, Dean and Chapter of Westminster).

William Kent (1744). However, Dr Eileen Harris's reassessment of Batty Langley, author of *Ancient Architecture Restored and Improved by a Great Variety of Grand and Usefull Designs, entirely new in the Gothick Mode for ornamenting of Buildings and Gardens* (1742), suggests that Langley was inspired to write the book by Hawksmoor's work at Westminster Abbey. This was the first book published on Gothic architecture, and one which was to be a major source for Gothic designers in the mid-eighteenth century, although not without a certain disapproval from the connoisseurs. But, as Dr Harris put it 'For the few articulate but equally frivolous "Goths" who fulminated loudly over Langley's massacre of the venerable style, there were many silent "church wardens and country gentlemen" willing to apply his new order to "minor purposes"'.[42]

Kent's real significance lay in the way that he differed from Wren and Hawksmoor by extending the use of

219   William Kent, Esher Place, Surrey, 1733.

Gothic architecture from ecclesiastical and collegiate buildings to domestic architecture. His work at Hampton Court, Middlesex, which Wren had largely remodelled in the 1690s without concern for the Tudor fabric, was the first evidence of this. Kent was called in to rebuild the Clock Court range in 1731, and, according to Horace Walpole, he too initially considered a Classical design, only to be prevailed upon by Sir Robert Walpole to work instead in a Gothic manner.[43] At about the same time Henry Pelham, an intimate of Sir Robert Walpole, approached Kent to design a house for him at Esher Place, Surrey, with its isolated fifteenth-century tower, which he had bought in 1729. Again, Kent at first considered a Classical solution, proposing a Palladian house on top of the hill looking down at the tower. He soon changed his mind, and in 1733 produced plans in which Gothic wings were added to the tower (Fig. 219).[44] Kent followed his domestic work at Esher with an ambitious plan for remodelling Honingham Hall, Norfolk, in 1737, for Walpole's nephew William Townshend, but this was prevented by Townshend's death the following year.[45] In 1738 Kent was able to begin the slightly less thorough-going Gothic remodelling of Rousham Hall, Oxfordshire.

Perhaps the most significant development of the Gothic Revival during the 1730s and 1740s was the fashion for informally laid-out gardens and parks ornamented with occasional buildings. As such buildings were relatively cheap and not restricted by the need to be functional, they encouraged architectural invention, and it was chiefly through this medium that the use of Gothic began to spread and become a fashion that was not restricted to alterations of old buildings.

Vanbrugh was a pioneer of this style of gardening, and made repeated use of towers and castellations at Castle Howard, Yorkshire, Claremont, Surrey (1715), and his own estate at Greenwich (1718 and 1721). His tower at Claremont was probably inspired by Elizabethan hunting towers, such as that at Chatsworth House, Derbyshire, which he would have known. For Vanbrugh, Elizabethan and Jacobean architecture was a source of deep inspiration, not for detail but for plan and, above all, silhouette. The influence of Wollaton Hall, Nottinghamshire, on Seaton Delaval, Northumberland,[46] and Blenheim Palace, Oxfordshire, has often been cited, but his use of Elizabethan sources went deeper. Burghley House, Northamptonshire, is a building he would probably have known well, situated as it is on the road from London to York. Its north front is the closest model for the dramatic semi-circular bows on the east and west fronts of Blenheim Palace, Oxfordshire, or the garden front of the 'New Design' for Eastbury House, Dorset. The idea of a pyramid or obelisk over a gateway, found in the courtyard at Burghley, can be seen in Vanbrugh's designs for Eastbury and in a more squat form in the pyramid gate at Castle Howard. Burghley's south front has distinct similarities with the unexecuted west front of Grimsthorpe Castle, Lincolnshire, illus-

220   Sir John Vanbrugh, Kimbolton Castle, Huntingdonshire, 1707.

trated in *Vitruvius Britannicus*. At Grimsthorpe the massive proportions of the towers flanking the north front
have never been explained. Such proportions were a
regular feature of sixteenth- and early seventeenth-century architecture to be seen, for instance at Audley End,
Essex, or at Drumlanrig Castle, Dumfriess-shire (also
illustrated in *Vitruvius Britannicus*). At Castle Howard the
way the towers of the service range rise above the square
building recalls Hardwick Hall, Derbyshire. The thin
turrets proposed to be added to Sir William Sanderson's
house in Greenwich can be paralleled on the Little Castle
at Bolsover, Derbyshire, and the unusual octagonal turrets at Seaton Delaval are anticipated by Sir William
Sharington's tower at Lacock Abbey, Wiltshire.[47] In his
smaller buildings Vanbrugh experimented with Tudor
and Jacobean plan forms, both H-plans, as at his own
house at Claremont in Surrey (1709), and compact
plans, such as that for example at Chastleton House,
Oxfordshire.[48]

Vanbrugh's appreciation of antiquarian feeling is well
known from his defence of the old ruins of Woodstock
Palace and is spelled out in a letter he wrote to the Earl
of Manchester in 1707 about his designs for Kimbolton
Castle (Fig. 220):

As to the Outside, I thought 'twas absolutely best, to
give it Something of the Castle Air, tho' at the Same
time to make it regular . . . This method was practic'd
at Windsor in King Charles's time, And has been

221   John Freeman, the Ruin, Fawley Court, Oxfordshire,
1732.

universally Approv'd . . . to have built a Front with Pillasters, and what the Orders require cou'd never have been born with the Rest of the Castle: I'm sure this will make a very Noble and Masculine Shew; and is of as Warrantable a kind of building as Any.[49]

What distinguishes Vanbrugh from others interested in English medieval and Tudor architecture is that it was not essentially decorative detail that interested him – all the houses are clad in Classical dress – but form and massing. In this he had more in common with the earlier architects of such houses as Burghley or Bolsover, who combined Gothic form and Classical detail, than with his contemporaries. The one exception to this, assuming it is by Vanbrugh, is the 'Jacobean' design of the lower part of the screen at Audley End.

The Belvedere at Claremont was probably the first in a series of towers built with increasing frequency during the eighteenth century, principally on hill tops.[50] Sometimes these gave the impression of being complete castles. Stainborough Castle built by the 3rd Earl of Strafford in 1728–30 at Wentworth Castle, Yorkshire, with a keep and bailey is one of the most important early examples.[51] Freestanding towers, such as that at Whitton Place, Middlesex – probably built in the 1730s and certainly before 1748 – were more common. At least seven examples can be found before 1750.[52] Parallel with these towers was a series of buildings that looked rather to ecclesiastical architecture for their models. Perhaps the earliest example is John Freeman's ruin at Fawley Court, Oxfordshire, finished in 1732 (Fig. 221),[53] although Alfred's Hall at Cirencester Park, Gloucestershire, as remodelled in 1732, had a traceried window. The grandest is James Gibbs's Gothic Temple at Stowe, Buckinghamshire (1741), but perhaps the most remarkable design, although sadly it was never built, was William Stukeley's design of 1744 for a Gothic bridge capped by a flying spire for the Duke of Montagu at Boughton, Northamptonshire. Stukeley had built a 'Hermitage' with Gothic elements in his garden at Stamford in 1738 and designed an unbuilt Gothic mausoleum to be added to Weekley Church for the duke.[54]

By the 1740s, Gothic garden buildings were becoming common, but this decade also saw increased antiquarian interest in the use of Gothic. The rebuilding of Welbeck Abbey, Nottinghamshire, by Henrietta Howard, Countess of Oxford, from 1742, was a key example of this. Like Lady Anne Clifford, Lady Oxford was profoundly aware of her descent, as Horace Walpole noted after her death: 'The poor woman who is just dead passed her whole widowhood . . . in collecting and monumenting the portraits and reliquies of all the great families from which she is descended, and which centred in her.' Widowed in 1742, she retired to her family's ancient seat, which she found 'in allmost Ruines', and

dedicated the remaining years of her life to restoring it, principally in the Gothic manner. Her description of the new dining-room in 1744 reveals the impression she was trying to create: 'ye ceiling is to be painted with ye armes of my family, and ye marriages into it in proper colours to be hung with full length pictures in cedar frames those you saw in the dining room here with more, a Gothick chimneypiece designed partly from a fine one at Bolsover . . .'[55] Horace Walpole was ecstatic:

> It is impossible to describe the bales of Cavendishes, Harleys, Holleses, Veres and Ogles: every chamber is tapestried with them; nay, and with 100 other fat morsels; all their institutions inscribed, all their arms, crests, devices sculpted on chimneypieces of various English marbles in ancient forms – mostly ugly. Then such a Gothic hall, with pendent fretwork in imitation of the old and with a chimneypiece like mine in the library . . . so much of every thing I like, that my party thought they would never get me away again.[56]

This was the Great Hall, rebuilt in 1751, and a Gothic *tour-de-force* which at this date had no equal (Fig. 222).

The Countess of Oxford was not alone in her extensive use of Gothic during the 1740s. In Buckinghamshire, the Gothic west front of Hampden House was designed in 1741. In Essex, Thomas Barrett-Lennard, a keen antiquary who inherited the ancient Dacre barony from his mother, set about repairing Tudor Belhus in 1745. Walpole, visiting in 1754, declared that 'What he has done is in Gothic and very true . . . The chimneypieces, except one little miscarriage . . . are all of a good King James I Gothic.'[57] In Sussex, Wiston House, a great Elizabethan mansion, was reduced in the 1740s – one of the wings is dated 1747 – and given new façades created out of a mixture of reused Elizabethan material and Gothic elements. Of the interior, only the Great Hall survives, but that was given a vast Gothic chimney-piece and overmantel, together with Gothic doorcases and niches, all taken from Batty Langley.[58] In Oxfordshire, Sanderson Miller remodelled the chapel of Wroxton Abbey, an incomplete early seventeenth-century house, in the Gothic style for Lord North in 1747. In Warwickshire, Philip Yorke visiting Warwick Castle in 1748 noted that Lord Brooke, who had come of age in 1740, had done substantial work to the castle, and picked out particularly the windows in the state apartment 'made in the Gothic style and very pretty' and the 'chapel fitting up, the ceiling of which is Gothic and ornamented with different coats of arms belonging to the family'.[59] Brooke was anxious to stress the family's antiquity and in 1759, claiming collateral descent from the Beauchamp Earls of Warwick, persuaded the king to create him Earl of Warwick as well as Earl Brooke within two months of the death of the last Rich Earl of Warwick. Brooke's bank account[60] suggests that the alterations were the

222   Anon., the Great Hall, Welbeck Abbey, Nottinghamshire, 1742.

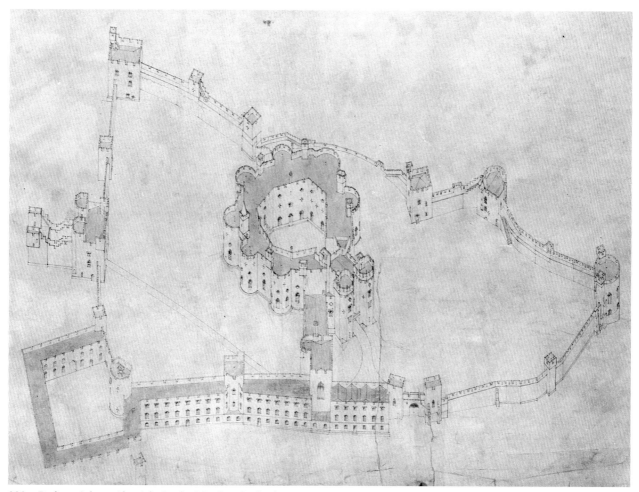

223   Robert Adam, Alnwick Castle, Northumberland, 1750.

work of Daniel Garrett who also worked in a Gothic manner for the 3rd Duke of Cleveland at Raby Castle, County Durham, from about 1745, and remodelled Kippax Park, Yorkshire, for Sir John Bland, which Dr Pococke noticed in 1750.[61]

The grandest contemporary example was at Alnwick Castle, Northumberland, which the Earl (Duke from 1766) and Countess of Northumberland extensively re-modelled in an exclusively Gothic fashion from 1750 (Fig. 223). Peter Waddell's description of the castle in 1785 shows that it was laden with heraldry. One hundred and ten eschutcheons bearing the arms of the principal families allied with the House of Percy decorated the great staircase. The duchess's portrait in the dining room was set in a frame with the arms of Percy, Lucy, Poynings, Fitpayn, Bryan and Latimer, while the ceiling was ornamented with coats-of-arms. The arms of the duke were placed above the breakfast room chimney-piece and his crest encircled by the Garter above that in the saloon, while the chapel was decorated with panels:

each Pannel round the Chapel has near its Top, a Coat of Arms, shewing the several Alliances with this great and noble Family; and for the information of those unacquainted with Heraldry a Label is affixed to each, on which is inscribed the Name of the Family whose arms are above it. The Centre pannels are much larger than any of the others, and on them are painted Labels shewing the Descent of this illustrious Family in direct line from Charlemaigne, and their Intermarriages with some of the most honourable and noble Houses of Europe.[62]

The earl and countess had good reason for this. No Percy had lived in Northumberland since the attainder of the 7th Earl in 1572, and indeed the male line had died out with the death of the 11th Earl in 1670. Since then the succession had twice gone through the female line to the countess whose husband, although a substantial Yorkshire baronet, was the great-grandson of a London haberdasher. By returning to Alnwick, rebuilding the castle in a Gothic manner and covering the interior with heraldry the Northumberlands were glossing over the recent rupture and reasserting their links with the medieval Percies.[63]

Thus by 1748, interest in Gothic architecture was spreading. It was to cash in on this that Batty Langley's *Ancient Architecture Restored* had been published in 1742. Only at this relatively late date, when his neighbour the Earl of Radnor had already given Radnor House a Gothic façade with crenellations, buttresses and traceried windows,[64] did Horace Walpole become interested in the style, writing to his friend Horace Mann that he was going to build 'a little Gothic castle'. Mann's response in February 1750 was not sympathetic: 'Why will you make it Gothic? I know it is the taste at present, but I am really sorry for it.'[65] Thus, even Mann in Italy was aware that Walpole was no prophet of a new style.

Although Walpole was later strident in his call for the accurate reproduction of Gothic detail, with Strawberry Hill becoming a pattern-book of medieval motifs, he was indebted to Batty Langley in the first phase of Strawberry Hill, begun in 1750 and completed in 1754.[66] Nor was he the first to apply archaeology to Gothic buildings. The Countess of Oxford had copied a chimney-piece from Bolsover at Welbeck in 1744 (Fig. 222),[67] while her Great Hall of 1751 is a remarkable essay in the manner of Henry VII's chapel at Westminster Abbey. The Welbeck hall is probably by Henry Keene, and the plaster ceiling of his church at Hartwell of 1753 was an even more impressive essay in Perpendicular vaulting. By contrast, it was only in about 1753 that Walpole began to be concerned with archaeological correctness, declaring to Sir Horace Mann that 'as Chiswick is a model of Grecian architecture, Strawberry Hill is to be so of Gothic' – although in application most of his carefully borrowed Gothic details are reapplied in a manner quite unrelated to their original context.[68]

Nevertheless, Walpole did help to popularise Gothic by building the first important Gothic house within easy reach of London. He also helped to develop it from being an antiquarian style associated with old buildings, for Strawberry Hill was effectively a new house. But Walpole was only able to build a Gothic house because Strawberry Hill was a suburban villa. Sanderson Miller's suggestion that Sir George Lyttelton rebuild Hagley Hall, Worcestershire, to a Gothic design in 1752 was quickly squashed and a standard Palladian great house was built instead.[69] Gothic was not considered a suitable style for a new seat, only a Classical building would do. Similarly, when Miller, who as early as 1744 had rebuilt the south and east fronts of his own Tudor house at Radway, Warwickshire, in a Gothic manner, designed the new Shire Hall at Warwick in 1754 there was no suggestion that Gothic would be an appropriate style for a public building, and a handsome Classical façade was built instead. As Walpole wrote to Mann 'The Grecian is proper only for magnificent and public building.'[70] Nor was Gothic deemed appropriate for London. Lady

Pomfret's house in Arlington Street, begun in 1757, is the one exception.[71]

By 1748, Gothic design had been accepted as a respectable way of completing earlier ecclesiastical and collegiate buildings, partly out of architectural propriety, partly out of antiquarian respect. It was seen as an appropriate way to alter older houses, particularly by owners anxious to stress the antiquity of their line, and as a suitable style for garden buildings intended to give a *frisson* of romance.

With the building boom that followed the Peace of Aix-la-Chapelle in 1748 the popularity of domestic Gothic began to spread. It seems to have been thought particularly appropriate for bishops' palaces. In 1753 Horace Walpole visiting Gloucester noted that 'The Bishop's house is pretty and restored to the Gothic by the last Bishop', that is Martin Benson, bishop from 1735 to 1752, who had commissioned Kent's Gothic screen for the cathedral.[72] Joseph Butler, Bishop of Durham employed Sanderson Miller to Gothicise the interior of Durham Castle in 1751–2, leaving it to Miller

> to settle the whole plan as he thinks best . . . as he is a master and I ignorant in these Matters, I ought to reform my Tastes by his, if I find them different, which I have ye beauty to say I do not', adding that 'Our People at Durham do not much understand the Kind of Antique Work.[73]

At Hartlebury Castle, Worcestershire, Keene refitted and reroofed the chapel in the Gothic manner with plaster vaulting based on Henry VII's chapel for the Bishop of Worcester in about 1750 (Fig. 226). That year Sanderson Miller added Gothic bays to Adlestrop Park, Gloucestershire, for Sir William Leigh, and first provided advice for Sir Roger Newdigate at Arbury Hall, Warwickshire, beginning another major scheme of Gothic remodelling that would last into the 1780s.

Despite the example of Lady Anne Clifford and Sir Robert Shirley, few Gothic parish churches were built in the first half of the eighteenth century. At Werrington, Cornwall, St Martin's was rebuilt on a new site in 1742 with a Gothic exterior and Classical interior, but as this arose from the laying-out of the park the choice of Gothic probably owes more to the fashion for Gothic garden buildings. In 1747–8 Sanderson Miller rebuilt the tower of Wroxton church with an 'octagon of stone', but that again was probably principally inspired by the role the tower could play in Lord North's garden. After 1748, this began to change and by 1751 Dr Pococke could notice that the church at Retford had been 'new modelled after the Modern Gothick taste',[74] and in the early 1750s a number of Gothic churches were built: Shobdon, Herefordshire (1752–6); Edward Woodward's Preston-on-Stour, Warwickshire (1752); Henry Keene's Hartwell church, Buckinghamshire

224   John Chute, Donington Grove, Berkshire, 1763.

225   John Townesend, ceiling of the Convocation House, Oxford, 1758.

226   Henry Keene, the chapel, Hartlebury Castle, Worcestershire, *c.*1750.

(1753); Wicken church, Northamptonshire, by Thomas Prowse and John Sanderson (1753); the chancel of Hagley church, Warwickshire, by Sanderson Miller (1754); William Robinson's church at Stone, Staffordshire (1754), and a new nave and transepts for Kineton church, Warwickshire, by Sanderson Miller (1756). However, despite these examples, Classicism remained the dominant style for new churches throughout the century. Even where old churches were improved or steeples rebuilt, the new work was as likely to be Classical as Gothic,[75] while many Gothic churches were little more than Classical buildings tricked out with Gothic detail. An exception to this was Francis Hiorn's Tetbury church of 1777 with its immensely tall, thin piers, but it was not until the nineteenth century, and particularly the Million Pound Act of 1818, that it became as common to build a Gothic church as a Classical one.

Completely new Gothic houses were slow to be built. Elvills, built by Stiff Leadbetter for Sir John Elwill between 1758 and 1763 at Englefield Green, near Windsor, a common area for villas, is perhaps the first. Away from London the first Gothic house that was not a villa was probably Donnington Grove, Berkshire, which was

designed in 1763 by John Chute for the antiquary James Pettit Andrews (Fig. 224). Andrews's antiquarian inclinations probably explain the style, but the land had Gothic associations: there had been a medieval priory at Donnington, and the ruined tower of Donnington Castle sat on the hill above. Classical authority was beginning to crumble but symmetry still prevailed.

However accurate its use of detail, Gothic architecture in eighteenth-century England was an associational and decorative movement. In particular, the structural tradition of Gothic vaulting was lost between the early eighteenth century – the last structural vault in England was that of the Convocation House in Oxford (Fig. 225), built by John Townesend in 1758–9, which ironically replaced a seventeenth-century plaster vault – and its revival at St Luke, Chelsea, in 1820.[76] Except, perhaps, in the case of James Essex, such research as there was into medieval architecture went into the accurate reproduction of detail not into the structural qualities of Gothic buildings. In this the English contrast strongly with the French, where interest in Gothic architecture was principally in its structural potential, not in its detail.

X

THE PALLADIAN INTERIOR AND THE IMPORTANCE OF GARDEN BUILDINGS

Any account of Classical architecture in the eighteenth century has to come to terms with the challenge presented by Rococo, Chinoiserie and Gothic architecture and decoration. Were these a threat to the authority of Classical architecture as some contemporary commentators believed? Isaac Ware sounded as if he feared that Rococo could have been when he wrote about ceilings in his *A Complete Body of Architecture* in 1756:

> The *French* have furnished us with abundance of fanciful decorations for these purposes, little less barbarous than the *Gothic*; and they were, like that species of building, (for we will not descend to call it architecture) received with great readiness: the art [of good design] seemed upon the point of being lost in *England*: but a better taste has now prevailed.[1]

Two years earlier *The Adventurer* had complained that 'the Greek and Roman architecture are discarded for the novelties of China; the RUINS OF PALMYRA, and the copies of the capital pictures of CORREGIO, are neglected for gothic designs'. Similarly, *The Monthly Review* argued in 1758 that:

> Of all the antiquities that have been communicated to the world; of all the remains of antient monuments brought from the East, none can be compared with the ruins of Palmyra and Balbec . . . Such specimens of architecture as have already been communicated to the public by the learned and ingenious Editor of the Ruins of Balbec, with others expected of Athens, &c. will, we hope, improve the taste of our countrymen, and expell the littleness and ugliness of the Chinese and the barbarity of the Goths.[2]

Did these styles, particularly Rococo, represent a backlash against Palladian orthodoxy? The case of Gothic has already been examined, but what about Rococo and Chinoiserie? As they were found principally in decoration it is necessary to examine Palladian attitudes towards interiors and towards the use of non-Classical styles,

attitudes that can be paralleled in mid-eighteenth-century park and garden buildings.

As an architectural style Palladianism concerned itself with exteriors and with planning, not with the decoration of interiors. In the *Quattro libri* Palladio's villas are illustrated with a ground-plan and an elevation, and while some of the palazzi have sections, none provides much lead on decoration. The only interiors illustrated are Palladio's reconstructions of Vitruvian room-types, principally atria, together with those of a number of Roman temples. Scamozzi's *Dell'idea dell'architettura universale* is no more informative. Thus, although the painted interiors of some of Palladio's villas, particularly that of the Villa Barbaro at Maser with its contemporary frescos by Veronese, represent one of the highpoints of European decoration, this was not considered an integral part of the Palladian tradition by succeeding revivalists. Each generation of Palladians had to create its own interiors in the shell which a Palladian design provided. Unlike the best Baroque buildings, interior and exterior did not necessarily have to form an integrated design. This gave Palladianism a flexibility which helps explain its long survival at the heart of English architecture, for interiors could react to changing fashions while the architectural framework remained little altered. Architects and patrons could chose the latest decorative style, whether it was that of the Jonesian revival, the Italian *stuccadore*, the French Rococo, neo-Classical *grottesche* or Louis XVI, without changing the architectural style of their building.

Nevertheless, for the early neo-Palladians, for Lord Burlington, Colen Campbell and William Kent, the search for an authentic Palladian interior formed an intrinsic part of their creation of a coherent neo-Palladian architecture. With neither Palladio's *Quattro libri* nor his drawings providing a lead, they turned to Inigo Jones's interiors, with perhaps surprising results, for, while Inigo Jones may have looked to sixteenth-century Italy for his exteriors, his interiors reveal a wide mix of sources, with contemporary (that is early seventeenth-century) French decoration being particularly important.[3]

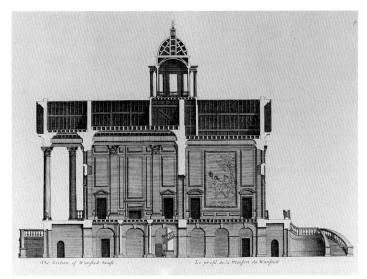

227   Colen Campbell, section of Wanstead House, Essex. *c*.1714, from *Vitruvius Britannicus* (1715) (demolished).

228   Colen Campbell, interior of Ebberston Lodge, Yorkshire, 1718.

In his interiors Jones made use of Classical details from Ancient Roman buildings, specifically using Palladio's fourth book as a source; of *grottesche* – as in the Queen's Presence Chamber at the Queen's House – an Ancient Roman form of decoration which had been revived by Raphael and his followers in Rome in the mid-sixteenth century and was used at a number of Palladio's villas; together with details from the work of more recent

Italian architects such as Domenico Fontana.[4] However, the presence of a French queen, Henrietta Maria, daughter of the King of France and one of Jones's chief patrons, had a powerful influence on Jones. A significant number of his designs for the queen at Somerset House and at the Queen's House, particularly of chimney-pieces, are taken directly from French models, either from drawings – some by an anonymous French draughtsman survive among Jones's own drawings – or from engravings. Chief among these were Jean Barbet's *Livre d'architecture, d'autels, et de cheminées* and Pierre Collot's *Pièces d'architecture où sont comprises plusieurs sortes de cheminées*, both published in 1633.[5] Trabeated, that is compartmented, beamed ceilings, such as those of the Banqueting House and of the hall at the Queen's House, were also important (Fig. 229). These probably derive from late sixteenth-century Italian examples. Jones's style of interior decoration remained influential into the 1650s, particularly at Wilton House, Wiltshire, and Thorpe Hall, Cambridgeshire, but after the Restoration it was displaced by lavish plaster ceilings inspired by contemporary French examples.

Jones did not see any contradiction between the restrained Palladian Classicism of his exteriors and the lavish decoration within. Nor, apparently, did he think there was anything incongruous about combining sixteenth- and seventeenth-century French and Italian decoration in the same set of rooms. As Gordon Higgott has shown, Jones's architectural beliefs were based on the concept of decorum, which in Jones's mind called for restrained exteriors but allowed greater licence inside. Jones compared a well-ordered building to a wise man who, outwardly 'carrieth a graviti in Publicke Places . . . & yt inwardly his Immaginacy set free, and sumtimes liccenciously flying out. as nature hirself doeth often tymes Stravagantly'. Thus, Jones argued that composed ornament, that is rich decoration, 'do not well in sollid Architecture and ye facciati of houses' but could be used on garden buildings and the inside of houses.[6] This was an attitude which subsequent Palladians were to follow, with interiors and garden buildings revealing a stylistic freedom of approach that is not to be found on the exteriors of important buildings.

Wanstead House, Essex, was Colen Campbell's first Palladian design, but the section of the house which he published in the first volume of *Vitruvius Britannicus* in 1715 (Fig. 227) shows that he had concentrated his efforts on the exterior and had not attempted to create a specifically Palladian interior. The hall and the saloon were intended to have raised, bolection-moulded panelling, characteristic of English interiors since the later seventeenth century, while the two-storey hall was decorated with giant pilasters. As houses such as Bramham Park and Beningbrough Hall in Yorkshire still show, such halls were particularly fashionable in the

229   Inigo Jones, the hall, the Queen's House, Greenwich, Kent, 1630.

230   John Webb, the Single and Double Cube Rooms at Wilton House, Wiltshire, 1648, from *Vitruvius Britannicus* (1717).

first two decades of the eighteenth century. Wanstead has gone, but Ebberston Lodge, Yorkshire, the only Campbell building with an interior that survives from before 1722, is firmly in this rather Baroque panelled manner (Fig. 228).

The only other interiors Campbell published in the first volume of *Vitruvius Britannicus* were sections of St Peter's in Rome, of the Banqueting House in Whitehall, of the hall at Castle Howard, Yorkshire, and of his own design for a church in the Vitruvian style. However, in the second volume, of 1717, Campbell illustrated sections of the Single and Double Cube Rooms at Wilton House (Fig. 230), together with a section of the grotto there, which Campbell believed to be by Jones. These engravings were to have a profound influence on Campbell's subsequent approach towards architectural interiors, of which he published a number in the third volume, of 1725, including a section of Mereworth Castle, Kent, and engravings showing the four walls of the hall at Houghton Hall, Norfolk, those of the Garden Room at Hall Barn, Buckinghamshire (also showing the decoration of the ceiling), and those of a great hall 'of my own invention'. In these Campbell moved away from the wooden panelled interior to the use of plain, plastered walls with architectural elements – chimney-pieces, pedimented doorcases, sculptural reliefs, niches, false windows – placed upon them. At the same time,

accurate Classical entablatures based on the orders took the place of the decorative cornices of such houses as Ebberston and Beningborough, where detail was often strongly influenced by Domenico de Rossi's *Studio d'architettura civile*. This change encapsulates the development of the neo-Palladian interior in the early 1720s.

These interiors show that Campbell had been looking closely at Palladio, the use of a shell motif above a door in the hall at Mereworth was taken from the exterior of the Palazzo Chiericati, but particularly at Jones. Houghton's two-storey square hall (Fig. 231) with its heavy bracketed balcony running round all four sides is modelled on the hall of the Queen's House at Greenwich (Fig. 229). Mereworth's hall is a circular, domed version of the same. The two flanking rooms in the section of Mereworth and the Garden Room at Hall Barn follow Wilton in the use of tabernacle-framed doors, dados and light-panels with ornamental drops between them.

Was this change one that Campbell worked out for himself or was it engineered by Lord Burlington? It is unlikely to be coincidence that the new style appears in Campbell's work after he came into contact with Burlington.[7] Certainly for Lord Burlington the question of an appropriate style of Palladian decoration was an important one which he worked out in his own interiors at Burlington House, at Chiswick and at other houses

231   Colen Campbell, the Stone Hall, Houghton Hall, Norfolk, 1722.

with which he was involved. His interiors rely on three main sources: Ancient Rome; *cinquecento* Italian interiors, particularly those in Rome; and Jones's work and drawings. Burlington recognised, around 1721, that Jones, unlike Palladio or Scamozzi, had used antique details culled from Palladio's book for his interiors.[8] Jones's own work was to prove particularly valuable as a model for the chimney-pieces and overmantels which played such a key part in early eighteenth-century decoration but for which there was no precedent in antiquity. The attention Burlington paid to the question of an appropriate Palladian interior and its dissemination to others can be seen in the proportion of his publications concerned with interiors. Through the publication of William Kent's *Designs of Inigo Jones, with some Additional Designs* in 1724, and subsequently of John Vardy's *Some Designs of Mr Inigo Jones and Mr William Kent* (1744) and Isaac Ware's undated *Designs of Inigo Jones and Others* (Fig. 232), such designs, particularly chimney-pieces with overmantels and trabeated ceilings, became a standard part of mid-eighteenth-century decoration.

It should come as no surprise to discover that Burlington and Campbell were joined by Nicholas Hawksmoor in this early development of a Palladian interior. Hawksmoor's use of Palladian and Jonesian motifs on his exteriors is paralleled within, where heavy coffered ceilings, decorated with guilloche but otherwise plain, were an important feature of his work in the 1720s. At Blenheim Palace, Oxfordshire, Hawksmoor was called back to fit up the Long Library and rooms on the south front from 1722 to 1725. The coffered ceilings on the south front could almost be mistaken for the work of Burlington, and are probably another example of Hawksmoor drawing directly on Jones.[9] In particular, the design of one of the ceilings, with an octagon set

232 William Kent, design for a chimney-piece from Isaac Ware's *Designs of Inigo Jones and Others* (n.d.).

within a square, follows that of the closet behind the King's Withdrawing Room at the Queen's House, a building which Hawksmoor, as Clerk of the Works at Greenwich Hospital, knew well. The same pattern was later used in the Claude Room at Holkham Hall, Norfolk, built under Burlington's direction. A more elaborately developed use of accurate Classical detail, including coffering, combined with a guilloche-decorated, trabeated ceiling can be seen at Hawksmoor's Christ Church, Spitalfields, roofed in 1722 and consecrated in 1729 (Fig. 233).

Early Palladian interiors reveal a marked tension between opulence and austerity, a tension born out of the conflicting evidence of antiquity, and, perhaps, out of tension between the views of Lord Burlington and other aristocratic amateurs and those of Burlington's protegé William Kent. It is a tension best seen in two houses only a few miles apart in Norfolk, both intimately associated with Kent, Houghton Hall and Holkham Hall. Kent, as seen in chapter six, spent ten years in Italy, mainly in Rome. There he examined Ancient Roman decoration and studied under Giuseppe Chiari who followed in the tradition of Raphael. He returned to England in 1719, working initally as a painter, but soon designing whole interiors and subsequently buildings.

At Houghton, Kent displaced Colen Campbell by 1725, the date of two designs for the saloon. Of the main rooms the Green Drawing Room is a relatively restrained example of a Jonesian interior with a guilloche-decorated, beamed ceiling based on that of the Banqueting House in Whitehall.[10] The others are much more elaborate, with brilliantly coloured decorative paintings combining scenes of the gods with luxuriant foliage set in a more complex pattern of decorated beams (Fig. 169). The ultimate source for this is Ancient Roman tomb and grotto decoration, something which was of particular interest to Roman sixteenth-century architects, particularly Raphael and his followers, including Giulio Romano. Cinzia Maria Sicca has shown how influenced Kent was by their work, the best-known example being the ceiling of the Blue Velvet Room at Chiswick, whose paired brackets can be paralled in a ceiling by Giulio Romano in the Palazzo del Tè in Mantua but which are taken from a drawing from about the 1540s wrongly attributed to Cherubino Alberti in Burlington's collection.[11] Another is the ceiling of the saloon at 44 Berkeley Square, which owes much to the concave niche of the loggia of the Villa Madama in Rome, and to the ceilings of the Sala dei Venti and the Sala di Psiche, both in the Palazzo del Tè. However, as was argued in chapter six, Kent's decoration at Houghton and elsewhere also owes much to his own direct study of Ancient Roman decoration.

Holkham is very different. Here, Kent began to fit up the interior but was only responsible for the hall and the

233 Nicholas Hawksmoor, interior of Christ Church, Spitalfields, London, 1722.

234 Giuseppe Artari, the saloon, Ditchley Park, Oxfordshire, 1725.

family wing. One drawing for the library in the family wing shows that Kent considered decorating the coving with elaborate painted foliage similar to his work at Houghton, but this was never executed. Compared to Houghton the feeling of the rooms at Holkham is one of the utmost restraint (Fig. 166). Instead of taking Ancient Roman tomb and grotto decoration as its model, the decoration of these rooms is restricted to the correct Classical ornament associated with the orders as illustrated in Palladio's engravings of Roman temples in the *Quattro libri*, with trabeated ceilings based on those of Jones.

The model set by Campbell, Burlington and Kent proved very influential. Elaborately painted decoration in Kent's manner is less common, probably because it was very expensive, although it can be found in his own later work such as 22 Arlington Street, in London, of 1741–50. It can also be seen at Mereworth where the date 1732 on one of the ceilings shows that some, at least, of the decoration dates from after Campbell's death in 1729. The influence of Bartoli is clear in the ceiling of

the West Dressing Room. The austere Classicism of the Holkham model is more common. On the grandest scale it is seen in the work of Henry Flitcroft at Wentworth Woodhouse, Yorkshire, but it proved particularly popular with such amateur architects as Sir Thomas Robinson at Rokeby Park, Yorkshire, and Thomas Worsley at Hovingham Hall, Yorkshire. In general, however, followers of the Burlington approach to the Palladian interior took a less extreme line, taking such elements as chimney-pieces, overmantels, doorcases and cornices from the illustrations in the various Burlingtonian publications (Fig. 232) or from the pattern-books which swiftly plundered them, but without feeling the need for the neo-Classical accuracy and Palladian austerity of Holkham. Often, Palladian elements were used as frameworks around which more lavish decoration, particularly involving plasterwork, was developed; and not every architect designing Palladian exteriors felt that they needed to be complemented with purely Palladian interiors.

The evolving Palladian interiors of Burlington,

235   William Kent, the hall, Ditchley Park, Oxfordshire, 1725.

Campbell and Kent were not without competition in the 1720s. The same years saw the arrival of Italian *stuccadore* who purveyed a very different, much more exuberant form of interior decoration based on elaborate stucco ceilings.[12] The first evidence for these is in 1710–12, when Giovanni Bagutti and one Plura worked at Castle Howard, but it was not until the 1720s that their work became common. In 1720 Bagutti and one of the Artari family – Giovanni Battista and his sons Giuseppe and Adalberto – executed the stucco decoration of the Octagon of James Johnston's house in Twickenham. In 1724 Adalberto Artari, together with Francesco Vassalli, is recorded working at Sutton Scarsdale, Derbyshire. This was a style particularly associated with James Gibbs, although fine examples of the *stuccadore* art from the 1730s can also be seen at Barnsley Park, Gloucestershire, Clandon Park, Surrey, and Moor Park, Hertfordshire. Gibbs's Octagon was followed by St Martin-in-the-Fields, the Senate House at Cambridge, St Peter, Vere Street, London, Ditchley Park, Oxfordshire, the Radcliffe Camera in Oxford and Ragley Hall, Warwickshire. However, it seems probable that the *stuccadore* rather than the architect were responsible for the designs they executed.

Like Gibbs's own early Italianate work, the rich Continental interiors of the *stuccadore* were in clear competition with the emerging Palladian style. And, as with Gibbs's exteriors, it was the Palladians who generally carried the day. At Wentworth Woodhouse where the vestibule in the west front of about 1725 had Baroque decoration, the great east range, begun about 1734, has correctly Palladian interiors. The clash of the two styles is clearest at Ditchley Park, where receipts from Artari, Francesco Vassalli and Francesco Serena survive for plasterwork dated around 1725, the most important example being the exuberant saloon (Fig. 234). By contrast the hall, for which a design drawing by Kent survives and for which Kent was paid for painting the ceiling in 1725–6, is immensely austere with great tabernacle frames for doors and niches, a clear example of the new Palladian manner (Fig. 235).[13] However, the division is not always clear cut. The work of the Anglo-Danish plasterer Charles Stanley, for instance, often takes the Palladian framework of tabernacle doorcases, bas-reliefs and trabeated ceilings and reinterprets it using the skills of the *stuccadore*.

Stuccadore interiors continue into the 1740s, but by the time building revived after the Peace of Aix-la-Chapelle in 1748 a rather more delicate style had taken its place as the fashionable way to design extravagant interiors – Rococo. This French style first appears in England in the early 1730s and is particularly connected with the St Martin's Lane Academy founded in 1735. Its chief strength was in the decorative arts, for example the work of the engraver and the silversmith, but it also had

considerable influence on architecture. Despite the efforts of Cornelius Johnston, whose engraved design for the British Museum of 1754 attempts a genuinely Rococo building, that influence was restricted to interiors and to garden buildings. It is debatable whether the architectural concept of 'movement' epitomised by the canted bay and by the work of an architect such as Sir Robert Taylor should be seen as influenced by the contemporary Rococo movement.

Although recognised, and often reviled, as a French import, English Rococo decoration developed in a very different way from its Continental source. Whereas in French interiors Rococo decoration is concentrated in carved panelling with the ceilings left plain,[14] in England such *boiseries* were rare, and decoration, whether in stucco or papier mâché, was concentrated on the ceiling. This was probably because the English fashion for collecting pictures required extensive wall space. One of the very few instances of a specifically English engraved design for such a wall scheme is a plate by Thomas Johnson dated 1758.[15] The finest executed example was at Chesterfield House in London, of which Lord Chesterfield wrote to Madame de Monconseil on 31 July 1747: 'je me ruine actuellement à bâtir une assez belle maison ici, qui sera finie à la Françoise, avec force sculptures et dorures.'[16] Other examples could be found at Northumberland House in London, Stratfield Saye, Hampshire, Woburn Abbey, Bedfordshire, where the doors in the Yellow Drawing Room are based on J.F. Blondel's *De la Distribution des maisons de plaisance* (1738), and Woodcote Park, Surrey – but were rare.[17]

As with some of the later *stuccadore*, for example Stanley, the English Rococo interior developed out of the Palladian interiors of such architects as Campbell and Kent, with wall surfaces still divided up into rigidly geometrical panels and the wayward curves of the Rococo restricted predominantly to stucco-work on the ceilings and to drops or festoons applied to the walls. This can be clearly seen at Kirtlington Park, Oxfordshire, fitted up in the late 1740s (Fig. 236). Here the forms – trabeated ceilings, pedimented doorcases, coffered niches, chimney-pieces with terms and elaborate overmantels – are all the commonplace of Palladian decoration, but overlaid with a Rococo freedom. Kirtlington also has a delightful room decorated with *singeries* painted by Andien de Clermont in 1745. Although ultimately derived from such late seventeenth-century grotesques as those of Berain, Audran and Gillot, *singeries* were to form a recognised part of the Rococo vocabulary. The first recorded example by Clermont, at Monkey Island at Bray, Berkshire, dates from 1738, and records of over half a dozen other examples can be found before he left England in 1754.[18]

At Kirtlington there is what might be described as a creative tension between the strict Palladian framework

236 William Smith, the dining-room, Kirtlington Park, Oxfordshire, 1745.

and Rococo freedom but this almost reaches parody at Claydon House, Buckinghamshire. Claydon was built for Lord Verney by Sir Thomas Robinson, a vigorous exponent of Palladian orthodoxy, but much of the decoration was in the hands of Luke Lightfoot, a carver. Robinson's firm Palladian bones can be seen in many of the rooms, but overlaying this, and frequently swamping it is some of the wildest Rococo decoration in the country, which reaches its apogee in the Oriental splendour of the Chinese Room on the first floor. Lightfoot's almost Irish extravagancies reduced Robinson to a state of virtual apoplexy:

> Mr Lightfoot's design for finishing the great eating room shocked me so much and is so much the ridicule of all who have seen or heard of it – and which when done yr Ldp will undo – that it would be want of friendship not to acquaint you thereof. I will undertake to do it on a different design in some measure parallel to and proper to the work of the Hall and the Ballroom. With regard to the Saloon and the Drawing Room, they are not so bad and their absurdities might be easily remedied. This may be done with regard to the great eating room at an easier expense than it will cost to finish what he has begun – and if done by him will indeed be what he expressed very justly – *such a Work as the World never saw*.[19]

This anglicisation of Rococo was noted by Isaac Ware in his *A Complete Body of Architecture*, published in 1756:

> the art [of good design] seemed upon the point of being lost in England: but a better taste has now prevailed. We should, in that danger, have declared for banishing whatever came under the denomination of *French* ornament; but, now we see it over, the art will be to receive these ornaments with discretion, to adapt them to the few uses for which they are proper; and to soften the luxuriant use, and blend them with better figures, till we have reduced them into a more decent appearance.[20]

Rococo is sometimes seen as a deliberate reaction to Palladian orthodoxy. The scurrilous lampoon of Lord Burlington, 'Man of Taste' of 1731, by William Hogarth is partly responsible for this. In 1735 Hogarth was one of the prime movers behind the foundation of the St Martin's Lane Academy, a centre of Rococo activity. But the relationship between orthodox Palladians and Rococo is a complex one, with some of the finest exponents of Rococo interiors, particularly Daniel Garrett and James Paine, emanating from Lord Burlington's circle. Isaac Ware epitomises this complexity. Ware was one of Burlington's protégés, publishing *Designs of Inigo Jones and Others* about 1733 and a translation of Palladio's *Quattro libri* in 1738. He was also a prominent member of the St Martin's Lane Academy and in the late 1740s he

designed some of the finest English Rococo interiors, those at Chesterfield House in London. However, in his *A Complete Body of Architecture*, which despite veering in some respects from standard Palladian thought was the nearest thing there was to a Palladian textbook, he violently attacked the use of Rococo. What is more, while some of the Chesterfield House interiors are Rococo, others are correctly Classical. Is this a case of severe stylistic schizophrenia?

One thing that should be considered is that *A Complete Body of Architecture* was published at the outbreak of the Seven Years' War and that its violently anti-French sentiment may not be representative of Ware's beliefs when he was designing Chesterfield House. Another clue comes in the division of decoration at Chesterfield House. The entrance hall, dining-room (Fig. 237), saloon or Great Room and library were restrained, relatively chaste Classical rooms. By contrast the French Room or drawing-room (Fig. 238) was lavish in its Rococo decoration, as were the boudoir and music room. Rather than explain this as the compromise result of the competing tastes of patron and builder,[21] the choice of style must lie instead in its appropriateness to certain rooms. Thus, the essentially feminine Rococo decoration is restricted to the two feminine rooms, the drawing-room and boudoir. Similarly, Isaac Ware's drawings for completing Leinster House, Dublin, in the late 1750s nearly all show relatively standard neo-Palladian interiors, but an elaborate Rococo scheme survives for Lady Kildare's dressing-room.[22]

As these two examples of genuine French Rococo show, the style was felt to be most appropriate for drawing-rooms, which were often decorated with festoons of flowers and musical instruments, and bedrooms and dressing-rooms, where *amorini* sometimes appear on billowing clouds with turtle-doves and cupids' bows. At times it did spread beyond the more feminine rooms, in particular to dining-rooms where garlands of vines, Bacchic emblems, goatskins and satyrs' masks such as those at Hagley Hall, Staffordshire, provide suitable motifs for the plasterer. In some cases, as in the staircase hall at Nostell Priory, Yorkshire, or in the domed hall at Nuthall Temple (Fig. 239), the principal public spaces were exuberantly decorated with Rococo ornament; but generally Rococo can be seen as fitting into the concept of propriety which overlays English Palladianism. It was certainly no threat to Palladian architecture. As Gervase Jackson-Stops pointed out: 'To a large extent rococo in fact became the official style of interior decoration, particularly for smaller and more intimate rooms, among this new generation of Palladians in the 1740s and '50s, but posed no threat to the established conventions of exterior architecture.'[23]

By the middle years of the eighteenth century there was a highly developed sense of different styles – not just

237 Isaac Ware, the dining-room, Chesterfield House, London, 1748 (demolished).

238 Isaac Ware, the French Room, Chesterfield House, London, 1748 (demolished).

239   Thomas Wright, the hall, Nuthall Temple, Nottinghamshire, 1754 (demolished).

Palladian and Rococo but also Gothic and Chinoiserie – being appropriate for different rooms. A clear example of this can be seen at The Vyne, Hampshire, which was remodelled by Horace Walpole's friend John Chute from 1754.[24] Here, commentators have been confused by the contrast of the new Gothic tomb chamber (Fig. 241) and Gothic alterations to the chapel with the Classical tomb of Chaloner Chute and staircase hall (Fig. 242). Moreover, the drawing-rooms have Rococo papier-mâché decoration. The Vyne was a complex house which had been built in the early sixteenth century for Lord Sandys and substantially altered and given a portico by John Webb in the 1650s for its new purchaser Chaloner Chute. The principal interiors to survive from Lord Sandys's day were the chapel, described by Walpole as 'the most heavenly Chapel in the world', and the Oak Gallery. It was in sympathy with this element of the house's history that John Chute added simple geometrical plasterwork to the ceiling of the gallery in what he presumably considered a Tudor manner; Gothic panelling to the ante-chapel, *trompe-l'oeil* Perpendicular fan tracery to the chapel and built a new Gothic tomb chamber. However, the monument to his seventeenth-century forebear Chaloner Chute was designed in a Webbian Classical manner, as was the staircase, which was principally inspired by that at Ashburnham House, Westminster, then believed to be by Webb. At the Vyne, Gothic and Classical were not alternatives, but arose from the same historicist concerns, while Rococo was felt to be appropriate for Chute's private drawing-rooms.

A similar historicist approach can be seen at Felbrigg Hall, Norfolk. William Windham inherited Felbrigg with its Jacobean south range and Restoration west range in 1749. He quickly set about improving it with James Paine as his architect. His first plans included Gothicising the Jacobean front, but that was never carried out. Instead, he created a Gothic hall in 1752, and a Gothic library in 1755. By contrast, both the eating-room and the cabinet have plasterwork which can be interpreted as a Rococo evocation of a Restoration interior, in sympathy with the rich plasterwork ceilings of the 1680s in the two adjoining rooms. In one of these, the drawing-room, the carving of the four new doorcases carefully echoes the earlier plasterwork.[25] Finally the bedrooms were hung with Chinese paper.

There seems to have been a sudden burst of enthusiasm for Chinoisere in the late 1740s and 1750s, in both

240 Anon, Chinese decoration in a bedroom at Saltram House, Devon, before 1768.

241   William Chute, the chapel chamber, the Vyne, Hampshire, 1754.

interiors and gardens. In 1749 Mrs Montagu wrote of how 'we must all seek the barbarous *gout* of the Chinese'.[26] Only rarely did this extend to the architecture of the house, the one known example being Richard Bateman's 'half Gothick, half Attic, half Chinese and completely fribble house' at Old Windsor.[27] Generally, Chinoiserie was reserved for bedrooms and dressing-rooms, the exoticism perhaps being thought appropriate for a room of dreams. This craze is particularly well preserved at Saltram House, Devon, where four Chinese bedrooms survive, presumably fitted up by John Parker the elder before his death in 1768 (Fig. 240). Chinese decoration in drawing-rooms or dining-rooms was rare but not unknown. Lady Cardigan had a Chinese dining-room in 1742 and William Hallett fitted up a Chinese dining-room at Marble Hill in 1755 for Lady Suffolk. The dining-room at Dalemain, Cumberland, with a fine paper of about 1760 and a related Rococo chimney-piece, is a rare survival.[28]

Far from challenging Classical authority, Gothic, Rococo and Chinoiserie fit well into the Classical concept of propriety. At this date the use of Gothic interiors was restricted to remodelled medieval or Tudor buildings. Even here it was considered most suitable in the hall, the chapel and the library. Nor was Rococo a challenge to Palladian orthodoxy, but, as with Jones's use of contemporary French decoration, it formed an appropriate response to the perennial demand for richly decorated interiors within an otherwise austere architectural shell.

Inigo Jones had also argued that richer architectural forms were appropriate for garden buildings as well as interiors, expressing this in his varied series of designs for gateways.[29] Again, the neo-Palladians would have agreed: Gothic ruins, castellated towers, Chinoiserie pavilions, rustic huts and rough-hewn grottos were mixed with Grecian temples, triumphal arches, rotundas and obelisks in the mid-eighteenth-century landscape garden. Garden buildings were not uncommon before the eighteenth century, but the years between 1720 and 1740 saw an explosion of interest. Park and garden buildings were probably the most numerous type of neo-Palladian buildings, while they also played important roles in the spread of neo-Classicism and of the Gothic and Chinoiserie styles. Such buildings form a microcosm of eighteenth-century architecture, with the added significance that they were often the experimental buildings that pioneered the way for mainstream architecture.

Dovecots had long been a feature of many gardens, as had gazebos, little garden houses often placed to command the view. Tree houses had their adherents, while mounts formed an architectural feature and were often topped by a seat. Sometimes such buildings played an important architectural part in the setting of a house. The Jacobean garden at Llanerch, Denbighshire, painted in 1662, had a series of three walled gardens dropping down the hill, the first with a pair of gazebos, the third with a little domed pavilion in the centre of one wall, and a pair of pedimented garden seats in the corners.[30] Generally, garden buildings of this date were of limited architectural significance, although there were exceptions, such as the mid-seventeenth-century pilastered water pavilion at Denham Place, Buckinghamshire;[31] or the pavilion at Westbury Court, Gloucestershire, built in 1702–3, a highly controlled Dutch building with a colonnaded ground floor supporting a pedimented gazebo, the whole topped by a little cupola. In the early eighteenth century this relatively restrained tradition was reinvented on an astonishing scale.

As the size of gardens grew in the early eighteenth century, so did that of the garden buildings within them. Wrest Park, Bedfordshire, created by the Duke of Kent from 1702, was one of the most renowned gardens of its day, with a half-mile long, tree-lined canal at its centre. At the far end of this was a domed garden pavilion the size of a small chapel, designed by Thomas Archer in 1709. But it was Vanbrugh who gave real architectural force to this movement, expanding the formal garden to a heroic scale and then breaking its bounds so that the garden, with its buildings, spread out into the surrounding countryside to form a landscaped park.

John Harris has suggested that in his gardens at Castle

242   William Chute, the stairs, The Vyne, Hampshire, 1754.

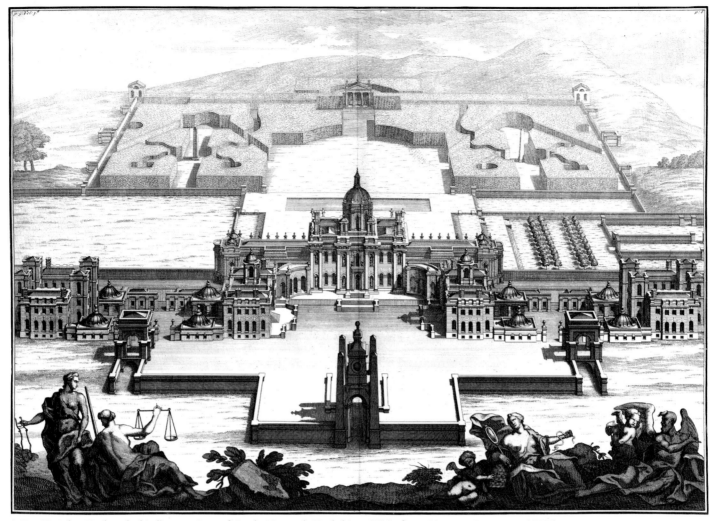

243   Sir John Vanbrugh, bird's-eye view of Castle Howard, Yorkshire, 1702, from *Vitruvius Britannicus* (1725).

Howard, Blenheim Palace and Eastbury, Dorset, Vanbrugh was trying to create a garden architecture based on the urban principles of Ancient Rome.[32] Unsurprisingly, garden buildings, specifically Classical temples, played a major part in this vision. At Castle Howard, illustrated in volume three of *Vitruvius Britannicus* in 1725, in an engraving intended for the second volume of 1717 (Fig. 243), Vanbrugh created an enormous parterre, supported by a bastioned wall, with a pair of obelisks placed as if in the centre of two piazzas, and a host of smaller ones in front of the house. At the end of the parterre sat a temple, probably the first erected in an English garden.[33] Blenheim was even larger, with another great bastioned parterre, a bridge built on the scale of a Roman acqueduct and, halfway down the immense avenue, a column of victory commemorating the great Duke of Marlborough, designed by Lord Herbert on the model of Trajan's Column in Rome.[34] The highpoint of Vanbrugh's grandiloquent, essentially urban manner was Eastbury, which had been bought by George Doddington in 1709, but where the designs in *Vitruvius Britannicus* are dated 1718. Here, a hexastyle

portico thirty feet high stood at the far end of the garden at the top of a series of terraces perhaps modelled on Praeneste, while to one side lay the bagnio, another substantial garden building, with a portico over a rusticated base.[35]

Among those gardens illustrated in *Vitruvius Britannicus*, Vanbrugh's are exceptional for the number of their ornamental buildings, but not unique. Volume three also includes a plan of the gardens at Narford Hall in Norfolk which has two vignettes, one of a portico, the other of a rusticated deerhouse.[36] Narford was owned by Burlington's friend, Sir Andrew Fountaine, whose intentions in building the portico are revealed in the reference by Sir Matthew Decker in 1728 to 'a little summer house, built in the Manner as a Temple'.[37] This was an Ionic tetrastyle temple raised on a podium, approached up a flight of steps, with a door leading through to a room beyond.[38] It survives at Narford, although relocated, and was almost certainly modelled on the Ionic Temple of Fortuna Virilis, one of the smaller but most complete temples in Rome. The exact date of the Narford temple is uncertain, but it must predate 1725.[39]

Only Vanbrugh has precedence in the accurate reconstruction of a temple as a garden building, at Castle Howard (assuming the temple there was executed) and at Stowe, Buckinghamshire, where the pair of Lake Pavilions erected between 1720 and 1724 are tetrastyle Doric temples.

Narford is the only garden illustrated in *Vitruvius Britannicus* with vignettes of garden buildings, but Badeslade and Rocque's abortive supplement (misspelt by them *Vitruvius Brittanicus*) of 1739 is very different. Vignettes are a common feature of the book – individual buildings at Kew, Claremont, and Esher, all in Surrey, Wrest, Chiswick, Middlesex, and Dalton, Yorkshire, are all illustrated in this way – while other garden buildings can be identified in the birdseye views. By the end of the 1720s garden buildings were no longer incidents in a garden, they were among its most important features.

In this development two gardens stand out, that developed by Lord Burlington at Chiswick, and Stowe, laid out for Sir Richard Temple, later Viscount Temple. The gardens at Chiswick were among those illustrated in *Vitruvius Brittanicus* in an engraving made in 1736, which includes eight different garden buildings (Fig. 245).[40] One of these was the Casina or Bagnio, 'the first essay of his Lordship's happy invention', designed by Burlington in 1717. Chiswick, where Burlington was subsequently assisted by William Kent, grew piecemeal throughout the 1720s and 1730s. It was a scene of constant changes and alterations, but the new axes and vistas were always formed around garden buildings or architectural features, at least three more of them, the Circular Temple, the Pavilion and the Orangery, designed by Burlington.

Stowe, where work began in 1715, was laid out on a much grander scale, as befitted a great country house rather than a suburban villa (Fig. 244). By 1719 Vanbrugh – who was responsible only for the buildings, Charles Bridgeman designed the garden – had begun Nelson's Seat and the Brick Temple (later renamed the Temple of Bacchus). With the extension of the gardens southwards between 1719 and 1724, Vanbrugh added the Lake Pavilions, the Rotondo, the Temple of Sleep, the Cold Bath and the Pyramid. Stowe was to be one of the most visited gardens in the country and work there continued for half a century, during which the gardens were repeatedly extended and remodelled. Again, garden buildings remained the dominant feature of the design, to an almost overwhelming degree.

Vanbrugh was the first architect to design garden buildings on a large scale. He left examples at Castle Howard, Blenheim, Eastbury, King's Weston, Claremont, Stowe and possibly at Duncombe Park, Yorkshire. His *oeuvre* includes temples, towers, a pyramid, obelisks, fake medieval walls, rotundas and a bridge. On

244   Sir John Vanbrugh, the rotondo, Stowe, Buckinghamshire, *c.*1719 (remodelled).

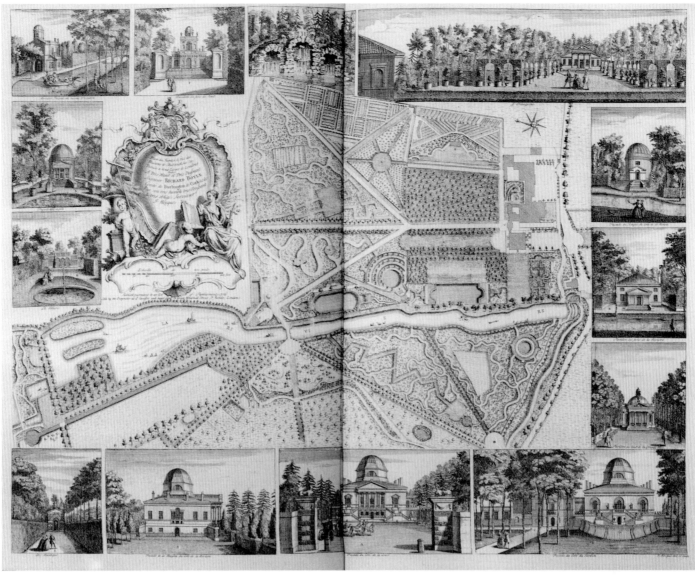

245   William Kent, plan of Chiswick, Middlesex, *c.*1730, from *Vitruvius Brittanicus* (1739).

his death in 1726 his position was effectively taken by William Kent. After an interlude in which James Gibbs was employed (he returned in 1739) Kent designed a series of temples and other garden buildings at Stowe, as he did at Claremont. At the latter, two of the garden buildings illustrated with vignettes in *Vitruvius Brittanicus* [*sic*] (Fig. 246) have been attributed to Vanbrugh, the other three to Kent (another building on the island, again by Kent, was added in a later state of the plate).[41] But there is no real stylistic division between the work of the two architects either here or at Stowe. In such garden buildings the conventional distinction between 'Palladian' Kent and 'non-Palladian' Vanbrugh becomes very tenuous. Vanbrugh anticipated many of the common forms of Georgian garden buildings and Kent was quite happy to follow him, and not only in conventional temples. One might note in particular the obelisk at Holkham Hall, on a scale matching Vanbrugh's at Castle

Howard; the rotunda on the river at Richmond,[42] emulating that at Stowe; the use of pyramids on the Worcester Gate at Badminton, Gloucestershire, anticipated by Vanbrugh in the Pyramid Gate at Castle Howard, and the repeated use of heavy rustication, as for instance, in the Hermitage at Stowe, which can be found in Vanbrugh's Robin Hood's Well at Skelbrooke in Yorkshire.[43] In an early design for Townesend's Building at Rousham, Oxfordshire, Kent even took as his model Vanbrugh's Temple of the Four Winds.[44] Indeed, if a contrast in the design of garden buildings in the 1720s must be made, it should not be between Vanbrugh and Kent but those two architects and the work of James Gibbs.

It was in his garden designs that Kent was at his freest as an architect, and there are times when his work comes close to that of Nicholas Hawksmoor. Unlike Vanbrugh, Hawksmoor did not design many garden and park buildings, and most of these are at Castle Howard. The parallels between Hawksmoor's Mausoleum and Kent's Temple of Ancient Virtue at Stowe are obvious,[45] while the Carrmire Gate at Castle Howard (for which Hawksmoor was probably responsible) and the Triumphal Arch at Holkham Hall, by Kent, reveal a very similar aesthetic sensibility.[46] More significantly, the Temple of Venus and the Temple of British Worthies at Stowe reveal an imaginative reinterpretation of antique buildings, possibly based on earlier drawings and engravings which has much in common with Hawksmoor's approach.[47] The similarities to be found in the garden buildings of Vanbrugh, Hawksmoor and Kent are a reminder that the parallels between the work of these architects are often as important as the differences.

Today, the English neo-Palladian house has become almost synonymous with the informal landscape garden in which grass comes sweeping up to the house without any apparent restraint. Indeed, so closely associated are the two that it is easy to forget that early examples were

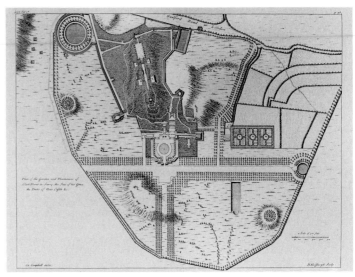

246 Sir John Vanbrugh, plan of Claremont, *c*.1726, from *Vitruvius Brittanicus* (1739).

247 Sir John Vanbrugh, the Castle Howard landscape, Yorkshire, *c*.1726.

usually set in formal landscapes. At Newby Hall, Yorkshire, Campbell's house was placed in a park that had
already been laid out by George London,[48] but a formal
garden was specially designed as the setting for the house
at Stourhead, Wiltshire. Among the early neo-Palladian
villas this was certainly the case at Chiswick, Marble
Hill, Rokeby Park, and Dalton, and was also true of
Campbell's abortive design for Goodwood House, Sussex. In nearly all these examples, the formal gardens were
soon swept away, but they survive at Dalton and have
been recreated at Chiswick.

Kent was the driving force in this change. In
December 1734 Sir Thomas Robinson wrote to Lord
Carlisle that

> a new taste in gardening has just arisen, which has
> been practised with so great success at the Prince's
> garden in town, that a general alteration of some of
> the most considerable gardens in the kingdom is
> begun, after Mr Kent's notion of gardening, viz. to
> lay them out, and work without either level or
> line . . . when finished it has the appearance of beau-
> tiful nature, and without being told one would imag-
> ine art had no part in the finishing, and is, according
> to what one hears of the Chinese, entirely after their
> model for works of this nature, where they never
> plant straight lines or make regular design.[49]

It would be interesting to know what Carlisle made of
this news, for he and Vanbrugh had already anticipated it
at Castle Howard.

Vanbrugh's first gardens had all been massively formal,
but at Claremont, from 1716, Vanbrugh broke all the
rules (Fig. 246).[50] Instead, of a symmetrical garden in
front of the house Vanbrugh surrounded the hill behind
with great irregular earthen ramparts with bastions at the
corners and wiggling paths running through the trees,
although the central axis of the garden, from the bowling
green to belvedere, remained formal.[51] At Castle
Howard in the mid-1720s this informality was taken
further (Fig. 247). Here Vanbrugh laid out an irregular
terrace, lined with statues, along the path of the former
village street leading to the Temple of the Four Winds of
1725, which sits on the edge of the garden, looking out
into the countryside. At the same time, he created the
irregular castellated, buttressed wall, approached through
the Pyramid Gate, on the main approach from York.
Carlisle continued to develop this landscape after
Vanbrugh's death with the aid of Hawksmoor who
added the Pyramid in 1728, the Mausoleum in 1729, the
Temple of Venus in 1731 and the Carrmire Gate on the
approach from York.

Whereas at Chiswick and Stowe garden buildings
were clearly set in the formal context of a garden, generally as the focus of an axial vista, at Castle Howard

buildings were placed apparently informally in the landscape in the manner of a painting by Claude or of ruins
in the Roman Campagna. Kent developed this idea,
particularly at Rousham and Esher (whose formal lines
had been carefully softened by the time it was re-engraved in 1738), and by the late 1730s the idea of a
temple or other garden building set in the landscape
rather than in a formal garden had begun to spread
rapidly across the country.

Antique Roman precedent undoubtedly lay behind
this idea. Such buildings are one of the most evident
features in Robert Castell's recreations of Pliny's gardens
in his *Villas of the Ancients* (1728). Robert Morris discussed the idea in his *Lectures on Architecture* of 1734–6:
'The ancient *Romans* planted their plots in this *rural*
manner and their *Temples*, dedicated to their peculiar
GODS, were dispersed among the *Groves* and Woods,
which Art or nature had made, with *Vistas* to them.'[52] It
was also taken up by Joseph Spence, a keen gardener
himself, in *Polymetis* (1747) where Polymetis's villa, in
which the book is set, clearly embodies Spence's ideas of
a Roman villa:

> They came early to the villa: and sat down to their tea,
> in the library; which looks directly upon the gardens,
> that were just finished and brought to their present
> perfection. You see, says Polymetis, I have followed
> the taste in fashion (which, as it happens, is certainly
> the best taste too) of making my gardens rather wild
> than regular. Their general air, I hope, has nothing
> stiff and unnatural in it; and the lower part, in particu-
> lar, joins in with the view of the country, as if it made
> a part of it. Indeed the mode has allowed me to have
> as many temples as I could wish, in such a space of
> ground.[53]

Inevitably, Roman precedent was also sought for the
precise form of such buildings. Vanbrugh does not seem
to have been concerned in the precise reconstruction of
Roman buildings when he designed his garden buildings; his temples are generic rather than specific. Both
Hawksmoor and Kent were more interested in neo-
Classical reconstruction, although their approach was
always strongly tempered by romantic imagination. But
for the Palladian neo-Classicists garden buildings were an
opportunity for archaeological reconstructions untram-
melled by the demands of practicality. The use of baseless
Doric columns is always a sign of neo-Classicism and
both the Temple of Piety at Studley Royal, Yorkshire,
and the colonnade at Shugborough Park, Staffordshire,
must have been intended as reconstructions of the
hexastyle Temple of Piety in the Forum Holitorum in
Rome, part of which survives incorporated in the
church of San Nicola in Carcere. Serlio was the first to
attempt to recreate it, and was followed by Antonio

248 Thomas Pitt, the Temple of Concord, Stowe, Buckinghamshire, 1752.

Labacco and Desgodetz, but the Studley Royal temple differs significantly from these, following instead Palladio's reconstruction in Lord Burlington's collection.[54]

Other early examples of garden temples, such as that at Narford, should probably be seen as neo-Classically inspired. The Temple of Fortuna Virilis must have been the source for a similar temple at the Rievaulx Terraces, built between 1749 and 1757, where there is also a baseless Doric rotunda. A rather more ambitious reconstruction of an antique temple was the Temple of Concord and Victory at Stowe of 1752 which is peripteral, with Ionic colonnades on all sides (Fig. 248). This is usually described as being based on the Corinthian and pseudoperipteral Maison Carrée in Nîmes. A more probable source is the Temple of Concord in Rome which is both Ionic and peripteral.

The gabled temple of antiquity looked best when it commanded a straight vista, but architects sometimes wanted temples that had equal effect from all sides, and for this rotundas based on the Temples of Vesta in Rome and Tivoli were ideal. Examples include Kent's Temple of Ancient Virtue at Stowe, of about 1734, and the Temple of Venus at Garendon, Leicestershire, which Ambrose Phillipps designed for himself before 1737. Both of these are Ionic, and it might at first seem strange that neither these, nor the Doric rotunda at Rievaulx, follow the original Corinthian order. Indeed, it is unusual to find Corinthian garden buildings. This is probably explained by Palladian respect for the proprieties of the orders. Most Roman temples had Corinthian capitals, suitable for religious buildings but inappropriate for garden buildings. Thus, a compromise was reached by designing buildings modelled on antique temples but with an Ionic or Doric order.

Mausolea were another obvious source for neo-Classical garden buildings. Indeed, the earliest example of the use of the baseless Doric column was a genuine mausoleum, that at Elmore, Gloucestershire, erected in memory of Sir John Guise who died in 1732. Guise stipulated such a mausoleum in his will and even specified the source to be followed, the sepulchre at Terracina outside Rome illustrated by Fréart as a particularly good example of the Doric order.[55] In 1764 Bishop Pococke visiting Lord Botetourt's park at Stoke Gifford, Gloucestershire, described how 'We then went to a brow of a Hill, on which his Lordship has built a model of ye Monument of ye Horatii at Albano, with four round Obeliscs upon an arch'd building adorn'd with a Pediment every way. On ye Frieze round ye four sides is this inscription, "Memoria Virtutis Heroicae SPQR".'[56] The Monument of the Horatii was a well-known remain near Rome, engraved by, among others, Piranesi, and Pococke had in 1750 identified it as the source for another garden building at Werrington, Devon. In Scotland, Sir James Clerk included a reconstruction of the Roman mausoleum known as 'Arthur's O'en', which William Stukeley had recorded, as the dovecote of the new stables he designed for himself at Penicuik House, Midlothian (c.1761).

Other examples can be identified of garden buildings modelled directly on Roman remains, that is neo-Classical reconstructions, but the fashion for garden and park temples was such that it is not always easy to distinguish neo-Classical reconstructions from those designed with only a generic regard for antique originals. Inevitably, the latter are far more numerous.

249 William Kent, unexecuted design for a Chinese building at Esher Place, Surrey, c.1735.

250   Anon., Shugborough Park, Staffordshire, c.1750.

As already mentioned, garden buildings, principally towers and mock forts were important in the rise of Gothic architecture in the 1730s and 1740s. Less widespread, but also popular were exotic Oriental buildings. Kent made three designs for Chinese garden buildings associated with Esher Place, dated about 1735 (Fig. 249), and may have been responsible for the Chinese House at Stowe, which had been placed in the Elysian Fields by 1738.[57] At Wroxton Abbey, Oxfordshire, Sanderson Miller remodelled the existing formal layout between 1737 and 1751 and replaced it with a Rococo garden decorated with a Chinese summerhouse (for which the lead for the roof was bought in 1739[58]), a Chinese lodge, a Chinese seat, as well as a Classical obelisk and a Gothic tower – with the rebuilt tower of the medieval church being an additional feature.

The designer of the Chinese buildings at Wroxton is not known, but whoever it was is unlikely to have been concerned with accuracy. As with early Gothic garden buildings it was a mood that was being they evoked. By contrast, Thomas Pennant described the Chinese Pavilion at Shugborough Park (built before 1748) as 'a true pattern of the architecture of that nation . . . not a mongrel invention of *British* carpenters'.[59] This was because Thomas Anson's brother, Admiral George Anson, brought back drawings of genuine Chinese buildings from Canton. The accuracy of the Chinese Pavilion – which was reached by two Chinese bridges and joined by a pagoda in 1752 – indicated a changing approach to garden buildings, a change already seen in the erection of archaeologically correct reconstructions of Classical tem-

ples. No longer was a vague resemblance enough, the building had to be an accurate example of what it set out to represent. Thus, it comes as no surprise that the park at Shugborough also included an accurate reconstruction of the baseless Roman Doric portico of the Temple of Piety in Rome; nor that this was followed together by the Triumphal Arch (1764), the Tower of the Winds (1764) and the Choragic Monument (1769), all from James Stuart's *Antiquities of Athens* (Fig. 250).

Less archaeological in its intention, but equally diverse in the range of garden buildings to be found there, was Dogmersfield Park, Hampshire. In 1754 Dr Pococke described seeing a Gothic arch of brick and flint in squares, an imitation Druid avenue, a colonnaded temple, an octagonal tower, a thatched house, a cottage built to resemble a Gothic chapel and 'a small low turret on four Gothick arches, called the Chinese building . . . rather defective in the execution'. Most of these are shown in two paintings, one of which is dated about 1747, and all would be important novelties if it could be proved that they were built in the late 1730s and early 1740s when the park is believed to have been laid out. However, all bar the tower and the Gothic Hunting Tower, possibly the cottage built to resemble a chapel, were demolished in 1790.[60]

The finest example of this postage-stamp collecting attitude towards garden buildings came in the late 1740s, the 1750s and early 1760s at Kew, Surrey (Fig. 251). Shortly before his death in 1751, Frederick Prince of Wales had begun to develop this in an exotic manner and his work was continued by his widow the Dowager

251 Sir William Chambers, the Menagery, Kew Gardens, Surrey, 1760 (pencil, Metropolitan Museum of Art, New York).

Princess of Wales under the direction of William Chambers. Kew had a 'House of Confucius', a Chinese bridge, a Chinese menagerie, a Pagoda, a Mosque, an Alhambra, a cottage, a Temple of the Sun based on that at Baalbek, a ruined Roman arch and a whole series of other Classical temples.[61] Chambers, whose *Designs of Chinese Buildings, Furniture, Dresses etc* (1757), was the first accurate English publication on Chinese buildings, subsequently published them as *Plans, Elevations, Sections and Perspective Views of the Gardens and Buildings at Kew in Surrey*, in 1763.

In park and garden buildings, as in interior decoration, different styles were not seen to be in competition. To build a Chinoiserie or a Gothic building was not to suggest that it was superior to a Palladian one. Different styles could coexist because each served a different purpose. At the same time there was no doubt of the ultimate superiority of Classicism. For all the scare-mongering of the newspapers writing about Gothic, Rococo or Chinoiserie, in the middle of the eighteenth century Classicism was not under threat.

THE PALLADIAN ASCENDANCY

Sɪʀ Fʀᴀɴᴄɪs Dᴀsʜᴡᴏᴏᴅ ᴡᴀs a passionate architec-tural enthusiast, a founder member of the Dilettanti Society, who inherited his estate at West Wycombe, Buckinghamshire, in 1724 as a boy of sixteen. He spent the next fifteen years travelling extensively, but by 1739 he was ready to rebuild West Wycombe Park. Drawings were prepared, work started on the park but in the event building work never began. It was not until 1748, nearly a decade later, that he was reported to be again consid-ering rebuilding. This time work was soon under way and continued throughout the next decade.[1]

A clue to Dashwood's behaviour can be found in London, where the rebuilding of St Bartholomew's Hospital by James Gibbs from 1730 was one of the most impressive developments of that decade. Work pro-gressed smoothly, and by 1739 the administration and south blocks had been completed. Four years later a subscription was launched to finance the west block, but this time problems quickly arose. The quarrymaster, John Allen of Bath, reported difficulty in transporting the stone because the necessary vessels were being used by the navy. In September 1745 he wrote to the gov-ernors regretting that he would not be able to supply the stone: 'this French War wil render it Impracticable for me to do it within five Years, and then it must be at an Exorbitant Expense'. The governors decided to await the return of peace and the foundations were covered with straw in December 1745. Peace was made in 1748, but it was only in 1749 that the price of freight had dropped sufficiently for building to resume, the block being finished in 1753.[2]

The 1710s, 1720s and 1730s had proved to be an un-usually peaceful interlude in seventeenth and eighteenth-century English history. After a quarter of a century of war with France between 1688 and 1713, interrupted only by the Five Year Peace of 1697–1702, the Treaty of Utrecht in 1713 ushered in a quarter of a century of peace broken only by a brief war with Spain in 1727. The result had been a marked economic boom, peaking in 1725, which had paid for a major expansion of Lon-don, financed the expensive porticos of the new London churches and allowed the wave of country-house build-ing which ushered in neo-Palladianism. The 1730s were

less prosperous – a contemporary noted in 1733 that 'the rage for building is much abated' – and the last years of the decade saw the economy in a marked decline. War with Spain in 1739, quickly followed by a general European war, the War of the Austrian Succession, which lasted until 1748, turned this into a slump. Timber imports, an important measure of building activity, show a falling off from 1736 that became precipitous in 1740. The same is true of deeds registered in the Middlesex Deeds Registry which gives an idea of speculative hous-ing market in London.[3] During the war, govern-ment expenditure rose from £4,725,000 in 1738 to £9,398,000 in 1744 and reached £12,544,000 in 1749.[4] Interest rates rose, particularly in 1744–5, making it difficult to borrow and uneconomic to realise capital held in stocks, and they did not recover until 1749.[5] Land tax, which particularly hit landowners, was in-creased to 4s. in the pound with the total sum collected rising from £1,134,000 in 1739 to £2,130,000 in 1741.[6] Matters were worsened by two appalling harvests in 1740 and 1741. Bankruptcies and riots were common. The same years saw successive severe winters causing the loss of half the country's sheep, a problem exacerbated by serious outbreaks of foot-rot in 1745 and 1747. Mean-while, the price of grain, of particular importance to landowners, hit a long-term low in 1743–4. Labour was tight, imports of timber expensive and, as has been have seen, freight difficult. The country even saw an invasion in 1745. It was not a time to build.[7]

It was not only Sir Francis Dashwood and the gover-nors of St Bartholomew's who found their building plans frustrated. All forms of building slumped in the ten years before 1748, particularly new country houses. This slump can be clearly charted in the careers of individual architects, but is also seen in the individual aspirations of patrons, as well as in the raw numbers of houses and other buildings erected.

James Gibbs was one of England's most prolific coun-try-house architects in the 1720s and early 1730s, but after providing designs for Quarrell, Stirlingshire, in 1735–6 he had virtually no such work for over a decade. A new house at Hampstead Marshall, Berkshire, was begun in 1739 but abandoned incomplete the same year;

the same happened to a scheme for remodelling Hartwell House, Buckinghamshire, in 1740; plans for remodelling and extending Kiveton Hall, Yorkshire, in 1741, came to nothing; and schemes for Wiston Park, Sussex, Kirtlington Hall, Oxfordshire, and Catton Hall, Derbyshire, were rejected (the latter two being awarded to William Smith instead). It was only in 1749 that his country-house practice picked up again with two new houses at Bank Hall, Lancashire, and Patshull Hall, Staffordshire,[8] and a major remodelling at Ragley Hall, Warwickshire. By then it was too late to revive his career and Gibbs's death in 1754 brought an end to this late rally. Terry Friedman, Gibbs's biographer, suggests that this break was largely self-imposed, arguing that Gibbs was so taken up with building the Radcliffe Camera that he devoted less time to his country-house practice and consequently accepted fewer commissions.[9] However, the number of rejected schemes suggests that Gibbs was anxious to maintain his country-house practice but was unable to gain employment.

Gibbs was not alone in this situation, a survey of other leading architects shows a similar pattern. Roger Morris, who was very busy until 1732, had no new countryhouse commissions after 1733 until he began Inveraray Castle, Argyllshire, in 1745. This was followed by Kirby Hall, Yorkshire, in 1747, and Brandenburg House, Hammersmith, in 1748, but again the rally came too late for Morris who died in 1749. Kirby Hall was built in association with Lord Burlington who had been involved at Northwick Park, Gloucestershire, Petersham Lodge, Surrey, and Holkham Hall, Norfolk, between 1730 and 1734, but thereafter designed no country houses until Kirby Hall. William Kent was also busy in the late 1720s and early 1730s, but his country-house work tailed off after Holkham in 1734. Apart from the remodelling of Rousham Hall, Oxfordshire, in 1738, his only work until he designed Wakefield Lodge, Northamptonshire, in 1748, the year of his death, was his remodelling of the main front at Badminton House, Gloucestershire, with its ancillary buildings from 1745.[10] John James had two commissions in 1733, Standlynch, Wiltshire, and Baylies House, Buckinghamshire, but no further work until he was called to remodel Welbeck Abbey, Nottinghamshire, in 1742. He died in 1746. James Leoni had five commissions in 1728–35, but received only three new ones between 1735 and his death in 1746, only one of which is firmly dated to the 1740s. Thomas Ripley had no work after 1738 although he did not die for another twenty years.

All these architects were established before 1730, but the paucity of new commissions was particularly hard for architects trying to establish themselves. John Sanderson built two substantial houses in 1730–1, Kelham Hall, Nottinghamshire, and Stratton Park, Hampshire, but this promising start fizzled out. It was not until 1747 that he

was called upon to work on another country house, the completion of Kirtlington Park, Oxfordshire, and it was only in 1750 that he was asked to design a new house. Isaac Ware was one of Lord Burlington's protégés, and, like Kent and Flitcroft, should have been well placed to receive commissions early in his career; but although he was a practising architect from 1733 when he was twenty-six, and may have begun remodelling Chicksands Priory, Bedfordshire, in 1739, his first significant house was the suburban Clifton Hill House, Bristol, of 1746. It was not until the 1750s that he was busy with country houses. Matthew Brettingham was also well known in the Burlingtonian circle as the executant architect at Holkham, but apart from minor work in Norfolk no significant country-house work can be definately attributed to him until he remodelled Euston Hall, Suffolk, in 1750–6 at the age of fifty-one. Between then and his death in 1769 he was well employed. John Vardy is another architect who might have been expected to establish a private practice in the 1740s. He was another protégé of Burlington's, and held a succession of clerkships in the Office of Works from 1736, but it was not until the 1750s that he designed any country houses.

At the same time, many of the larger building projects begun about 1735 such as Holkham Hall, Wentworth Woodhouse, Yorkshire, Prior Park, Bath, and Nostell Priory, Yorkshire, progressed only slowly, and were not completed until the 1750s or 1760s. Gibbs's plans to remodel Hartwell House were abandoned in 1740 when only the Great Hall had been done, and work was not revived until 1759.[11] Other projects such as Thorndon Hall, Essex, begun in 1734, and Hampstead Marshall, Berkshire, were abandoned unfinished. Elsewhere, as at West Wycombe, owners restricted their work to the gardens, where alterations did not require such a large capital injection. At Newnham Paddox, Warwickshire, Lord Denbigh began to remodel the park in 1742, employing Lancelot Brown from 1745, but it was only in 1753 that work began on rebuilding the house.[12]

Of course, the circumstances of individual landowners varied and some were determined to build. The Countess of Oxford, a great heiress in her own right, was widowed in 1741, and devoted the rest of her life to rebuilding her ancestral home, Welbeck Abbey, Nottinghamshire. In Scotland the Duke of Argyll was already sixty-one when he succeeded to the title in 1743 and was not prepared to delay rebuilding the uninhabitable Inveraray Castle, Argyllshire. He visited Inveraray for the first time in 1744 and work began the following year. Sir James Dashwood had a large enough fortune, especially as his wife was an heiress, to ignore the economic climate when he rebuilt Kirtlington Hall, Oxfordshire, in 1742–6. The same is true of William Wrightson of Cusworth Hall, Yorkshire, and Robert More of Linley Hall, Shropshire, both of whom had acquired substantial for-

252   William Kent, the Horse Guards, London, 1750 (Antonio Canaletto, oil, private collection).

tunes through marriage or inheritance. However, even More seems to have been forced to suspend his activities in 1744–5, and the roof was not completed until 1746.[13]

Not all architects were hit equally. The practical Henry Flitcroft maintained a steady practice throughout the decade, but his recorded works at this time are all alterations. In the provinces, William Smith of Warwick, who took over his father Francis Smith's practice on the latter's death in 1738, had a substantial volume of work until his death in 1747, as did Daniel Garrett in Yorkshire and Northumberland. (It may be that pressures on provincial architects were less intense than on those who relied on work gained in London.) Similarly, war brought prosperity to some, particularly to such cities as Bristol which flourished from the demand for its iron-foundries and shipping and could afford to erect an important series of civic and ecclesiastical buildings during the 1740s, including the Exchange, Cooper's Hall, the Infirmary, Redland Chapel, Market Archway and Post Office together with substantial private houses such as 40 Prince Street, Clifton Court and Clifton Hill House. Indeed, according to Michael Jenner, 'the 1740s were a decade of achievement in Bristol's architecture only nearly rivalled in the boom years of the 1860s'.[14] Except for the case of Isaac Ware at Clifton Hill House the architects of all these buildings were local men. But one has to search for new country houses built between 1740 and 1748 – remodellings, which did not require the same financial commitments were more common but still not numerous. This is in marked comparison to the volume of building carried out in the 1720s and early

1730s and the boom of the 1750s which will be discussed below.

Urban domestic architecture also suffered during these years. Although William Kent had three important town-house commissions in the 1740s – 22 Arlington Street (1741–50), 44 Berkeley Square (1742–4) and 16 St James's Place (c.1740–43) – this was exceptional. Gibbs and Leoni, who had both been active in London in the 1730s, had no urban commissions, and other architects had little work. John Summerson has shown how the expansion of London slowed down in the 1730s, and that by the end of the decade at least fifteen hundred houses were uninhabited in St Martin's and adjacent parishes, with very little being built in the 1740s.[15] In Bath, John Wood's grandiose schemes for rebuilding the city ground to a halt during the early 1740s, and it was only in 1753–4 that he was able to revive them.[16]

The 1740s saw relatively few new churches, and public buildings were also scarce, although there was a handful of exceptions: Gibbs continued to build the Radcliffe Library in Oxford which was begun in 1737, but it took ten years to complete; the Foundling Hospital in London, begun in 1742, also took a decade to build; and James Paine built the Mansion House at Doncaster, Yorkshire, in 1745–8. But in Whitehall, William Kent's programme, which had included new Royal Mews in 1731–3, a new Treasury in 1733–7, and new law courts in 1739–41 was brought to a halt. His Parliament building was never executed and his Horse Guards had to wait until 1750 (Fig. 252).

The Peace of Aix-la-Chapelle in 1748 brought a

marked change. Government debt meant that the land tax was slow to come down, but the sum collected fell from £2,212,000 in 1750 to £1,288,000 in 1754. Interest rates were low and trade boomed, with Pelham's conversion of the public debt in 1751 making money even cheaper and adding a further stimulus to activity. Timber imports rose sharply reaching a peak in 1753.[17] In agriculture the years between 1751 and 1753 were years of high grain prices. This economic stimulus coupled with a decade's pent-up demand was reflected in the building of country houses, although London building, while climbing out of the trough of the mid-1740s and peaking in 1753, failed to recover to the levels of the 1730s and remained on a plateau for most of the 1750s.[18] Nearly all the architects established before 1735 mentioned above who had had little work in the following decade, received country-house commissions in the years that immediately followed the Peace of Aix-la-Chapelle. More significantly, these years saw a sudden rash of new architects. No important architect established a successful career between 1735 and 1745, but the number of architects who appear at the end of the 1740s and in the 1750s and 1760s is legion.

James Paine started slowly with Heath Hall, Yorkshire, in 1744, then Hickleton Hall, Yorkshire, in 1747, but from 1749 he was continually busy. William Hiorn, born in about 1712, suddenly became active in 1748 and produced a string of houses over the next decade. John Carr, born in 1723, built his first house in 1748 and thereafter was never short of work. Thomas Wright built a house for the dowager Duchess of Kent at Old Windsor in 1743, but his career did not take off until 1748, while his namesake Stephen Wright had plenty of work from 1751. Sir Robert Taylor, who had a successful career as a master mason and monumental sculptor, turned to architecture with enormous success in 1753 when he was nearly forty, perhaps as a result of the surge in demand for architects. Stiff Leadbetter followed the same path; born in about 1705, he established himself in Eton, Berkshire, as a builder. There is no evidence of him working as an architect before 1753, but by 1759 he was so busy that he had to turn down the offer of work at Hartwell House, Buckinghamshire. The commission went instead to Henry Keene, born in 1726, for whom the boom meant that he could establish himself as an independent architect in his early twenties.

The 1750s were an expansive decade for new country houses. The Seven Years' War of 1756 to 1763 brought some falling off, as would have been expected when land taxes rose sharply to cover increased government spending which in turn led to high interest rates (rising from 2.9 per cent in 1754 to 4.2 per cent in 1762), but this certainly does not compare with the slump in the 1740s. Speculative housing, which in London had reached a minor peak in 1756, also fell off and there is a decline in the number of deeds registered in the Middlesex Deeds Registry, but nothing compared to the dramatic and continuing fall in the 1740s. Instead of declining markedly as during the previous war, the major economic indicators remained relatively static, perhaps suggesting that the underlying health of the economy was strong. It was certainly helped by a massive programme of public works, canals, roads, bridges, ironworks and hospitals.[19]

This underlying strength of the economy was shown by dramatic economic boom that followed the declaration of peace in 1763, which even a financial crisis that year failed to stem. Sheppard describes the upturn as being as sudden and dramatic as if a dam had burst. That year imports of timber leapt to their highest level for forty years and thereafter the building cycle seems to have changed, no longer showing long periods of static or even declining growth but a continual upward climb. With the end of the war the yield on Consols fell sharply and the pent-up demand of a rising population suddenly liberated by cheap money led to a building boom.[20] Twice as many new houses were begun in London in 1766 as in 1761. Thomas Malton wrote thirty years later in *A picturesque tour through the Cities of London and Westminster*: 'the riches which flowed into the country, after the peace . . . had excited a rage for building, and houses rose like exhalations'.[21] Contemporaries commented on the fast rate of building, noting 'many piles of building that are daily rising in the metropolis' (1764), the 'rage or at least hurry of building' (1765) and the 'thousands of houses' built in last few years (1767). In 1766, the year that the preface to John Gwynn's *London and Westminster Improved* spoke of 'the rage of building has been carried to so great a height for several years past, as to have increased his metropolis in an astonishing manner', the number of property transactions in the Middlesex Deeds Register was twice that in 1761.[22] In Edinburgh the New Town was laid out in 1766, and in Bath the Royal Crescent was begun in 1767.

It was on the back of this boom that there was room in the late 1750s and 1760s for another group of architects to join those who had launched their careers so dramatically after the Peace of Aix-la-Chapelle, men such as William Chambers, Robert Adam, Robert Mylne, James Stuart, Lancelot Brown and James Wyatt. There was also space for a whole new school of provincial architects, such men as James Essex in Cambridge, Anthony Keck in Gloucestershire, Thomas Atkinson in Yorkshire and Thomas Pritchard in the Welsh borders.

By identifying the effective break in country-house building it is also possible to show that what is sometimes seen to be a neo-Palladian 'villa revival' in the 1750s is better explained as a part of a general revival of country-house building. The villa never went out of fashion, but, like all types of country-house, few examples were built in the 1740s. However, it is clear that after 1748 the

253   Henry Flitcroft, the entrance hall, Woburn Abbey, Bedfordshire, 1748.

254 Stiff Leadbetter, Nuneham Park, Oxfordshire, 1756.

great house was increasingly displaced by the villa as the model for the seats of landed families. The key period for this was the decade between 1755 and 1765.

Flitcroft's remodelling of Woburn Abbey, Bedfordshire (Fig. 253), which began in November 1748, a month after the signing of the Peace of Aix-la-Chapelle,[23] initiated a new wave of great houses: Brettingham's remodelling of Euston Hall (1750), and Packington Hall, Warwickshire, (1766); Brown's Croome Court, Worcestershire (1751), Newnham Paddox (1754), and Fisherwick Park, Staffordshire (1774); Sanderson Miller's Hagley Hall, Worcestershire (1753); Paine's unfinished designs for rebuilding Glentworth Hall, Lincolnshire (1753), Worksop Manor, Nottinghamshire (1762), Sandbeck Hall, Yorkshire (c.1763), and Thorndon Hall (1764); Mr Hoare's Fonthill, Wiltshire (c.1757); John Carr's Harewood House, Yorkshire (1759); Robert Adam's Luton Park, Bedfordshire (1766); Samuel Wyatt's Doddington Hall, Cheshire (1776); Sir Robert Taylor's Heveningham Hall, Suffolk (1778). These show that the great house was still a significant building type, but it was increasingly challenged by the villa in its enlarged form.

In 1756 the 1st Earl Harcourt commissioned Stiff Leadbetter to build him a new seat at Nuneham Courtenay near Oxford (Fig. 254). The Earl – he had been raised to the title in 1749 – was a consummate courtier, one-time governor of the Prince of Wales, the future George III, for whom he stood proxy in his marriage to Princess Charlotte of Mecklenburg-Strelitz.

He was deeply proud of his ancient lineage, the Harcourts had owned Stanton Harcourt since the twelfth century, and keenly aware of his dignity. He was not a man who would commit an architectural impropriety. However, he was also a strong architectural enthusiast, a leading member of the Society of Dilettanti and, at Nuneham, was the first person to incorporate Greek motifs brought back by James Stuart into a building. Before 1740 one would have expected a man in his position to build a great house, instead, he deliberately decided to build a villa.[24]

Nuneham Park was not the first villa Leadbetter had designed. He had begun one the previous year for the Duke of Marlborough at Langley Park, Buckinghamshire, but that was a suburban retreat, the Duke's seat remained Blenheim. At Langley, Leadbetter was doing no more than earlier architects for whom the neo-Palladian villa had been suitable for suburban retreats, and for heirs, younger sons and newly rich merchants, but not family seats. At Nuneham he was asserting that the villa, not the Palladianised great house, was the suitable form for a nobleman's seat.

Shortly after Lord Harcourt set to work at Nuneham, Sir Nathaniel Curzon succeeded to his father's estate at Kedleston in Derbyshire. He inherited an income approaching £10,000 a year and a substantial red-brick house built about 1700. In December 1758, only a month after Curzon succeeded, Matthew Brettingham visited Kedleston. It was the first stage in a plan to rebuild the house, part of a wider scheme to assert the

255   Robert Adam, Kedleston Hall and the fishing lodge, Derbyshire, 1758 (George Cuitt (attrib.), oil, National Trust).

family as Tory rivals in the county to the Whig Dukes of Devonshires at Chatsworth. Curzon's ambitions were rewarded when he was granted a peerage as Lord Scarsdale in 1761.[25] Unsurprisingly, Brettingham took Holkham as his model, repeating in particular the great colonnaded entrance hall and the four quadrant pavilions. Brettingham was soon dismissed, but his basic plan was left unchanged. This differed from Holkham in one important respect. Holkham with its four pavilion towers lay clearly in the tradition of the great house. At Kedleston the towers were dropped, and the house was designed as a villa, though on a dramatic scale (Fig. 255). Like Lord Harcourt, Curzon was at the forefront of architectural fashion, Brettingham was replaced by the more sophisticated Paine, James Stuart, recently returned from Greece, was consulted and finally Robert Adam, fresh from Italy, took over. Clearly Curzon, like Harcourt, thought the villa the type of house most likely to impress.

Nuneham and Kedleston were in the vanguard of the move to establish the villa as a suitable model for a seat, but there could be no further doubts when even a duke was prepared to build a villa for his seat. Thoresby House, the great late seventeenth-century Nottinghamshire seat of the dukes of Kingston, had burnt down in 1745. The 2nd Duke, perhaps in view of the difficult wartime circumstances, decided not to rebuild immediately but fitted up the stables as a temporary house. It was not until 1767 that he turned to John Carr to build him a new seat, an elaborate villa which takes pride of

place, together with Kent's Horse Guards and Adam's Shelburne House in London, in the fifth volume of *Vitruvius Britannicus*, published in 1771 (Fig. 255). By then the idea of the villa as a seat was well established. Eight great houses begun after the Peace of Aix-la-Chapelle appear in the two volumes of *Vitruvius Britannicus* published by Woolfe and Gandon in 1767 and 1771, all started before 1760.[26] By contrast, of the nine villa-seats, three date from the 1750s and six from the 1760s.[27] With a further six of the suburban villas illustrated built after 1748,[28] the villa clearly predominates in these two volumes.

256   John Carr, Thoresby Park, Nottinghamshire, 1767, from *Vitruvius Britannicus* (1771) (demolished).

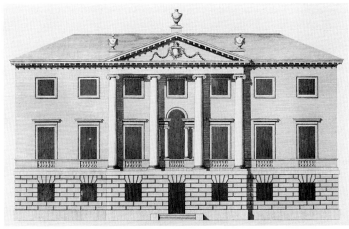

Houghton Hall was the model for many of these great houses, particularly those built by such architects as Miller at Hagley (Fig. 257) and Brown at Croome Court who were not at the forefront of the profession. Fonthill, Fisherwick, Thorndon and Doddington follow the same pattern, although without towers. Isaac Ware's Amisfield House, East Lothian (1756), published in his *A Complete Body of Architecture* in 1756, was an inventive adaptation of the Hougton model and was followed at Sandbeck and Packington. A similar design, possibly by Ware, had already been used on the south front of West Wycombe Park (*c*.1749).

The predominance of the Houghton-type shows the difficulties architects faced when trying to design a Palladian great house, but a handful of architects were more ambitious. The only architect who tried to find an innovative neo-Palladian design for the great house was Sir Thomas Robinson when he built the west wing at Castle Howard, Yorkshire (1753), in effect a separate great house tacked on to the end of Vanbrugh's house (Fig. 258). Robinson did not turn to the tired Houghton model but took one of Kent's unexecuted Parliament designs, with a domed centrepiece and pavilion towers that have subsequently been removed.[29] It was one of the most imaginative designs of the 1750s but had no imitators. At Luton Park, begun in 1766, Robert Adam,

working for the 3rd Earl of Bute, a client with an advanced architectural taste, came up with a sophisticated if rather gaunt design whose entrance front was to have been formed by a screen of giant columns. It was never completed.[30] Sir Robert Taylor's solution to the problem was Heveningham Hall (Fig. 332), a condensed version of his incomplete Stone Buildings at Lincoln's Inn of 1774, which would have looked happier forming one side of a London square.

Meanwhile, at complete variance with the rise of the villa was the continuing popularity in certain circles of the courtyard house, still seen by some as the grandest of all housing types. Thus the 4th Duke of Bedford, who was described as 'haughty, imperious and insolent in his general demeanour' and as possessing 'exalted ideas of his rank', emphasised his grandeur by turning the irregular plan of Woburn Abbey into an orderly quadrangle rather than reduce it to a compact pile.[31] Not that it proved easy to adapt such long, low façades to a Palladian design. Flitcroft's west front takes certain elements from John Sanderson's work at Stratton Park, Hampshire, in 1731, for the Duke before he succeeded,[32] in particular the three-bay columned centrepiece, but despite the accent of the towers at each end the result is uninspired. By contrast, the twin stable quadrangles which Flitcroft also built at Woburn are not the result of compromises and

257   Sanderson Miller, Hagley Hall, Worcestershire, 1751.

258   Sir Thomas Robinson, the west wing of Castle Howard, Yorkshire, 1753.

259   James Paine, Worksop Manor, Nottinghamshire (William Hodges, oil, His Grace the Duke of Norfolk) (demolished).

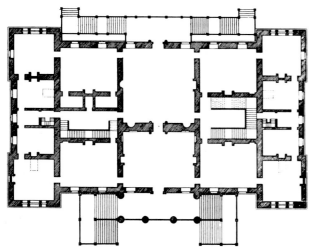

260   James Gibbs, ground-plan of Houghton Hall, Norfolk, 1722, from *Vitruvius Britannicus* (1725).

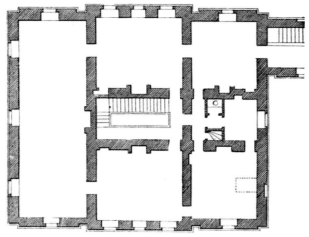

261   William Kent, plan of the family wing, Holkham Hall, Norfolk, 1734, from *Vitruvius Britannicus* (1771).

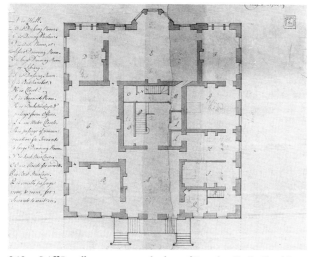

262   Stiff Leadbetter, ground-plan of Langley Park, Buckinghamshire, 1755.

are much more forceful designs. A similar air of unsatisfactory compromise hangs about Matthew Brettingham's rebuilding of another courtyard house, Euston Hall, for the Duke of Grafton. The continuing popularity of the courtyard house among those with a grand opinion of themselves is shown by the decision of Francis Child and the Duke of Northumberland to remodel rather than rebuild their respective quadrangular houses to the west of London, Osterley Park (remodelled from 1756) and Syon Park (from 1762).

The most ambitious courtyard house stylistically, and indeed in scale, was Paine's vast scheme of 1763 for rebuilding Worksop Manor for the Duke of Norfolk as a great quadrangle with a central Egyptian Hall (Fig. 259). Here there was no excuse of rebuilding an existing quadrangular house. Old Worksop House, which had burnt down, had been a tall house without a courtyard, much like Hardwick Hall, Derbyshire. Paine's design, which is a not unsuccessful attempt to create a neo-Palladian palace, looks back to Inigo Jones's designs for Whitehall published in 1727, and implies a knowledge of Jones and Webb's designs for Whitehall and for Durham House at Worcester College.[33] Perhaps unsurprisingly, only one range was ever built. It is clear that the Duke of Kingston was more in tune with fashion than the dukes of Bedford, Grafton or Norfolk, for these houses appear like dinosaurs in a changing world dominated by the villa. The only comparable scheme to Worksop was William Chambers's design for a new palace for George III at Richmond of 1765, and that was never built.

Adapting the villa to the needs of a great house was not without difficulties, and a number of compromise designs show architects trying to compress houses so that they have the appearance but not the plan of a villa. At Kirby Hall, Yorkshire, Lord Burlington and Roger Morris designed a house in 1747 with a central villa block with a 1.3.1 rhythm, extended discretely on either side by lower wings. At Wrotham Park, Middlesex (1754), Isaac Ware again designed a central villa block flanked by two pavilions connected by three-bay link ranges and stretched the *piano nobile* across the whole house, allowing a run of seven rooms across the front. John Carr did the same on a grander scale, and to a more carefully considered design, at Harewood House, as did James Wyatt at Heaton Hall, Lancashire (*c*.1772). However, this solution, which meant that the interior of the house could not be read through the disposition of the exterior, went against Palladian standards of honesty and was never widespread.

As suited their self-consciously grand manner, both Woburn and Worksop were designed with a pair of state apartments flanking a central saloon – although at Woburn only the north side of the west range was fitted up as a state apartment, on the south side what should have been the bedchamber was left as the library.[34] In this

263   James Paine, Stockeld Park, Yorkshire, 1758.

264 Sir Robert Taylor, Asgill House, Surrey, c.1760 (aquatint after Thomas Malton).

they were as outdated as they were in their quadrangular plans. The idea of a pair of apartments running along the principal front had been one of the dominant features of the Baroque house, and also characterised such early Palladian great houses as Wanstead, Wentworth Wood-house and Nostell. But the Baroque idea of the state apartment with a series of drawing-rooms leading to a bedchamber and closet, all in an enfilade, was already falling out of fashion in the 1720s and 1730s as the highly formalised aristocratic life of the turn of the century gave way to greater informality. Instead, the state apartment contracted to no more than one suite of rooms consisting of the bedroom and dressing-room and perhaps an ante-room – as at Kedleston – but no drawing rooms. At the same time, the idea of a pair of suites, preferably symmetrical, for the owner and his wife was replaced by a single bedroom and a pair of dressing rooms, the hus-band's often adjacent to the library. Nor was it expected that these suites should be in an enfilade. These develop-ments were to be important in making it possible for the villa to serve as a seat.

Houghton Hall and Ditchley Park built in the 1720s, were important forerunners in the move away from Baroque planning. Neither had state apartments, and

although Campbell's plan makes Houghton look as if it was a symmetrical house with pairs of apartments on either front, both were, in fact, designed to divide into two semi-independent units each centred around an internal staircase, separated by the hall and saloon (Fig. 260). One side was essentially for the family, the other for public use.[35] It is possible that this layout derives from French example.

Sanderson Miller used such a plan at Hagley House as did Carr on a grander scale at Harewood, and it was followed almost exactly by Samuel Wyatt at Doddington Hall, Cheshire as late as 1776. But by the 1750s the idea of the double circuit was already being superseded by the single circuit, which was probably pioneered at Holk-ham in the 1730s. Here, the family rooms were in a detached pavilion organised, like the family part of the house at Houghton, around a central internal staircase (Fig. 261).

This was a momentous move which had profound implications both for grand London houses and for the development of the villa. In London, Matthew Brettingham, the executant architect at Holkham, de-signed Norfolk House in St James's Square, completed in 1752, with a circuit of rooms around a central staircase.

265   Pierre Bullet, Château de Champs, Seine-et-Marne, France 1693.

As Mark Girouard has shown, this rapidly became the fashion for great London houses, while those that did not have the space to allow a full circuit were designed as a D, with the staircase along one side rather than in the centre.[36] York House in Pall Mall, another Brettingham house with this plan, built for the Duke of York in 1761, was one of the few London houses to be published in the fifth volume of *Vitruvius Britannicus*.

Brettingham's country house designs were less innovative, following the main block of Holkham, but others were swift to follow his lead and introduce the idea of a central staircase and surrounding circuit of rooms to the villa. James Paine built an important series of villas in the north of England, some of which, such as Gosforth Hall and Axwell Park, Northumberland (1755 and 1758), revolved around a central staircase, but one of the first

266   Jean Courtonne, Hôtel de Matignon, Paris, France, 1721.

267   William Talman, unexecuted plan for Castle Howard, Yorkshire, 1698.

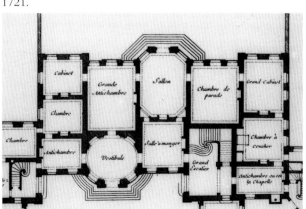

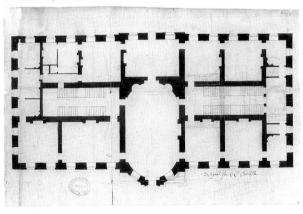

important examples was Langley Park, designed by Leadbetter in 1755 (Fig. 262). Lady Pomfret visiting in 1759 noted with a degree of surprise that 'It is a large plainstone building with three pair of stairs, & many Rooms, but nothing like an Apartment'.[37] The house was entered through a hall and revolved round a handsome central top-lit staircase. To the left of the hall were the public rooms, a dressing-room, dining-room, lesser drawing-room and large drawing-room or library which lay opposite the hall. To the right were the Duke's private apartments, a bedroom, dressing-room, closet, servant's room and back stairs. All the rooms opened one from another, allowing a sequence of different circuits.

Dr Pococke, who visited the house in 1757 remarked that 'the Duke of Marlborough has built a very handsome new house of hewn stone, with four fronts'.[38] This again marked an important change for the villa. Campbell and Burlington's villas in the 1720s and 1730s had generally had a strong central axis running through the hall and saloon. At Langley Park this axis disappeared, and as a result the house had four fronts of equal significance, all consequently with a pediment. Sir Robert Taylor was the first fully to exploit this in 1755 at Harleyford House, Buckinghamshire.

At Harleyford, Taylor gave each front a different elevation, one has a pediment, the next a canted bay, the third a bow and the fourth a flat wall with no pediment. The canted bay, a semi-hexagonal or semi-octagonal structure projecting from a building, was a persistent element in Taylor's houses (Fig. 264) and a marked feature of English architecture in the 1750s and 1760s, when Isaac Ware described it in his *Complete Body of Architecture* in 1756 as an 'absurdity that reigns at present'.[39] During these years it appears in the work of virtually every leading neo-Palladian architect – eleven examples are illustrated in Woolfe and Gandon's *Vitruvius Britannicus* (1767 and 1771). But its origins do not lie in the work of Palladio or Inigo Jones and no examples appear in the first three volumes of *Vitruvius Britannicus*; instead they need to be sought in French architecture a century earlier.

The origins of the canted bay lie with a handful of innovative buildings designed by Louis Le Vau in France in the middle of the seventeenth century. Here at the Château de Raincy, designed before 1645, at the Louvre from 1654 and at Vaux-le-Vicomte, of 1657, Le Vau broke his façades with a centrally-placed projecting bow.[40] His inspiration is unclear, as there seems to be no direct Italian precedent. Bernini's curved design for the Louvre was not made until 1664, and remained unexecuted, while in Italy the first comparable curved façade is Guarini's Palazzo Carignano in Turin of 1679. A possible link can be made with the oval salon in the garden front of the Palazzo Barberini in Rome, designed

by 1628. Oval spaces in Italy, particularly in secular buildings, are rare before 1628 and so this salon was an important innovation, but while the *salone* of the Palazzo Barberini does project slightly the façade is not curved.[41]

After Le Vau the idea of a bow-fronted house seems to have fallen out of favour in France for much of the rest of the century, in particular not appearing in the work of Jules Hardouin-Mansart, the dominant architect of the middle years of Louis XIV's reign. The two exceptions are the Château de Turny, which is strongly in the Le Vau manner, and Antoine le Pautre's Hôtel de Beauvais in Paris, which has a bow-fronted first-floor vestibule overlooking the courtyard. The end of the century saw a revival of the bow, possibly as a conscious reaction to the monumentalism of such buildings as Versailles, since the bow broke up the façade and brought movement to a building. The key example seems to have been the Château de Champs which has an oval salon with a projecting bow (Fig. 265). This has a complicated building history. Work was in hand in 1693, but the house received its final form about 1701 under Pierre Bullet.[42]

Bullet's example was quickly followed by J.-S. Cartaud at the Château de Montmorency (1702); Jacques Gabriel at the Hôtel de Varangeville (1704); and Germain Boffrand at the Hôtel Amelot (1712) and the design for Château de la Malgrange (1712). By 1720 the projecting bow or canted bay was a standard feature of fashionable French houses.[43] Initially these examples had curved bows with their ends squared off, following the example of the Châteaux de Champs and Montmorency. Others, such as the Hôtel Amelot and the Hôtel de Lassay, were curved and not squared off. Alternatively, the bays are canted not curved, as on the garden front of the Hôtel de Matignon (Fig. 266), the stables at Chantilly, the Palais Bourbon and Hôtel Peyrenc de Moras-Biron.

A similar interest in projecting bows and canted bays can be seen at the same time in England. William Talman, always alive to architectural ideas, was the first to experiment with an oval salon and projecting bow on the garden front of one of his unexecuted designs for Castle Howard, Yorkshire, of 1698 or 1699 (Fig. 267). This innovation does not seem to have been favourably received, for a pencilled emendation shows the curves converted to a more conventional square projection. Talman also designed a small villa, generally associated with the Thames Ditton project of about 1699, with a canted bay.[44] In 1708 his son John placed a projecting oval bay holding a staircase in the centre of his design for a new building at All Souls College, Oxford.[45]

It was Talman's successful rival at Castle Howard, John Vanbrugh, who first incorporated bow windows on an executed scheme, on the two side elevations of Blenheim Palace, Oxfordshire, of 1705 (Fig. 268). Thereafter, he used them at Castle Howard (1706);

268   Sir John Vanbrugh, side elevation of Blenheim Palace, Oxfordshire, 1705.

269   William Kent, 22 Arlington St, London, 1741, seen from Green Park. Number 22 lies on the left, with canted bays.

270   William Talman, Panton Hall, Lincolnshire, c.1719 (demolished)

the Royal Military Academy at Woolwich (1718); Vanbrugh Castle (1718); and Mincepie House, Greenwich (1721).[46] While the source of Talman's bow would definitely appear to be France, Vanbrugh's bows do not seem specifically French. Unlike Talman and Bullet his bows never express oval salons but are projections from rectangular rooms. They are generally formed by three-bay semicircular bows, often pilastered, flanked by slightly projecting bays often pierced by pairs of windows. One possibility, as suggested by Pierre du Prey, is that Vanbrugh developed the idea from Talman's rejected Castle Howard design.[47] Alternatively, as Kerry Downes has argued and Gervase Jackson-Stops has reiterated, Vanbrugh may have derived the motif from his interest in Elizabethan and Jacobean prodigy houses.[48] This seems more probable, for the bow as a projection from galleries or other rooms has a continuous history in English architecture from Henry VIII's Queen's Gallery at Hampton Court to Lilford Hall, Northamptonshire, in 1635.[49] Either way, the influence of Vanbrugh's bows seems to have been relatively limited.[50]

With Thomas Archer we are on firmer ground. The north front at Chatsworth House, Derbyshire (1704), has an oval curve, perhaps inspired by Vaux-le-Vicomte but with the pedimented frontispiece removed, as its central feature. Chettle House, Dorset, built after 1711 with a central bow and further bows at the end of each wing, lies firmly in the contemporary French tradition, despite its original great broken pediment and detailing from Rossi's *Studio d'architettura civile*.

It was, however, from about 1720 that there was a surge of interest in the canted bay. This may have been sparked off by the fashion in France. Panton Hall, Lincolnshire, which was probably being built by William Talman when he died in 1719, is the most important example (Fig. 270).[51] Here, on a much smaller scale, Talman finally used the idea of an oval salon projecting through the façade to create a canted bay, which he had first suggested at Castle Howard two decades earlier. At about the same time the same idea appeared at Orford House in Ugley, Essex, where a canted bay is placed in the centre of a seven-bay façade.[52] These were followed by an undated design for a square house at Abbotstone, Hampshire, with a canted bay on each façade (Fig. 271);[53] the design for the 'House for a Merchant' at Bristol of 1724 in the King's Weston book of drawings which was to have had a canted bay for its entrance hall;[54] and the wings at Gilling Castle, Yorkshire, designed by William Wakefield, which must date between 1719 when work began and Wakefield's death in 1730. Then, in 1726 Nicholas Hawksmoor, who seems to have completed Panton after Talman's death, included two canted bays on the garden front of the rectory of Christ Church, Spitalfields. This may have encouraged Colen Campbell, who did not use canted bays in any of his other buildings, to leave an existing Tudor canted bay at Compton Place, Sussex, when it was refaced in 1726–31. Shortly afterwards, in about 1727, Sir Robert Walpole rebuilt Thatched House Lodge in Richmond Park with a canted bay. The architect is unknown, but William

Kent, then at work for Walpole at Houghton Hall, must be the most likely candidate.

Throughout the 1730s this growing interest in the canted bay continued. William Kent used them on four Gothic designs: at Esher Place, Surrey (1731); in his unexecuted design for Honingham Hall, Norfolk, of 1737; on the wings he added to Rousham House, Oxfordshire, in 1738–41; and in the Gothic screen enclosing the Courts of Chancery and King's Bench in Westminster Hall of 1739. Roger Morris, who had been closely involved with Campbell in his last years and seems to have completed the work at Compton Place after his death in 1729,[55] designed a canted bay on the garden front of his design for Whitton Place, Middlesex, in about 1732 (Fig. 272). This was built for the Earl of Ilay (later Duke of Argyll) for whom he subsequently designed a library in London in 1742 with a pair of canted bays.[56] Canted bays were to be a regular feature of the work of Henry Flitcroft, and early examples could be found on the side elevation of Montagu House, Whitehall (1731), and over the front door of 9 St James's Square (1736). In about 1732, Carlton House was remodelled for the Prince of Wales with a canted bay in the centre of the garden front.

What little building there was in the 1740s often included a canted bay. Kent used a pair at 22 Arlington Street overlooking Green Park in 1741 (Fig. 269), while his Banqueting House at Euston, Suffolk, of 1746, incorporates a canted bay under a dome. Following Kent's Gothic example, Sanderson Miller included bays at Radway Grange, Warwickshire (1744). They were also used by Henry Joynes at Linley Hall, Shropshire (1742); by Flitcroft on the Green Park front of the house he built for the Duke of Kingston in Arlington Street (c.1742)[57] and on the wings and in the centre of the north front at Wimpole Hall, Cambridgeshire in 1745 (Fig. 275); and by Morris at the Banqueting Pavilion on Monkey Island, near Bray, built for the Duke of Marlborough in 1745. In 1747, together with Burlington (who had never used them before) he designed canted bays at each end of the wings at Kirby Hall, Yorkshire.

After the Peace of Aix-la-Chapelle in 1748, the canted bay ceased to be a marginal element in neo-Palladian architecture and became one of its central features, first appearing in print in 1750 in Robert Morris's *Rural Architecture*.[58] It was at its most popular in the 1750s and continued to be used extensively in the 1760s, but this decade also marked the beginning of its gradual replacement by the projecting bow. This had been relatively rare during the middle years of the century.[59] Only two projecting bows are illustrated in Woolfe and Gandon's *Vitruvius Britannicus* (1767 and 1771), compared to eleven uses of the canted bay. Although this demonstrates the dominance of the canted bay, the fact that Asgill House, Surrey, was the only house by Sir Robert

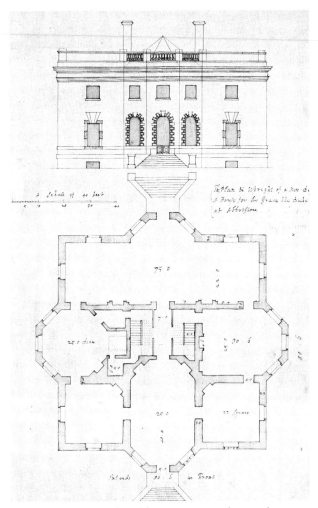

271   Anon., design for Abbotstone, Hampshire, n.d.

Taylor that was illustrated means that it misses the growing popularity of the bow. In three houses built in 1755–6, Harleyford Manor, Buckinghamshire, Coptfold Hall, Essex, and Barlaston Hall, Staffordshire, Taylor introduced the idea of a curved bow on the garden front rising the whole height of a building. Surprisingly, Taylor does not seem to have developed this innovation and his later houses rely on canted bays alone.

Paine experimented with a colonnaded bow in his Kedleston design (Fig. 293), exhibited in 1759, but apart from two London houses, Lord Petre's House in Park Lane (1766) and 105 Pall Mall (1779), where they appear on the garden front, he never repeated the motif. However, James Wyatt did develop the Kedleston design at Heaton Hall, Lancashire (c.1772). Robert Mylne used a Taylorian bow at Cally House, Kirkudbrightshire, in 1763, but it was Robert Adam who took up the bow. It appears in his first house, Hatch House, Kent, (1762) (Fig. 273) and thereafter was a regular feature of his work, particularly in his minor houses of the 1770s.[60]

The replacement of the canted bay by the bow is

272   Roger Morris, Whitton Place, Middlesex, *c.*1732 (demolished).

shown in the two volumes of the *New Vitruvius Britannicus* of 1802–8 which have eleven curved bows, some colonnaded, most not, and only four canted bays. The 1770s seem to have been the turning point, although the canted bay was not completely displaced. John Carr of York, ever-conscious of metropolitan fashion, perhaps acts as a weathercock: three of the examples of canted bays in Woolfe and Gandon are his, as are two in the *New Vitruvius Britannicus*, Denton Hall, Yorkshire, and Basildon Park, Berkshire, of 1770 and 1776. However, Thornes Hall, Yorkshire, of 1779, has a curved bow instead. Curved bays were to be a standard feature of Regency architecture, particularly on smaller houses, such as Sir John Soane's Tendring Hall, Suffolk (Fig. 328), and on town houses where the view was important, as at Brighton.

There were two main reasons for the popularity of the canted bay and for the projecting bow. One was practicality. They allowed an oval-shaped room, let more light into the room and took advantage of the view. It was not by chance that Stiff Leadbetter added a canted bay to the garden front of Nuneham Park, with its fine situation above the Thames looking towards the spires of Oxford, for, as Lord Harcourt admitted, the 'charming view . . . was my chief inducement to build'.[61] Similarly, when the Earl of Chesterfield added a gallery at the Ranger's House in Blackheath in 1748 he gave it three bow windows commanding 'three different, and the finest, prospects in the world'.[62] Many of the early canted bays were clearly built for the views they brought:

Thatched House Lodge on the top of the escarpment in Richmond Park; the two Arlington Street houses looking over Green Park (Fig. 269); Carlton House over its gardens and St James's Park; Whitton Place looking out over the famous gardens there.

Equally important was the architectural effect the canted bay allowed, breaking up a façade and bringing movement through the advance and recession of the building. This seems to have been the reason why projecting bows and canted bays were first introduced into French architecture. This sense of movement also helps to explain their varying popularity in England. It can clearly be seen in the work of the Baroque architects, but the early neo-Palladians, particularly Campbell and Burlington, reacted against it. During the 1720s and 1730s their buildings were essentially static, with elevations that are flat planes. This began to change with Kent, but it is not surprising that the canted bay achieved only limited popularity during these years and was generally used where the view encouraged it. By the 1750s this had changed; the buildings of such second generation neo-Palladian architects as James Paine, Robert Taylor and Henry Keene, who came of age in the 1750s, have a marked sense of movement which can be seen both through the manipulation of the orders and other architectural elements and through the spatial ambiguity inherent in the canted bay. Thus, it is no coincidence that the canted bay was at the height of its popularity in the 1750s, although by then the motif's French origin had probably been forgotten.

The slump of the 1740s had its effect on architectural style as clearly as it did on architectural careers. Its first effect was to kill off finally the Baroque strand of country-house design. If, by 1730, neo-Palladianism had gained the high ground of the architectural establishment, particularly in the Office of Works, its victory in the country was not yet complete. There still remained a strain of country-house design that owed nothing to neo-Palladianism and looked back to an essentially Baroque tradition. This was strongest in the work of provincial master-builders and, although its most successful exponent, Francis Smith of Warwick, had already moved towards Palladianism before his death in 1738, it can still be found in the work of a man such as Nathaniel Ireson at Crowcombe Court, Somerset (1734). The slump of the 1740s starved this strain of oxygen and when the new wave of country-house building began at the end of the forties it had been largely extinguished. Ireson's rejected first design for the north front of Corsham Court, Wiltshire, of 1747, with its Archer-like capitals represents its dying whisper (Fig. 274).[63]

By 1748 a Palladian orthodoxy had been established. Many of the first generation of neo-Palladians, for example Burlington, Kent, Flitcroft and Morris survived – if only just – to contribute to the new country-house

273   Robert Adam, Hatch House, Kent, 1762.

274 Nathaniel Ireson, unexecuted design for Corsham Court, Wiltshire, 1747.

boom, as did many of their protégés – Ware, Bretting-ham, Garrett and Vardy. More significantly, a whole generation had grown up for whom neo-Palladianism was the accepted style of building, such men as Paine, Taylor, Carr, Adam and Chambers who, stimulated by

275 Henry Flitcroft, Wimpole Hall, Cambridgeshire, 1745.

the volume of building in the 1750s and 1760s, were able to develop the style to new heights. It may be true that for the mass of builders from the 1730s James Gibbs had greater direct influence than Burlington, but for the metropolitan architects who came of age in the 1750s it was Burlingtonian Palladianism, not a simplified Gibbsian version, that inspired their work. It was in their hands that English neo-Palladianism reached its ascendancy.

Nevertheless, not everyone aspired to these heights. A more idiosyncratic aspect of the spread of neo-Palladianism in the 1750s and 1760s was the way in which certain of its motifs, principally Serlian and Diocletian windows, were taken up by provincial builders to create a vibrant vernacular Palladianism. Ironically, it was a work of Burlington's, one of his very first, the remodelling of old Chiswick House in about 1723, which probably provided the germ for the style: refacing the entrance, Burlington placed a Diocletian window over Serlian window. It was not a combination he used again, but it was followed by Isaac Ware on the wings at St George's Hospital at Hyde Park Corner in 1733 (Fig. 276), and by Henry Joynes at Linley Hall in 1743. Henry Flitcroft, Burlington's former assistant, used the motif most consistently (Fig. 275),[64] and it was quickly picked up by such others as the Hiorn brothers, Joseph Pickford and James Essex.[65] Variations on the combination became the common currency of local builders. The Langwith family in Grantham were typical. Vine House, built in 1764, has a Serlian window on either side of the front door and a pair of Diocletian windows in the attic; numbers 16–17 Watergate, of five bays, had canted bays on either side of the front door, flanked by two tripartite

276   Isaac Ware, St George's Hospital, London, 1733 (demolished).

windows with a Diocletian window above; the Vicarage, built in 1789, is dominated by the Venetian windows on either side of the front door. Meanwhile in Bristol, which had flourished during the 1740s, vigorous, un-scholarly commercial Classicism remained strong.

These were also the years when Palladianism reached new heights on the Continent. In the Veneto the con-tinued strength of the Palladian revival in the hands of such architects as Giorgio Massari and Ottone Calderari spawned a series of scholarly publications. The first of these was Francesco Muttoni's *Architettura di A. Palladio con le osservazioni del l'architetto NN*, published in nine volumes between 1740 and 1760. It was followed by O. Bertotti-Scamozzi's four volumes *Le fabbriche ed i disegni di A. Palladio raccolti ed illustrati* in 1776–83, and D. Cerato's *Nuovo metodo per disgnare li cinque ordini di architettura civile conforme le regole di A. Palladio e V. Scamozzi* in 1784.[66]

In Germany, the influence of English Palladianism proved almost as powerful as that of the master himself.[67] Wenzelaus von Knobelsdorf's Opera in Berlin (1743) was a puffed-up version of Campbell's Stourhead. Von Knobelsdorf's patron was Frederick the Great, who ordered his ambassador in London to acquire a copy of the plans for Burlington's house for General Wade, so that he could copy it at Potsdam. Indeed, Burlington also gave him a copy of the *Fabbriche antiche*. Frederick's Palladian obsession was stoked by the Venetan Francesco Algarotti, who frequented Lord Burlington's circle in London, where Frederick had met him in 1739. It led in the 1750s to a series of Potsdam houses being built as reduced versions of Palladio's palazzi, but this was only one among a number of styles Frederick used in this architectural zoo. As Algarotti described it, Potsdam be-came 'une école d'architecture autant qu'il est une école de guerre'.

More conventional in his approach was Friederich Wilhelm von Ermansdorf, who worked solely for Leopold Franz von Anhalt-Dessau. Von Ermansdorf made two trips to Italy, in 1761 and 1765, on the second occasion visiting Vicenza and studying the villas and palazzi of Palladio. He also visited England in 1763 where he saw buildings by Campbell and other archi-tects. The result was Schloss Worlitz (1769), another extended version of Campbell's Stourhead. In the last decades of the eighteenth century numerous examples of such Palladian houses, probably owing as much to Eng-land as Italy, spread across Germany and into Hungary and Poland.

XII

ADAM, 'MOVEMENT' AND NEO-CLASSICISM

WAS SIR WILLIAM CHAMBERS A neo-Classical architect? Was Robert Adam a neo-Palladian architect? Convention would give a positive answer to the
first question and a negative one to the second, for, as
Damie Stillman stated in his monumental two-volume
English Neo-Classical Architecture (1988), neo-Classicism
'has come to be accepted as the usual designation for the
art, and especially the architecture, of the last four decades of the eighteenth century and, in some cases, the
early part of the century following'.[1] And yet, few theorists have inveighed as powerfully as Chambers against
the primacy of archaeological precedent, which lies at
the heart of the concept of neo-Classicism, while objec-
tive study of Adam's architectural designs shows that for
all his violent attacks on earlier styles his buildings are
heavily indebted to those of Lord Burlington and the
other neo-Palladians.

The confusion lies with the definition of what is
meant by neo-Classical. As has been argued above, neo-
Classicism is an attitude towards the architecture of antiquity which can be present at any time. It is dangerous
to use it to describe a period of architecture or indeed a
style. Neo-Classicism was a feature of English architecture from the time of Inigo Jones and was particularly
strong among amateur architects in the first half of the
eighteenth century. In the second half of the century
interest in neo-Classicism became more pervasive, particularly among professional architects, but it was neither
novel, nor was it all-embracing. Indeed, it would be fair
to argue that neo-Palladianism remained the dominant
force in English architecture into the 1780s, despite the
increasing importance of neo-Classicism. It is the buildings of Chambers and Adam which best demonstrate this
point.

Chambers returned to England in 1755 after five years
in Rome preceded by a year studying architecture in
Blondel's Ecole des Arts in Paris. In Rome he had mixed
with advanced French thinkers centred around Marie-
Joseph Peyre and Charles de Wailly, such as Jean-
Laurent Le Geay and Louis-Joseph Le Lorrain, and his
most famous design of these years, a mausoleum for
Frederick, Prince of Wales, of 1751, reflects their influence. The French circle in Rome was in part influenced

by a new approach to antiquity and so is generally
described as neo-Classical – although David Watkin was
perhaps more accurate in referring instead to Franco-
Italian Classicism – but their influence on Chambers's
work once he had established his practice in England was
minimal. His first substantial country-house design, that
for Harewood House, Yorkshire (1756), betrays a certain
influence from his Roman days – although that of the
High Renaissance is equally strong – but was rejected by
the client. Of his executed works, only the Triumphal
Arch at Wilton, Wiltshire, of 1757 and the Casino at
Marino, near Dublin, of 1758 (Fig. 277), represent the
spirit of what had been discussed in Rome, but it would
be difficult to identify anything about these buildings
that was specifically neo-Classical in the sense of being
derived directly from antiquity.

Instead, Chambers slipped into the established English
neo-Palladian tradition which he upheld for the rest of
his career. His work reveals a close study of Palladio
and Scamozzi and of Colen Campbell and later neo-
Palladians. Campbell's Newby Hall, Yorkshire (Fig.
278), was the source for his unexecuted design for
Llanaeron, Cardigan (*c*.1761), as it was for Duddingston
House, East Lothian (1763) (Fig. 279), although with
freestanding rather than attached porticos. Duntish
Court, Dorset (*c*.1760) (Fig. 280), can be read as an
astylar version of Stourhead Wiltshire, (Fig. 132), with
the balustrade replaced by a pitched roof. Lord
Bessborough's villa at Roehampton, with its hexastyle
portico and square attic windows above the cornice,
could be seen as a reinterpretation without the dome of
Campbell's Mereworth, Kent, or as an adaptation of
Isaac Ware's Foots Cray, Kent. Peper Harow, Surrey
(*c*.1765), follows Ware's Wrotham Park, Middlesex, in
flanking the centrepiece with Serlian windows, while
Charlemont House, Dublin (1763), is adapted from
Ware's Chesterfield House, London.

Other Chambers schemes show similar neo-Palladian
influence. His unexecuted design of 1768 for a hunting
lodge for Lord Charlemont is a paraphrase of Roger
Morris's Whitton Place, which he had acquired in 1765.[2]
At the other end of the architectural scale, the four
different projects for a palace at Richmond, which date

277   Sir William Chambers, the Casino at Marino, Dublin, 1758.

between 1762 and 1775, lie firmly in the neo-Palladian tradition. Similarly, the riding house at Buckingham House follows the standard neo-Palladian design for a stable or riding house, of Diocletian windows set in blank arcading, which William Kent had established at the Royal Mews. However, Chambers differed from contemporaries like Paine in that he seldom quotes directly from Lord Burlington and William Kent, or indeed from Palladio.

However, the work which best sums up Chambers's architectural beliefs is Somerset House, to which he devoted the last twenty years of his career from 1776 (Fig. 281). Although the influence of contemporary French buildings which Chambers had seen in Paris in 1774 is often emphasised, John Newman's account of the building rightly stresses that 'Somerset House is fundamentally Palladian'.[3] Here, Chambers achieved the synthesis that he stressed in his theoretical writings. As the anonymous author of 1778 (widely taken to be Chambers) quoted in Baretti's *Guide* of 1781 explained: 'It [Somerset House] is an attempt to unite the chastity and order of the Venetian Masters with the majestick grandeur of the Roman.'[4] Jones, Webb, Palladio, Antonio da Sangallo – whose Farnese Palace in Rome provided the source for the delightful triple-vaulted vestibule – all played their part.

Writing of the Adams' 'presumptuous book' in 1773, Chambers complained that 'They boast of having first brought the True style of Decoration into England, and that all architects of the present day are only servile copyers of their excellence', but compared his own work at Melbourne House, 'decorated in a manner almost diametrically opposite to theirs; and more, as I flatter

myself, in the true Style, as approaching nearer to the most approved style of the ancients'.[5] But for Chambers 'the most approved style of the ancients' was not achieved by slavishly following antique precedent. One can hear his beliefs in his pupil James Gandon's disparaging remark about Stuart and Adam 'rummaging even the dunghills of antiquity, producing specimens to shew what architecture was in its infancy and in its decline'.[6] Chambers's approach to architecture is explained in a letter he wrote to Edward Stevens on the eve of the latter's departure for Italy in 1774:

> Do not, as some have done, begin your studies where they ought to be left off, and instead of forming yourself upon those noble remains, whence the great masters of the fifteenth and sixteenth centuries collected their knowledge, trifle away your time in collecting little poor ornaments and extravagant forms, from the remains of barbarous times. Our taste here has been sufficiently poisoned by this unlucky mistake. Work in the same quarry with M. Angelo, Vignola, Peruzzi and Palladio, use their materials, search for more and endeavour to unite the grand manner of the two first with the elegant simplicity and purity of the last.

He went on to stress the point, stating that Palladio's and Scamozzi's works

> which are numerous, require your particular attention. Study them carefully and correct that luxuriant, bold and perhaps licentious style which you will have acquired at Rome, Florence, Genoa and Bologna by their simple, chaste but rather tame manner; form if you can a style of your own in which endeavour to avoid the faults and blend the perfections of all.[7]

English neo-Palladians had always mixed the Venetian and the Roman *cinquecento* schools in varying degrees – as can be seen particularly in the work of William Kent. Chambers forms the ultimate expression of this tendency.

Chambers's Palladianism did not extend to sympathy for a neo-Classical approach to antiquity. The only building of his that can correctly be described as neo-Classical is the Temple of the Sun in Kew Gardens, of 1761, based on the eponymous temple at Baalbek. He presumably considered such direct reproduction acceptable in a garden where the buildings formed a pattern book of architectural styles ranging from China to Rome. Chambers is often portrayed as a Roman antipathetic to Greek architecture, but – as his advice to Edward Stevens makes clear – his real rejection was of the idea of antique architecture, whether Greek or Roman, being inherently superior. This was a belief he shared with Paine. Thus, he rejected the fundamental neo-Classical idea that the Roman Doric order should

278 Colen Campbell, Newby Hall, Yorkshire, 1720, from *Vitruvius Britannicus* (1725)

279 Sir William Chambers, Duddingston House, Midlothian, 1763.

be baseless because it was so in antiquity. His statement 'if columns without bases are now set aside, it is a mark of the wisdom of our Architects, rather than an indication of their being governed by prejudice, as some adorers of antiquity would insinuate'[8] is a strictly anti-neo-Classical statement. He had no more time for the structural theories of Laugier: the primitive hut, he argued, is not a model of perfection but merely the first step in the evolutionary development of architecture. As Eileen Harris stated: 'He accepts nothing as pre-ordained, no authority as infallible. Everything is examined critically and impartially . . . Perfection consists for him in mediums between extremes, discovered by experience and ratified by the universal consent of the ancients and moderns.'[9] Chambers's approach to architecture can be compared with that of Wren, and, like Wren, he cannot be described as a neo-Classicist.

Chambers never denied his fundamental neo-Palladianism. Robert Adam on the other hand declared vociferously that he was completely uninfluenced by those who had come before him. He had no doubt about having revolutionised architecture, and commentators have generally taken him at his word: 'The novelty and variety of the following designs', declared the introduction to *The Works in Architecture of Robert and James Adam* (1773)

280 Sir William Chambers, Duntish Court, Dorset, *c.*1760 (demolished).

will, we flatter ourselves, not only excuse, but justify our conduct to the world. We have not trod in the path of others, nor derived aid from their labours . . . To enter upon an enquiry into the state of this art in Great Britain, till the late changes it has undergone, is not part of our present design. We leave that subject to the observation of the skilful; who we doubt not, will easily perceive, within these few years, a remarkable improvement in the form, convenience, arrangement, and relief of apartments; a greater movement and variety, in the outside composition, and in the decoration of the inside, an almost total change.

Nevertheless, the more Adam's work is compared with that of his contemporaries the less accurate his statement becomes. Despite his anxious, self-proclaimed novelty, Adam's buildings display many features which, in another architect, would be explained as neo-Palladian: numerous Serlian windows, particularly in recessed arches, rustication, especially of the ground floor, the common use of the *piano nobile*, porticos both attached and freestanding. Much of his work – including exteriors, planning and interior decoration – is anticipated by Lord Burlington and subsequent neo-Palladians, particularly James Paine and Robert Taylor.

281   Sir William Chambers, Somerset House, London, 1776 (Jean-Louis Desprez, pen and watercolour, Yale Center for British Art, New Haven, Conn. (detail)).

There is no explanation for this contradiction in Adam's writings; Adam never credited a source. In fact it is a common feature of his writing that he tended to disparage anyone whose work paralleled or anticipated his own. The best-known examples of this are his dismissive remarks about James Stuart, whose work at Spencer House in London was 'pityfulissimo', and his designs for Kedleston Hall, Derbyshire, 'so excessively and ridiculously bad'[10] that they 'beggared all description', but the same tendency can be found when Adam mentions Palladio and the later neo-Palladians. In Italy he dismissed Palladio in a letter as 'one of those fortunate geniuses who have purchased reputation at an easy rate'[11] and promised 'in imitation of Scotch heroes, to become author, to attack Vitruvius, Palladio and those blackguards of ancient and modern architecture, sword in hand'.[12] It would not have been possible to guess this opinion from his use of interlocking pediments on the design for the Royal College of Physicians in Edinburgh,

one of the first buildings he worked on after his return to London in 1758. Anyone informed in architecture in the mid-eighteenth century would have been well aware that this motif derives from Palladio's Venetian churches. The library was never built, but Adam returned to the theme with his first (unexecuted) design for Great Saxham House, Suffolk, of 1762,[13] and at Witham Park, Somerset (Fig. 282), which was begun in the same year but never finished.

Similarly, Burlington and Kent are the obvious targets of one particular attack in the introduction to the *Works*: 'The massive entablature, the ponderous compartment ceiling, the tabernacle frame, almost the only form of ornament formerly known, in this country, are now universally exploded.' This statement sits strangely with the fact that one of the rooms most extensively illustrated in the first volume of the *Works*, the entrance hall at Syon House, Middlesex (1762–9), is graced with a massive entablature and ponderous compartment ceiling,

while the (admittedly unillustrated) dining-room has a tabernacle frame over the chimney-piece (Fig. 284). Nor is Syon House alone. The library at Harewood House, of about 1769, has a similar tabernacle frame over its chimney-piece; so does the great eating-room at Headfort House, County Meath, of 1775; there are more in the entrance hall at Wormleybury, Hertfordshire, of 1777. Just because Adam condemned a motif or the work of an architect is no reason to assume that he did not use that motif or was not influenced by that architect.

Adam more than any other eighteenth-century British architect realised the importance of novelty as an enticement for clients and of publishing as a means of self-promotion, as Eileen Harris demonstrated in *British Architectural Books and Writers* (1990). Any stylistic comment he made, whether in a private letter or printed book, needs to be compared with his executed work (and that of his contemporaries) before being accepted as a true statement of fact.

If Adam can be defined as a neo-Palladian it is not because the direct influence of Palladio is strong in his work. Indeed, there seems to be no evidence in Adam's buildings of a considered study of Palladio. Instead, the link, even between Palladio's Venetian churches and Adam's interlocking pediment designs, is at one remove. Interlocking pediments had already been anticipated in the circle around Lord Burlington with the Orangery at Chiswick, Burlington's designs for the Council House at Chichester and Kent's Temple in the Woods at Holkham Hall, Norfolk, and by James Paine at Serlby Hall, Nottinghamshire (1754) (Fig. 283), and probably at Milnsbridge Hall, Yorkshire (*c.*1750).[14] The Palladian tenor of Adam's work derives from the English neo-Palladians who formed the dominant architectural school during his formative years and on his return to England.

Burlington and Kent were pervasive influences on Adam's work, as they were on that of James Paine. The influence comes both in direct borrowings, sometimes of

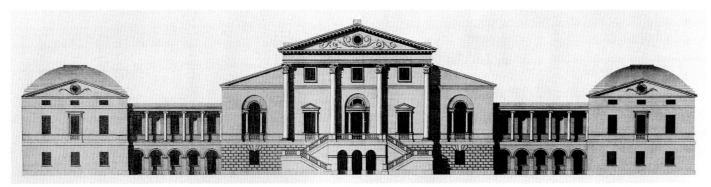

282   Robert Adam, Witham Park, Somerset, 1762, from *Vitruvius Britannicus* (1771) (demolished).

283   James Paine, Serlby Hall, Nottinghamshire, 1754, from *Plans, Sections and Elevations of Noblemen and Gentlemen's Houses* (1767) (remodelled).

whole façades, and in attitudes towards planning and the antique. Holkham (extensively published in 1761 and possibly visited by Adam in 1759) was a particularly important influence on both Adam and Paine. The entrance front of Adam's February 1767 scheme for Luton Park, Bedfordshire, with its hexastyle portico flanked by corner pavilions with Venetian windows and pyramidal caps, is taken directly from the garden front at Holkham.[15] At Gosford House, Lothian, of 1791, Adam took the essential form of Holkham, with its great central villa-like structure flanked by smaller tripartite wings, but used the north front of Chiswick, with its three Venetian windows in recessed arches interspersed by niches and topped by a central dome, as the framework for the west elevation, adding a central portico and pilasters. The fishing lodge at Kedleston of 1770 (Fig. 255) derives from the wings at Holkham (Fig. 151), while Adam probably took Holkham's sculpture gallery, with its plain niches along the walls, as the model for those which can be found at Croome Court, Worcestershire, Shelburne House and in the dining-room at Syon House. Finally, the hall at Kedleston, one of Adam's great *coups de théâtre*, is the child of that at Holkham, although here the midwives were Brettingham and Paine.

Burlington and Kent are intimately mixed at Holkham, but the influence of Kent alone can also be seen in some of Adam's interiors. One of Adam's most successful spaces is the imperial staircase, with its niche at the landing, at 20 Portman Square (Fig. 286); this was probably inspired by Kent's 44 Berkeley Square (Fig. 285). Nor should it be forgotten that Kent anticipated Adam in designing complete interiors, furniture as well as the architectural framework and decoration.

Equally important is the precedent Burlington and Kent provided for Adam's interest in neo-Classicism. Burlington anticipated Adam in collecting drawings of Classical remains and in using them as sources for his designs. Indeed, in a building such as the York Assembly Rooms Burlington was a far more thorough going neo-Classicist than Adam. Similarly at Holkham, Chiswick and York, Burlington, taking his cue from the Roman Baths, anticipated the variety of shapes of room – octagonal rooms, circular rooms, rectangular rooms with apses at each end, rooms with niches – of which Adam made such effective use (Figs. 287 and 288).

One feature particularly associated with Adam does not seem to have been used by Burlington, apses screened by pairs of columns carrying an architrave, as in the library at Kenwood. (The first floor room in the link building at Chiswick does have pairs of columns at each end supporting an architrave but the walls behind are not

284   Robert Adam, the entrance hall, Syon House, Middlesex, 1762.

285   William Kent, the staircase, 44 Berkeley Square, London, 1742.

286   Robert Adam, the staircase, 20 Portman Square, London, 1773.

curved.) However, this motif was not introduced by Adam; Kent used it externally on the façade of the Temple of Venus at Stowe (1729), and Burlington's protégé Isaac Ware included a hall with a pair of columned apses in his competition design for the Mansion House of 1737, subsequently engraved.[16] It was not until the late 1750s and early 1760s that the fashion for columned apses suddenly emerged. James Stuart included one in the Painted Room at Spencer House of 1759, while in the same year Paine exhibited his designs for Kedleston with columned apses at either end of the staircase hall. In 1762 he exhibited his Banqueting House at Forcett Park, Yorkshire, which has three colonnaded apses. That year also, he designed Worksop Manor, Nottinghamshire, which was intended to have a great room in the west range with colonnaded apses. Adam planned such apses at Compton Verney, Warwickshire, in 1760, and Witham Park, Somerset, in 1762, and they first seem to appear in his work in the dining-room and hall at Syon of 1761.

Generally, Adam did not follow Burlington's interpretation of Roman interior decoration, the internal use of complete entablatures taken from specific temples as at Holkham. What he did favour, especially in the early years after his return from Italy, was decorating ceilings with paintings in imitation of those found in antique tombs. Here again, Adam did not introduce the idea to England. As already seen, Kent had done so thirty years earlier, and had been followed by Sir Andrew Fountaine and Sir Francis Dashwood. Adam was aware of this but, typically, dismissed Kent's examples as 'evidently those of a beginner'.[17]

Burlington and Kent form the foundation on which much of Adam's work stands, but the most interesting parallels are with his immediate contemporaries, particularly James Paine and Robert Taylor, the two architects who, according to Thomas Hardwick, 'nearly divided the practice of the profession between them till Mr Robert Adam entered the lists'.[18] Of the two it was Paine, who had been practising for well over a decade and had more than a score of houses to his credit, many for aristocratic clients, whom Adam was keenest to displace; as he did at Kedleston Hall, Nostell Priory, Yorkshire, and Alnwick Castle, Northumberland.

It would be wrong, however, to think that Adam displaced Paine because his architecture was exciting and new while Paine's was old-fashioned and dull. When comparing individual buildings it is often the similarities that are most apparent. If the prominent position of Kenwood House, Middlesex, of 1767, in the *Works* is evidence, this is a house of which Adam was particularly proud (Fig. 289). And yet the composition of the south front – two-and-a-half storeys with a rusticated basement, a pediment supported by paired pilasters and a façade defined at each end by further paired pilasters set over niches – was one that appeared repeatedly in Paine's work from his first independent commission, Heath House, Yorkshire, in 1744. The only feature that distinguishes Kenwood from examples by Paine is the decorative treatment of the pilasters and the plaques above the first-floor windows.

Similarly, the design for the south front of Stowe House, Buckinghamshire, of 1771 (Fig. 291), the largest Adam ever made for a country house, can be read as a combination of the hexastyle portico of Paine's north front at Kedleston (Fig. 293) with the flanking Venetian windows and twin attached columns (reduced to pilasters) of the south front. The wings of the Stowe design would have had three Serlian windows above a low rustic framed by pilasters, with a balustraded cornice, a combination – with the pilasters replaced by pairs of attached columns – considered by Paine for the west front of Sir Matthew Featherstonhaugh's house in

Whitehall (illustrated in the first volume of Paine's *Works* in 1767). It could even be argued that Adam's Deputy Ranger's Lodge in Green Park, of 1768 (Fig. 331), should be read as a reduced and simplified form of Paine's garden front at Kedleston (Fig. 293) with a central, domed, circular room, expressed externally by a colonnade above an arcade, breaking out of a rectangular block.

Internally, Paine's suggestions for the decoration of Kedleston anticipate many of Adam's neo-Classical features there:[19] the hall was to be lined with Corinthian columns flanking statues in niches; the circular saloon was to have a coffered ceiling (Paine's preliminary saloon design suggested octagonal coffering such as Adam used); while the staircase was to have apsed ends with colonnaded screens.

It is in the elevations of Kedleston that Adam is generally seen to have broken away from Paine's dull Palladianism, replacing it with his own concept of 'movement'. By April 1760, when Adam took over the commission, building had already begun and so it has been assumed that he had to accept the neo-Palladian formality of the north or entrance front, but was able to

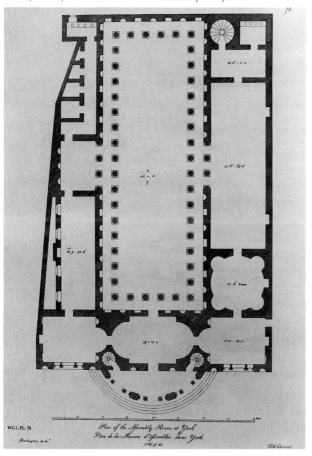

287   Lord Burlington, ground-plan of the Assembly Rooms, York, 1731, from *Vitruvius Britannicus* (1767).

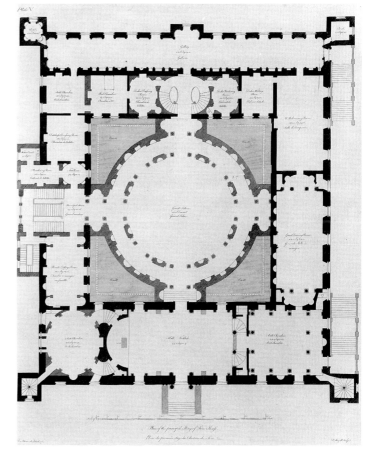

288   Robert Adam, ground-plan of Syon House, Middlesex, 1762, from *Works in Architecture* (1773).

289   Robert Adam, Kenwood House, Middlesex, 1767, from *Works in Architecture* (1773).

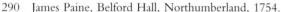
290   James Paine, Belford Hall, Northumberland, 1754.

redesign the south front as he preferred. However, as Leslie Harris has shown, the house was not built from north to south but from east to west. According to Harris, 'Adam would have had ample time to make serious changes to the north front had he or Lord Scarsdale decided to do so'.[20] Despite its neo-Palladianism, Adam had no objections to the north front. Indeed, he went on to repeat it in the second design for the entrance front of Luton Park, for the Earl of Bute in December 1766.[21]

So what of the south front of Kedleston which is usually held up as the model of 'movement' (Fig. 292)? This was the quality which, according to the *Works*, Adam introduced to architecture: '*Movement* is meant to express, the rise and fall, the advance and recess, with other diversity of form, in the different parts of a building, so as to add greatly to the picturesque of the composition.'[22] The south front is probably best seen as a novel variation on the classic tripartite Palladian villa with its rustic and *piano nobile*, but replacing the standard temple front of the centrepiece with a triumphal arch topped by a dome. This is always hailed as a masterpiece, but looked at objectively, would this be so if it were not by Adam? For all the acclaim it now receives, Adam

291   Robert Adam, unexecuted design for the south front of Stowe, Buckinghamshire, 1771.

292   Robert Adam, south front of Kedleston Hall, Derbyshire, 1760.

293   James Paine, unexecuted design for the south front of Kedleston Hall, Derbyshire, 1758, from *Plans, Sections and Elevations of Noblemen and Gentlemen's Houses* (1783).

cannot have considered the south front a great success: he never illustrated it in his *Works* and the triumphal arch motif only reappears once in his buildings, in the unexecuted design for the north front at Luton Park of 1772. It could be argued that Adam's scheme was a rather forced attempt at novelty by an inexperienced architect.

The result certainly has a greater sense of 'movement' than his own north front, but can it really be said to have more 'movement' than Paine's intended south front with its circular, colonnaded, domed rotunda breaking from the square mass of the house (Fig. 293)? Barely a square foot of wall in Paine's scheme is without some form of ornament, some advance or recession of the wall plane, some contrast between solid and void – emphasised by the colonnade and the Venetian windows.

Looking at Paine's design for the south front of Kedleston and at houses by him such as Belford Hall, Northumberland (Fig. 290), all the attributes of 'movement' may be seen in Paine quite as much, if not more so, than in Adam. Similarly, Robert Taylor's villa designs, for example Harleyford House, Buckinghamshire, of 1755, or Asgill House, Surrey, of 1761 (Fig. 264), seem to epitomise the concept of 'movement' with their subtle use of canted and semi-circular bays, their sense of advance and recession, their varied use of height. Adam certainly found Taylor's intricate planning fascinating, returning to the same idea in his late villa plans. Nor are Paine and Taylor alone among successful architects of the 1750s whose work is often best described through the concept of 'movement'. Henry Keene is another.

While the Adam brothers can be credited with defining and publishing the concept of 'movement', what they were saying was hardly novel by the time it was published in 1773. Given that James Adam first composed the passage for his unfinished essay on architecture in 1762 this is not surprising.[23] But even then what he was describing was an aesthetic which was at its height in the 1750s. By 1773 the concept of 'movement' was positively old fashioned, for advanced architectural thinking had reacted against it in favour of a much greater sense of austerity, which will be discussed in chapter fourteen.

Thus Adam did not arrive in London with a novel style which he quickly used to break the power of older, established architects, but took up and refined the dominant style which he found on his arrival.[24] Nor was neo-Palladianism a temporary influence on Adam. The importance of Chiswick and Holkham as sources for Gosford in 1791 has already been pointed out. In the same year Adam designed Charlotte Square in Edinburgh, a scheme whose domestic element would have caused little surprise forty years earlier (Fig. 294). The central part of the north side, for instance, with its rusticated ground floor, its advance and recession, its

pairs of attached columns at the ends shows no real stylistic advance on houses of the 1750s such as Paine's Belford Hall, Northumberland (Fig. 290), or Axwell Hall, County Durham. This is not to say that Adam did not differ from his neo-Palladian contemporaries, just as they differed from each other. Two distinguishing external features are his use of giant colonnades, such as that planned for Luton Park, and his porticos supported at each end by pairs of columns: a motif which seems to appear first on the stables at Bowood around 1770, and which he used repeatedly during the 1780s and 1790s. But what really distinguished Adam from his contemporaries, and was recognised at the time for being revolutionary, was his use of decoration both internally and externally.

It is in his interiors that Adam's claim to be a neo-Classicist lies. Before considering these, however, his success needs to be set in the context of a growing interest in neo-Classicism evident in the 1750s. Like Palladian neo-Classicism, this was dominated by the enthusiasms of amateurs, and indeed it grew directly out of Palladian neo-Classicism. But where in the earlier part of the century neo-Classicism had been advanced by such individuals as Burlington and Mead, the moving force behind neo-Classicism in the middle years of the century was the Society of Dilettanti. This had been founded in 1732 as a dining society arising out of friendships made in Italy on the Grand Tour. Horace Walpole claimed that while the ostensible qualification for membership was foreign travel, the real one was a propensity to drunkenness. His attack was almost certainly unfair; while there can be no doubt about the ability of a leading Dilettanti such as Sir Francis Dashwood to organise a good party, it was founder members of the 1730s, including Dashwood, who were to prove the moving forces in the new wave of neo-Classicism which accompanied the building boom of the 1750s.

Because the Dilettanti Society is best known for its support for publications on Greek antiquities – particularly Stuart and Revett's *The Antiquities of Athens* (1762) and the subsequent *The Antiquities of Ionia* (1769), which the society published – it is sometimes assumed that its interests were overwhelmingly Greek. Indeed, it has been argued that *The Antiquities of Athens* was the manifesto for an architectural style based exclusively on that of Greece, the Greek Revival, which was then expressed in James Stuart's work: 'from the 1760s onwards, Greek Revivalism is a continuous and expanding theme in British architecture and decoration'.[25] Only the success of Robert Adam 'the man who forestalled the Greek Revival' and Stuart's lack of application is seen as having prevented the Greek Revival becoming widespread until the end of the century. Certainly, this was the view of the Greek Revivalist writers in the next century: 'No event that ever occured in the history of architecture in

294 Robert Adam, Charlotte Square, Edinburgh, 1791.

England, and thence throughout all Europe, produced so sudden, decided, and beneficial effect as did the works of James Stuart', wrote James Elmes in 1847.[26] But this hypothesis is not supported by the writings or actions of the Dilettanti Society and its members. Indeed, when the society considered the model for their proposed club-house in Cavendish Square in 1753, under the direction of a committee which included Sir Francis Dashwood

258 CLASSICAL ARCHITECTURE IN BRITAIN

and Colonel Gray, the guiding force at Spencer House, they ignored Greece and settled on the Roman temple at Pola which Stuart had praised.

The architectural enthusiasms of Sir Francis Dashwood, whose uncle and guardian, the 7th Earl of Westmorland, had been responsible for the remarkable Vitruvian basilica at Mereworth, make the point neatly.[27] As a young man Dashwood travelled extensively, visiting Italy twice as well as the Eastern Mediterranean. He was also a keen collector of archaeological books, both English and foreign, and kept in touch with new discoveries through his correspondence. His first essay in neo-Classicism was a column and ball intended as a milestone erected opposite the park gates at West Wycombe around 1752. This was based on a drawing in Dashwood's collection, possibly by the antiquary Dr William Stukeley, of a similar column erected by the Emperor Vespasian near Rome. The remodelled south front of the house, with its baseless Roman Doric columns, modelled, as we have seen, on Palladio's reconstruction of the peristyle of a Roman house, soon followed. But Dashwood was also one of the first to turn the new information from Greece into architecture. In 1759 he built a Temple of the Winds, based on one of the buildings illustrated in the first volume of *The Antiquities of Athens*; then in 1770 he employed Nicholas Revett to add a west portico to the house. This Greek Ionic portico was a reconstruction of the Temple of Bacchus at Teos, which Revett had just published in *Ionian Antiquities*, and was the first Greek portico to be built on a country house (Fig. 165).

In decorating West Wycombe Park, Dashwood was equally eclectic in his sources, although all the interiors seem to have been intended as neo-Classical reconstructions. No information on Greek decoration was known, but Dashwood made use of Robert Wood's *Ruins of Palmyra* (1753), drawings of antique ceilings by Bartoli and copies of ceiling paintings after the school of Raphael. He also based the floor of the entrance hall, heated by a Roman-style hypocaust, on Roman mosaic pavements.[28]

Thomas Anson was another dilettante who reveals the continuity between Roman and Greek neo-Classicism. At Shugborough, Staffordshire, he littered his park with a selection of garden buildings lifted straight from *The Antiquities of Athens* (Fig. 250). There was a temple with baseless Greek Doric columns modelled on the Hephaesteion, a Tower of the Winds, a triumphal arch copied from the Arch of Hadrian all built in about 1764, and a monument copied from the Choragic Monument of Lysicrates of 1770. These joined an earlier temple with baseless Roman Doric columns intended as a reconstruction of the Temple of Piety in Rome.

It was because of their adherence to Vitruvian ideals that the Dilettanti sought to learn more about the remains of Ancient Greece, not because they wished to replace those ideals. Stuart's declaration of the superiority of Greek architecture was not revolutionary. The Vitruvian tradition that lay at the heart of Burlington and the Palladian neo-Classicists' approach to antiquity always acknowledged Greek architecture as the fount of beauty. Stuart's various proposals for *The Antiquities of Athens* stress that his work also arose out of his respect for Vitruvius:

> We shall likewise endeavour ... to illustrate each Print with such explanations and descriptions as will be necessary to make them useful, and intelligible, which will be chiefly done by pointing out the relation they may have to the Doctrine of Vitruvius, or the Description of Pausanius, Strabo, &c.[29]

This point is made even clearer in Revett's introduction to *Ionian Antiquities* (1769):

> Among the Remains of Antiquity which have hitherto escaped the Injuries of Time there are none in which our Curiosity is more interested than those Buildings which were distinguished by VITRUVIUS, and other antient Writers, for their Elegance and magnificence ... However mutilated and decayed these Buildings now are, yet surely every Fragment is valuable, which preserves, in some degree, the Ideas of symmetry and Proportion which prevailed at that happy Period of Taste.[30]

The well-publicised quarrel between Johann Winckelmann and Giambattista Piranesi during the 1760s and 1770s over the relative merits of Greek and Roman architecture, and the subsequent rise of the exclusivist Greek Revival, which was based on the primacy of the Greek orders and of column and lintel construction and considered Roman architecture as unworthy of imitation, has created a false dichotomy in mid-eighteenth-century English architecture. At that time, interest in Greek and Roman buildings was part of a single desire to increase knowledge of antique buildings.

The Palladian neo-Classicists had largely relied on published sources and on the researches of Italians such as the Bartolis for their information on antiquity. In the 1750s this changed, as British architects and artists based in Rome and encouraged by amateurs began to produce their own archaeological studies. It was the subsequent return of these architects to London that turned neo-Classicism from being the activity of amateurs to one equally dominated by professionals.

James Stuart, who had set out for Rome in 1742, was the first off the mark with 'Proposals for publishing an Accurate Description of the Antiquities of Athens' in 1748. This project was slow to come to fruition and, in the meantime, Stuart measured the obelisk found in the Campus Martius in Rome, his drawings being published by Bandini in *De obelisco Caesaris Augusti* in 1750. It was not until 1751 that Stuart reached Greece, and, although he returned to England in 1755, the first volume of *The Antiquities of Athens* was not published until 1762. By then Robert Wood had published his *Ruins of Palmyra* in 1753 and his *Ruins of Balbec* in 1757, studies of late-Roman architecture in two Syrian cities. Robert Adam, then studying in Rome, considered a revised version of Desgodetz's *Edifices antiques* and a study of Hadrian's villa at Tivoli before settling on a survey of Diocletian's palace at Split which he visited in 1757, leading to the publication in 1764 of *Ruins of the Palace of the Emperor Diocletian at Spalatro*. In this he was encouraged by Robert Wood and by the painter Allan Ramsay, who had been responsible for bringing back Bartoli drawings for Dr Mead, and was now spending his time gathering information for an essay on Horace's Sabine villa.[31] Adam's Scottish contemporary Robert Mylne travelled to Sicily in 1757 to survey the Greek temples there with the intention of publishing a volume on the 'Antiquities of Sicily', but his dramatic success in winning the Blackfriars Bridge competition almost immediately on returning to England meant that he had neither the time nor the need to do so. These works were followed in 1768 by Thomas Major's *The Ruins of Posidonia* (or Paestum); by the Society of Dilettanti's first volume of *The Antiquities of Ionia* in 1769; by George Marshall's new edition of Desgodetz's *The Ancient Buildings of Rome* in 1771; and by Charles Cameron's *The Baths of the Romans explained and illustrated, with the Restorations of Palladio corrected and explained* in 1772.

As the list of publications shows, Greece had no monopoly at this date. No one period of architecture predominated, and this phase of neo-Classicism is marked by an interest in the breadth of Classical antiquity, something reflected in neo-Classical works built in England in the 1750s and 1760s.

Patrons, particularly dilettanti, were anxious to apply new found knowledge of antiquity to interiors as well as to garden buildings. Neo-Classicism ceased to be a minority concern and became a fashion, rising in importance as interest in Rococo decoration waned. The difficulty lay in finding architects with the skill to create such interiors, and so anyone with a direct knowledge of antiquity was eagerly welcomed.

The first to meet this demand was Giovanni Battista Borra, draughtsman on Robert Wood's expeditions to Palmyra and Baalbek. He is recorded at Norfolk House, London, in 1755 and Stowe, Buckinghamshire, in 1760, and may have worked at Stratfield Saye, Hampshire, and Spencer House, London (*c*.1758).[32] However, Borra's popularity was short-lived. His style mixed antique with Piedmontese Rococo elements, and with the arrival of

'Athenian' Stuart in London in 1755 he was displaced in the favour of the neo-Classicists. This may literally have happened at Spencer House, where Colonel Gray, a leading dilettante, was responsible for the most advanced neo-Classical house of its day.

Stuart's reputation has suffered from the assumption that he wished to introduce a Greek style and failed, but nowhere does Stuart declare a desire to supersede Roman architecture with a system on the column and lintel[33] or a belief that the Greek orders alone should be used. His interest in the buildings that were to become the archetypes of the Greek Revival, in particular the Parthenon, was limited. The first volume of *The Antiquities of Athens* included none of the great monuments of Ancient Greece and concentrated instead on Hellenistic remains. The first Greek motif to be used by Stuart on his return to England, the unusual Serlian windows at Nuneham Park, Oxfordshire, of 1756, derives from the Hellenistic Aqueduct of Hadrian at Athens (Fig. 295).[34] Hellenistic architecture was then seen as an intrinsic part of Greek architecture, not as a later degeneration, as Greek Revivalists would consider it. Chambers was only following popular opinion when he referred in the same breath to buildings 'erected by Pericles or Alexander; while the Grecian flourished most'.[35] The Parthenon and the Erectheum had to wait for the publication of the second volume in 1789, after Stuart's death, while the Greek Doric order played a very minor role in the neo-Classical movement of the 1750s, 1760s and 1770s. It appears only in a handful of park and garden buildings as an archaeological curiosity, not as the central element of a new style.

Stuart had a high opinion of Roman architecture. In his initial proposals for *The Antiquities of Athens* he described the temple at Pola, which he had surveyed, as 'built in the most exquisite taste of the Augustan age'. His aim was not to replace the Roman orders by the Greek ones but to increase the range available:

> a greater number of Examples than those we already have, are necessary in order to form a true judgement of the ancient Architecture; for though many Treatises on this subject have been published, it cannot be truly said we have any Author except Desgodets, on whose authenticity we can entirely depend; and although his Book contains many excellent Examples of the Corinthian Order; yet unless the Coliseo and the Theatre of Marcellus can be supposed Models fit for our imitation in Buildings of a less gigantic structure, he must be allowed very deficient in what he regards the Doric and Ionic Orders.[36]

Elsewhere he commented:

> we thought it would be a work not unacceptable to the lovers of Architecture, if we added to those Col-

295   Stiff Leadbetter, one of the Venetian windows at Nuneham Park, Oxfordshire, 1756.

296   Robert Adam, design for the west portico, West Wycombe, Buckinghamshire, c.1771.

lections, some examples drawn from the Antiquities of Greece . . . it must then be granted that every such example of a beautiful Form or Proportion, wherever it may be found is a valuable addition to the former stock.[37]

Stuart's domestic architecture shows a similar mix of Greece and Rome. His interest in Greek architecture lay primarily in its decorative potential. As was explained in the preface to the second volume of *The Antiquities of Athens*, the purpose of the first volume was to ensure that subscribers 'might find in it something interesting concerning the different Grecian modes of decorating buildings'. In his interiors, Stuart was happy to mix motifs from Roman, Greek and Hellenistic periods. At Holdernesse House and 15 St James's Square he used the ceiling from the Temple of the Sun at Palmyra. In the painted room at Spencer House (Fig. 297) the only Greek elements are the painted Ionic capitals, otherwise the room is almost entirely Roman, including a copy of a surviving Roman painting, the '*Aldobrandini Wedding*' (Rome, Vatican Museums), and Corinthian columns from the Temple of Antoninus and Faustina in Rome. However, the room is, above all, a tribute to Raphael's Vatican Loggie. Nor was Stuart alone at the time in valuing Raphael's work in the Vatican. According to Horace Walpole, Lord Strafford's dining-room at 5 St James's Square was decorated by Andien de Clermont after Raphael's Loggie in the Vatican. Walpole commented that Strafford 'chose all the ornaments'.[38] The exact date of the room is unclear, but as the house was built in 1748–9 and Clermont left England in 1754 it must have anticipated Stuart's work at Spencer House.

Stuart hoped to increase the range of decorative motifs, and in particular to introduce a new Ionic order. In this he was successful. Much of his decorative detail became a standard part of British architecture in the 1760s and 1770s, when the Greek Ionic capital flourished, ironically under the patronage of Robert Adam, and largely superseded the Roman Ionic capital. It is generally assumed that Stuart was pushed aside by Adam because of his own incompetence and sloth. This is probably unfair, for Stuart had a much more successful career than is generally credited, working repeatedly for a small circle of patrons, many connected with the Society of Dilettanti, and developing his own impressive version of antique decoration.[39] Nevertheless, it was Adam, with his ruthless ambition and well-financed office, who seized the fashionable high ground when he returned to London in 1758, in particular displacing Stuart at Kedleston.

Adam was well aware of contemporary interest in neo-Classicism and much of his time in Rome was spent developing an appropriate knowledge of Classical motifs. As a friend of Allan Ramsay he could draw on the latter's knowledge of domestic Roman buildings and the preliminary version of his introduction for the *Ruins . . . of Spalatro* shows this was initially planned to provide similar assistance: 'what still further excited my curiosity was the Hopes of throwing some new Lights upon the private Buildings of the Ancients, A Subject which had

297 James Stuart, the Painted Room, Spencer House, London, 1759.

hitherto been so Superficially handled that I doubted not It would render such an undertaking still more accept-able to the Publick'.[40] In the event, Spalatro turned out to be something of a disappointment and proved to be only of limited help to those trying to recreate Roman domestic architecture. Even Adam made little use of what he found there.

Adam's agressive claim that he had not 'trod in the paths of others, nor derived from their labours' ignored the fact that he had been anticipated by William Kent, Sir Andrew Fountaine and Sir Francis Dashwood in the use of *grottesche*. It also ignores the debt Adam owed to Stuart, who had anticipated him in devising a new style of interior decoration in which Classical motifs, particu-larly those recently published, were used to create inte-riors in which walls, paintings, ceilings and furniture were combined in one integrated design. This was to be

Adam's approach, and one of his first interiors to attempt this, the Painted Breakfast Room at Kedleston (1760) (Fig. 299), although described as being 'quite in a new taste', is heavily indebted to Stuart's Painted Room at Spencer House.[41] Later, Adam was to claim precedence for the Etruscan style which James Wyatt had already used at the temple at Fawley Court, Oxfordshire (1771) – although whether Adam was aware of that or not is unclear.[42]

Adam had no need to be obsessed with primacy, for he soon developed his neo-Classical style with a fluency that outshone Burlington and Stuart. One reason for his success was that, like Stuart, he had a very different attitude towards the antique from the Palladian neo-Classicists. They had wanted to recreate antique build-ings or parts of antique buildings, something that could only be of limited interest to most people. Adam's aim

299 Robert Adam, design for the ceiling of the Painted Breakfast-Room, Kedleston Hall, Derbyshire, 1760.

was 'to seize . . . the beautiful spirit of antiquity and to transfuse it, with novelty and variety'.[43] Archaeological accuracy was not an important consideration. As Eileen Harris noted,

> regarding the whole difficult question of the nature of the influence that Adam's archaeological experiences and publishing projects had on the formation of his style, it is worth stressing the degree to which this influence was in no sense pure or 'exclusive', either in the sense of being 'uncontaminated' by other sources

of inspiration, or of ever being the basis for displacing or combating earlier classical norms on principle.[44]

Instead, antique remains were quarried to serve as inspiration for his imagination. This point is revealingly made by comparing Adam's design for the west portico at West Wycombe (Fig. 296) with that built by Revett (Fig. 165), Adam's being elegant but with no hint of archaeology, while Revett's was an accurate reconstruction of a building mentioned by Vitruvius. Although Adam began by making some fairly literal copies of

298 Robert Adam, the Long Gallery, Syon House, Middlesex, 1762.

300 John Carr, the dining-room, Farnley Hall, Yorkshire, 1786.

301 John Johnson, ceiling at 63 New Cavendish St, London, 1776.

antique ceilings and decoration he soon developed beyond this, using motifs and ideas he had learnt from antiquity in combinations that were his own.

Adam's success in the 1760s was dramatic and in 1774 William Pain acknowledged 'the very great Revolution . . . which of late has so generally prevailed in the Stile of Architecture especially in the decorative and ornamental department'.[45] At Harewood, Kedleston, Syon (Fig. 298), Osterley, Audley End, Nostell, Kenwood, Northumberland House, Saltram and elsewhere he created dazzling interior after interior. He may not have broken entirely with neo-Palladian precedents, but it is fair to say that he transformed them through the lightness of his detail. But his dominance was short-lived; despite all efforts to keep the style exclusive it inevitably filtered down to lesser architects. In July 1773 when the first number of the *Works* appeared, English pattern-books showed little evidence of Adam's influence, but with the launch of the monthly *Builder's Magazine*, and the publication by Adam's former draughtsman George Richardson of *A book of Ceilings composed in the Stile of the Antique Grotesque* and William Pain's *Practical Builder*, all in 1774, Adam-derived ornament and decoration were instantly available to builders, architects and patrons who before would have needed direct contact with the Adam office.[46] John Carr, who worked with Adam at Harewood, was capable of a very creditable version at such houses as Basildon House, Berkshire (1776), and Farnley Hall, Yorkshire (1786) (Fig. 300). Other architects developed simpler versions. The work of John Johnson, the Essex builder who had much work in the 1770s and 1780s, is typical of the sub-Adam style that became common (Fig. 301). But Adam's expensive, fashionable manner carried within it the seeds of its own downfall. The greater the fashion the greater the chance of a violent reaction and in Adam's case the expence of his style meant that it was highly vulnerable when the outbreak of war in 1776 brought an end to the boom years of the 1760s and 1770s and with it the demand for extravagantly expensive interiors.

PALLADIANISM ON THE PERIPHERIES: SCOTLAND, IRELAND AND THE AMERICAS AFTER 1748

B Y 1815 THE PERIPHERIES OF the British architectural world had seen a political revolution, a revolution which was reflected in brick and stone. Despite the Act of Union in 1707, Scotland still seemed almost a foreign country in 1748 – only three years earlier a Scottish army had penetrated as far as Derby. By 1815 the idea of a British state which subsumed England and Scotland had been accepted. Just as it was then accurate to talk of a British Empire and a British army, so it would be correct to talk of British architecture rather than separate English and Scottish architectures. In Ireland the 1770s and 1780s had seen growing prosperity and confidence leading to parliamentary independence in 1782. This was reflected in Dublin's innovative architecture, as advanced as anything in England. The Act of Union in 1801 destroyed Dublin's pretensions and brought Irish, like Scottish, architecture firmly within London's orbit. Meanwhile, with the economic growth of the 1750s and 1760s, American architecture had almost closed the stylistic gap with England that was still obvious in 1748. Then, just at the moment when English – or rather British – architecture experienced marked stylistic advance, American architecture was cut off from its mainspring, first by war in 1776 and then in 1782 by independence. The result was a stylistic recession that took several decades to overcome.

Scotland

In *Britons: Forging the Nation 1707–1837* (1992), Linda Colley has shown how it was only in the years after 1748 that the Act of Union really changed the relationship between England and Scotland. For the Scots these were years of prosperity, years in which the Scottish economy expanded faster than ever before. Between 1750 and 1800 overseas commerce grew by 300 per cent while the proportion of Scots in towns doubled.[1] In Edinburgh the New Town was laid out in 1767 and still represents

the finest expression of late eighteenth-century North British optimism. It was also a symbol of the way Edinburgh was now seen as a British rather than an exclusively Scottish town, with the three main streets named after the King, Queen and Prince of Wales – George, Queen and Prince's Streets – while two of the lesser ones were named after the dynasty (Hanover Street) and the king's father (Frederick Street). The union of the two nations was epitomised – or at least it was in the initial plan – in the squares at each end of the New Town, named after the two patron saints, Andrew and George. Glasgow saw an equally rapid expansion, although there the nineteenth century now dominates. Nor was growth restricted to the cities and towns. Agricultural advance was rapid in the Lowlands and much of the landscape, with its network of farms, dates from these years. As John Martin Robinson showed in *Georgian Model Farms* (1983), model farms, most of which date from these years, were relatively far commoner in Scotland than in the agriculturally more advanced south. Growing Scottish prosperity, coupled with the rich pickings to be gained in England and the empire, meant that there was more money to be spent on country houses. This volume of building was accompanied by rapid stylistic advance, advance which drew English and Scottish architecture close together. However, just as Linda Colley observes that for the Scots becoming British did not mean ceasing to be Scottish as well, so in architecture certain distinctively Scottish traits survived.

'Far from succumbing helplessly to an alien identity imposed by others, in moving south they [the Scots] helped construct what being British was all about.'[2] This is particularly true of architecture. Ever since Colen Campbell and James Gibbs had made their way to London in the first decades of the century – just after the Act of Union – the Scots had been an important force in English architecture. But before 1748 poor communications meant that an architect setting out for London effectively abandoned any Scottish practice. Campbell is not known to have designed anything that was built in Scotland once he had settled in the south, and although Gibbs designed Balveny House, Banffshire, in 1724, and St Nicholas Church West in Aberdeen in 1741, and was involved at Quarrell, Stirlingshire, in 1735, this was only a very small part of his practice.

Nor was there much trade the other way. Despite the marked influence of Sir Christopher Wren and of Prattian Palladianism on Sir William Bruce and James Smith, direct English involvement in eighteenth-century Scottish architecture before the death of William Adam in 1748 was minimal. The 2nd Duke of Argyll obtained a sketch for rebuilding Inveraray Castle, Argyllshire, from Sir John Vanbrugh in about 1720 but nothing came of it. It was to another English architect, Roger Morris, that the Duke's brother, the 3rd Duke of Argyll, turned when he revived the same project in 1745 – an understandable choice as the Duke had previously employed Morris extensively in England. The Duke had already built a new house for himself at Whim, Peebleshire, in 1731–43, before he succeeded to the title, and a sketch-plan dated October 1744 and inscribed 'pr Mr. Morris' suggests that Morris was involved in the formation of the gardens there.[3] He also produced unexecuted designs for coach houses and other offices at Blair Atholl, Perthshire, in 1742, and may have been responsible for drawings for remodelling Rosneath, Dunbartonshire, dated 1744 and 1747.[4] Despite this, Morris's impact north of the border was limited.

By the 1760s an architect moving to London no longer had to abandon his Scottish practice. A British practice was now possible thanks to improved communications. Robert Adam and his brother James are the archetypal Scottish architects in London, but there were others, including Robert Mylne and James Playfair, while both William Chambers and James Stuart were of Scottish extraction. Adam maintained an office in Edinburgh with the help of his elder brother John, who never left Scotland. Indeed, after the collapse of his English practice during the American Revolutionary War Adam concentrated on Scottish work. For Mylne, Scotland was probably as important a source of commissions as England, while Playfair (who died aged only thirty-nine) found that his work was almost exclusively Scottish, despite his office being in London.

By the time of William Adam's death his sons must have been aware that their father's style was increasingly old-fashioned and indeed provincial. To John Adam, who carried on the family business, this fact must have become painfully clear on the concentrated architectural tour of England he made in 1748, the year his father died, during which he made a detailed study of neo-Palladian buildings such as Combe Bank, Kent, which he recorded in his sketchbook.[5] The result was a marked change of architectural direction away from William

302   James Adam, unexecuted design for Gunsgreen House, Berwickshire, c.1755.

Adam's exuberant use of Classical detail in favour of restrained English Palladianism. While the Exchange in Edinburgh of 1753 could be a work of William Adam, John Adam's first major country house, Dumfries House, Ayrshire (Fig. 303), begun the next year, could pass almost without comment in England. Tripartite, with a central pediment, rustic, *piano nobile* and flanking wings, only the pulvinated frieze and the (for England) old-fashioned ground-plan sets it apart from the work of an English contemporary such as Stiff Leadbetter. Contemporary drawings by James Adam, such as that for Gunsgreen House, Berwickshire (c.1755) (Fig. 302), with its rusticated ground floor and *piano nobile*, show how English Palladianism had become the house style of the brothers' practice. The design for Gunsgreen House would have looked quite at home in Isaac Ware's *A Complete Body of Architecture*, published in 1756. Nor was it only on exteriors that the Adams were influenced by Ware. Much of the detail for the fitting up of Dumfries House and of Hopetoun House, West Lothian (c.1755), was taken from Ware.[6]

More ambitiously Palladian is Paxton House, Berwickshire, (1758) (Fig. 304). Although often ascribed to the Adam family, documentary evidence is lacking, and if it is by the Adams it seems strange that it was not included in *Vitruvius Scoticus*, as Dumfries is. This has a portico-in-antis and a pulvinated frieze with a full Doric entablature. If Dumfries is reminiscent of Leadbetter, Paxton could almost be the work of John Carr of York, but James Gibbs's unexecuted design for Whitton

303 John Adam, Dumfries House, Dumfriess-shire, 1754.

304 Anon., Paxton House, Berwickshire, 1758.

305 William Adam, model of Mavisbank, Midlothian, 1723.

306 John Clerk, Penicuik House, Midlothian, 1761.

307   Robert Adam, Register House, Edinburgh, 1774, from *Works in Architecture* (1773).

Place, illustrated in *A Book of Architecture* in 1728, is a more plausible source than any overtly neo-Palladian publication.[7]

If any two buildings represent the changing face of Scottish architecture in the middle years of the eighteenth century they are the country houses built by successive Clerk baronets. Mavisbank, Midlothian (Fig. 305), built by Sir John Clerk with William Adam in 1723, follows the ideal of the Palladian tripartite villa but with a classic Scottish ground-plan and marked idiosyncracy in the details – it has French-style quoins, for instance, and lavish stone garlands over the windows of the *piano nobile*. It was not a house of which Lord Burlington would have approved and indeed Clerk was critical of Burlington's Chiswick House. Penicuik House, Midlothian, rebuilt to his own designs by Clerk's son Sir James Clerk in 1761 with John Baxter, formerly mason at Mavisbank, as his executant architect, was very different (Fig. 306). With its hexastyle Ionic portico, its dominant *piano nobile* (the bedroom floor is treated as an attic), and its pavilion towers with Serlian windows, Penicuik is essentially an attenuated version of the most influential English Palladian house of the 1730s, Burlington, Leicester and Kent's Holkham Hall, Norfolk.

Although English style penetrated north of the border after 1748, few English architects did. One who did have good Scottish contacts was Isaac Ware, who not only built Amisfield, East Lothian, in 1756, but also published designs in his *Complete Body* for Cally House, Kirkudbrightshire, and Carnsalloch, Dumfriess-shire. Apart

from Ware, the only major mid-eighteenth-century English architect to practice in Scotland was William Chambers who built Duddingston House, Lothian, for the Earl of Abercorn in 1763, together with two houses in Edinburgh, 26 St Andrew's Square, in 1769, and Dundas House (the greatest of the Edinburgh townhouses) for Sir Lawrence Dundas, in 1771. Other English architects who tried their hand in Scotland include Henry Holland and Thomas Harrison, but these incursions were relatively minor. No English architect established a long-distance Scottish practice as extensive as that of James Wyatt in Ireland – indeed, the prolific James Wyatt is conspicuous by his absence in Scotland. Nor did any Englishman settle in Scotland as James Gandon did in Dublin. In the creation of a British architecture it was the Scots who gained, creating extensive practices in England while effectively maintaining a closed shop in their native land.

In the middle years of the eighteenth century English Palladianism become the new British style in Scotland. It can be seen in the designs of such Englishmen working in Scotland, as Ware and Chambers, as well as in those of Scots working in Scotland, for example the Adams and Mylne. It was only really with the effective return of Robert Adam to Scotland after 1778 that a distinctively Scottish strand can again be identified. Adam had always kept up his Scottish connections and these grew increasingly important in the 1770s. After 1778 his English practice was restricted to minor works, while in Scotland it flourished until his death in 1792. As with his brothers,

308   Robert Adam, Culzean Castle, Ayrshire, 1777 (Alexander Nasmith, oil, National Trust for Scotland).

Palladianism was an important element of Robert Adam's Scottish practice. The façade of the Register House in Edinburgh, begun in 1774, is a straightforward, if rather attenuated, Palladian design (Fig. 307), while the complex floor-plans of his late villas continue the work of Robert Taylor in the 1750s and 1760s. The years after 1778 also saw the perfection of a very different manner, Adam's symmetrical castle style. This had first been experimented with in England at, for example Ugbrooke House, Devon, of 1763, but was developed into a genuinely Scottish style continuing the tradition of the tower house at such places as Culzean Castle, Ayrshire (1777–92) (Fig. 308), and Dalquharran Castle, Ayrshire (1790). Adam's castle style never caught on in England – Willersley Castle in Derbyshire by William Thomas (1789) is perhaps the only example – but was continued in Scotland by such architects as John Paterson and Richard Crichton. In England, however, James Wyatt was developing medievalising architecture in a very different direction, towards the asymmetrical ecclesiastical Gothic of Lee Priory, Kent (Fig. 348), and Fonthill Abbey, Wiltshire.

If there was one architect who might have set Scottish architecture on its own distinguished path it was James Playfair. Despite having an office in London and exhibiting regularly at the Royal Academy, Playfair's practice was almost exclusively Scottish. At Cairness House, Aberdeenshire (1791), he designed a building of international importance. Sadly, he died in 1794, while it was still building. Playfair would almost certainly have developed into a great neo-Classical architect, for it was in the years after 1815 that Scottish Classical architecture really flourished, taking the Greek Revival to its heart in a way that the English never did.

Ireland

The architectural history of Ireland between 1748 and 1815 is in many ways the reverse of that of Scotland. While England and Scotland with their joint Parliament were increasingly merged within a British ideal, the Protestants in Ireland were growing confident of their own identity. In 1782 they were able to force parliamentary independence on a British government distracted by the demands of the American War. This growing independence was reflected in the architectural embellishment of the capital, Dublin, which gained a series of public buildings as fine as any in London, innovative buildings which must be seen as architecturally distinct from those in Britain.

However, while politically Ireland was making clear

its distinction from Britain, when it came to architects it was almost entirely dependent. Unlike Scotland, there was no educated surplus of architects in Ireland setting out to make their fortunes in London while continuing to dominate the home market. Ireland was a net importer of architects, both those who settled there permanently such as Thomas Cooley and James Gandon, and those who conducted business at a remove, often without visiting Ireland at all. These include most of the leading architects practising in London including Robert Adam, Lancelot Brown, William Chambers, John Soane, James Stuart, Robert Taylor, Isaac Ware and James Wyatt.

Briefly, under Sir Edward Lovett Pearce, Irish architecture had shone forth as being as advanced as anything in England and considerably more so than anything in Scotland or America. His untimely death in 1733 cut down Irish architecture in its prime. Richard Castle, who developed what he had learnt from Pearce, was a good architect but lacked Pearce's imagination. His final design, the Lying-in Hospital in Dublin, begun shortly after his death in 1751, reveals a confident Gibbsian Classicism such as he had already shown on the entrance front of Leinster House. With his death the two leading Irish architects were essentially minor, provincial figures, Nathaniel Clements, whose career spans two decades from about 1751, and Davis Ducart, first heard of in 1765 and last recorded in 1771. Clements was an amateur architect and only a handful of works by him are known, none at any distance from Dublin. At his own house outside Dublin, later the Viceregal Lodge, at Newberry Hall, County Kildare (Fig. 309), and probably Colganstown, County Dublin, all built in the 1750s or

1760s, Clements developed his own Irish Palladian idiom with small compact villas flanked by extensive wings, decorated with restrained Palladian detail, particularly first floor Diocletian windows and Serlian-type doorcases. Ducart or Daviso de Arcort, described as a Sardinian and so probably Savoyard or Piedmontese, was more idiosyncratic. His work owes little to contemporary English Palladianism and reveals a marked dash of the Baroque. He was, however, the last to design country houses such as Castletown Cox, County Kilkenny (Fig. 310), in the classic Irish Palladian manner introduced by Pearce, with elaborate complexes of arcades and pavilions holding stables and farm buildings. Later Irish houses, of which Castle Coole, County Fermanagh (Fig. 313), is the classic example, isolate the house from its offices which, although sometimes vast, are generally hidden from sight, often linked to the house by a tunnel.

Clements, and particularly Ducart, reveal how distant the Irish remained from the mainstream of English Palladianism. Strong Palladian elements can be seen in their work, particularly in the extensive wings of villas, but, like those of Pearce and Castle before, their buildings remain at one remove (or in Ducart's case several removes) from the English example. That there was a call for a more precise Palladianism can be seen from the Provost's House at Trinity College, Dublin, of 1759 (Fig. 311). Its elevation is closely derived from General Wade's house in London, designed by Burlington in 1723, although the plan, particularly with its top-lit upper landing, seems to speak more of Ireland. The Provost's House has stubbornly resisted revealing its authorship, but John Smyth, a Dublin architect, was paid

309   Nathaniel Clements, Newberry Hall, Co. Kildare, 1760s.

310   Davis Ducart, Castletown Cox, Co. Kilkenny, 1767.

for producing drawings. As the entrance front of Smyth's St Thomas, Marlborough Street, Dublin, of 1758, was a version of Palladio's Redentore in Venice, it is possible that he was responsible for at least the elevation. The Provost's House, St Thomas and Mount Ievers, County Clare, of 1736 (Fig. 189) are evidence of a subtradition of literal Palladianism in Ireland, but above all reveal the lack of confident knowledge of the style to be found in that country. It is not surprising, therefore, that, with growing prosperity, Irish patrons turned to England for architects who did have that confidence.

Perhaps the first to play this part was Theodore Jacobsen, who designed the new quadrangle at Trinity College in Dublin in 1752. Jacobsen was already the architect of the Foundling Hospital in London (1742) and the Royal Naval Hospital at Gosport, Hampshire (1751), but he was only an amateur architect and his façade is a rather unhappy, overblown version of Colen Campbell's third design for Wanstead. Much more significant was the work of William Chambers who carried out alterations to Marino House near Dublin for the 1st Earl of Charlemont in 1758. Charlemont was an Irish peer and a connoisseur who determined to set an example by living in Ireland. Revealingly, his Irish patriotism did not extend to employing an Irish architect. Presumably he felt none was good enough. Chambers's most impressive work for Charlemont was the Casino at Marino (Fig. 277) in which he turned the fantasies of the

Franco-Italian style he had learnt in Rome into stone. This was to prove much more influential on those working in the architectural vacuum in Ireland than in England, but when Chambers came to build Charlemont House in Dublin in 1763 he returned safely to the Palladian mainstream with a design modelled on Ware's Chesterfield House in London.

Despite Chambers's work for Charlemont and that by Isaac Ware for the Earl of Kildare – he designed a bridge at Carton House, County Kildare, which was illustrated in *A Complete Body of Architecture* (1756) and completed the decoration of Leinster House in the late 1750s[8] – it was really in the 1770s that the English invasion of Ireland took place. In about 1770 Lancelot Brown designed stables at Slane Castle, County Meath. In 1773, Chambers charged Agmodisham Vesey of Lucan House outside Dublin for 'various plans, elevations, sketches and designs for a villa'. This was followed by extensive plans for Trinity College, Dublin, in 1775, of which the Theatre was built in 1777 and the Chapel in 1787. Chambers also worked at Rathfarnham House on the outskirts of Dublin in 1770, but complained about the problem of supervising the workmen at such a distance. This does not seem to have been a problem for James Stuart, who also worked at Rathfarnham. The quality of his work is exceptionally high, suggesting, perhaps, that he may have supervised it himself. Stuart's rival Robert Adam, who had been responsible for the drawing-room

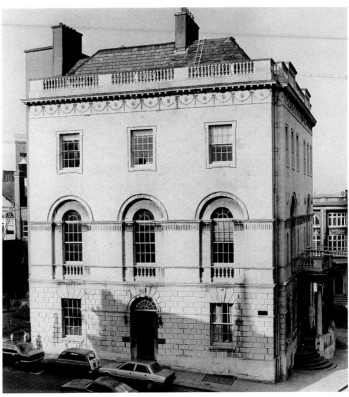

311   Anon., Provost's House, Trinity College, Dublin, 1759.

312   Thomas Ivory, Newcomen's Bank, Dublin, 1781.

313   James Wyatt, Castle Coole, Co. Fermanagh, 1790.

314 Thomas Cooley, interior of the Royal Exchange, Dublin, 1766 (Thomas Malton, watercolour, National Gallery of Ireland, Dublin) (remodelled).

ceiling of Langford House, Mary Street, in Dublin in 1765, sent designs for Headfort House, County Meath (1772), and for alterations to Castle Upton, County Antrim, in 1783.

Of all the English architects at work in Ireland, James Wyatt was the only one who could be said to have established a major practice there. In 1772 he sent designs to General Cunninghame for Mount Kennedy, County Wicklow; although these were not executed until about 1782, when they were carried out by Thomas Cooley. After 1773 Wyatt had a large number of Irish commissions, some for new houses, some for alterations or decoration including Abbeyleix, County Leix (1773); Downhill, County Londonderry (c.1776); Curraghmore, County Waterford (c.1778); Westport, County Mayo (1781); Slane Castle, County Meath

(1785); Castle Coole, County Fermanagh (1790) (Fig. 313); and Leinster House, Dublin (before 1794).

Wyatt's only recorded visit to Ireland was in 1785. This suggests that he had a well-developed team of executant architects. Irish architects or builders must also have carried out the designs of Adam and Chambers. This direct involvement with the latest British fashions had a significant effect on bringing Irish architecture into line with that in England. It has been suggested, for instance, that Richard Morrison could have worked at some stage for Wyatt, and that this explains why Morrison was the first Irish architect to work in Wyatt's Gothic manner.[9]

Particularly influential in this process were the two English architects who settled in Dublin in the late eighteenth century, Thomas Cooley and James Gandon.

315 James Gandon, Four Courts, Dublin, 1786 (Thomas Malton, watercolour, National Gallery of Ireland, Dublin).

316 James Gandon, Custom House, Dublin, 1781 (Thomas Malton, watercolour, National Gallery of Ireland, Dublin).

Cooley, a London carpenter, was a protegé of Robert Mylne and of James Wyatt and won the competition for the Dublin Royal Exchange in 1766 (Fig. 314). This was an ambitious and architecturally complex building which owes much to Chambers's Casino. It represented a marked advance on anything to be found before in Dublin and heralded a spate of impressive buildings in the city. As Maurice Craig suggested, Cooley's sophistication had a positive effect on at least one older Irish architect, Thomas Ivory, who had been made drawing master to the Dublin Society by 1764. His Marine School (1768) and Bluecoat School (1773) would both have sat happily in England. His Newgate Prison (1773) looks rather more to William Kent than to George Dance's contemporary Newgate in London, but his Newcomen's Bank in Castle Street facing the Royal Exchange (1781) (Fig. 312) reveals the architect to have been sensitive to the latest fashions in London.

Both Cooley and Ivory died relatively young, Cooley in 1784 aged forty-three, Ivory in 1786 aged fifty-four, but the arrival of James Gandon in 1781 meant that they had already been eclipsed. Gandon was a pupil of Chambers and the author, with John Woolfe, of the two volume continuation of *Vitruvius Britannicus* (1767 and 1771). He had not found it easy to establish himself in England and was approaching forty when he managed to get the commission to build a new Custom House in Dublin in 1781 (Fig. 316). He did not look back. The Custom House was followed by extensions to the Parliament House in 1785, the Four Courts in 1786 (Fig. 315) and the King's Inns in 1795. In Gandon, Ireland at last found another architect fit to rival any in England. His four main public buildings show him developing the Palladianism he had learnt under Chambers to new, but restrained, heights. It was a display of opulence only made possible by Dublin's pretensions to rival London, pretensions ruthlessly cut down by the Act of Union in 1801 which meant that Dublin lost its Parliament. But if Dublin suffered something of an eclipse, the Act of Union had very positive architectural effects on the country as a whole, for the financial recompense former borough holders received often went on rebuilding and enlarging their country houses and on the erection of the numerous courthouses which are among the finest features of early nineteenth-century Irish architecture. By 1815, Irish architecture, while maintaining its own distinctive elements and now served by confident school of Irish architects, for example Francis and Richard Johnston, Robert and Edward Parke and Richard Morrison, should be seen as part of a broader, more homogenous British architecture in a way that it could not be in 1748.

★ ★ ★

America

British America remained a grouping of thirteen colonies with no single capital to provide a focus for its architectural development, an architectural development which anyway was marked by strong regional variations thanks to the varying climates and economic systems. Porticos and verandas appropriate in the sultry South made less sense in temperate New England, while the South's plantation system encouraged the development of country houses in a way that New England's network of small farms did not. Nevertheless, the three decades between 1748 and the outbreak of the American Revolution in 1776, years of rapid economic growth for America, particularly after the end of the Seven Years' (or French and Indian) War in 1763, saw sophisticated and fashionable architecture finally cross the Atlantic.

America was too far away for English architects to attempt to create a long-distance practice. A journey to Dublin may have been an expedition taking days to accomplish, but Boston or Charles Town were weeks away. The only non-emigrant English architect to work on the other side of the Atlantic was Sir Thomas Robinson, but as Governor of Barbados from 1742 to 1747 he was somewhat exceptional, designing buildings which he commissioned himself in his capacity as governor. It is an interesting question, however, as to why no Americans seem to have sought plans for their houses from English architects in the way that they acquired other luxury goods from London. Sophisticated Americans were well aware of English fashions and had well-developed links with London. By the middle of the century larger American houses, particularly plantation houses, rivalled English villas and manor houses in scale and there were builders and craftsmen quite capable of carrying them out. If a house of the sophistication of Castle Coole, County Fermanagh, could be built in the wilds of Ireland without a visit from the architect, it might be thought the same could have happened in America. But Wyatt could rely on capable executant architects in Ireland; comparably skilled architects capable of carrying out sophisticated metropolitan designs were lacking in America. Nor could Wyatt have hoped for stonework of the quality found at Castle Coole in America. Indeed, the tradition of stone-masonry was largely lacking in that country. Timber was the most popular material, even for some quite sophisticated buildings, a fact that needs to be borne in mind when analysing the differences between English and American buildings.

There is no evidence of American architects coming to England in search of work in the way that Scots did. The idea is not quite as absurd as it might at first seem – by the middle of the century the American artistic fraternity was sufficiently advanced to produce Benjamin

317 Anon., Mathias Hammond House, Annapolis, Maryland, 1774.

West, who began as a portrait painter in Philadelphia but subsequently moved to England. On the other hand, America was a land of opportunity for young or unsuccessful architects, as Ireland was, and by the second half of the century its economy was at last sufficiently developed to support a small architectural profession. This was to have an important effect on America's architectural position, bringing it in a few decades into line with the English mainstream. It is important, however, not to see American architecture solely through an English prism. Commercial links between Ireland and America were strong, and Ireland was a major source of American immigrants. The influence of Irish on American architecture during the eighteenth century would repay further study. For instance Samuel Cardy, architect of St Michael's church in Charles Town, was an Irishman. So was James Hoban, a pupil of Thomas Ivory at the Dublin Society Drawing School, who designed the White House.

One thing that the Americans did not lack was English architectural books. In Charles Town, for instance, in 1767, Robert Wells sold Campbell's *Vitruvius Britannicus*, William Halfpenny's *The Modern Builder's Assistant* (1757), William Pain's *The Builder's Companion* (1758) and other 'treatises on architecture'. In 1769 he offered

Abraham Swan's *Collection of Designs in Architecture* (1757), *The British Architect* (1745) and his *Carpenter's Complete Instructor* (1768); William Halfpenny's *The Modern Builder's Assistant* (1757) and John Crunden's *Convenient and Ornamental Architecture* (1767). In 1772, Wells had 'just received from London' John Miller's edition of Palladio's *Elements of Architecture* (1759); Ware's edition of *The First Book of Andrea Palladio's Architecture* (1742); Matthew Darly's *The Ornamental Architect* (1770); Halfpenny's *The Country Gentleman's Pocket Companion* (1753) and Robert Morris's *Architecture Improved* (1755). By 1770, the Charles Town Library Society owned Chambers's *Treatise on Civil Architecture* (1759); Gibbs's *Rules of Drawing* (1732) and his *Book of Architecture* (1728), together with Leoni's edition of Palladio (1716– 20) and Pain's *Builder's Companion* (1728).[10] Particularly popular books were even reprinted in America, as was Abraham Swan's *The British Architect* of 1745, published in Philadelphia in 1775.[11]

Given the fact that leading British architects did not practice in America, the plentiful supply of architectural books was crucial in bringing American architecture into line with that in the home country. An advertisement in the *Maryland Gazette* in 1751 declares that John Ariss, 'lately from Great Britain', was prepared to 'undertake

Buildings of all Sorts and Dimensions . . . either of the ancient or Modern Order of Gibb's Architect'.[12] The influence of James Gibbs's *A Book of Architecture* (1728) is evident down the whole east coast of America in the steeples inspired by that of St Martin-in-the-Fields. St Michael, Charles Town, of 1752, is a Doric version of St Martin's, with a multi-story octagonal spire rising from immediately behind the portico. It was a model repeated throughout the thirteen colonies. Gibbs's influence was not just ecclesiastical. The design for Mount Airy in Richmond (*c*.1748–58), a house with a rusticated three-bay centrepiece with a ground-floor arcade, clearly derived from one of the plates in Gibbs's book.[13]

The libraries of two important early architects, William Buckland, who died in 1774, and Peter Harrison, are known, and prove to have been well-filled with architectural books. Buckland's included Thomas Chippendale's *Gentleman and Cabinet Maker's Director* (1754); James Gibbs's *A Book of Architecture* (1728); Edward Hoppus's *The Gentleman's and Builder's Repository of Architecture Displayed* (1737); Batty Langley's *The City and Country Builder's and Workman's Treasury of Designs* and his *Gothic Architecture* (1747); Timothy Lightoler's *Gentleman and Farmer's Architect* (1762);

Robert Morris's *Select Architecture* (1757); William Salmon's *Palladio London-iensis*; Abraham Swan's *The British Architect* (1745) and his *Designs in Carpentry* (1759), and Isaac Ware's *A Complete Body of Architecture* (1756).[14] Harrison's library was even more impressive; it would have reflected well on an English amateur, and indeed it is as an amateur that one should probably consider Harrison. However, it is important not to deduce from Harrison's or even Buckland's libraries that these books were generally available. While it is possible to identify what books arrived in America by a certain date, it is less easy to say how widespread their use was and, particularly, whether they reached the hands of relatively poor craftsmen.

It was often details of interiors which crossed the Atlantic most successfully in book form. Faithful borrowings can often be identified in houses. At Drayton Hall, South Carolina (1738–42), the overmantel of the first-floor chimney-piece was taken from plate 64 of William Kent's *Designs of Inigo Jones* (1727). The elaborate chimney-piece in the dining room at Mount Vernon, Virginia, derived from plate 50 of Swan's *British Architecture*, a book that proved almost more popular in America than it did in England. Sometimes the source to

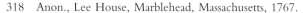

318   Anon., Lee House, Marblehead, Massachusetts, 1767.

319   Peter Harrison, the Redwood Library, Newport, Rhode Island, 1748.

be copied is mentioned in the contract, as when the vestry of Pohick Church, Virginia, instructed the mason William Copein to carve a stone font 'according to a draught in the 150th Plate' of Batty Langley's *City and Country Builder's and Workman's Treasury of Designs* (1740).[15] Inevitably, it was easier for joiners to copy a single sophisticated doorcase or chimney-piece than for a builder to interpret a complete building. The result is that sometimes, as at William Buckland's Gunston Hall, Virginia (1755), elaborate joinery derived from English pattern-books could be found in houses of little external architectural distinction. From the outside, Gunston Hall is no more than an overblown single-storey farmhouse with dormer windows, but a veneer of sophistication anticipating the quality of the interior is added to this essentially vernacular exterior by the elaborate Serlian porch and quoining.[16]

Governor Bladen's 1740s Annapolis house was possibly the first tripartite, astylar, pedimented house to be built in America. This was a model that had been popular in England since the middle of the previous century, but which enjoyed renewed popularity in the middle decades of the century as may be seen in such houses as Thomas Ripley's Wolterton Hall, Norfolk (1727) (Fig.

147), and James Gibbs's Kelmarsh Hall, Northamptonshire (1728) (Fig. 146), and remained fashionable until the end of the century. A succession of American examples, starting with the William Hammersley House, Maryland, in 1749, can be found in the quarter of a century before the American Revolution: the George Milligan House, Maryland (c.1765); the Upton Scott House, Annapolis (1762); Blandfield, Virginia (c.1769); the Mathias Hammond House, Annapolis (1774) (Fig. 317); the Thomas Snowden House, Maryland (c.1774). They include at least two examples which have an extra half storey, a common feature in England, Lee House, Marblehead, Massachusetts (1767) (Fig. 318) and the Samuel Chase-Edward Lloud IV House, Annapolis (1769). The model was also chosen by Joseph Anderson for the Maryland State House, Annapolis (1769), although here the dramatic dome rising behind means that it would never be mistaken for an ordinary house. None of these houses would have looked out of place in the work of a contemporary lesser English architect such as Stiff Leadbetter. Indeed, one of the finest examples, Tryon Palace at New Bern in North Carolina, was built by a former workman of Leadbetter's, John Hawkes, in 1767–70. Like many of these houses, Tryon Palace imi-

320 Thomas Jefferson, first design for Monticello, Virginia, 1768.

321 Anon., Whitehall, Annapolis, Maryland, 1765.

322   Anon., Miles Brewton House, Charleston, South Carolina, 1765.

tated the Palladian model not only in its tripartite villa-form but in its use of flanking pavilions, sometimes brought forward to form a courtyard, sometimes set in line with the house.

Thus, the years after 1748 saw the establishment in America of the classic Palladian villa-form of a tripartite, pedimented villa with flanking pavilions. During the 1760s and early 1770s it was paralleled within by a fashion for Rococo ornament.[17] But these years also saw a more overtly neo-Palladian movement in America, a movement whose origins have already been seen in the porticos of Drayton Hall (Fig. 200) and the Charles Pinckney House in Charles Town (Fig. 201). This was continued in South Carolina by Prince William's church, Sheldon (1753) a temple-form church with tetrastyle portico and attached columns that would not have looked out of place in the park of an English peer and remains impressive even as a ruin. Further north at Newport, Rhode Island, was the Redwood Library built by Peter Harrison in 1748 (Fig. 319). Harrison was born in York in 1716 and emigrated to Newport in 1740. He was not a fulltime architect or a builder but worked as a sea-captain and a custom officer and should probably be

considered an amateur enthusiast. The Redwood Library had a correct tetrastyle Doric portico and interlocking pediments, derived ultimately from Palladio's Venetian churches, but was itself based exactly on a garden building by William Kent illustrated in Isaac Ware's *Designs of Inigo Jones and others* (published in 1731) and in Edward Hoppus's *Andrea Palladio's Architecture* (1735), which stole a number of plates including the relevant source for the Redwood Library from Ware. The rear elevation had triple Venetian windows in the manner of Lord Burlington's villa at Chiswick. Harrison is known to have owned both books. Harrison was equally derivative in his sources in the Brick Market at Newport (1761). This has two and a half stories with a ground-floor arcade (subsequently filled in), alternately segmental and round-headed first-floor windows, separated by pilasters, with pairs of pilasters at each end, and is based on the *Vitruvius Britannicus* engraving of Webb's Somerset House, although with seven rather than five bays and with Ionic rather than Corinthian pilasters. Another house of this date in Newport that has been attributed to Harrison was the Charles Dudley House of about 1750. John Harris has pointed out how sophisticated this

323   Thomas Jefferson, unexecuted design for the President's House, Washington, 1792.

design is, for, although altered in the early nineteenth century, it is clear that the house, with its tetrastyle Ionic portico and uncharacteristic cupola, was a reduced version of Scamozzi's Villa Molini.[18]

More ambitious, if rather less successful, was the Exchange and Custom House at Charles Town by William Naylor, a draughtsman and purveyor of building materials, for which the provincial Assembly voted £60,000 in 1767.[19] This was liberally decked out with Palladian motifs, pediments, rusticated colonnades, balustrades, Serlian windows, but all combined in an unsophisticated manner which showed that Naylor had no real understanding of Palladian composition or proportion. Nevertheless, the result would not have looked out of place among Bristol's mercantile Classicism.

Sometimes, indiscriminate borrowings from English books led to Palladian developments that were never seen on the other side of the Atlantic. Among the illustrations in Robert Morris's *Select Architecture* of 1755 was one of a villa based on the plate of the villa of the ancients in Palladio's *Quattro libri*. This has a two-storey centre of three bays, flanked by two-bay, single-storey ranges, with offices beyond them in a line. It proved impressively popular in America (although it was never followed in England), perhaps because it allowed the apparent sophistication of a villa for a small, single-storey building. At least three examples were built in Virginia: Tazewell Hall (*c.*1760), Brandon (*c.*1765) and Battersea (*c.*1765). Each of these appears to have had a single-storey portico in the centre, but a more elaborate version of the same plan was Whitehall, a villa built by Governor Horatio Sharpe in 1765 outside Annapolis (Fig. 321). This had a freestanding tetrastyle Corinthian portico in the centre, perhaps the earliest such domestic portico in America. It was this model that Thomas Jefferson followed in his first design for Monticello, Virginia (1768) (Fig. 320), which was to have had a two-storey central portico between single-bay wings (although Jefferson planned to have an extra half storey over the flanking ranges).[20]

Perhaps the most distinctive feature of American Palladianism before the Revolution was its use of the two-storey portico. (Ironically, Palladian architecture was probably better suited to America than to England, particularly to the South, where the hot summers made porticos practical, not impractical as they were in Eng-

324   Thomas Jefferson, Monticello, Virginia, 1793.

land.) As well as at Drayton and in Jefferson's first design for Monticello, it could be found on the rebuilt Williamsburg Capitol (1752), whose proportions were criticised by Jefferson; the Miles Brewton House, Charles Town (1765) (Fig. 322), whose proportions were impeccable; and Lansdowne, Philadelphia, built for Governor John Penn (1773). Although a common feature of Palladio's villas, the English never used such two-storey porticos. Their popularity in America shows that native architects were looking directly at Palladio, although their intellectual framework remained that of the English Palladians.

This was particularly true of Thomas Jefferson, the most renowned of all eighteenth-century American architects, who declared that 'Architecture is my delight, and putting up and pulling down one of my favourite amusements'.[21] Any discussion of Jefferson's architecture is inevitably coloured by his position as one of America's founding fathers, but his distinction as a statesman, the charm of his buildings and his undoubted appeal as a man should not lead to the importance of his buildings being overstated.

Jefferson needs to be understood within two parameters. The first is the American Palladian movement of the pre-Revolutionary decades that has just been discussed. In the context of such houses as the Miles Brewton House in Charles Town (1765) and Whitehall outside Annapolis (1765), there was nothing novel was

325   Thomas Jefferson, Virginia State Capitol, Richmond, Virginia, 1785.

about Jefferson's 1768 design for Monticello. It was in the advanced colonial style of the day but no more. Monticello remained incomplete because of the American Revolution, but when Jefferson returned to architecture in the 1780s and 1790s his Palladian outlook remained the same. All his later buildings grew out of his initial pre-war Palladianism, although inevitably greater study and experience meant that the designs were more sophisticated.

A gentleman and a landowner, Jefferson also needs to be seen in the context of the English amateur. Like Lord Burlington and other English eighteenth-century amateurs, Jefferson was obsessed with Palladio and, through Palladio, with the Antique. English amateurs could have been responsible for virtually all Jefferson's buildings. Some had been anticipated by them on paper if not in practice. Ambrose Phillipps of Garendon's 1730s scheme for the Place Royale du Peyrou in Montpellier with a series of pavilions in front of a Pantheon-like church is based on Louis XIV's Marly, with the church in the place of the King's Building. Jefferson followed the same scheme when laying out the University of Virginia (1817–26) with the Pantheon-like building holding a library not a church. But then the idea of using the Pantheon as the model for a library had been suggested by Robert Trevor for the Radcliffe Library in Oxford in 1737. Recreations of Roman temples had been an English Palladian obsession long before Jefferson took the Maison Carrée in Nîmes as the model for his Virginia Capitol in Richmond in 1785 (Fig. 325). None, admittedly, was on a comparable scale, although at the time of the Fifty New Churches Act numerous British architects had experimented with the idea of designing a church in the form of a temple. However, full-scale temple reconstructions could be found at Stowe, Buckinghamshire (1749), in the Temple of Concord (Fig. 248), and in the Ionic Temple at Rievaulx, Yorkshire (c.1749–57). Jefferson's designs for the governor's mansion at Richmond and the President's House in Washington (Fig. 323) were both based closely on Palladio's Villa Rotunda, a source which had already been used four times by English Palladians.[22]

Jefferson's obsession with complex small villas based around a canted bay, which first appears at Monticello in 1768 and which he was following as late as 1817 in his design for Barboursville, Virginia,[23] was for a form developed by Sir Robert Taylor in the 1750s; the parallels with Asgill House, Surrey (c.1760), illustrated in the fourth volume of Vitruvius Britannicus in 1767, are particularly close. His octagonal Poplar House, Virginia, followed a design by Inigo Jones illustrated in the Burlington-sponsored The Designs of Inigo Jones (1727) by William Kent. Nor was Jefferson above directly following Burlington. The garden front of Monticello is repeatedly compared to the Hôtel de Salm in Paris. But Burlington's villa at Chiswick is a closer source (Fig. 137), despite Jefferson's comment that 'the Octagonal dome has an ill effect, both within and without'.[24] Like Monticello (Fig. 324), the Chiswick villa has an octagonal dome rising behind a tetrastyle portico, flanked by single-storey, and single-bay wings, although at Monticello the rustic has been reduced to almost nothing.

Jefferson's well-known architectural quotations need to be seen in context. When he criticised Williamsburg architecture, and particularly the College of William and Mary, which was dismissed as looking like a brick-kiln, he was not attacking up-to-date American Palladian architecture but a Virginian conservatism that meant the Maltravers-type house design was still considered fashionable.[25] Similarly, his attacks on English architecture – 'Their architecture is the most wretched style I ever saw'[26] – were obviously laced with political antipathy and may be based on his dislike of the direction English architecture was taking in the 1780s, away from Palladianism. Finally, his praise of French architecture – 'Were I to proceed to tell you how much I enjoy their architecture, sculpture, painting and music, I should want words' – and, in particular, of the Hôtel de Salm – 'While at Paris, I was violently smitten with the Hotel de Salm, and used to go to the Tuilleries almost daily, to look at it'[27] – should not lead to assumptions that Jefferson imitated French architecture when he returned to America. For the idea of living on a single floor (which he is usually cited as taking from France) he had no need to look across the Atlantic. It was a common feature of many American Palladian villas. Jefferson's initial design for Monticello, made before he ever visited France, was based on a single storey with a mezzanine, and this is how Monticello was completed on his return. What Jefferson probably did learn from the French, as the English Palladians had learnt before him, was how to plan a house for maximum convenience, something that at Monticello became almost an obsession for Jefferson.

To see Jefferson as an innovative neo-Classicist breaking the trammels of British architecture to create a new independent style worthy of a young republic is grossly to misrepresent his work. Jefferson was the culmination, the very worthy culmination, of English neo-Palladianism, but far from leading the independent republic's architecture into new fields he could be seen to be holding it back in a distinctly conservative manner, designing buildings in the 1820s which would not have looked out of place in the 1760s.

The 1770s–1790s were years of dramatic change in British architecture, with the work of such men as Robert Mylne, James Stuart, Henry Holland and James Wyatt breaking the bounds of Palladianism. This sense of innovation is lacking during these years in America. In many ways this is not surprising. The American Revolution broke the immediate links with Britain, the mainspring of American architectural innovation. The war caused immense economic and social upheaval, bringing building to a halt between 1776 and 1783, so that it was not until the late 1790s that the economy was again prospering. Nevertheless, the conservatism of the entries for the the competition for the President's House in the new federal capital of Washington in 1792, a building that would have been expected to attract the most advanced architectural ideas around, comes as a surprise.[28] Compared to schemes by Jacob Small, James Diamond and Andrew Mayfield Carshore, Jefferson's Palladian Villa Rotonda seems almost advanced (Fig. 323). The competition was won by James Hoban with a 'design competently based on Gibbs' which would have been derided as absurdly old-fashioned in England.[29]

Thus, it comes as no surprise to read Benjamin Latrobe's comment on arriving in Norfolk in 1796 (which had been largely rebuilt since the Revolution) that the architecture there was 'plain and decent but of the fashion of 30 years ago'. Nor to discover Asher Benjamin complaining in 1806 that 'Old fashioned workmen, who have for many years followed the footsteps of Palladio and Langley, will no doubt leave their old path with great reluctance.'[30] The style which American architects took to when the economy recovered was the Adam, or Federal Style, arriving in America thirty years after it has first been fashionable in England. It is a style mainly found in interiors, but occasionally in exteriors, as in the central pavilion of Charles Bulfinch's Tontine Crescent in Boston (c.1793), with its echoes of Adam's Society of Arts building in the Adelphi in London (1772). Bulfinch's most ambitious building, the Massachusetts State House in Boston of 1795 was deliberately modelled on William Chambers's Somerset House in London of 1776–86.[31] (Bulfinch had spent two years in England in 1785–7.)

A similar conservatism can be found in the planning of Federal-style buildings. In American terms, Jefferson had been innovative in intending a canted bay for the 1768 scheme for Monticello, although by then English interest in the canted bay, at its height in the late 1750s, was beginning to wane. His lead was picked up after independence and Federal buildings show a fascination with canted bays and bows into the nineteenth century, as can be seen at such houses as William Birch's Montebello,

326 Benjamin Latrobe, Baltimore Cathedral, Maryland, 1804.

Baltimore (c.1796), Gabriel Manigault's Joseph Manigault House, Charleston (c.1803), and Latrobe's Benjamin James Harris House, Richmond (1804).

It was only with the arrival of Benjamin Latrobe in 1793, a pupil of S.P. Cockerell, whose Hammerwood Lodge, Sussex (1790), was in an advanced neo-Classical style inspired by French architects of the Boullée–Ledoux school, that America moved beyond Palladianism and the Adam style and again began to catch up with advanced English thought. Latrobe's State Penitentiary at Richmond (1797) shows the influence of George Dance – both his Newgate Gaol (1770) and his St Luke's Hospital (1782). As Derek Linstrum has pointed out, the rotunda of his Baltimore Cathedral (1804) (Fig. 326) was built to the same scale and to the same basic design as James Wyatt's Pantheon (1769). With such works by Latrobe and such buildings as the Monumental Church in Richmond (1812) by Latrobe's pupil and rival Robert Mills, American architecture had by 1815 at last achieved its own identity, an identity that placed it on a par with European architecture and no longer meant that it always seemed to be trailing a couple of decades behind what was going on on the other side of the Atlantic.

XIV

THE END OF PALLADIAN PRIMACY

T HE AMERICAN REVOLUTIONARY WAR which broke out in 1776 brought an end to the building boom that had run so impressively since the Peace of Paris in 1763. For the Adam brothers it spelt the end of the preeminent architectural position they had held since the early 1760s. Horace Walpole's comments on Henry Holland's Carlton House, begun in 1783, the year the war ended, were only too accurate: 'How sick one shall be, after this chaste palace, of Mr Adam's gingerbread and sippets of embroidery.'[1] But Adam's position was already being challenged in the early 1770s by new talents such as James Wyatt, George Dance, Charles Cameron, James Gandon and Henry Holland. Nor was it was only Adam's pre-eminence that was under threat. As in the first decades of the century, the sheer volume of building encouraged architectural experiment. At Blackfriars Bridge in 1760 and All Hallows, London Wall, in 1765, Robert Mylne and George Dance introduced new, structurally based, Continental theories of neo-Classicism; West Wycombe Park, Buckinghamshire, in 1771, was the first country house to be given an accurate Greek portico; the first major asymmetrical country house, Downton Castle, Herefordshire, was built in 1772; 1776 was the date of James Wyatt's first Gothic house, Sheffield Place, Sussex, with its asymmetrical east front. Neo-Palladianism, the dominant architectural style in England since the 1720s, the style into which Adam's exteriors fall despite his protests, was in danger of losing its primacy. The outbreak of the American War reduced the volume of building so dramatically that the rate of stylistic change was dampened, but by the time building picked up in the mid-1780s, Britain was heading for a period of stylistic plurality and neo-Palladianism was increasingly marginalised.

The post war boom which saw the number of new houses begun in London double between 1761 and 1766 was unsustainable, and the inevitable correction came in 1767, but the overall volume of building remained high, 50 per cent higher in 1770, the trough of this recession, than it had been in 1760. Recovery in 1771 was impeded by a major financial crisis in June 1772, but only briefly, and building rose to another peak in 1777 before falling away dramatically.[2] These were the years of the

Adams' ambitious schemes for the Adelphi – begun in 1771, temporarily threatened by the crash of 1772, but finished that year – and Portland Place; of Sir Robert Taylor's Grafton Street (1771), and Bedford Square (1776). Such was the volume of house building that the City authorities thought it timely to bring out the great London Building Act of 1774. Speculative housing was joined by a rash of public building: James Wyatt's Pantheon was begun in 1769; George Dance's Newgate Prison in 1770; ambitious plans for the Stone Buildings at Lincoln's Inn were sought in 1771 and work on Taylor's scheme started in 1774. Even the government was induced to rebuild Somerset House from 1776, the greatest public building of the century. The demand for new country houses was equally high, as the young James Wyatt and Henry Holland found to their satisfaction when they were able to establish themselves as architects, primarily through country-house work, in their early twenties. Wyatt's success was such that he was able to challenge Adam, with interiors like those at Heveningham Hall, Suffolk, that were quite as fine as anything by Adam (Fig. 327).

The first rumours of war in America did little to reduce enthusiasm, even when small-scale skirmishing in 1775 gave way to full-scale campaigning in 1776. The entry of the French in 1778, followed by the Spanish in 1779, changed all this. A colonial conflict had turned into a major European war. Government borrowing increased dramatically, as did taxes. The national debt more than doubled, and with the price of Consols falling sharply, high interest rates meant private loans dried up.[3] The volume of building fell away and those who were committed to major speculative schemes were often badly burnt. William Scott and Robert Grews signed contracts to build Bedford Square in Bloomsbury, an ambitious regular palace-fronted square, in 1776. At first everything went well, and by the end of 1777 thirty-four houses had been leased, but the following year only a further three were added to the list and none during the next two and a half years. Only financial support from the Bedford Estate kept the scheme afloat, but it took seven years for the square to be completed. In 1784 Grews admitted that 'The great scarcity of Money, occasioned by the unhappy American War, so severely affected many of the persons concerned under us, that some were compelled to stop, and we found ourselves under the unfortunate necessity of taking back the Ground, and completing the Houses thereon.'[4]

The Bedford Square developers were lucky to have the financial support of a large aristocratic estate which allowed them to complete their scheme in the middle of an economic slump. Others were not so fortunate. A few hundred yards from Bedford Square the young John Nash, who had recently set up on his own after leaving Sir Robert Taylor's office, signed an agreement in 1777 to redevelop the site of Sir John Rushout's house in Bloomsbury Square. Eight houses were built, two large and six small. The speculation was a disaster. Nash was unable to let the houses he had built and, forced into bankruptcy in 1783, he left for Wales to begin his career again. But it is the Adam brothers who show most clearly the effect of the American War. Bouncing back from the Adelphi crisis, William Adam and Company accumulated a profit of over £35,000 between 1772 and 1777. Then things went wrong; the number of speculative building leases signed by the brothers slumped from twenty-five in 1778 to thirteen in 1780 and two in 1782. Despite a brief rally in 1783 when twelve leases were signed, it was not until 1789 that figures moved consistently again into double figures.[5] The Portland Square development, begun with high hopes in 1773, struggled on through the 1780s with fifteen houses still unfinished at Robert Adam's death in 1792. The Register House in Edinburgh, Robert Adam's chance at last to design a great public building, was started in 1774 with completion intended for 1777. In the event, work was suspended, with only part of the building in use, in 1778 and was not resumed until 1785. Some £30,000 was lost in the Battersea and Sand End Company, and other branches of the Adam empire were also in difficulty. Indeed William Adam and Company never really recovered, and although it struggled on, it finally collapsed in 1801. William Adam writing in 1787, had no doubt about the underlying cause of the company's problems: these were 'above all' owed to 'the diminution of the value of buildings from the fatal American war', adding that as far as Robert and James Adam had been concerned the war 'proved as destructive to their business of architecture as it had been to the building business'.[6]

The result is a marked break in the Adam practice. The early 1770s were the years of the Adelphi and Portland Place; a succession of public buildings – the Chelsea Hospital Commission (1771), the Royal Society of Arts (1772), the Edinburgh Register House (1774), Bury St Edmunds Theatre and Market Hall (1775), Drury Lane Theatre (1775); London houses – Northumberland House (1770–5), 20 St James's Square (1771–4), Derby House (1773–4) and Home House (1773–6); as well as a substantial number of country houses. Apart from Culzean Castle, Ayrshire, begun in 1777 but where much of the present house dates from a second phase started in 1785, the late 1770s and early 1780s saw little more than minor work, mainly alterations. A further casualty of the war was the elaborate Adam style, which had reached its apogee of expense at the Northumberland House Glass Drawing-room of 1770 and which had inspired such comparable extravagances as the saloon at Brocket Hall, Hertfordshire (1772), and James Wyatt's cupola room at Heaton Hall, Lancashire (c.1772). This was displaced by a growing tendency for simpler interiors, largely because the money was no longer there to pay for such extravagances. But fashion also intervened. A tendency towards simpler decoration in the 1770s, perhaps based on French example, can already be seen in the work of Chambers, as at Gower House, London, and Milton Park, Northamptonshire (1770), and of Holland, at Claremont House, Surrey (1771), Brookes's Club (1778) and Berrington Hall, Shropshire (1778). This was something Holland was to take to an extreme at houses such as Althorp, Northamptonshire (1787), and Southill House, Bedfordshire (1796), in the late 1780s and early 1790s.

The Adam practice recovered in the late 1780s and 1790s but thereafter work was mainly confined to Scotland, where a wave of public buildings followed the return of prosperity: Edinburgh University, begun 1789; the Bridewell in Edinburgh (1791); the Trades House, Glasgow (1791); the Royal Infirmary, Glasgow (1792); and the Glasgow Assembly Rooms (1796). These were accompanied by a series of smaller houses, again mainly in Scotland, and new monumental urban domestic schemes, Fitzroy Square in London (1790), Charlotte Square, Edinburgh (1791), and Glasgow High Street (1793). But the Adams had lost their national primacy and in England were largely irrelevant after 1778.

The 1770s also brought to a close the careers, through death or retirement, of a whole generation of architects whose roots lay in the 1750s or even earlier. John Vardy had died in 1765; Stiff Leadbetter and Isaac Ware in 1766; Matthew Brettingham and Henry Flitcroft in 1769. William Hiorn and Henry Keene died in 1776, although Hiorn had built little since the mid-1760s. James Paine was not to die until 1789, but he took on no important commissions after 1771. Instead, he established himself in prosperous retirement on the estate he bought at Sayes Court in Surrey in 1773. Sir Robert Taylor had two last great houses, Gorhambury, Hertfordshire (1777), and Heveningham Hall, Suffolk (1778), but little else after 1778, and he died in 1788. Similarly, Lancelot Brown, who was very active in the early 1770s, had little work after 1776 and died in 1783. James Stuart had commissions at Montagu House in London and the Belvedere, Kent, in about 1775, but little after that,

327 James Wyatt, the entrance hall, Heveningham Hall, Suffolk, c.1780.

except the rebuilding of the chapel at Greenwich Hospital following a fire in 1780 (Fig. 329), before his death in 1788.

By the time the economy recovered after the Peace of Versailles in 1783, the only architects in the neo-Palladian tradition still practising were Robert Adam and William Chambers, who worked on until their deaths in 1792 and 1796. Chambers, however, had effectively abandoned his private practice to concentrate on building Somerset House from 1776, and, as we have seen,

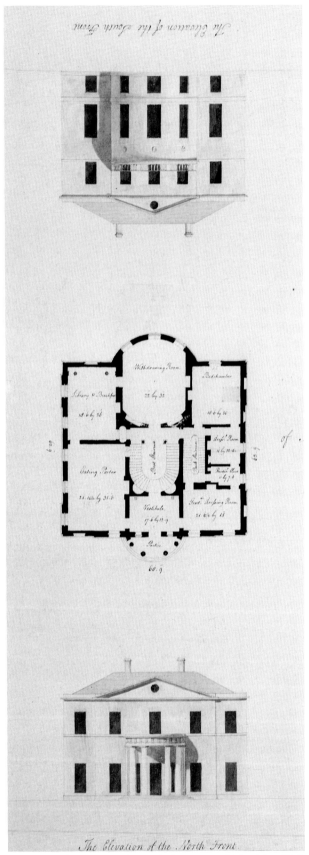

328   Sir John Soane, plan and elevations of Tendring Hall, Suffolk, 1784 (demolished).

Adam was largely restricted to Scotland. The departure of this generation brought an end to those who had looked back to Colen Campbell and Lord Burlington, to Inigo Jones, and to Palladio and other Italian *cinquecento* architects for direct inspiration. Those who now dominated the profession, such men as James and Samuel Wyatt, George Dance, Henry Holland, Robert Mylne and Thomas Leverton, had already been experimenting with ideas that owed little to neo-Palladianism when they first established themselves as young men in the late 1760s or 1770s. Those architects who emerged in the late 1780s and early 1790s, S.P. Cockerell, Joseph Bonomi, Thomas Harrison and John Soane, had neither interest nor grounding in neo-Palladianism.

These architects had ten years in which to make their mark, ten years between the Peace of Versailles in 1783 and the outbreak of a new war with France in 1793. The economy slowly recovered with the return of peace, although it was not until 1785, when it was at last possible to borrow for building again, that real recovery began. Another postwar boom led to over expansion and a severe crash in 1788. By 1790 brick production in the twelve months to the middle of the year was higher than ever before. Output from the textile industry was at a record level, harvests were good, incomes increasing, interest rates falling. Building boomed and architects and speculators thrived. In 1791 Horace Walpole wrote of 'the rage for building' and added that 'There will soon be one street from London to Brentford, ay and from London to every village ten miles round'.[7] Michael Searles, a south London surveyor, architect and developer, had an income of about £2,000 in 1792.[8] John Johnson made enough to build and endow a charitable foundation for his poor relatives in 1792.[9] John Soane, who had found it hard to establish himself after his return to England from Italy in 1780, was inundated with work from 1784; over fifty commissions are known between then and 1793, including at least fourteen new houses.

As in 1778, the economy was halted in its tracks by the outbreak of war with France, this time revolutionary France, in 1793. There are signs that the economy was already under strain, and the outbreak of war bringing a rise in interest rates and a shortage of credit, helped by a wet harvest, intensified a depression that was probably already naturally due. Brick production fell 40 per cent in two years.[10] Many speculators were bankrupted. Others, such as Michael Searles, only avoided bankruptcy through severe retrenchment. S.P. Cockerell said it all when he was subsequently accused, in 1807, of having allowed shoddy workmanship:

if I had pressed the builders to the extent of the power I possessed under their contracts, most of them would have failed, and the Foundling estate have been left in the condition of those estates in Bath, Bristol, and

9   James Stuart, the chapel, Greenwich Hospital, Kent, 1780.

other places where from the effects of the war . . . whole acres remain in a state of ruin and desolation.[11]

Decline continued until 1799, when the economy picked up again, helped by the brief Peace of Amiens of 1802. This time the resumption of war in 1803 caused only a brief interruption, and throughout the rest of the decade, despite continuing conflict with France, the building industry boomed.[12] The ten years between 1783 and 1793 had seen a flowering of British architecture, a return to stylistic diversity unparalleled since the early years of the century. The decade of 1800–10 confirmed English architecture in that path.

One of the ironies of the decline of neo-Palladianism was that the simple Prattian Palladian ideal of a country house as a plain tripartite block, with only an astylar pediment for decoration, returned to prominence (Figs. 33 and 34). This had been an undercurrent throughout the century, with such houses as Henry Flitcroft's Bower House, Essex (1729), Baggrave Hall, Leicestershire, and Burswell Hall, Lincolnshire (c.1760), and can be found, for instance, in the work of Sir John Soane at Tendring Hall, Suffolk (1784) (Fig. 328). The principal changes since Pratt's day were to the roof, which lost its heavy cornice, dormer windows and cupola. To make up for the resulting loss of space, it became increasingly common in the second half of the century to add an extra half storey, making a tall two-and-a-half-storey block, something which Talman and Wren had pioneered at Kimberley Hall, Norfolk, and Winslow Hall, Buckinghamshire (Fig. 83), in the very first years of the century.

This was probably the most economical way to build a substantial dignified house and, as a result, was in great demand from country squires, prosperous inhabitants of small towns and aristocrats for their London seats (as at Egremont House by Brettingham (1756), Shelburne House by Adam (c.1765), Melbourne House by Chambers (1771) and Aldborough House by Richard Edwin (1773)). It was a design of considerable flexibility which could be built with no more decoration than a pediment and a couple of string courses, or alternatively elaborately dressed up with a rusticated ground floor, Serlian window, blind relieving arch, decorated frieze and balustrade.

At the same time, during the second half of the century the rustic and *piano nobile* gradually disappeared. Lord Harcourt had agonised whether to build an external staircase at Nuneham Park in 1755, and decided ultimately that he would, because 'a house without an outside staircase seems to want one of its great monuments'. By contrast, Leadbetter's other major houses, Langley Park, Buckinghamshire, Hatchlands, Surrey, and Newton Park, Somerset, have no *piano nobile*. Harcourt's son, who succeeded in 1777, swept away the external staircase, creating a front door on the ground-

floor and remodelling the rustic – previously given over to offices – as family rooms.[13] At Houghton Hall, Norfolk, William Kent's external staircase was removed in about 1780 by the 3rd Earl of Orford, presumably as a response to the same fashion. The move was not absolute. Taylor's houses were fairly evenly divided with Gorhambury Park, Hertfordshire (1777), following the traditional ideal of a villa with rustic and *piano nobile*. But it was marked, and by the end of the century it would have been unusual to suggest designing a house with a *piano nobile*.

At the same time, the porticoed villa pioneered by Colen Campbell's Newby Hall, Yorkshire, remained popular into the nineteenth century. Its austerity meant that it could easily be adapted to the Greek Revival by replacing a Roman order with a Greek one. James Wyatt's Castle Coole, County Fermanagh (1790) (Fig. 313), is perhaps the finest example of the style which had changed little when his nephew Sir Jeffry Wyatville built Dinton House, Wiltshire, in 1814, or indeed when Wyatville's pupil Edward Haycock built Millichope, Shropshire, in 1835.

The rise of this more austere approach to country-house design should be seen as a reaction to the sense of movement in country-house architecture so prevalent in the 1750s and 1760s. As the examples of Colen Campbell and then Chambers show, the model was Palladian, but Robert Mylne seems to have added a new theoretical dimension. Howard Colvin noted of Mylne that the 'exteriors of his houses are characterised by a fastidious restraint that is prophetic of the neo-classical simplicity of the 1790s',[14] but his significance as an innovative architect has been underplayed.

The key to understanding Mylne's importance lies in his only publication, the pamphlet *Observations on Bridge Building*, which appeared in 1760 to support his entry for the Blackfriars Bridge competition. Mylne was another of the British architects who flocked to Rome in the 1750s. In 1754 Robert Adam, ever alert to possible competition, had written to his family:

> There are two sons of Deacon Mylne's in Rome at present, studying architecture. One of them has studied in France and has accordingly that abominable taste to perfection; the other, who came straight from Scotland, has made great progress and begins to draw extremely well, so that if he goes on he may become much better than any of those beggarly fellows who torment our native city.[15]

In Rome, Mylne moved among advanced neo-Classical circles, studying under Piranesi. He was the first Briton to win the Silver Medal for architecture in the Concorso Clementino at the Academy of St Luke in 1758, and the following year he was elected a member of the Academy, being also a member of the academies of Florence and

330 Robert Mylne, Tusmore Park, Oxfordshire, 1766 (demolished).

331 Robert Adam, the Deputy Rangers's Lodge, Green Park, London, 1768, from *Works in Architecture* (1773) (demolished).

Bologna. In 1757 he visited Sicily with Richard Phelps, where he made drawings of the Greek temples for a volume on the 'Antiquities of Sicily'. This was never published – his success on his return to England meant that he never had the time and indeed made it unnecessary – but Piranesi and Winckelmann were both indebted to him for information, Winckelmann using the drawings for his account of the temple at Agrigento. Mylne remained in close contact with Piranesi on his return to England, acting as his agent in London, while Piranesi later engraved Mylne's design for Blackfriars Bridge.

Mylne returned in 1759, and, contrary to Adam's expectation, moved to London, where his arrival coincided with the competition to build Blackfriars Bridge. It was to boost his chances as the youngest and least known of the eight shortlisted candidates that he produced his pamphlet. Eileen Harris's analysis of this reveals that Mylne's 'fastidious restraint' did not arise by chance, but was the product of the application of the radical principles of the Venetian Franciscan Carlo Lodoli.[16] Lodoli's theories, which he never published but which were set down by Francesco Algarotti in *Saggio sopra l'architettura* (1759), eliminated everything in building that did not bear the sanction of utility, or that deviated from the 'certain circuit of forms in architecture produced by the material of which it is composed'. Mylne could have met Lodoli in Venice in 1759, but his passion on the subject almost certainly arose from the influence of Piranesi, who had been much taken by Lodoli's ideas during his early years in Venice. Piranesi argued in his polemical publications that the most monumental works of the Romans, their aqueducts and sewers, were the most perfect fulfilment of Lodoli's functionalist principles, and so it was appropriate for Mylne to apply those principles to designing Blackfriars Bridge. As Eileen Harris noted, Mylne's faith in Lodoli seems to have been even more constant than Piranesi's.

Blackfriars Bridge was an enormous commission costing £152,840 (£163 under the estimate), and much of Mylne's subsequent career was spent as a civil engineer on bridges and canals. He held a clutch of valuable surveyorships, including those for St Paul's and Canterbury Cathedrals, the New River Company and the Stationers' Company, but he also maintained his architectural interests, and his first major country house, Tusmore Park, Oxfordshire (1766) (Fig. 330), demonstrates his Lodolian principles, making a remarkable contrast with Paine's recent Kedleston designs. Mylne was fortunate in his client at Tusmore, William Fermor, who had gone to Italy on his Grand Tour with the intention of learning about architecture so that on his return he could rebuild his house. To this end, he had taken regular lessons from Mylne in 1758.[17] Presumably Mylne managed to imbue Fermor with his own ideals. Certainly, there is a thorough going radicalism about Tusmore which exceeds any of his other houses. Ornament and movement are reduced to a minimum: a string course to mark the rustic from the *piano nobile*, a low rusticated arcade to support the portico on the garden front, the plainest of entablatures over the Ionic porticos on the entrance and garden fronts and only a very plain cornice with no entablature around the rest of the house; windows are set unrelieved in the façade. Even Chambers's Duddingston House, Midlothian (Fig. 279), with its fluted Corinthian portico, elegant entablature and elaborate window surrounds, seems ornate in comparison. A certain austerity could always be found in neo-Palladianism, in many of Burlington's buildings, Kent's Devonshire House, Ware's Clifton Hill House or Taylor's frequent use of windows set bare in the wall without surrounds, but Mylne brings a new rigour borne of radical theorising.

Adam, always aware of fashion and nervous of competitors, particularly those schooled in Rome, experimented with a similar austerity at the Deputy Ranger's Lodge in Green Park of 1768 (Fig. 331). The resulting chillness does not seem to have appealed to him and none of his subsequent buildings was reduced so dramatically to the bare essentials. Other architects seem to have been more receptive. Sir Robert Taylor was one of the most distinguished architects of his day; a marked austerity of detail is a frequent feature in his work, but generally coupled with a sense of movement derived from his subtle use of canted bays. However, his late works at the Stone Building at Lincoln's Inn (1774), Gorhambury, Hertfordshire (1777), and Heveningham Hall, Suffolk (1777) (Fig. 332), have a stillness about them that contrasts with the restless activity an earlier building such as Asgill House (Fig. 264).[18] James Wyatt's Castle Coole is perhaps the finest example of this austerity (Fig. 313). James Gandon's Nottingham County Hall of 1770, of which he published a larger version in the second volume of his new edition of *Vitruvius Britannicus* in 1771, keeps architectural detail to a minimum, with an Ionic portico flanked by blank walls relieved only by arches (Fig. 333). What makes the County Hall remarkable is the lack of an architrave, usually considered an advanced feature of French neo-Classical architecture, in particular of Jacques Gondoin's École de Chirugie in Paris, begun in 1769 but not published until 1780.[19] Not that Gandon was the first English architect to reduce the entablature in this way. The same volume of *Vitruvius Britannicus* also illustrates John Carr's Constable Burton House, Yorkshire (c.1762–8), and Thoresby Park, Nottinghamshire (1767) (Fig. 256), without architraves.[20]

Before Mylne, the new structurally based Continental neo-Classical theories seem to have had little serious impact in England. The only important work to have been translated into English was that of the French

332   Sir Robert Taylor, Heveningham Hall, Suffolk, 1777.

333   James Gandon, unexecuted design for the County Hall, Nottingham, 1770, from *Vitruvius Britannicus* (1771).

334   George Dance, the Common Council Chamber, Guildhall, City of London, 1777, (from Pugin and Rowlandson's *Microcosm of London* (1808)) (demolished).

theorist Abbé Laugier, whose *Essai sur l'architecture* was published in 1753 and appeared in English two years later. Laugier's ideas had much in common with those of Lodoli, indeed, it was once thought that Laugier was influenced by Lodoli but this is now discounted. Laugier believed that the fixed and immutable laws of architecture were to be found in simple nature exemplified by the primitive hut. Isaac Ware quoted from Laugier extensively in his *A Complete Body of Architecture* of 1756; Chambers attacked the book vigorously in his *Treatise on Civil Architecture* in 1759; and Adam echoed it in the *Works in Architecture* (1771). But none of these writers nor their contemporaries seems to have grasped its truly revolutionary message; the tendency was 'to feed off Laugier's maxims, the superstructure, as it were, of his *Essai*, and leave behind their foundation'.[21] As Eileen Harris has said of Ware, Laugier

> offered him a fresh and bold way – using reason and nature as the true standards of perfection – to rid English architects of their undiscriminating attachment to a single authority . . . there is no mention of the rustic cabin embodying the fundamental principles of architecture, which Laugier insisted must always be kept in mind. Ware, it seems, was really not ready to

submit the rich architectural vocabulary amassed since the Renaissance to the rational purge demanded by Laugier.[22]

No British architect reacted to Laugier as Soufflot did at Sainte-Geneviève in Paris.

The one exception that is often cited, is George Dance's All Hallows, London Wall, of 1765 (Fig. 335). All Hallows is renowned for the fact that the entablature within the building is reduced to a frieze alone. This is usually claimed to be proof that Dance was influenced by Laugier, but Laugier would not have approved of the frieze being used on its own: 'The entablature is divided in all Orders into architrave, frieze and cornice. Of these three parts only the architrave could and should be used singly whenever there are several stories. The frieze and cornice can only be used jointly and with the architrave'.[23] So where did Dance get this idea from? Sir John Soane was clear on this point when he discussed All Hallows in his Royal Academy lectures and, given his closeness to Dance, there can be no doubt that he is here passing on his former master's views. In the lecture Soane did not justify All Hallows in terms of structural theory but of direct observation of Ancient Roman buildings:

> When either of the Orders of Architecture are used in the interior of buildings, such parts of the entablature as apply to external decoration should be suppressed. Thus the Ancients preserved the characteristic beauty of the column, and at the same time pleased the eye, and satisfied the most correct judgement.

This was particularly observable in Roman buildings: 'The suppression of those parts of the entablature which can only apply to external decoration is also attended to in many Roman buildings.'[24] He cites six different examples to prove his point.

Dance spent six years in Rome, arriving in May 1759, just after Mylne had left for England. Much of his time was spent on a detailed study of antique buildings, some of his drawings survive in the Soane Museum, and, like Mylne, he was admitted to the Academy of St Luke where he won a prize, the gold medal at Parma, in 1763 for 'a Public Gallery for Statues, Pictures, etc.'. He also became a member of the Society of Arcadia, a fashionable body of Italian intellectuals. Unlike Adam, Dance remained in contact with Continental theorists when he returned to England; this happened in 1764, after six years training and, thanks presumably to his father's influence as Clerk of the City Works, he immediately obtained the commission to rebuild All Hallows. All Hallows is the product of these six years, and its origins lie clearly in Ancient Rome. The church's three-bay vaulted interior with a single column between each arcade is closely modelled on the Basilica of Maxentius,

335   George Dance, interior of All Hallows, London Wall, City of London, 1765.

then known at the Temple of Peace, but without the aisles of the original. Only one side of the basilica remains and its vaulting has completely disappeared so that the form of the roof could only be conjectured. At All Hallows, Dance provided a barrel vault with decoration based on Roman originals, while the coffering in the apse is derived from the Temple of the Sun and the Moon, as that on the Basilica of Maxentius had been lost.

Dance's fascination with late-Roman architecture, with vaulted structures such as the Basilica of Maxentius, the Roman Baths and Hadrian's Villa, where the key element is the dome and its vaulting rather than the column, was developed in his later work. Robert Adam used vaulted ceilings on a number of occasions, the most renowned being the Third Drawing Room at Derby House (1773), while the best surviving examples were probably done the same year in 20 St James's Square. Most of his ceilings, however, are flat or have a shallow cove. Dance developed this use of vaults in a much more dramatic manner at Cranbury Park, Hampshire (c.1778), where the Ballroom has a superbly decorated cross-vaulted ceiling with lavish coffered decoration, perhaps inspired by vaulting at Hadrian's Villa. Perhaps the most remarkable of Dance's experiments with vaulted structures was the Common Council Chamber in the Guildhall of 1777 (Fig. 334). As at Cranbury, the vaulting springs from the four corners, but as a pendentive dome without apses, and rising to a central oculus, a common feature of domed Roman structures. David Watkin has suggested that the fluting in the dome may be derived from the ruin of the Serapeum at Hadrian's Villa.

Dance was not alone in his experiments with domes in the 1770s. In about 1775 Thomas Leverton designed a domed entrance hall at 1 Bedford Square with pendentives supporting a saucer dome, while at 6 Bedford Square he used such a dome with the saucer dome replaced by a lantern, flanked by apses. Sir Robert Taylor took this a step further at the Reduced Annuities Office at the Bank of England in 1782, where the saucer dome was replaced by a circle of windows. This may have been an empirical development, but it had been anticipated in Near Eastern basilican architecture, particularly in the Monks' Choir of the church of the Holy Sepulchre in Jerusalem, illustrated by Corneille Lebrun in *Voyage en Levant* in 1714. But it was Soane who was most influenced by Dance's use of vaulting and his experiments with the effects of top-lighting.

Dance's study of the Basilica of Maxentius becomes particularly pertinent when considering Soane's Bank Stock Office, the first of his vaulted interiors in the Bank of England.[25] Among the Soane drawings relating to the Bank Stock Office, the first of the great halls Soane designed at the Bank of England, is a series of sketches plausibly attributed to George Dance. The sketches are again based on the Basilica of Maxentius, but this time

keeping the aisles. One example has a central lantern in the vaulting. To underscore the Roman origins of these astylar buildings, the author has sketched in decorative Roman detail in the spandrels and incised reliefs on the piers. This helped form the basis of the Bank Stock Office as it was finally designed by Soane. Thus, faced with the need to design large unencumbered top-lit halls, Soane, with Dance's prompting, turned to those Roman buildings which he had studied in Italy that fulfilled these requirements, in particular elements of Hadrian's Villa at Tivoli, the Basilica of Maxentius, the so-called Temple of Minerva Medica, the Pantheon and the Roman Baths. While the Basilica of Maxentius formed the model for the Bank Stock Office, the Temple of Minerva Medica, a circular domed building with niches in the walls and round-headed clerestorey windows, lies behind the Rotunda (Fig. 336).

The greatest difficulty lay with the lighting. Side-lighting was not difficult; as Dance had shown at All Hallows, half-light lunette windows fitted neatly under the vaulting. But what about top-lighting? An open oculus, as in the Pantheon, which let in rain was hardly practical in London. Soane experimented with a number of solutions. In the Rotunda, which has an unbroken curved dome, he did use a central oculus, but closed by a lantern. At the Bank Stock Office, the Consols Office, the five per cent Office and the Old Dividend Office he designed saucer domes topped by wide colonnaded openings. He presumably based these on Taylor's design for the Reduced Annuities Office.

Given Soane's study of this late, essentially astylar, Roman architecture, his astylar treatment of the domed Bank interiors becomes understandable. Indeed, much of what seems most original in Soane can also be traced back to his study of Ancient Rome. The best-known example of this is Soane's frequent use of a starfish vault as in the breakfast-room at Lincoln's Inn Fields or the Privy Council Chamber. This was based one of the vaulted ceilings illustrated in P.S. Bartoli's *Gli antichi sepolchri*. Equally important were Campanella's engravings of a very complete set of wall paintings found in a Roman villa excavated in the grounds of the Villa Negroni in 1777. As nothing comparable had been found in Rome and those uncovered in Pompeii were only beginning to be known, these provoked intense interest. They were quickly copied by Thomas Hardwick, subsequently Soane's sketching companion in Rome, soon after which the originals were bought by Soane's putative Roman patron, the Bishop of Derry. Soane subsequently purchased eight of the engravings which were published between 1778 and 1802.[26] He was clearly influenced by these, particularly in the decoration of the front parlour of Pitshanger Manor, while the very thin elongated columns which support the responds of the arches separating the library from the dining-room in

336   Sir John Soane, the Rotunda of the Bank of England, City of London, 1794 (demolished)

Lincoln's Inn Fields are probably based on similar elongated columns found in the engravings. It could also be argued that the complex sense of space and use of side-lighting found in Lincoln's Inn Fields also derives at least in part from Campanella's engravings.

But what of Laugier, who is usually seen as central to Soane's philosophy, and of whose *Essai sur l'architecture* Soane owned no less that ten copies? Laugier believed that architecture should be reduced to its structural essentials, as epitomised by the primitive hut: 'in an architectural Order only the column, the entablature and the pediment may form an essential part of its composition.'[27] Anything else is superfluous and should be avoided where possible. But an examination of Soane's buildings raises severe doubts about Laugier's influence. Laugier's book is a straightforward account of the differ-

ent structural elements of architecture, punctuated by a list of common faults which should be avoided. Nearly every fault can be found at the Bank of England. An analysis of the block of shops in Regent Street designed by Soane in 1820, which seems to develop his astylar manner to its extreme, shows the weakness of relying on Laugier to explain Soane (Fig. 338). The key decorative element is the use of pilasters: Laugier disapproved of pilasters above nearly everything else, as he believed that only columns were permissible. He would have been equally critical of the use of square piers to support the porches. As Laugier believed that a void cannot support a solid he would have disapproved of the wide shop-front openings below elements of wall, and indeed pilasters. He would also have criticised the round-headed windows, the use of an attic and the purely decorative

337 Sir John Soane, the Infirmary, the Royal Hospital, London, 1810 (demolished).

338 Sir John Soane, Regent Street Buildings, London, 1820 (demolished).

339 Sir John Soane, the New Bank Buildings, City of London, 1807 (demolished).

340   Sir John Soane, the Threadneedle Street front of the Bank of England, City of London, 1825.

features which punctuate the skyline. Above all, Laugier, for whom the orders were the height of beauty – the Corinthian order was 'the greatest, the most majestic and most sublime architectural creation'[28] – would have been shocked by Soane's paring away of the detail of the orders. While Laugier believed that it was possible to design buildings without the orders, completely astylar buildings, where economy demanded, these are seldom found in Soane's work where the orders are usually present, even if reduced to a brick pilaster with no mouldings. There is nothing in Laugier to sanction Soane's pared-down orders.

Laugier almost certainly did have an influence on Soane. As Arthur Bolton pointed out, Soane's unexecuted design of 1800 for a church at Tyringham follows Laugier's recommendations for the ideal church closely.[29] But another architectural doctrine, that of *convenance* or decorum, is of greater use in explaining Soane's buildings. According to this well-established Classical belief, the hierarchy of the Classical orders should reflect the relative importance of the buildings to which they are applied. Thus, the Corinthian order (or sometimes the Composite), as the most beautiful, was appropriate for such buildings as churches and palaces, while the Tuscan order as the rudest was suitable for barns, factories and stables. Soane developed the theory more thoroughly than any other English architect. This explains the wide contrast in Soane's buildings between

those of exceptional elaboration with lavish use of the Classical Orders and where hardly an inch of wall or ceiling is left undecorated and those of extreme austerity with scarcely a moulding. In the latter case, Soane was following a long tradition in Georgian architecture, particularly urban architecture, where the orders were pared away, sometimes in their entirety, but remained the framework around which buildings were designed.

When analysing Soane's buildings it is possible to take a single basic structure and then see how, as he embellishes it, it gains in importance. The Infirmary at the Royal Hospital (1810) (Fig. 337), the Regent Street buildings (1820) (Fig. 338), the New Bank Buildings (1807) (Fig. 339) and the Threedneedle Street front for the Bank of England (1825) (Fig. 340) demonstrate such a progression. The Infirmary, a military hospital, lay close to the bottom of the scale, its basic structure is made up of brick arcades and round-headed windows relieved by stone dressings and a Coadestone coat of arms over the cornice on the north front. The Regent Street buildings, a row of shops, but on the grandest street in London, is still dominated by round-headed windows, but with square piers supporting the porches, pilasters without mouldings, and some embellishment along the skyline. The New Bank Buildings, five commercial offices set on one of the most prominent sites in the City, follows the same basic framework but with a more developed cornice, more elaborate pilasters, pairs

341 Henry Holland, the entrance hall, Berrington Hall, Herefordshire, 1778.

of freestanding Ionic columns at each end of the façade, Ionic columns supporting a porch in the centre, and greater relief around the windows. The Threedneedle Street front of the Bank of England, a quasi-governmental building of great national importance, maintains the use of round-headed windows, but with an attached Corinthian Order supporting a full entablature, rusticated walls, and elaborate window surrounds in the attic.

The immediate philosophical background to Soane's architecture can probably be found in Chambers's *Treatise on Civil Architecture* of 1759, the standard Classical textbook of late eighteenth-century England, rather than Laugier's *Essai*. Soane's style is only comprehensible when all his buildings are considered, not just that hand-

ful of astylar buildings which is sometimes identified as representing Soane's 'personal style'.

Dance had been one influence on Soane's early career. The other was Henry Holland, whose office he joined in 1772. It was an office where French influence was particularly important, as can be seen in *Designs in Architecture*, Soane's first book, published in 1778, just before he left for Italy. Both Chambers and Adam acknowledged debts to France, Adam particularly in planning, noting that the 'proper arrangement and relief of apartments are branches of architecture in which the French have excelled all other nations'.[30] Chambers was a francophile by training and retained strong friendships in France. However, French influence in his work is limited largely to decorative details and to interior decoration. Even after his trip to Paris in 1774 to study recent buildings, the designs for Somerset House look primarily to *cinquecento* Italy and to England, although French influence is evident in the details.[31]

Chambers had good reason to visit Paris, as he remarked before he left: 'Many great things have been done since I last saw Paris which I must examine with Care and make Proper remarks upon.'[32] The years that followed the Peace of Paris in 1763 were particularly vibrant ones for French architecture, with the rise of such architects as Jacques-Germain Soufflot, Marie-Joseph Peyre, Charles de Wailly, Pierre-Louis Moreau, Jacques Gondoin, Étienne-Louis Boullée and Claude-Nicolas Ledoux. They were also years, particularly after the Peace of Versailles in 1783, in which relationships between France and England were closer than they had been for at least a century. These links reached their peak in 1786 with the signing of the Anglo-French Treaty of Commerce. With the weakening hold of neo-Palladianism, French influence spread from being a matter of decoration, as with the Rococo and in Chambers's work, to become a direct architectural influence in the work of such architects as Henry Holland, S.P. Cockerell, Joseph Bonomi and Thomas Harrison. It was a brief flourishing, for twenty-two years of almost continual war from 1793 broke this close relationship, and direct French influence, except in the Empire style of decoration, largely disappeared in the first years of the nineteenth century, being pushed out by the Greek Revival.

Walpole's comments on Carlton House in 1785 show that Holland's French leanings were not unnoticed:

> It will be the most perfect in Europe. There is an august simplicity that astonished me. You cannot call it magnificent; it is the taste and propriety that strike. Every ornament is at a proper distance, and not one too large, but all delicate and new, with more freedom and variety than Greek ornament, and though probably borrowed from the Hôtel de Condé, and other new palaces, not one that is not rather classic than French.[33]

The sources of Holland's manner are unclear, for he did not visit France until 1785, but elements appear in the decoration of Brooks's Club in 1776 and Berrington Hall begun in 1778 (Fig. 341).[34] The Brooks's commission was probably critical as it introduced Holland to a circle of Gallic sympathising Whig aristocrats who were to form the core of his patrons. Not that Holland was the only source of French ideas at this date. French decorators worked at Chatsworth in 1781 under Guillaume Gaubert, who subsequently worked for the Prince of Wales at Carlton House. Before he visited France, Holland must have derived his knowledge of French taste

342 Thomas Hope, house in Portland Place, London, 1799 (demolished).

chiefly from the works of such architects as Patte, Peyre and Gondoin, but he also relied on French craftsmen and a French assistant J.-P. Trecourt.

Of the generation of architects who emerge in the 1780s, Thomas Harrison's design for a commemorative edifice and for a national Valhalla take after Boullée's visionary schemes, but it is his Chester Castle (1788) that looks most strongly towards France. The Shire Hall range, which was the first to be built, shows the influence of Brogniart's Couvent des Capucins (1779) in the extreme austerity of the exterior, with its simple block cornice and in the use of an unfluted Greek Doric order. Similarly, the idea of a screened, colonnaded courtyard leading to a portico behind which was a semi-circular meeting room with a coffered ceiling, derives from Gondoin's École de Chirugie of 1769. However, as Chester Castle evolved – it was not finished until 1822 – it moved away from French sources to a more thoroughly Greek approach. S.P. Cockerell is not known to have visited France, but some of his designs show 'very marked French influence of an advanced kind',[35] notably Daylesford House, Gloucestershire (1788), the colonnaded façade of Gore Court, Kent (1792), the destroyed church of St Martin Outwich, London (1796), and the tower of St Anne, Soho (1802). Joseph Bonomi's work is markedly austere, and the circular belvedere at Rosneath, Dunbartonshire (1803), suggests a knowledge of Ledoux's work.

French influence did not mean the end of the English

343   Nicholas Revett, portico at Standlynch House, Wiltshire, 1766.

344   Henry Holland, the sculpture gallery, Woburn Abbey, Bedfordshire, 1787.

archaeologically based neo-Classical tradition, as seen with Dance and Soane's studies of Roman vaulted structures. The most remarkable antique interiors of these years were those created with archaeological correctness by the amateur Thomas Hope, first in his London house from 1799 and then at Deepdene, Surrey, from 1807, some of which he published in *Household Furniture and Interior Decoration executed from Designs by Thomas Hope* in 1807 (Fig. 342). Hope championed the idea of the Greek Revival, something which finally began to have an impact on British architecture in the 1780s and 1790s. The initial impact of newly discovered Greek buildings on

British architecture had been largely decorative, with the Greek Ionic order becoming accepted as a standard element of Classical design. The Greek Doric order, by contrast, had largely been ignored except for a handful of garden buildings. Use of the Greek orders in the design of buildings, rather than for decoration, remained limited to a small circle of Dilettanti employing James Stuart or his fellow partner in the *Antiquities of Athens*, Nicholas Revett. Stuart designed an attached Greek Ionic portico in 1764 for Thomas Anson, a member of the Society of Dilettanti, at Lichfield House, St James's Square. Revett added an entrance portico to Standlynch House, Wiltshire (fig. 343), for Henry Dawkins, another Dilettanti and one of Robert Wood's companions on the Baalbek and Palmyra expeditions in 1766; a Greek Ionic portico, modelled on the Temple of Bacchus at Teos illustrated in *Ionian Antiquities* (1769), to West Wycombe Park in 1771 for Sir Francis Dashwood, another Dilettanti (Fig. 165); and designed the church of St Lawrence at Ayot St Lawrence, Hertfordshire, based on the Temple of Apollo at Delos in 1778. All these lay firmly in the Dilettanti tradition which encompassed both Greece and Rome and there is no evidence that they were doctrinaire attempts to introduce a Greek Revival. More challenging was Thomas Johnson's County Gaol, Warwick (1779), which has a giant Greek Doric order and complete entablature, although in execution the columns were not fluted as intended. This is built as a single façade but should probably be read as a tetrastyle temple with side ranges laid flat. It is hard to believe that this innovative work was the idea of the Warwick masterbuilder Johnson. The whole design has the feel of the amateur about it, so it may be that, as has been suggested, the ideas of someone like Sanderson Miller, or more probably the Earl of Aylesford, lie behind it.

It was only after the Peace of Versailles in 1783 that Greek architecture became more than a minor interest of amateurs and dilettanti. Henry Holland used the Greek Doric order on the *porte-cochère* at Woburn Abbey, Bedfordshire (1787–9), where he also designed a full Greek Ionic portico in the sculpture gallery (Fig. 344). In 1789 the Earl of Aylesford, assisted by Joseph Bonomi, used squat Greek Doric columns to support the crossvault of the remarkable church at Great Packington, Warwickshire (Fig. 345). The first serious monument of the Greek Revival, Thomas Harrison's Chester Castle, was begun in 1788. In the following year the second volume of the *Antiquities of Athens*, with the great monuments of Periclean Athens, including the Parthenon, was finally published, and this was followed in 1797 by the second volume of the *Ionian Antiquities*. These are signs of a growing interest in Greece, confirmed by a violent attack on Greek architecture by Chambers in his *A Treatise on the Decorative Part of Civil Architecture* in 1791, which C.H. Tatham noted in 1795 in a letter to Henry

345   Joseph Bonomi, interior of Packington church, Warwickshire, 1789.

Holland from Rome writing that 'It is with pleasure I read your remarks on the subject of Greek architecture gaining ground in England.'[36]

However, evidence of interest in Greek architecture remains limited before the outbreak of war in 1793, and the rest of the decade was unpropitious for building. It was only in the first decade of the nineteenth century that the Greek Revival was finally established as an accepted style, although not without controversy. A handful of key examples tells the story, George Dance's unfluted Greek Doric portico at Stratton Park, Hampshire (1803); William Wilkins's remodelling of the Grange, Hampshire, as a reconstruction of the Theseion in Athens (1804); Wilkins's defeat of James Wyatt's Roman designs for Downing College, Cambridge, with his own Greek designs (1804); Soane's Prince's Street Vestibule for the Bank of England (1804); Robert Smirke's austere Theatre Royal, Covent Garden (1808); William Stark's Glasgow Courthouse (1807); and Sir Charles Monck's imaginative Greek essay at Belsay Hall, Northumberland (1810) (Fig. 346).

This was a very different sort of architecture to that of James Stuart, a militant movement convinced that architecture should subscribe to the rules of Ancient Greece, to the primacy of the Greek Doric order and to a structural system based on the column and lintel. But, just as the Greek Revival was preaching a doctrine of Athenian purity, two other architectural developments arose to challenge such exclusivity, the concept of asymmetry and the increasing acceptance of Gothic architecture as more than just an associational style.

Symmetry was an essential feature of post-Renaissance Classical architecture, and its dominance meant that even eighteenth-century Gothic buildings were strictly symmetrical. There were two renowned exceptions, Sir John Vanbrugh's Vanbrugh Castle, Greenwich (1718 on), and Horace Walpole's Strawberry Hill, Twickenham (1748 on), but in neither case was asymmetry originally intended. At Vanbrugh Castle, marriage forced Vanbrugh to add to the existing symmetrical building, but the lie of the land meant that this could only be done asymmetrically. At Strawberry Hill, asymmetry grew out

346   Sir Charles Monck, Belsay Hall, Northumberland, 1810.

347 Richard Payne Knight, Downton Castle, Shropshire, 1772.

of the reuse of an existing building and the constrictions of the site. Deliberate asymmetry was the result of a growing interest in the Picturesque, and it is no surprise to discover that one of the first deliberately asymmetrical buildings was a *cottage orné*, as rustic cottages, which by their nature tended to be asymmetrical, were a popular subject for painters, for example Gainsborough, who fed the passion for the Picturesque. Hans Stanley, Governor of the Isle of Wight from 1764, built himself an L-shaped thatched cottage called Steephill on the south side of the island soon after being appointed governor.[37] It soon became one of the most famed sites on the island.

Although this marked a decisive break with Classical tradition, Steephill was only a temporary retreat, not a seat, and for this type of house a certain degree of architectural licence had always been tolerated. Much more significant was the erection by Richard Payne Knight, author of *The Landscape, A Didactic Poem* (1794) and *Analytical Inquiry into Principles of Taste* (1805), both key works of the Picturesque, of Downton Castle, Herefordshire, in 1772–8 (Fig. 347). While Downton has often been thought of as a Gothic house because of its

crenellations, Andrew Ballantyne argued, probably correctly, that it should be read as a Classical house. Following his belief that Classical houses were not symmetrical, and for reasons of the Picturesque, Knight built a house in which rational planning prevailed over symmetry.[38] As the house was his seat, this was a major aesthetic statement.

Knight did not build any other houses, but his acceptance of asymmetry was taken up by James Wyatt and John Nash. In about 1785 Wyatt designed Lee Priory, Kent, an asymmetical Gothic house which led Horace Walpole to claim the house as 'a child of Strawberry' (Fig. 348). According to Edward Hasted, the three fronts of the house conveyed 'an idea of a small convent, never attempted to be demolished, but partly modernized, and adapted to the habitation of a gentleman's family'.[39] Wyatt's Dodington Park, Gloucestershire (1798) (Fig. 349), shows him applying the same fluidity to a Classical design. But it was Nash who really made asymmetry his own, designing what was probably his first example in about 1796, soon after returning to London. This was Point Pleasant, Kingston-upon-Thames, Surrey, de-

348   James Wyatt, Dodington Park, Gloucestershire, 1798.

signed to take advantage of its view over Richmond Hill and described by Humphry Repton as having a 'new and unexampled plan by my ingenious friend'.[40] Point Place was Classical and was swiftly followed by Nash's own East Cowes Castle (1798) in the castellated style; The Warrens, Hampshire (1800), which was Classical; Luscombe Castle, Devon (1800), Gothic; and Cronkhill, Shropshire (1802), which was Italianate.

Wyatt and Nash's acceptance of asymmetry was particularly powerful for it was combined with a new attitude towards Gothic architecture which regarded it as being morally equal to Classical architecture. Under Wren, Hawksmoor, Kent and the Gothic Revivalists of the mid-century, Gothic architecture never challenged the primacy of Classical architecture. It was used to complete or remodel existing buildings. In a handful of cases it was used to design a villa, but it was not appropriate for a new-built family seat. This assumption began to crumble towards the end of the century, largely thanks to Wyatt, who began his career as a Classicist but by the end was working almost exclusively in the Gothic style.

Sheffield Place, Sussex, was his first Gothic house, and is important as an early example of a Gothic seat, being extensively remodelled for John Holroyd, subsequently Earl of Sheffield, in about 1776. Wyatt created symmetrical north and south fronts, but an asymmetrical east front, with a great traceried window on the left, intended purely as an eyecatcher from the lake below. This was followed by the remodelling of Sandleford Priory, Berkshire (1780), and of Pishiobury Park, Herefordshire (1782), but the key house was Lee Priory (Fig. 348). Here, with a house designed to suggest that it had developed over many years, Wyatt was at last able to throw away the Classical straightjacket of symmetry and design a house that could not be accused of being no more than Classical architecture tricked up. Gothic architecture was established as a valid style in its own right, as appropriate for designing a landed seat as Classical architecture. The dramatic result of this was Fonthill Abbey, Wiltshire (1795), where symmetry was thrown away in the exuberance of Gothic. By the first decade of the nineteenth century Gothic was no longer just a manner for remo-

349   James Wyatt, Lee Priory, Kent, *c.*1785 (British School, oil, Yale Center for British Art, New Haven, Conn. (detail)).

350   James Wyatt, Oriel College Library, Oxford, 1788 (from the *Oxford Almanac*)

delling old houses or for villas, it was an accepted style for great houses, Wyatt's, Cassiobury, Hertfordshire (1800), and Ashridge Park, Hertfordshire (1808), and Robert Smirke's Lowther Castle, Westmorland (1806). The seal on the respectability of the new style was set in 1804 when George III turned to Gothic for his new palace at Kew.

Arbitrary cut-off dates are always hard to find in architectural history, but 1815, with building in the trough of another depression and the ending of the long war with France heralding many decades of peace, is better than most. It was a year of potential. No one architectural style was dominant, and many architects such as Wyatt and Nash accepted Thomas Hopper's dictum that 'it is an architect's business to understand all styles and be prejudiced in favour of none'. Palladianism

and neo-Palladianism had been increasingly sidelined, although not entirely abandoned. James Wyatt's library for Oriel College, Oxford (1788) (Fig. 350), still lies recognisably in the neo-Palladian tradition, as does Benjamin Wyatt's half-executed design for the Theatre Royal, Drury Lane, of 1812. Many Greek Revival buildings, such as Richmond Terrace in Whitehall (1822) could be described as neo-Palladian structures tricked out with Greek detail. The compact Palladian house remained a popular way to design country houses. But in the last decades of the eighteenth century the Palladian consensus which had dominated English architecture since the middle of the seventeenth-century – despite the eruptions of the Baroque in the early eighteenth-century – had been destroyed.

NOTES

CHAPTER I

1. Peter Paul Rubens, *Palazzi di Genova* (Antwerp, 1622), introduction.
2. Erich Hubala, 'Il Palladio e l'architettura del '600 in Germania', *BCISAP*, III (1961), pp. 50–52, fig. 39; Erik Forssman, 'Il Palladianesimo in Germania', *Palladio la sua eredita nel mondo* (exh. cat., Milan, 1980), p. 13.
3. Werner Hager, 'Uno studio sul Palladianesimo di Elias Holl', *BCISAP*, IX (1967), p. 85. There are interesting parallels between the composition of the Augsburg Town Hall and Inigo Jones's early designs, particularly that of a town house for Fulke Greville *c*.1617, despite the completely different scale of the two buildings. Could Jones have visited Augsburg on his way from Heidelberg to Italy? There is no evidence to suggest that he did, the Earl of Arundel's party is known to have progressed down the Rhine from Heidelberg to Italy, not to have gone through Germany.
4. Forssman (1980), p. 15.
5. John Harris, 'Heidelberg, Holl, Jones und das serlianische Zwischenspiel', in *Elias Holl und das Augsburger Rathaus* (exh. cat., Regensburg, 1985), pp. 118–26; id. 'Inigo Jones and the mystery of Heidelberg Castle', *Apollo* (March, 1993), pp. 147–52.
6. David Howarth, *Lord Arundel and his Circle* (New Haven and London, 1985), p. 244, fn. 52.
7. British Library, Egerton MS 2593, fol. 147; quoted in Howarth (1985), p. 236, fn. 22.
8. John Summerson, 'The Book of Architecture of John Thorpe', *Walpole Society*, XL (1966), p. 48. Begun *c*.1622 for Sir John Danvers, and perhaps the first English villa in the Italian tradition, Danvers House was a compact tripartite structure raised on a basement after the Italian example with a central range containing west hall, stairs and hall and flanking ranges with the chapel and parlour. The tripartite plan comes from Palladio, although not from one specific villa, but the projecting stair turrets look back to Jacobean domestic tradition. The façade is austere, dominated by a central Serlian window on the first floor.
9. Built for the 1st Earl of Northampton, and dated 1624 by the inscription that runs along the balustrade, this arcaded structure with Tuscan pilasters and niches owes much to Serlio's third and fourth books. See Sebastiano Serlio, *The Five Books of Architecture* (London, 1611), III, chap. 4, fol. 66*v*; IV, chap. 5, fol. 15, chap. 8, fols. 50, 54; V, chap. 14, fol. 10*v*.
10. Linda Campbell, 'Documentary Evidence for the building of Raynham Hall', *AH*, 32 (1989), pp. 52–67.
11. It has generally been assumed that these were added by James Clitherow during work on the house around 1670, but no evidence of the necessary disturbance of the brickwork was found when the house was restored in 1963, and Clitherow's work was probably restricted to rebuilding the office wing. The Classical ornament found at Boston Manor is not characteristic of the 1670s but precedents can be found in contemporary work by Jones.
12. Gervase Jackson-Stops, 'Castle Ashby, Northamptonshire', *CL* (30 Jan. 1986).
13. Kevin Sharpe, *The Personal Rule of Charles I* (New Haven and London, 1992), pp. 124–6, 605–7.
14. *City of Cambridge*, RCHM (London, 1959), p. lxxxii; Jennifer Sherwood and Nikolaus Pevsner, *Oxfordshire*, The Buildings of England (London, 1974), pp. 34–8.
15. Howard Colvin, *Unbuilt Oxford* (New Haven and London, 1983), p. 11.
16. *Architecture in Britain*, chap. 10.
17. The first design for Somerset House, for instance, is firmly indebted to the illustration on p. 249 in Scamozzi's book. In the second design Jones returned on a more ambitious scale to the themes he addressed in his first scheme for the Banqueting House.
18. John Newman, 'Inigo Jones's architectural education before 1614', *AH*, 35 (1992), p. 20.
19. John Summerson, *The Unromantic Castle* (London, 1990), pp. 50–52.
20. John Newman, 'Nicholas Stone's Goldsmiths' Hall: Design and Practice in the 1630s', *AH*, 14 (1971), pp. 30–9.
21. John Harris, *The Artist and the Country House* (London, 1979), fig. 278. *The Earl of Strafforde's Letters and Despatches* (London, 1739), II, p. 118.
22. It appears in Jones's work at the Prince's Lodgings, in a masque design for Cupid's Palace (*c*.1619), at the east and west ends of the Chapel Royal at St James's Palace, and at Sir Peter Killigrew's house (*c*.1630). Elsewhere it is used at Raynham Hall; Danvers House; Nicholas Stone's Goldsmiths' Hall, London (1635), and Chilham Church, Kent (1631–2); Woburn Abbey, Beds (*c*.1630); on the chapel and entrance screen at Castle Ashby, Northants (*c*.1630); at the east end of Stanmore Church, Middx; Copthall, Essex (1639); extensively at St Gregory-by-St Paul (*c*.1641) which had largely been demolished by Jones when working on the cathedral; Holy Trinity, Berwick-on-Tweed, by John Young (1650), which owes much to St Gregory; Forde Abbey, Dorset (*c*.1650); Thorpe Hall, Cambs (1653); and Bloxholm Hall, Lincs.
23. Jones used the round-headed window at the Queen's House, St Paul, Covent Garden, St Paul's Cathedral and in the design for a seven-bay pergolaed house. Other architects used it at Raynham Hall; Stoke Bruern, Northants (*c*.1629–35), and Woburn Abbey, Beds (before 1630); Fonthill House, Wilts (*c*.1630); the Goldsmiths' Hall (1635); Wilton, Wilts (1636); Balls Park, Herts (1638); Kirby Hall, Northants (1638); Tart Hall, Middx (1638).
24. Used by Jones in the early design for a riding house; in the design for Sir Fulke Greville's house; St Paul, Covent Garden; St Paul's Cathedral; and Sir Peter Killigrew's house. Other architects used them at Raynham Hall; Danvers House; Goldsmiths' Hall; Tart Hall; Wilton House; Kirby Hall. An alternative was the *oeil-de-boeuf* window used in the stables at Ramsbury Manor, Wilts, probably built by the 4th Earl of Pembroke before his death in 1650, and at Tythrop House, built by his son James Herbert between 1646 and his death in 1676. (Giles Worsley, 'The Design and Development of the Stable and Riding House in Great Britain from the Thirteenth Century to 1914', Courtauld Institute PhD, 1989, p. 80.)
25. Used by Jones in the first design for the Prince's Lodging at Newmarket; in the second design for a riding house and on the rear of Sir Peter Killigrew's house. Elsewhere it appears at Stanmore Church, and on the gallery at Castle Ashby. The aediculed niches behind the gallery at Castle Ashby are also Serlian.

26. Used by Jones on the early design for a riding house; preliminary side elevation of the Queen's House; at the Prince's Lodging, Newmarket; the side range to the Chapel Royal at St James's Palace; the Queen's House and Sir Peter Killigrew's house. Used by other architects at Raynham Hall; Boston Manor; Cornbury Hall and Lindsey House.

27. John Harris and Gordon Higgott, *Inigo Jones, Complete Architectural Drawings* (London, 1989), pp. 96–7; John Harris and A.A. Tait, *Catalogue of the Drawings by Inigo Jones, John Webb and Isaac de Caus at Worcester College, Oxford* (Oxford, 1979), pls. 120–21.

28. Newman (1971), p. 33.

29. John Bold, *Wilton House and English Palladianism* (London, 1988), p. 33. Timothy Mowl and Brian Earnshaw have suggested that Inigo Jones alone should be credited with the design of Wilton and that de Caux was only an executant architect (Timothy Mowl and Brian Earnshaw, 'Inigo Jones Restored', *CL*, 30 Jan. 1992). However, Gordon Higgott does not believe that either the Grand Design for Wilton at Worcester College nor the Reduced Design in the RIBA Drawings Collection are in Jones's hand, and there seems to be no reason to doubt John Aubrey's account which fits in with what is known independently of Jones's method of working at the Goldsmiths' Hall.

30. Newman (1971), pp. 33–4.

31. *BDBA*, p. 787.

32. Sebastiano Serlio, *Tutte l'opera d'architettura* (Venice, 1619), VII, fol. 41.

33. Harris and Higgott (1989), pp. 192, 257, 312; J.T. Smith, *Sixty-Two Additional Plates to Smith's Antiquities of Westminster* (London, 1809), p. 5.

34. H.M. Colvin (ed.), *The History of the King's Works*, IV (London, 1982), p. 159.

35. Licence to build dated 12 Dec. 1640, from the Privy Council, among the Bedford Papers at Woburn Abbey.

36. Geoffrey Webb pointed out the importance of the Maltravers type of house, which he christened the 'Genoese type', in an important article 'The Architectural Antecedents of Sir Christopher Wren', *RIBA Journal*, 40 (1933), pp. 573–87. This emphasises the contrast between this group of houses and Jones's other work, and notes the similarities between them and similar houses which are conventionally distinguished from his work as Artisan Mannerist. I am grateful to Mr Howard Colvin for drawing my attention to this article.

37. A row of shops similar to Jones's Lothbury warehouses appears in the background of Hollar's engraving *Winter* (1643) which is set in the City of London (Malcolm Warner, *The Image of London: Views by Travellers and Emigrés 1550–1920*, London, 1987, p.106, fig. 12). As the other engravings in this series have been associated with Arundel properties it is tempting to link these shops with Jones's design. However, it is clear that the street shown is Cornhill, not Lothbury. Nevertheless, this engraving is important evidence that Jones's severe astylar manner was already influential in the City.

38. It should be noted, however, that Leicester House was altered in the 1670s and in the eighteenth century (information from Dr John Adamson).

39. Although greatly extended in the nineteenth century and subsequently reduced, the original appearance of West Woodhay is known from early photographs and its present state closely follows what was there before. Gervase Jackson-Stops, 'West Woodhay House, Berkshire', *CL* (22 Jan. 1987).

40. John Harris, *The Design of the Country House 1620–1920* (London, 1985), fig. 23.

41. John Newman, who examined Chevening when it was restored in 1969, points out that the change in the type of stone used for the quoins two-thirds of the way up the façade may be evidence of a break in building, perhaps when the 13th Lord Dacre died in 1630 and was succeeded by a minor who did not come of age until 1640. He suggests that if this is the case the house may not originally have been planned with a hipped roof but could have been intended as a compact pile with gables like Boston Manor (John Newman, *West Kent and the Weald*, The Buildings of England, London, 1980, pp. 210–12).

42. An early eighteenth-century drawing of St Clere shows the house before it was altered with a hipped roof and dormers,

43. a central row of chimneys and octagonal caps on the turrets (*CL*, 18 April 1968).

It has been suggested that Forty Hall was much altered in 1708 as there is a rainwater head of that date (*Middlesex*, V, Victoria History of the Counties of England, London, 1976, p. 277) and as Daniel Lysons (*The Environs of London*, London, 1795, II, p. 299) states that Forty Hall was 'repaired and modernised' by the Wolstenholmes in 1700. However, it cannot be assumed from this statement that the roof was altered. Alison Maguire and Andor Gomme have established that the roof structure is all of one piece and that if it dated from *c.*1700 the entire structure, including the top-floor ceiling beams and joists would all have had to be new. Its design would seem to militate against the roof originally being gabled, but the carpentry of the roof is definitely pre-Classical of a type that would have been extremely unlikely in the reconstruction of a major house near London *c.*1700. Their conclusion is that the entire roof structure is in its original condition and dates from *c.*1630 (information from Professor Andor Gomme).

44. Serlio (1619), VII, fols. 103, 105.

45. *Architecture in Britain*, pp. 164–5.

46. Harris and Higgott (1989), p. 300, fig. 97. Although this engraving is believed to be of Tart Hall there is uncertainty about its precise identification.

47. A.A. Tait, 'Post-Modernism in the 1650s', in Charles Hind (ed.), *Inigo Jones and the Spread of Classicism* (London, 1987), pp. 23–35.

48. *BDBA*, p. 474.

49. Howard Colvin, 'Inigo Jones and the Church of St Michael le Querne', *The London Journal*, 12/1 (1986), pp. 36–9.

50. Howard Colvin, *The Canterbury Quadrangle, St John's College, Oxford* (Oxford, 1988), pp. 13–52.

51. See especially fols. 33, 41, 103, 105, 155.

52. *Ibid.*, fol. 155.

53. *Holl* (1985), p. 344.

54. Gordon Higgott, '"Varying with Reason": Inigo Jones's Theory of Design', *AH*, 35 (1992), pp. 51–77.

55. *Ibid.*, pp. 59–61.

56. '[Wilton and Coleshill] serve to bridge a period of ten years during which few other houses were built'. (Summerson, 1977, p. 165.)

57. Although he fought with the Royalists in the Civil War, Blount subsequently came round to the Commonwealth and served on several of its commissions.

58. Pratt, although accused of Royalist sympathies, actively supported the Commonwealth government; during the 1650s he sat on the Committee for Berkshire, was a JP and a sheriff of the county. Indeed the nature of his activities meant he had to be pardoned by Charles II in 1662. (Nigel Silcox-Crowe, 'Sir Roger Pratt', in Roderick Brown (ed.), *The Architectural Outsiders*, London, 1985, p. 6.)

59. Other houses probably built or substantially altered at this date include Edward Peyto's Chesterton House, Warwicks; Sir John Lewis's Ledston, Yorks; Moulton Manor and Hall, Yorks; Highnam Court, Glos, built by William Cooke who originally supported the Crown and then turned to Parliament; Norgrove Court, Worcs; Syndale House, Kent; and Yotes Court, Kent.

60. Mowl and Earnshaw (1992).

61. Howard Colvin, 'Chesterton, Warwickshire', *Architectural Review* (August 1955).

62. Giles Worsley, 'Thorpe Hall in Context', *GGJ* (1993), pp. 6, 7.

63. The suggestion has often been made that the source for Thorpe Hall and for other similar three-storey houses such as Chevening can be found in Rubens's *Palazzi di Genova* (1622) (see, for example, Oliver Hill and John Cornforth, *English Country Houses: Caroline*, London, 1966, pp. 102–3). Rubens's book was not without influence, John Webb's Worcester College drawings include a sheet with six house plans taken from the *Palazzi di Genova* and another with two window openings drawn from the same source (W. Grant Keith, 'Six Houses in search of an Architect', *RIBA Journal*, 40, 1933, p. 733), while the Duke of Newcastle's Nottingham Castle, Notts (1674–9), has details taken from the book (Hill and Cornforth, 1966, p. 35). However, the complexity of most of Rubens's illustrations does not fit in with the studied simplicity of Jones's Maltravers-type houses. It would

seem that any influence was, at best, tangential, and that the source for Chevening and Thorpe lies instead in the logical addition of an extra half storey to Jones's two-storey Maltravers-type house, as happened in the Lothbury warehouses.

64. The will of Sir Henry Pratt, dated 2 July 1645, and proved on 14 April 1649, exhorts his executors to finish 'my building in Colcell if I shall leave and part of thereof unfinished at my decease' (Malcolm Pinhorn, 'A Note on the Date of Construction of Coleshill, Berkshire', *Blackmansbury*, I/1 (April 1964), pp. 5–7). His son Sir George Pratt must have sought designs, perhaps for completing this house, from John Webb. Webb's book of capitals at Chatsworth includes three for Coleshill, for the front (showing that Webb's design was not astylar as the completed Coleshill was), atrium and Great Chamber, and a design by Webb for a chimney-piece and overmantel is inscribed for 'Sir George Pratt's Great Chamber' (John Harris, *Catalogue of Drawings Collection of the RIBA: Inigo Jones and John Webb*, Farnborough, 1972, p. 23). According to Sir Mark Pleydell, owner of Coleshill from 1728, the house was burnt down 'soon after' Sir George Pratt's wedding in 1647. It was presumably after this that Sir George Pratt began to build a new house in the cucumber garden which had got as far as the first storey when he was persuaded by Pratt – and perhaps Jones – to demolish it and build the final house on an adjacent site (Silcox-Crowe, 1985, pp. 6–7; John Bold, *John Webb: Architectural Theory and Practice in the Seventeenth Century*, Oxford, 1989, pp. 157–8).
65. Mowl and Earnshaw (1992).
66. Silcox-Crowe (1985), pp. 6–7.
67. H. Avray Tipping, 'Coleshill House, Berkshire', *CL* (26 July 1919).

CHAPTER II

1. John Bold, *John Webb: Architectural Theory and Practice in the Seventeenth Century* (Oxford, 1989), p. 181.
2. E.S. de Beer (ed.), *The Diary of John Evelyn* (London, 1955), III, pp. 300–1.
3. Giles Worsley, 'Milton Manor, Berkshire', *CL* (14 Nov. 1991).
4. Society of Antiquaries, Prattindon Collections of Worcestershire History I (18).
5. Daniel D. Reiff's *Small Georgian Houses in England and Virginia* (London and Toronto, 1986), illustrates the prevalence of this type.
6. Oliver Hill and John Cornforth, *English Country Houses: Caroline* (London, 1966), pp. 174–6.
7. H.M. Colvin (ed.), *History of the King's Works*, IV (London, 1982), p. 177.
8. *Architecture in Britain*, pp. 190–2.
9. Arline Meyer (ed.), *John Wootton 1682–1764* (London, 1984), p. 32.
10. R.T. Gunther (ed.), *The Architecture of Sir Roger Pratt* (Oxford, 1928), p. 23.
11. *Ibid.*, p. 285.
12. *Ibid.*, p. 298.
13. W. Bray (ed.), *The Diary and Correspondence of John Evelyn* (London, 1852), III, p. 177.
14. Gunther (1928), p. 290.
15. *Ibid.*
16. *Ibid.*, p. 11.
17. *Ibid.*, p. 289.
18. *Ibid.*, pp. 34–9, 292.
19. *Ibid.*, pp. 24, 290.
20. *Ibid.*, p. 60.
21. *Ibid.*, pp. 34, 70, 75, 76, 151, 212, 264.
22. *Ibid.*, pp. 68, 74, 76, 196–7.
23. *Ibid.*, pp. 290, 298.
24. *Ibid.*, p. 290.
25. *Ibid.*, p. 37.
26. Vitruvius, *The Ten Books of Architecture*, ed. M.H. Morgan (New York, 1960), p. 170.
27. Gunther (1928), p. 37.
28. *Ibid.*, p. 194.
29. *Ibid.*, pp. 26, 37, 69, 76, 232, 260–61.

30. Samwell's is perhaps a name that should be considered for Burlington House, given the similarities with the west wing at Felbrigg Hall, Norfolk.
31. Henry Wotton, *The Elements of Architecture* (London, 1624), p. 1.
32. Rudolf Wittkower, *Palladio and English Palladianism* (London, 1983), pp. 95–100.
33. Roland Fréart, *A Parallel of the Antient Architecture with the Modern*, trans. John Evelyn (London, 1664), p. 118.
34. *Ibid.*, p. 6.
35. *Ibid.*, p. 22.
36. *Ibid.*, p. 84.
37. *Ibid.*, p. 99.
38. *Ibid.*, p. 28.
39. *Ibid.*, p. 24.
40. *Ibid.*, p. 22.
41. De Beer (1955), II, p. 461.
42. Fréart (1664), p. 122.
43. De Beer (1955), p. 483.
44. *Ibid.*, p. 455.
45. Eileen Harris, *British Architectural Books and Writers* (Cambridge, 1990), p. 462.
46. De Beer (1955), p. 455.
47. H.M. Colvin *et al*, *Architectural Drawings from Lowther Castle, Westmorland* (London, 1980), pp. 7–8, pls. 2, 4, 5, 7b. It should be noted that the stables at Lowther were of two storeys, while the central range of those at Cornbury is single storey.
48. Roger North, *Autobiography*, ed. A. Jessop (London, 1887), p. 62.
49. Gunther (1928), p. 60.
50. D.J. Watkin (ed.), *Sale Catalogues of Libraries of Eminent Persons. IV: Architects* (London, 1972), p. 2.
51. Kerry Downes (ed.), *Sir Christopher Wren* (exh. cat., London, Whitechapel Art Gallery, 1982), III, figs. 3 and 4.
52. *Architecture in Britain*, p. 253.
53. Howard Colvin (ed.), *History of the King's Works*, V (London, 1976), pl. 44A.
54. John Harris, *The Palladians* (London, 1981), p. 15.
55. W. Kuyper, *Dutch Classicist Architecture* (Delft, 1980), p. 58.
56. Erik Forssman, 'L'interpretazione del Palladio nei paesi dell'Europa del Nord', *BCISAP*, XII (1970), p. 157.
57. Jan Terwen, 'Il Palladianesimo in Olanda', in *Palladio: la sua eredita nel mondo* (exh. cat., Milan, 1980), pp. 84–8.
58. Forssman (1970), pp. 155–8; Erik Forssman, 'Il Palladianesimo dei paesi Scandinavi', in *Palladio* (1980), pp. 97–9.
59. Terwen (1980), p. 74.
60. H.J. Louw, 'Anglo-Netherlandish Architectural Interchange c.1600–c.1660', *AH*, 24 (1981), p. 17.
61. *Ibid.*, p. 16.
62. The Star Chamber, the preliminary design for the Queen's House at Greenwich, the first scheme for the Banqueting House and the designs for the Prince's Lodgings at Newmarket all have tripartite elevations.
63. Jean Perouse de Montclos, 'Palladio et la theorie classique dans l'architecture française du XVIIème siècle', *BCISAP*, XII (1970), p. 97–8.
64. Anthony Blunt, 'Palladio e l'architettura Francese', *BCISAP*, II (1960), p. 15.
65. Claude Mignot, 'Lettura del Palladio nel XVII secolo: una riservata ammirazione', in *Palladio: la sua eredita nel mondo* (exh. cat., Milan, 1980), p. 207.
66. H. Sauval, *Histoire et recherches des antiquités de la ville de Paris* (Paris, 1733), III, p. 7: 'far-sighted, judicious, profound, sound, in a word, the first architect of our century. In short, if he was not the Vitruvius of our time, he was at least the Palladio.'
67. See Robert W. Berger, *Antoine le Pautre* (New York, 1969), pl. 39. One should, however, be careful to ensure that apparently Palladian quotations do not come from earlier sources: the second design in *Desseins de plusiers palais* seems at first sight to be inspired by the Villa Rotunda, but a more direct source would probably be Serlio's design for a villa based on the Odeo Cornaro illustrated in his seventh book (see Berger, 1969, pls. 21–2, and Robert Tavernor, *Palladio and Palladianism*, London, 1991, pl. 58).
68. Blunt (1960), p. 15.
69. Louis Hautecoeur, *Histoire de l'architecture classique en France*, II (Paris, 1948), fig. 228.

70. *Ibid.*, figs. 145, 112.
71. *Ibid.*, fig. 254.
72. *Ibid.*, fig. 697. Other similar examples that Hautcoeur cites include the Châteaux de Troarn, Vaux, Vauleville (Calvados), de Vernay à Airvault (Deux Sèvres), and la Saulaie à Martigne-Briand (Maine et Loire).

CHAPTER III

1. John Summerson, 'Inigo Jones: Covent Garden and the Restoration of St Paul's Cathedral', *The Unromantic Castle* (London, 1990), pp. 43–62.
2. Gordon Higgott, '"Varying with Reason": Inigo Jones's Theory of Design', *AH*, 35 (1992), p. 53.
3. *Inigo Jones on Palladio* (facsimile of Jones's annotated Palladio), ed. B. Allsopp (Newcastle, 1970), I, p. 62.
4. John Harris and Gordon Higgott, *Inigo Jones: Complete Architectural Drawings* (London, 1989), p. 240.
5. *The Parish of St-Giles-in-the-Fields*, Survey of London, V (London, 1914), p. 136.
6. Esther Eisenthal, 'John Webb's Reconstruction of the Ancient House', *AH*, 28 (1985), pp. 7–31.
7. John Bold, *John Webb: Architectural Theory and Practice in the Seventeenth Century* (Oxford, 1989), p. 74.
8. John Harris and A.A. Tait, *Catalogue of the Drawings by Inigo Jones, John Webb and Isaac de Caus at Worcester College, Oxford* (Oxford, 1979), p. 79.
9. Bold (1989), pp. 107–25.
10. Sebastiano Serlio, *The Five Books of Architecture* (London, 1611), III, fols. 42–3.
11. Bold (1989), p. 19.
12. H.W. Robinson and W. Adams (eds.), *The Diary of Robert Hooke* (London, 1935), p. 179.
13. Mark Girouard, 'Solomon in Nottingham', *CL* (3 Oct. 1991).
14. Eileen Harris, *British Architectural Books and Writers* (Cambridge, 1990), pp. 480–3.
15. *Ibid.*, p. 209.
16. Wolfgang Herrmann, 'Unknown Designs for the 'Temple of Jerusalem' by Claude Perrault, *Essays in the History of Architecture Presented to Rudolf Wittkower*, ed. Douglas Fraser, Howard Hibbard and Milton J. Lawine (London, 1967), pp. 143–55. This includes a detailed list of seventeenth- and eighteenth-century literary attempts at reconstructing the temple.
17. Christopher Wren, *Parentalia* (London, 1750), p. 360.
18. Pliny, *Natural History*, ed. D.E. Eichholz, (London, 1962), XXXVI, pp. 91–3.
19. This is transcribed as 'hersepolis' in Robinson and Adams (1935), pp. 320–1.
20. *Ibid.*, pp. 317, 320–1, 322.
21. Wren (1750), p. 356, also MS p. 24 in the annotated edition in the RIBA Library.
22. Harris (1990), p. 505.
23. *Ibid.*, pp. 194–5.
24. Wren (1750), pp. 351–66.
25. Kerry Downes, *Hawksmoor* (London, 1979), p. 31.
26. Wren (1750), p. 353.
27. *Ibid.*, 'Discourse on Architecture. By Sr.C:W:' appended to the heirloom copy in the RIBA, fol. 1.
28. Wren (1750), p. 360.
29. *Ibid.*, p. 354.
30. Howard Colvin, *Unbuilt Oxford* (New Haven and London, 1983), p. 13.
31. *Architecture in Britain*, p. 199.
32. Serlio (1611), bk 1, I, fol. 12. Mr Donald Insall has pointed out that this form of roof is still known as a Serlian roof.
33. Robert Plot, *Natural History of Oxfordshire* (Oxford, [1676]), pp. 271–6.
34. Colvin (1983), p. 20.
35. *Ibid.*, p. 18.
36. Wren (1750), p. 335.
37. *Ibid.*, p. 314.
38. *Ibid.*, pp. 321–2. The latter is now known as the column of

Marcus Aurelius. In the seventeenth century it was mistakenly attributed to his uncle Antoninus Pius.
39. *Ibid.*, pp. 321–3.
40. G.B. Montano, *Li Tempii e sepolcri antichi* (Rome, 1638), pls. XXXIII, XXXV, XXXX; R.A. Beddard, 'Wren's Mausoleum for Charles I and the Cult of the Royal Martyr', *AH*, 27 (1984), pp. 36–41. Apart from Renaissance feel of the dome, the one major variant is the attached Corinthian colonnade. *Parentalia* suggests this is inspired by the Temple of Vesta, but there are several such colonnades in Montano.
41. Giovanni Antonio Rusconi, *Della architettura . . . secondo i precetti di Vitruvio* (Venice, 1590), p. 19; Vitruvius, *Architecture ou art de bien bastir*, trans. Jean Martin (Paris, 1547), fol. 11*v*.
42. *Architecture in Britain*, p. 218.
43. 'Catalogue of the Pictures etc. of Nicholas Hawksmoor and Colonel John Mercer', *Sale Catalogues of Libraries of Eminent Persons*, ed. David Watkin, IV (London, 1972), p. 29.
44. *Architecture in Britain*, p. 301.
45. G.F. Webb, 'The Letters and Drawings of Nicholas Hawksmoor Relating to the Building of the Mausoleum at Castle Howard', *Walpole Society*, XIX (1931), p. 137.
46. Mrs Arundell Esdaile, Lord Ilchester and H.M. Hake, eds., 'The Vertue Notebooks III', *Walpole Society*, XXII (1934), p. 76.
47. 'Family Memoris of The Rev. William Stukeley: III', *Surtees Society*, 80 (1887), p. 9.
48. Webb (1931), p. 117.
49. *Ibid.*, p. 148.
50. Downes (1979), p. 244.
51. Howard Colvin, *Architecture and the After-life* (New Haven and London, 1991), pp. 317–18.
52. *Ibid.*, p. 57.
53. Kerry Downes, *Hawksmoor* (London, 1970), pp. 195–7.
54. *Ibid.*, pp. 183–4.
55. Serlio (1611), III, fol. 44.
56. Hawksmoor drawings, Worcester College, Oxford, A.4.
57. Downes (1970), figs. 77–8.
58. *VB*, II, pl. 27; Ilaria Toesca, 'Alessandro Galilei in Inghilterra', *English Miscellany*, III (1952), figs. 7, 8; Terry Friedman, *James Gibbs* (New Haven and London, 1984), pp. 56–8.
59. Howard Colvin, 'Fifty New Churches', *Architectural Review* (1957), pp. 189–96.
60. Watkin (1972). Mr Hugh Pagan has commented that Du Cerceau's temple suite is a scarce item and that if Hawksmoor had a set of it, complete or incomplete, it would have been one of the rarest things in his library. He also points out that the absence of a reference to it in his library list is not necessarily significant, as suites of engravings are not necessarily catalogued when listing a library.

CHAPTER IV

1. Roger North, *Of Building*, ed. Howard Colvin and John Newman (Oxford, 1981), p. 62.
2. *Ibid.*, pp. 63, 68.
3. *Ibid.*, pp. 68–9.
4. *Ibid.*, p. 76.
5. Giles Worsley, 'Impractical but Proper', *CL*, (22 Nov. 1990).
6. Mark Girouard (ed.), 'The Smythson Collection', *AH*, 5 (1962), III/1 (4), p. 128.
7. Giles Worsley, 'Thorpe Hall in Context', *GGJ* (1993), p. 9.
8. Giles Worsley, 'Hollin Hall, Yorkshire', *CL* (14 July 1988).
9. H.M. Colvin *et al*, *Architectural Drawings from Lowther Castle Westmorland* (London, 1980), p. 9, pls. 3a, 4.
10. W. Kuyper, *Dutch Classicist Architecture* (Delft, 1980), figs. 229–30.
11. RIBA Drawings Collection, G1/7: ground plan of the College of Physicians in Warwick Lane, built after the Great Fire in 1666. Hooke's diary shows that he purchased architectural books from France and Holland, and it is known that his friend Wren, with whom he often discussed architecture, owned a copy of Le Pautre's *Oeuvre d'architecture* (D.J. Watkin, ed.), *Sale Catalogues of Libraries of Eminent Persons. IV: Architects* (London, 1972), p. 36. Hooke's diary (ed. H.W. Robinson and W. Adams, London,

1935) shows that Hooke bought Le Pautre's 'cuts' on 1 Aug. 1673.

12. John Bold, *John Webb: Architectural Theory and Practice in the Seventeenth-Century* (Oxford, 1989), pp. 136–7.
13. Kerry Downes, *Sir Christopher Wren: The Design of St Paul's Cathedral* (London, 1988), pp. 15–22, 50–51, 108.
14. Bold (1989), pp. 28–30.
15. Wren's use of flying butresses is often cited as another Gothic influence, but Mr Howard Colvin has suggested to the author that these would not have been considered specifically Gothic but would have simply been seen as a convenient structural technique. He suggests that they are more common on Italian churches than has been appreciated.
16. Howard Colvin (ed.), *History of the King's Works*, v (London, 1976), pp. 316–20.
17. Edward Croft-Murray, *Decorative Painting in England 1537–1837* (London, 1962), i, p. 55.
18. Colvin (1976), pp. 316–20.
19. John Harris, *William Talman: Maverick Architect* (London, 1982), figs. 14, 18, 57, 62, 68.
20. James Lees-Milne, *English Country Houses: Baroque* (London, 1970), p. 16.
21. John Harris, 'Diverting Labyrinths', *CL* (11 Jan. 1990).
22. *BDBA*, p. 283.
23. Harris (1982), pls. 44, 53; see chap. 11.
24. George Clark, *The Later Stuarts 1660–1714* (Oxford, 1956), 174–7.
25. J. Parry Lewis, *Building Cycles and Britain's Growth* (London, 1965), p. 15; T.S. Ashton, *An Economic History of England; The Eighteenth Century* (London, 1955), p. 170.
26. Andor Gomme, 'Smith and Rossi', *AH*, 35 (1992), pp. 183–8.
27. Paul Jeffery, 'Thomas Archer's Deptford Rectory: A Reconstruction', *GGJ* (1993), pp. 32–42.

CHAPTER V

1. *Architecture in Britain*, p. 317.
2. *A computation of the Increase of London and Parts Adjacent* (1719), quoted in T.S. Ashton, *Economic Fluctuations* (Oxford, 1959), p. 92.
3. Daniel Defoe, *A Tour through London about the year 1725*, ed. Sir Mayson M. Beeton and E. Beresford Chancellor (London, 1929), pp. 97–8.
4. Francis Sheppard, Victor Belcher and Philip Cotterell, 'The Middlesex and and Yorkshire Deeds Registries and the Study of Building Fluctuations', *London Journal*, v (1979), pp. 183–4.
5. John Summerson, 'The Classical Country House in Eighteenth-century England', *The Unromantic Castle* (London, 1990), pp. 81–2.
6. For a fuller discussion of Talman's stylistic range, see Giles Worsley, 'William Talman: Some Stylistic Suggestions', *GGJ* (1992), pp. 6–18.
7. *Ibid.*, fig. 14.
8. Howard Colvin, *Unbuilt Oxford* (New Haven and London, 1983), p. 38.
9. Andrea Palladio, *I quattro libri dell'architettura* (Venice, 1570), IV, p. 32.
10. Colvin (1983), p. 39; John Harris and A.A. Tait, *Catalogue of the Drawings by Inigo Jones, John Webb and Isaac de Caus at Worcester College, Oxford* (Oxford, 1979), pl. 55.
11. *BDBA*, p. 64.
12. Eileen Harris, *British Architectural Books and Writers* (Cambridge, 1990), pp. 110–12.
13. Bodleian Library, MS Rawlinson B. 376, fol. 8.
14. John Bold, *Wilton House and English Palladianism* (London, 1988), pp. 66–8.
15. Giles Worsley, 'Nicholas Hawksmoor: A Pioneer neo-Palladian?', *AH*, 33 (1990), pp. 60–74.
16. Kerry Downes, *Hawksmoor* (London, 1979), pl. 24a.
17. The building history of the Writing School is not entirely clear. *The Wren Society*, XI, pp. 61 and 80, says that the building was altered in 1776, although this is not entirely reliable as it also states

that the Writing School was demolished in 1790, which it was not until 1902. Mr John Newman has pointed out to me the similarity between the twin brackets and those in the entrance hall of Thomas Leverton's 1 Bedford Square of 1780 (illus. in *Architecture in Britain*, fig. 373) and suggested that as none of the preliminary drawings shows a pediment this was added in 1776. It is true that the brackets have no parallel in Hawksmoor's work, but this may mean no more than that the brackets were added in 1776 to enliven a gaunt façade. Hawksmoor used broken-based pediments elsewhere in designs for All Souls, Queen's College, St George Bloomsbury and the chapel in the 'first' and 'third' designs for Greenwich Hospital.
18. Worcester College, Oxford, Clarke Collection, 354.
19. The same motif of a giant order on a high base, framing a half pilaster supporting a heavy cornice and flanking a void forms the basis of the central tower of the entrance front of Hawksmoor's Queen's College Proposition IV, although here the cornice is given a full Doric order and the Palazzo Valmarana motif is reduced to a single bay.
20. Downes (1979), cat. 253.
21. Kerry Downes, *Vanbrugh* (London, 1977), p. 84.
22. Broken-based pediments appear in the gates of the Castle Howard kitchen court (*c*.1710–16); at Goose-pie House, Whitehall, (1701); at the Nunnery, Greenwich (1719–20). Pavilion towers like those at Wilton appear on the Morpeth Town Hall, Northumb. (1714). He used Serlian windows in the first design for Easbury House, Dorset (*c*.1715); on the loggia at King's Weston, Avon (*c*.1718); in the towers of Seaton Delaval, Northumb. (1720); and at Grimsthorpe Castle, Lincs (*c*.1722).
23. Deborah Howard, *The Architectural History of Venice* (London, 1980), pp. 193–206; Renato Cevese, *Ville della Provincia di Vicenza* (Milano, 1980); Fausto Franco, 'Francesco Muttoni, l'architetto di Vicenza', *BCISAP*, IV (1962), pp. 147–55; Renato Cevese, 'Palladio e l'architettura del seicento Veneto', *BCISAP*, XII (1970), pp. 107–10.
24. Wend Graf Kalnein and Michael Levey, *Art and Architecture of the Eighteenth-Century in France* (Harmondsworth, 1972), pp. 207–17.
25. Jorg Gamer, *Matteo Alberti* (Düsseldorf, 1978); John Harris, review of Robert Tavernor, *Palladio and British Palladianism* (London, 1991) in *GGJ* (1992), p. 114.
26. Richard Hewlings, 'James Leoni: An Anglicized Venetian', in *The Architectural Outsiders*, ed. Roderick Brown (London, 1985), p. 30.
27. Harris (1990), pp. 139–44.
28. Howard Colvin, 'A Scottish Origin for English Palladianism?', *AH*, 17 (1974), pp. 5–11.
29. *VB*, I, pp. 1–2.
30. Roland Fréart, *A Parallel of the Antient Architecture with the Modern*, trans. John Evelyn (London, 1664), pp. 22, 84, 99, epistle dedicatory.
31. *VB*, II, p. 1.
32. *VB*, I, pp. 3–5, 7.
33. *Ibid.*, p. 5; (1717), pp. 1–2.
34. *VB*, II, pp. 2, 4, 5.
35. *VB*, I, pp. 4, 5.
36. *VB*, I, p. 5; *VB*, II, p. 3; *VB*, III, p. 7; Lindsay Boynton, 'Newby Park, the First Palladian Villa in England', in H.M. Colvin and J. Harris, *The Country Seat* (London, 1970), p. 100.
37. Downes (1977), pp. 257–8.
38. *VB*, I, p. 3.
39. Bodleian Library, MS Rawlinson B. 376, fol. 8.
40. Giles Worsley, 'Colour and Movement', *CL* (26 March 1992).
41. Howard Colvin and John Newman (eds.), *Of Building: Roger North's Writings on Architecture* (Oxford, 1981), fig. 1; Andrea Palladio, *I quattro libri dell'architettura* (Venice, 1570), II, pp. 57, 62.
42. John Harris, *Catalogue of the Drawings Collection of the Royal Institute of British Architects: Colen Campbell* (Farnborough, 1973), p. 16.
43. *VB*, I, p. 4.
44. Colvin (1983), pp. 38, 52.
45. *Architecture in Britain*, pp. 317–18.
46. *VB*, II, pp. 1, 2.

CHAPTER VI

1. Giles Worsley, 'Nicholas Hawksmoor: A pioneer neo-Palladian?', *AH*, 33 (1990), pp. 66–73.
2. Howard Colvin, *Catalogue of Architectural Drawings of the 18th and 19th-centuries in the Library of Worcester College* (Oxford, 1964), 465–8.
3. Vitruvius, *Ten Books of Architecture*, I, chap. 5, verse iv.
4. Colvin (1964), cat. 81.
5. Howard Colvin, *Unbuilt Oxford* (New Haven and London, 1983), p. 150; Colvin (1964), pl. 88.
6. John Harris and A.A. Tait, *Catalogue of the Drawings by Inigo Jones, John Webb and Isaac de Caus at Worcester College, Oxford* (Oxford, 1979), cat. 17, pls. 55, 106.
7. Colvin (1983), p. 85.
8. Compare *VB*, III, pl. 47, with John Harris, *The Artist and the Country House* (London, 1979), figs. 195a–c. Some of the detail at Ebberston, particularly the urns, may have been added by masons without Campbell's approbation, but in *Vitruvius Britannicus* Campbell was clearly 'improving' his own original design.
9. *VB*, III, p. 46. The date of Newby Hall is important, but its early building history is confused because the key letters referring to it (Leeds Archive Office, Vyner MSS [VR] and Newby Hall MSS [NH]) do not give their year and therefore have to be dated internally or by comparison with contemporary accounts. Lindsay Boynton ('Newby Park, the First Palladian Villa in England', in H.M. Colvin and J. Harris (ed.), *The Country Seat*, London, 1970, pp. 97–105) assumed that Campbell's 'model' for the whole house was in Robinson's hands by 1718, and that the house was therefore designed in 1718. However, Robinson did not refer to following Campbell's 'model' until 10 Aug. 1720 (NH 2863/1). He began building work in 1718, but only on one of the pavilions, and his reference to not being able to 'begin to case the old house till June the bricks not being ready' (VR 6002/13834) suggests that he initially planned to remodel rather than rebuild the old house. This would explain the reference to half the house being pulled down (VR 6002/13846) if the house had, for instance, unfashionable projecting wings that he wished to remove. Robinson presumably changed his mind, but as the foundation of the new house was laid in June 1720 there is no reason to doubt Campbell's statement that the house was designed that year.
10. *VB*, I, p. 9.
11. *Ibid.*, p. 8.
12. John Harris and Gordon Higgott, *Inigo Jones: Complete Architectural Drawings* (London, 1989), pp. 68–9.
13. John Harris, 'James Gibbs – Eminence Grise at Houghton', in *New Light on English Palladianism*, ed. Charles Hind (London, 1990), pp. 5–9.
14. Andor Gomme, 'Architects and Craftsmen at Ditchley', *AH*, 32 (1989), pp. 85–8.
15. Roger North, *Of Building*, ed. Howard Colvin and John Newman, (Oxford, 1981), p. 62.
16. Gibbs's first design with such a rusticated door or window surround is probably that for St George, Hanover Square (1720).
17. An early example of Campbell's rusticated windows and doors being copied is Gilling Castle, Yorks, by William Wakefield. Towneley Hall, Lancs, has the same arrangement and can probably also be attributed to Wakefield.
18. Terry Friedman, *James Gibbs* (New Haven and London, 1984), pp. 200–2.
19. Cinzia Sicca, however, suggested that the volume of Palladio's drawings which Burlington is generally believed to have acquired in Italy were in fact bought from John Talman in London (Cinzia Sicca, 'The Architecture of the Wall: Astylism in the Architecture of Lord Burlington', *AH*, 33, 1990, pp. 96–7).
20. John Harris, 'Some Disputatious Thoughts on Chiswick', *GGJ* (1993), pp. 86–90.
21. Sicca suggested that this separation may even have happened before Burlington's trip to Italy. She argued that when Lord Bruce wrote to Burlington in July 1719 'I should not regularly suppose you still in England, but after so many differings, who knows' (Chatsworth 144.0.) this refers to problems with Campbell. The reference would seem to me too scant to prove such a hypothesis (Sicca, 1990, p. 86).
22. Compare, for instance, Plumtre House, Houghton Hall and the Rolls House.
23. *The Parish of St James Westminster: Part II, North of Piccadilly*, Survey of London, XXXII (London, 1963), pp. 500, 505, pls. 80, 85–7, fig. 92.
24. Kent to Burrell Massingberd, 15 Nov. 1719 (Lincolnshire Diocesan Archives 2MM, B19A). I owe this reference to Mr John Harris. One could compare, for instance, the apse of the loggia on the first floor of the Villa Cambiaso in Genoa (1548) with those of the Sculpture Gallery at Holkham Hall, Norfolk, although these may have a common source in the Temple of the Sun and the Moon in Rome. The best work on Alessi is the catalogue of the 1974 exhibition *Galeazzo Alessi*, (Genoa, 1974).
25. Sicca (1990), pp. 83–101.
26. Harris (1981), pp. 72, 78.
27. Richard Hewlings, 'Chiswick House: Intentions and Meanings', lecture given at the Friends of Chiswick House 1991 symposium *3rd Earl of Burlington – the Man and his Politics* (unpublished); Richard Hewlings, *Chiswick House and Gardens*, English Heritage Guidebook (London, 1989).
28. Jane Clark, 'For Kings and Senates Fit', *GGJ* (1989), pp. 55–63; *idem*, 'Palladianism and the Divine Right of Kings', *Apollo* (April 1992), p. 135; *idem*, 'The Mysterious Mr Buck', *Apollo*, CXXIX (May 1989), pp. 317–22.
29. RIBA, Palladio Drawings, XVI 19(b).
30. Robert Morris, *An Essay in Defence of Ancient Architecture* (London, 1728), p. xiii.
31. Eileen Harris, *British Architectural Books and Writers 1556–1785* (Cambridge, 1990), pp. 264–6.
32. *BDBA*, p. 131.
33. Giles Worsley, 'Rokeby Park, Yorkshire', *CL* (19 March 1987).
34. Ilaria Toesca, 'Alessandro Galilei in Inghilterra', *English Miscellany*, III (1952), p. 220.
35. Earl of Ilchester (ed.), *Lord Hervey and His Friends 1726–38* (London, 1950), pp. 70–2.
36. W.S. Lewis (ed.), *Horace Walpole's Correspondence*, XXXV (London, 1973), p. 143.
37. Harris (1990), p. 189.
38. Allan Ramsay, *A Dialogue of Taste* (London, 1762), p. 33.
39. *Letters to and from Henrietta Howard, Countess of Suffolk* (London, 1824), I, p. 306.
40. Giles Worsley, 'The Wicked Woman of Marl', *CL* (14 March 1991).
41. See chap. 5.
42. Richard Hewlings, 'James Leoni: An Anglicized Venetian', in *The Architectural Outsiders*, ed. Roderick Brown (London, 1985), pp. 21–43.
43. John Brushe, 'Wricklemarsh and the Collections of Sir Gregory Page', *Apollo* (Nov. 1985).
44. Harris (1990), p. 208.
45. Terry Friedman, *James Gibbs* (New Haven and London, 1984), pp. 62–3.
46. *Ibid.*, p. 110.
47. *Ibid.*, pp. 226–30.
48. *Ibid.*, pp. 140, 268, figs. 150, 297, 299.
49. *Ibid.*, pp. 140–5, 166–70.
50. *Ibid.*, pp. 138–40.
51. *Ibid.*, pp. 128–31, 241.
52. Harris (1990), p. 211 fn. 4.
53. *BDBA*, p. 332.
54. Harris (1990), pp. 348–51.
55. Harris (1990), pp. 317–22.
56. Harris (1981), p. 38.
57. Sampson's design is an intelligent reworking of ideas from *Vitruvius Britannicus*. In particular, the columned section of the centrepiece and the cornice come from the centrepiece of Newby Park, less the pediment, and the side ranges from Lindsey House.
58. Philip Ayres, 'Pope's *Epistle to Burlington*: The Vitruvian Analogies', *Studies in English Literature 1500–1900*, XXX/3 (Summer 1990), pp. 429–44.
59. Harris (1981), p. 81.
60. 'Vertue Notebooks: III', ed. Mrs Arundell Esdaile, Lord Ilchester and Mr Hake, *Walpole Society*, 22 (1934), p. 139.

61. Cinzia Maria Sicca, 'On William Kent's Roman Sources', *AH*, 29 (1986), pp. 134–57.
62. Harris (1981), p. 76.
63. Rudolf Wittkower, *Palladio and English Palladianism* (London, 1974), p. 141.
64. Mark Girouard, 'Ambrose Phillipps of Garendon', *AH*, 8 (1965), p. 28, fig. 6.
65. Harris (1990), p. 210.
66. *Ibid.*, p. 238.
67. *Ibid.*, p. 263.
68. *Ibid.*, pp. 210–11.
69. *Ibid.*, p. 407.
70. *Ibid.*, p. 266.
71. *Ibid.*, p. 221.
72. Alexander Pope, *Epistle to Lord Burlington* (London, 1731).

CHAPTER VII

1. G.F. Webb, 'The Letters and Drawings of Nicholas Hawksmoor Relating to the Building of the Mausoleum at Castle Howard', *Walpole Society*, XIX (1931), p. 131.
2. Kerry Downes, *Hawksmoor* (London, 1979), fig. 40.
3. A catalogue of the library survives at Chatsworth. See also Philip Ayres, 'Burlington's Library at Chiswick', *Studies in Bibliography*, XLV (1992), pp. 113–27.
4. Elements at least of the libraries of these three survive at Holkham Hall, Norfolk, Hovingham Hall, York, and West Wycombe Park, Bucks. Contemporary catalogues of the libraries at Hovingham and West Wycombe at Hovingham and in the Bodleian Library, Oxford (Bodleian Library Dashwood Papers B12/3, 3, 4, 11, 12), show that both Worsley and Dashwood owned more archaeological books than remain today.
5. Eileen Harris, *British Architectural Books and Writers* (London, 1990), pp. 150, 348.
6. *Ibid.*, pp. 350–1.
7. *Ibid.*, pp. 149–54.
8. Hugh Honour, 'John Talman and William Kent in Italy', *Connoisseur* (Aug. 1954), p. 3.
9. Cinzia Maria Sicca, 'On William Kent's Roman Sources', *AH*, 29 (1986), pp. 139–40.
10. Claire Pace, 'Pietro Santi Bartoli: Drawings in Glasgow University Library after Roman Paintings and Mosaics', *Papers of the British School at Rome*, XLVII (1979), pp. 117–39.
11. Paul Quarrie, *Treasures of Eton College Library* (exh. cat., New York, 1990), pp. 43, 106.
12. Thomas Ashby, 'Drawings of Ancient Paintings in English Collections', *Papers of the British School at Rome*, VII (1914), p. 3.
13. Harris (1990), p. 352.
14. John Fleming, *Robert Adam and his Circle* (London, 1962), p. 332.
15. It has been suggested that Dr Mead's drawings should be identified with those now in the Glasgow University Library (Pace, 1979). Another volume of drawings by Pietro Santi Bartoli survives in the RIBA Drawings Collection, together with 43 copies of drawings made by Francesco Bartoli *c.*1721. The provenance of these drawings is not known.
16. This letter, which is at Chatsworth, is reproduced in John Dixon Hunt, *William Kent: Landscape Garden Designer* (London, 1987), p. 14.
17. Quarrie (1990), p. 47.
18. Andrew Wilton and Anne Lyles, *The Great Age of British Watercolours 1750–1880* (exh. cat., London, Royal Academy, 1992), figs. 13, 15.
19. Francis Drake, *Eboracum* (London, 1736), dedication, p. 60.
20. 'The Family Memoirs of the Rev. William Stukeley: III', *Surtees Society*, 80 (1885), pp. 358–9.
21. Stuart Piggott, *William Stukeley* (London, 1985), p. 18.
22. *Ibid.*, pp. 53–6, 58, 70.
23. Giles Worsley, 'The Baseless Roman Doric Column in Mid-eighteenth-century English Architecture: A Study in Neo-classicism', *BM* (May 1986), pp. 331–9.
24. *Ibid.*
25. Howard Colvin, 'A Roman Mausoleum in Gloucestershire: The Guise Monument at Elmore', *GGJ* (1991), pp. 41–9.

26. Worsley (1986), p. 336.
27. S.G. Gillam (ed.), 'Building Accounts of the Radcliffe Camera', *Oxford Historical Society*, n.s. XIII (1958), pp. 161–2.
28. Allan Ramsay, 'A Dialogue of Taste', *The Investigator* (London, 1762), p. 52.
29. M. Bellicard, *Observations upon the Antiquities of the Town of Herculaneum* (London, 1753), pp. 37–8.
30. Giles Worsley, 'Taking the Ancients Literally: Archaeological Neo-Classicism in Mid-eighteenth-century Britain', in Charles Hind (ed.), *New Light on English Palladianism* (London, 1990), pp. 74, 80, fn. 80.
31. Paper given by Richard Hewlings at the conference *The Third Earl of Burlington: The Man and his Politics*, organised by the Friends of Chiswick House, 22 February 1991 (unpublished).
32. Giles Worsley, 'Rokeby Park, Yorkshire', *CL* (19 March 1987).
33. G. Sherburn (ed.), *Correspondence of Alexander Pope* (Oxford, 1956), I, pp. 45–6.
34. Worsley 'Taking the Ancients Literally' (1990), pp. 69–73.
35. Matthew Brettingham, *The Plans, Elevations and Sections of Holkham in Norfolk* (London, 1773), pp. ix–x, 1.
36. *Ibid.*, I, pp. ix–x.
37. British Library, King's Maps XXXI, 42b. Leo Schmidt stated that these drawings were made by Brettingham, probably to Lord Coke's designs, in 1726 and thus predate any involvement by Kent and Burlington. However, the drawings are not dated and Schmidt has not proved that these are the same as those for which Brettingham was paid in 1726. (Leo Schmidt, 'Holkham Hall, Norfolk: I', *CL*, 24 Jan. 1980.)
38. Giles Worsley, 'Thomas Worsley, 1710–1778: An Eighteenth-century Amateur Architect' (Oxford University BA Diss., 1982).
39. Giles Worsley, 'West Wycombe Park, Buckinghamshire', *CL* (6 Sept. 1990).
40. Worsley, 'Taking the Ancients Literally' (1990), p. 78.
41. *Ibid.*, 76–8.
42. Vitruvius, *Ten Books of Architecture*, VII, chap. 5, verse iii.
43. Bellicard (1753), p. 84.
44. Michael Wilson, *William Kent* (London, 1984), p. 15.
45. H.M. Colvin, *History of the King's Works*, V (London, 1976), pp. 73, 197–8.
46. See particularly p. 191, Perrault's reconstruction of the interior of a Roman bath.
47. Colvin (1976), p. 50.
48. Giles Worsley, 'Houghton Hall, Norfolk', *CL* (4 March 1993).
49. Giles Worsley, 'Antique Assumptions', *CL* (6 Aug. 1992); Richard Hewlings, *Chiswick House*, English Heritage Guidebook (London, 1989), p. 16.
50. Ingrid Roscoe, 'Andien de Clermont, Decorative Painter to the Leicester House Set', *Apollo* (February, 1986).
51. Steven Parissien, John Harris and Howard Colvin, 'Narford Hall, Norfolk', *Georgian Group Report and Journal* (1987), pp. 51–3; Wiltshire Record Office, Wilton Papers 2057 F 5/2; I am indebted to Dr Ivan Hall for drawing this ceiling to my attention and pointing out its connection with Caylus's work. 'Vertue Note Books: III', *Walpole Society*, XXII (1934), pp. 156–7.
52. Ivan Hall, 'Adam and Carr', in Giles Worsley (ed.), *Adam in Context*, Symposium (London, 1993), p. 32, fn. 3.
53. P.S. Bartoli, *Gli antichi sepolchri* (Rome, 1704), pl. 8; Marcus Binney, 'Hereford Cathedral Close', *CL* (9 Sept. 1980).
54. Worsley, 'West Wycombe Park' (1990).
55. Harris (1990), p. 151.
56. Vitruvius, *Ten Books of Architecture*, VI, introduction.
57. Robert Morris, *An Essay in defence of Ancient Architecture; or, a Parallel of the Ancient Buildings with the Modern* (London, 1728), pp. 38–9.
58. Isaac Ware, *A Complete Body of Architecture* (London, 1756), p. 155.
59. William Chambers, *A Treatise on Civil Architecture* (London, 1759), p. 155.
60. Richard Hewlings advances the interesting suggestion that amateurs' interest in recreating antique buildings had a political, essentially reactionary, motivation (Hewlings, 1991). This is an approach that would repay investigation.

CHAPTER VIII

1. James Macaulay, *The Classical Country House in Scotland 1660–1800* (London, 1987), is the main source for information about individual houses in this section.
2. *Architecture in Britain*, pp. 534–5.
3. Macaulay (1987), p. 1.
4. John Cornforth, 'Was there a Scottish Baroque?', *CL* (15 June 1989).
5. Ian Gow, 'William Adam: A Planner of Genius', *Architectural Heritage*, i (1990), pp. 62–73.
6. Daniel Defoe, *A Tour through the whole Island of Great Britain* iii (London, 1727), p. 192.
7. Macaulay (1987), p. 38.
8. Howard Colvin, 'A Scottish Origin for English Palladianism?', *AH*, 17 (1974), pp. 5–12.
9. Macaulay (1987), p. 36.
10. *Ibid.*, pp. 3, 10.
11. *Ibid.*, p. 65.
12. Alexander Pope, *Epistle to the Right Honourable Richard Earl of Burlington* (London, 1731), lines 23ff.
13. John Gifford, *William Adam* (Edinburgh, 1989), p. 78.
14. *VB*, i, p. 42.
15. *Ibid.*, p. 20.
16. Gifford (1989), p. 78.
17. Alistair Rowan, 'William Adam's Library', *Architectural Heritage*, i (1990), pp. 8–33.
18. R. Loeber, 'Irish Country Houses and Castles of the Late Caroline Period: An Unremembered Past Recaptured', *Bulletin of the Irish Georgian Society*, xvi/i (Jan.–June 1973), p. 29.
19. L.M. Cullen, *An Economic History of Ireland since 1660* (London, 1972), pp. 7–25; Loeber (Jan.–June 1973), p. 5.
20. Rolf Loeber, *A Biographical Dictionary of Architects in Ireland 1600–1720* (London, 1981), pp. 60–61.
21. *BDBA*, p. 474.
22. Loeber (1981), pp. 63–4.
23. Loeber (Jan.–June 1973), p. 35.
24. Loeber (1981), pp. 70–1.
25. *Ibid.*, pp. 89, 113.
26. *Ibid.*, pp. 112–13.
27. Loeber (Jan.–June 1973), p. 35.
28. If the surviving drawing of 1716–26 is, as has been assumed, a survey drawing, Crom was a five-bay house with a three-bay pediment and flanking single-bay wings. It had a particularly interesting central horseshoe-shaped staircase and an arcaded terrace that have been a marked similarity with those at Drumlanrig Castle, Dumfries (Gervase Jackson-Stops, 'Crom Castle, Co. Fermanagh', *CL*, (26 May 1988).
29. I owe this observation to Dr Edward McParland.
30. Intriguing references to porticos suggest attempts at greater sophistication, particularly at Dunmore Castle, Co. Kilkenny, rebuilt in 1663–4, but in the absence of any visual evidence it is hard to be certain what these references really describe (R. Loeber, 'Early Classicism in Ireland: Architecture before the Georgian era', *AH*, 22 (1979), p. 57).
31. Loeber (1979), p. 59.
32. Cullen (1972), pp. 26–49.
33. Loeber (1979), p. 59.
34. Rolf Loeber, 'The Building of Castle Durrow', *Bulletin of the Irish Georgian Society*, xvi/iii (July–Sept. 1973), pp. 103–6.
35. Maurice Craig and the Knight of Glin, 'Castletown, Co. Kildare', *CL* (27 March 1969).
36. *BDBA*, p. 325.
37. Cullen (1972), pp. 50–76; Maurice Craig, *The Architecture of Ireland* (London, 1982), p. 180.
38. I am indebted to Dr Edward McParland for discussions about Pearce. Any thorough account of Pearce must await Dr McParland's book on the subject.
39. Howard Colvin and Maurice Craig, *Architectural Drawings in the Library of Elton Hall by Sir John Vanbrugh and Sir Edward Lovett Pearce* (Oxford, 1964), p. xli.
40. *Ibid.*, cat. 114, pl. xlb.
41. *Ibid.*, pl. lxxvii.
42. *Ibid.*, pl. xix.
43. Compare Colvin and Craig (1964), pl. lxxv with *VB*, iii, pl. 32.
44. Compare Colvin and Craig (1964), pl. lxiii and *VB*, iii, pl. 43.
45. Colvin and Craig (1964), pls. lxxiv–lxxvi.
46. Edward McParland, 'Edward Lovett Pearce and the Parliament House in Dublin', *BM* (Feb. 1989), pp. 91–100.
47. See chap. 3.
48. McParland (1989), p. 100.
49. Colvin and Craig (1964), pl. lviii.
50. G.B. Nash, 'Social Development' in J.P. Greene and J.R. Pole (eds), *Colonial British America* (Baltimore and London, 1984), p. 247.
51. Gervase Jackson-Stops, 'A Future for a Colonial Past', *CL* (25 Sept. 1986).
52. Mills Lane, *Architecture of the Old South: Virginia* (New York, 1989), pp. 12–18.
53. Marcus Binney *et al.*, *Jamaica's Heritage: An Untapped Resource* (Kingston, Jan., 1991), p. 78.
54. Mills Lane, *Architecture of the Old South: Maryland* (New York, 1991), p. 14.
55. Mills Lane, *Architecture of the Old South: South Carolina* (New York, 1989), pp. 15, 35.
56. Lane, *Virginia*, p. 15.
57. Lane, *Virginia*, p. 19.
58. Lane, *Virginia*, pp. 25–60.
59. Lane, *South Carolina*, p. 34.
60. Lane, *South Carolina*, p. 38.
61. Lane, *South Carolina*, pp. 20–1.
62. Lane, *Virginia*, pp. 41–2.
63. Lane, *Virginia*, pp. 50–60.
64. Jackson-Stops (1986).
65. Lane, *South Carolina*, pp. 39–54.
66. Lane (1991), pp. 30–2.

CHAPTER IX

1. The most recent study of the Gothic Revival is *The Origins of the Gothic Revival* by Michael McCarthy (New Haven and London, 1987). This sets out to shift attention away from Horace Walpole but in the end concentrates primarily on Walpole and his circle.
2. Quoted by Mark Girouard, 'Elizabethan Architecture and the Gothic Tradition', *AH*, 6 (1963), p. 30.
3. Mark Girouard, *Robert Smythson and the Elizabethan Country House* (London, 1983), pp. 30–5.
4. Mark Girouard, 'Burghley House, Lincolnshire', *CL* (23 April 1992).
5. Giles Worsley, 'Snape Castle, Yorkshire', *CL* (6 March 1986).
6. Mark Girouard, 'Wardour Castle, Wiltshire: I', *CL* (14 Feb. 1991).
7. The importance of temporary architectural settings for fireworks deserves further examination. Gereon Sievernich's *Das Buch der Feuerwerkskunst* (Nordlingen, 1987), is a useful source of such illustrations.
8. John Evelyn, *Account of Architects and Architecture* (London, 1723), p. 9.
9. Henry Wotton, *The Elements of Architecture* (London, 1624), p. 51.
10. Jennifer Sherwood and Nikolaus Pevsner, *Oxfordshire*, The Buildings of England (London, 1974), p. 35.
11. Howard Colvin, *Unbuilt Oxford* (New Haven and London, 1983), pp. 10–12.
12. *City of Cambridge*, RCHM (London, 1959), i, pp. 196–7; Sherwood and Pevsner (1974), p. 35; *Dictionary of National Biography*, iii (1917), p. 1161.
13. Howard Colvin, *Architecture and the After-life* (New Haven and London, 1991), p. 264.
14. Thomas Cocke, 'Repairer of the Breach', *CL* (25 Oct. 1990).
15. *Dictionary of National Biography*, xviii (1889), pp. 137–8.
16. Richard Haslam, 'Lambeth Palace, London: II', *CL* (25 Oct. 1990).
17. Nikolaus Pevsner, *County Durham*, The Buildings of England (London, 1983), pp. 195–9.
18. *Ibid.*, pp. 213–17; Marcus Binney, 'Durham Castle, Co. Durham', *CL* (28 Sept. 1991).

19. John Cornforth, 'Auckland Castle, Co. Durham', *CL* (27 Jan. and 3 Feb. 1972).
20. Giles Worsley, 'Bishopthorpe Palace, York', *CL* (18 July 1991).
21. *Staffordshire*, Victoria County History, xiv (London, 1990), p. 52.
22. This mixed style was not confined to England: St Eustache in Paris (1532) is a good example. An interesting parallel can be found in contemporary Italian projects for completing the façades of Gothic churches, as in the designs of Girolamo Rainaldi for San Petronio, Bologna (1626), and those of Francesco Castelli and Carlo Buzzi for the Duomo in Milan of 1648 and 1653. (Rudolf Wittkower, *Gothic vs. Classic*, New York, 1974, figs. 60–67, p. 111.) John Onians also sheds valuable light on the use of combined Classical and Gothic schemes in Renaissance Italy in *Bearers of Meaning* (Cambridge, 1988).
23. It could be argued that the towers added to Westwood Park, Worcs, by Sir John Packington in the ten years after the Civil War in a manner that accurately follows the form of the original design of *c.*1598 emulates this spirit. Packington, like Shirley, was a determined Royalist, and Westwood was the home of numerous High Church Anglicans during the Civil War.
24. *Chirk Castle*, National Trust Guide (London, 1985), p. 43.
25. John Martin Robinson, 'Hoghton Tower, Lancashire', *CL* (23 July 1992).
26. John Cornforth, 'Drayton House, Northamptonshire: II', *CL* (20 May 1965).
27. Kerry Downes, *English Baroque Architecture* (London, 1966), p. 16.
28. John Cornforth, 'Hampton Court, Herefordshire', *CL* (22 and 29 Feb. 1973).
29. Timoth Mowl and Brian Earnshaw, 'The Origins of 18th-Century Neo-Medievalism in a Georgian Norman Castle', *Journal of the Society of Architectural Historians*, xl/4 (Dec. 1981), pp. 289–94.
30. John Cornforth, 'St Michael's Mount, Cornwall', *CL* (13 June 1993); see especially fig. 2.
31. Alistair Rowan, 'Clearwell Castle, Gloucestershire', in H.M. Colvin and J. Harris (ed.), *The Country Seat* (London, 1970), pp. 145–9.
32. *BDBA*, pp. 555–6; John Cornforth, 'Castles for a Georgian Duke', *CL* (8 Oct. 1992).
33. *The Wren Society* (1928), v, p. 17.
34. Howard Colvin, 'The Church of St Mary Aldermary and its Rebuilding after the Great Fire of London', *AH*, 24 (1981), pp. 24–31.
35. Quoted by Paul Frankl, *The Gothic: Literary Sources and Interpretations through Eight-Centuries* (Princeton, 1960), p. 364.
36. Quoted by Terry Friedman, *James Gibbs* (London, 1984), p. 199–200.
37. *The Wren Society* (1928), v, p. 17.
38. *Explanation of Designs for All Souls by Nicholas Hawksmoor* (Oxford, 1960), p. 5.
39. *Architecture in Britain*, p. 396; Michael McCarthy's *The Origins of the Gothic Revival* (London, 1987), ignores the Office of Works Gothic tradition.
40. Juliet Allan, 'New Light on William Kent at Hampton Court Palace', *AH*, 27 (1984), pp. 52–3.
41. Giles Worsley, 'Drawn to a Find', *CL* (20 May 1993).
42. Eileen Harris, *British Architectural Books and Writers* (Cambridge, 1990), p. 267–8.
43. Allan (1984), p. 51.
44. John Harris, 'William Kent and Esher Place', in Gervase Jackson-Stops (ed.), *The Fashioning and Functioning of the British Country House*, Symposium (Hanover and London, 1989), p. 14.
45. John Harris, *The Palladians* (London, 1981), p. 82.
46. Wollaton is not the only possible source that influenced Seaton Delaval; there are also distinct parallels to the twin towers with Serlian windows and the projecting pedimented pavilion in the centre in one of Serlio's church designs (Sebastiano Serlio, *The Five Books of Architecture*, London, 1611, v, ch. 14. fol. 15).
47. Howard Colvin and Maurice Craig, *Architectural Drawings in the Library of Elton Hall* (Oxford, 1964), fig. xla.
48. *Ibid.*, pls. ivb, xxviiib.
49. Kerry Downes, *Vanbrugh* (London, 1977), p. 48.
50. Sarah Markham (ed.) *John Loveday of Caversham* (Wilton, 1984), p. 139. It has been suggested, although without documentary proof, that the great triangular tower at Horton, Dorset, could be as early as 1726. Edmund Marsden, 'A Gothic Folly by Thomas Archer?', *CL* (13 April 1978).
51. Clearwell Castle, Glos, a small castellated Gothic house begun in 1728 by Roger Morris for Thomas Wyndham should perhaps be placed in this tradition. Other early examples include the castle at Castle Hill, Devon (before 1741); Rothley Castle, Wallington, Northumb. (*c.*1745), and an early, but undated Gothic castle at the end of the canal at Hurstborne Park, Hants, known only from a painting of 1748.
52. The castellated tower at Erddig, Clwyd (built before 1739); the demolished Gothic tower at Gibside, Co. Durham (1743); the Gothic Tower at Studley Royal, Yorks (before 1744); Sanderson Miller's tower at Edgehill, Warwicks, modelled on Guy's Tower at Warwick Castle (1745); Culloden Tower at Richmond, Yorks (1746); the castle at Hagley Hall, Worcs (1747), and that at Hackfall, Yorks (before 1751).
53. It has been suggested, without documentary proof, that the Gothic temple at Shotover dates from *c.*1718. This seems unlikely but it almost certainly dates from before the death of James Tyrell (who commissioned two other garden buildings from William Kent before 1733) in 1742. Mavis Batey, 'An Early Naturalistic Garden, Shotover: I', *CL* (22 Dec. 1977). Sherwood and Pevsner (1984), p. 765, plausibly compares the building with Gibbs's Gothic Temple at Stowe.
54. Stuart Piggott, *William Stukeley* (Oxford, 1950), pp. 144, 146.
55. British Library Add MSS 70432, Countess of Oxford to Mrs Montagu, 7 June 1744.
56. W.S. Lewis (ed.), *Horace Walpole's Correspondence* (London, 1977), xxxv, pp. 270–1.
57. *Ibid.*, pp. 183–4
58. Roger White, 'Wiston House Remodelled', *AH*, 27 (1984), pp. 241–8.
59. Joyce Godber, 'The Marchioness Grey of Wrest Park', *Publications of the Bedfordshire Historical Record Society*, xlvii (1968), p. 138.
60. Hoare's Bank Accounts, S 446.
61. J.J. Cartwright (ed.), 'The Travels through England of Dr Richard Pococke', *Camden Society*, 131 (1888), p. 62.
62. Alnwick Castle Papers, Peter Waddell, 'Alnwick Castle Described and Illustrated' (1785).
63. Giles Worsley, 'Alnwick Castle, Northumberland: II', *CL* (8 Dec. 1988).
64. T.H.R. Cashmore, D.H. Simpson and A.C.B. Urwin, 'Alexander Pope's Twickenham: Eighteenth-century Views of his 'Classic Village', *Borough of Twickenham Local History Society, Occasional Paper*, 3 (1988), pl. 21.
65. Lewis (1977), xx, p. 119.
66. McCarthy (1987), p. 66.
67. British Library Add MS 70432, Countess of Oxford to Mrs Montagu, 7 June 1744.
68. Lewis (1977), xx, p. 361.
69. McCarthy (1987), p. 116.
70. *Ibid.*, p. 127.
71. John Harris, 'Lady Pomfret's House: The Case for Richard Biggs', *GGJ* (1991), pp. 45–9.
72. Lewis (1977), xxxv, p. 153.
73. L. Dickins and M. Stanton, *An Eighteenth-century Correspondence*, (London, 1910), p. 279.
74. Cartwright (1888), p. 170.
75. Terry Friedman, 'High and Bold Structures: A Georgian Steeple Sampler', *GGJ* (1991), p. 16.
76. This is a point for which I am indebted to Mr Howard Colvin.

CHAPTER X

1. Isaac Ware, *A Complete Body of Architecture* (London, 1756), p. 571.
2. Quoted in Dora Wiebenson, *Sources of Greek Revival Architecture* (London, 1969), pp. 93, 98.
3. John Harris, 'Inigo Jones and his French Sources', *Bulletin of the Metropolitan Museum of Art* (May 1961).
4. *Ibid.*, pp. 106, 182, 198–9.

5. John Harris and Gordon Higgott, *Inigo Jones: Complete Architectural Drawings* (London, 1989), pp. 206–9, 217–19, 228–35.

6. Gordon Higgott, ' "Varying with Reason": Inigo Jones's Theory of Design', *AH*, 35 (1992), pp. 55–6.

7. Cinzia Sicca argues that it was William Kent who created the neo-Palladian interior at Kensington Palace, in particular the Cupola Room ('On William Kent's Roman Sources', *AH*, 29, 1986, p. 142.) However, the architectural form of the cupola room, specifically the use of pilasters, predates Kent's involvement. Kent is first mentioned in 1722 as being commissioned to paint the vault of the Cupola Room. It is only subsequently, after Campbell had designed the interior of Mereworth in 1723, that Kent came into his own as an interior designer at Kensington Palace. H.M. Colvin (ed.), *The History of the King's Works* (London, 1976), v, pp. 195–203.

8. I owe this important observation to Mr John Harris.

9. Kerry Downes, *Hawksmoor* (London, 1979), figs. 82–4.

10. It is uncertain whether Kent was involved with the design of the Green Drawing Room at Houghton. It may be that he only designed the State Apartments and that Thomas Ripley was responsible for the decoration of the family apartments.

11. Sicca (1986), pp. 134–57.

12. The work of these craftsmen is fully covered in Alistair Laing, 'Foreign Decorators and Plasterers in England', in Charles Hind (ed.), *The Rococo in England*, Symposium (London, 1986), pp. 21–45.

13. John Cornforth, 'Ditchley Park, Oxfordshire', *CL* (17 Nov. 1988); Andor Gomme, 'Architects and Craftsmen at Ditchley', *AH*, 32 (1989), pp. 89–91.

14. Roger White, 'Isaac Ware and Chesterfield House', in Hind (1986), p. 182.

15. Michael Snodin (ed.), *Rococo: Art and Design in Hogarth's England* (exh. cat., London, Victoria and Albert Museum, 1984), p. 205, cat. M18.

16. Quoted in White (1986), p. 180.

17. Until recently it was thought that the White and Gold Room at Petworth House, Sussex, was of this date. However, newly discovered drawings show that the room was designed in 1828. (Gervase Jackson-Stops, 'Living with Louis', *CL* (1 Oct. 1992).

18. Ingrid Roscoe, 'Andien de Clermont, Decorative Painter to the Leicester House Set', *Apollo* (Feb. 1986).

19. Christopher Hussey, *English Country Houses: Early Georgian* (London, 1955), p. 244.

20. Ware (1756), p. 521.

21. White (1986), pp. 180–1.

22. This was not executed. David J. Griffin, 'Leinster House and Isaac Ware', in *Decantations: A Tribute to Maurice Craig*, ed. Agnes Bernelle (Dublin, 1992), pp. 60–70.

23. Gervase Jackson-Stops, 'Rococo Architecture and Interiors', in Snodin (1984), p. 190.

24. Giles Worsley, 'The Vyne, Hampshire', *CL* (9 May 1991).

25. A contemporary similarly sympathetic approach to Carolean decoration can be found at Hagley Hall, where the saloon was intended to strike visitors with its seventeenth-century allusions. John Cornforth, 'Hagley Hall, Worcestershire: I', *CL* (27 April 1989).

26. John Cornforth, 'A Role for Chinoiserie', *CL* (7 Dec. 1989).

27. *BDBA*, p. 566.

28. Cornforth (1989); M. Jourdain and R. Saane Jenyns, *Chinese Export Art in the Eighteenth-Century* (London, 1950), p. 51.

29. Harris and Higgott (1989), pp. 76–83, 124–40.

30. John Harris, *The Artist and the Country House* (London, 1979), pl. III.

31. *Ibid.*, p. 121.

32. John Harris, 'Diverting Labyrinths', *CL* (11 Jan. 1990).

33. *VB*, II, pls. 5–6.

34. *Ibid.*, pls. 71–2.

35. *Ibid.*, pl. 15; Kerry Downes, *Vanbrugh* (London, 1977), p. 114.

36. *Ibid*, pl. 95.

37. 'An Account of a Journey done into Hartford, Cambridgeshire, Suffolk, Norfolk, and Essex', Wiltshire Record Office 2057 F5/2.

38. *VB*, III, p. 95.

39. It is possible that the survey on which the temple appears could have been prepared for the second volume of *Vitruvius Britannicus* which came out in 1717. However, this seems unlikely, given that there are no elevations or plans of the house as there are for other plates of gardens that were displaced to the third volume. (Eileen Harris, 'Vitruvius Britannicus before Colen Campbell', *BM* (May 1986), pp. 340–6.) It seems more likely that Fountaine built the temple after his return from his second Grand Tour, which lasted from 1714 until at least late 1716. (Brinsley Ford, 'Sir Andrew Fountaine, One of the Keenest Virtuosi of his Age', *Apollo*, Nov. 1985.)

40. J. Badeslade and J. Rocque, *Vitruvius Brittannicus* (London, 1739), pls. 82–3.

41. Gervase Jackson-Stops, *An English Arcadia 1600–1900* (London, 1992), pp. 58–60. The pyramidal temple is certainly by Vanbrugh as a design for it can be found in the Elton Hall album, now in the Victoria and Albert Museum (Howard Colvin and Maurice Craig, *Architectural Drawings in the Library of Elton Hall*, Oxford, 1964, pl. XXXVIIa). Jackson-Stops also attributed Mr Greening's House to Vanbrugh. The Bowling Green House is credited to Kent in Isaac Ware, *Designs of Iniqo Jones and others* (London, 1731), p. 40, as is a further garden building at Claremont not illustrated by Rocque. The rustic Tuscan temple in the Ninepin alley can be compared with the entrance to the grotto in the *Vitruvius Brittanicus* engraving of Esher and to the two porticos of the pavilions in Kent's 'Ionic rotunda with lawn flanked by two pavilions' (John Dixon Hunt, *William Kent, Landscape Garden Designer*, London, 1987, p. 144).

42. Badeslade and Rocque (1739), pls. 8–9.

43. Downes, (1977), pl. 147.

44. Hunt (1987), p. 166.

45. They are even clearer in a drawing by Kent in the British Museum for a similar but unexecuted building (Hunt, 1987, p. 144).

46. Compare in particular Hunt (1987), p. 138.

47. Hunt (1987), pp. 16–18, 51–5, 65–6, but see also Sebastiano Serlio, *The Five Books of Architecture* (London, 1611), III, fol. 25v, for a possible inspiration for the Temple of Venus at Stowe.

48. The drawings survive at Newby Park, Yorks.

49. Michael Wilson, *William Kent* (London, 1984), p. 192.

50. Harris (1990); John Harris, 'The Beginnings of Claremont', *Apollo* (April 1993).

51. *VB*, III, pl. 77.

52. Quoted in J. Dixon Hunt, *Garden and Grove* (London, 1986), pp. 217–18.

53. Joseph Spence, *Polymetis* (London, 1747), pp. 1, 2.

54. Giles Worsley, 'The Baseless Roman doric Column in Mid-eighteenth-century English Architecture: A Study in Neo-Classicism', *BM* (May 1986), figs. 18–20.

55. Howard Colvin, 'A Roman Mausoleum in Gloucestershire: The Guise Monument at Elmore', *GGJ* (1991), pp. 41–4.

56. Stewart Harding and David Lambert, 'Saving the Wizard's Landscape', *CL* (14 April, 1988).

57. Gervase Jackson-Stops, 'Sharawadgi Rediscovered', *Apollo* (April 1993).

58. John Cornforth, 'Wroxton Abbey, Oxfordshire', *CL* (10 Sept. 1981).

59. Thomas Pennant, *The Journey from Chester to London* (London, 1782), p. 69.

60. J.J. Cartwright, 'The Travels through England of Doctor Pococke', *Camden Society*, n.s. 44 (1889), II, p. 161; Mark Girouard, 'Echoes of a Georgian Romantic', *CL* (2 Jan. 1964).

61. Information from Mr John Harris.

CHAPTER XI

1. Giles Worsley, 'West Wycombe Park, Buckinghamshire', *CL* (6 Sept. 1990).

2. Terry Friedman, *James Gibbs* (New Haven and London, 1984), pp. 215–16.

3. J. Parry Lewis, *Building Cycles and Britain's Growth* (London, 1965), pp. 15–18; Francis Sheppard, Victor Belcher and Philip Cotterell, 'The Middlesex and Yorkshire Deeds Registries and

the Study of Building Fluctuations', *London Journal*, v (1979), pp. 182–5.

4. B.R. Mitchell, *Abstract of British Historical Statistics* (Cambridge, 1962), pp. 390–91.

5. T.S. Ashton, *An Economic History of England. The Eighteenth-Century* (London, 1955), pp. 27, 170.

6. Mitchell (1962), pp. 390–1.

7. Ashton (1955), pp. 54, 57; Sheppard, Belcher and Cotterell (1979), pp. 185–6.

8. Friedman (1984), pp. 149–50, states that Gibbs's work at Patshull post-dates his return from France in 1749; however, Dr Andor Gomme informs me that building work was going on at Patshull under Francis Smith before his death in 1738.

9. Friedman (1984), p. 145.

10. Richard Hewlings, 'Wakefield Lodge and Other Houses of the Second Duke of Grafton', *GGJ* (1993), pp. 43–61; Gervase Jackson-Stops, 'Badminton House, Gloucestershire', *CL* (9 April 1987).

11. Gervase Jackson-Stops, 'Hartwell House, Buckinghamshire', *CL* (22 Nov. 1990).

12. Dorothy Stroud, *Capability Brown* (London, 1975), pp. 54, 71.

13. Arthur Oswald, 'Linley Hall, Shropshire', *CL* (7 Sept. 1961).

14. Andor Gomme, Michael Jenner and Bryan Little, *Bristol: An Architectural History* (London, 1979), p. 143.

15. John Summerson, *Georgian London* (London, 1988), pp. 84–5.

16. Tim Mowl and Brian Earnshaw, *John Wood* (Bath, 1988), pp. 140–47.

17. Mitchell (1962), pp. 386–7; Lewis (1965), p. 19; Ashton (1955), p. 40.

18. Sheppard, Belcher and Cotterell (1979), p. 184.

19. Lewis (1965), p. 19; Sheppard, Belcher and Cottrell (1979), p. 182.

20. Sheppard, Belcher and Cotterell (1979), p. 186; Lewis (1965), p. 20.

21. Thomas Malton, *A Picturesque Tour through the Cities of London and Westminster* (London, 1792), ii, p. 100.

22. Ashton (1955), pp. 128–9.

23. Giles Worsley, 'Woburn Abbey, Bedfordshire', *CL* (22 April 1993).

24. Giles Worsley, 'Nuneham Park Revisited: I', *CL* (3 Jan. 1985).

25. Leslie Harris, *Robert Adam and Kedleston* (London, 1987), pp. 8–11.

26. Hagley Hall (1753), Harewood House (1759), Croome Park (1751), Foremark Hall (1759), Wrotham Park (1754), West Wycombe Park (1749), Gopsall Hall (*c*.1750), Fonthill House (*c*.1757).

27. Nuthall Temple (1754), Nuneham Park (1756), Kedleston Hall (1758), Castle Hill (*c*.1760), Tabley Hall (*c*.1760), Constable Burton (*c*.1762), Witham Park (*c*.1762), Thoresby Park (1767), Sandon Park (1769). John Wood's Buckland House, Berks (1755) is a villa in the country, but as Tim Mowl ('An Air of Irregularity', *CL*, 11 Nov. 1990) makes clear it was not initially built as a seat (the Throckmorton seat being Coughton Court, Warwicks), but as a secondary house.

28. Brandenburg House (1748), Foot's Cray (1754), Lord Bessborough's villa (1760), Asgill House (*c*.1760), Duddingstone (1763), Botleys (1765).

29. Giles Worsley, 'A Palladian Loose at Castle Howard', *CL* (30 Jan. 1986).

30. Francis Russell, 'Luton Hoo, Bedfordshire', *CL* (16 Jan. 1992).

31. Giles Worsley, 'Woburn Abbey'.

32. Marie P.G. Draper, 'The Houses of the Russell Family', *Apollo* (June 1988).

33. These were certainly accessible, Philip Yorke records looking at them as part of a sightseeing tour of Oxford in 1750. Joyce Godber, 'The Marchioness Grey of Wrest Park', *Publications of the Bedfordshire Historical Record Society*, xlvii (1968), p. 147.

34. At Woburn only the north side of the west front was fitted up as a complete state apartment with a bedchamber, on the south side the place of the drawing room was taken by the best parlour, and the bedchamber by the library.

35. John Cornforth, 'Ditchley Park, Oxfordshire: I', *CL* (17 Nov. 1988).

36. Mark Girouard, *Life in the English Country House* (New Haven and London, 1978), pp. 194–8.

37. Giles Worsley, 'Stiff but not Dull', *CL* (25 July 1991).

38. 'The Travels through England of Dr Richard Pococke', ed. J.J. Cartwright, *Camden Society*, n.s. xliv (1889), p. 260.

39. Isaac Ware, *A Complete Body of Architecture* (London, 1756), p. 300.

40. The Château de Raincy was published in the 'Petit Marot', the Château de Vaux-le-Vicomte in the 'Grand Marot', both *c*.1670.

41. Patricia Waddy, *Seventeenth-century Roman Palaces: Use and the Art of the Plan* (New York, 1990), pp. 220–3; on p. 285 Waddy also illustrates an unexecuted design by Bernini for the Barberini casino at Mompecchio with a similar oval salon, but again, although this breaks forward, the façade is not curved.

42. Runar Strandberg, *Pierre Bullet and J.-B. de Chamblain* (Stockholm, 1971), p. 108, fig.1.

43. Gabriel used it at the Hôtel Blonin (1718), the Hôtel Gabriel (1724) and Hôtel Peyrenc de Moras-Biron (1728–31). So did Jean Courtonne at the Hôtel de Matignon (1720) and the Hôtel de Noirmoutier (1722); Pierre Lassurance at the Palais Bourbon (1722) and the Hôtel de Lassay (1722); Jean Aubert, at the stables at Chantilly (1721–36), and the Hôtel de Lassay (1722); and Boffrand at the Chateau de Vaux à Foucheres (1723). J.F. Blondel illustrates two houses with canted bays in *De la Distribution des maisons de plaisance* (1737).

44. John Harris, *William Talman; Maverick Architect* (London, 1982), pls. 44, 53.

45. Howard Colvin, *Unbuilt Oxford* (New Haven and London, 1983), pl.1.

46. They also appear in unexecuted designs for bows at the end of the wings at Cholmondeley Castle, Ches. (1713); on the garden front of the second design for Eastbury House, Dorset (1717); and at Sacombe Park, Herts.

47. Jackson-Stops (ed.), *The Fashioning and Functioning of the British Country-House*, Symposium (Hanover and London, 1989), p. 31.

48. Kerry Downes, *Vanbrugh* (1977), p. 69; Jackson-Stops (1989), p. 9.

49. I owe this observation to Mr Howard Colvin.

50. There is an unexecuted drawing by Colen Campbell for a house with two projecting bays which seems to be influenced by Vanbrugh (John Harris, *Catalogue of the RIBA Drawings Collection: Campbell*, Farnborough, 1973, fig. 138) while the same may be true of Nicholas Hawksmoor's unexecuted designs for Ockham Park. Otherwise the two architects did not use projecting bows.

51. Harris (1982), pls. 76, 77.

52. Stylistically one would expect Orford House to date from *c*.1720, direct comparisons for the fenestration can be found on Hanover Square (*c*.1717) and at 808–10 Tottenham High Road (1715–25). This is also a plausible date for the canted bay. However, it has been suggested that the house dates from *c*.1700 and it could be earlier as it was built for Edward Russell, created Earl of Orford in 1697, who died in 1727. (P. Morant, *History and Antiquities of Essex*, London, 1768, ii, p. 618.)

53. Bodleian Library, Oxford, Gough Maps 10, fol. 37; Ashmolean Museum, Oxford, Gibbs Collection ii, p. 28.

54. John Bold, 'The Design of a House for a Merchant, 1724', *AH*, 33 (1990), p. 77.

55. Christopher Hussey, *English Country Houses: Early Georgian* (London, 1955), pp. 87–92.

56. Mary Cosh, 'Lord Ilay's Eccentric Building Schemes', *CL* (20 July 1972). The house, with its canted bays, is clearly visible in the junction of Argyle Street and Great Marlborough Street in John Rocque's 1746 survey of London.

57. Contemporary illustrations of the Green Park front of Arlington Street show a canted bay in Flitcroft's idiosyncratic manner. The parish rate books for the parish of St George, Hanover Square, Dover Street Ward (Westminster City Archives, 148–256) suggest that the house was rebuilt about 1742 when the Duke of Kingston's account at Hoare's Bank shows Flitcroft was carrying out extensive work for the duke.

58. Thomas Wright included them at Stoke Park, Glos, in 1749. James Paine used them consistently from 1749 when he placed them on the end of the wings he added to Cusworth Hall, Yorks. In about the same year he included one in the centre of the

garden front at Wadworth Hall, Yorks. He followed these in the 1750s with examples at Ormsby Hall, Lincs (1751); Felbrigg Hall, Norfolk (1751); Kirkstall Grange, Yorks (1752); Serlby Hall, Notts (1754), and Stockeld Park, Yorks (1758). Numerous other examples can be found in the 1750s: Richard Biggs at 18 Arlington Street, London, (1757); Matthew Brettingham at Egremont House, London (1756); Lancelot Brown on the side elevation of Croome Court (1751), and in his proposed design for Peper Harow, Surrey (1752); John Chute at Strawberry Hill, Middx (1753); Flitcroft at Amesbury Abbey, Wilts (c.1750), and Milton House, Northants (1750); William Hiorn at Kyre Park, Worcs (1753), and Foremarke Hall, Derbys (1759); Henry Keene at Bowood House, Wilts (1755), and Hartwell House, Bucks (1759); Stiff Leadbetter at Langley Park, Bucks, (1755), and Nuneham Park, Oxon, and Hatchlands, Kent (1756); Sanderson Miller at Adlestrop Park, Glos (1750), and Arbury Hall, Warwicks (1751); Sir Robert Taylor at Harleyford Manor, Bucks (1755), Coptfold Hall, Essex (1756), and Barlaston Hall, Staffs (1756); Isaac Ware at Wrotham Park, Middx (1754), and Amisfield House, East Lothian (1756). Other examples include Saltram House, Devon (c.1750); Dorchester House, London (1751); Rode Hall, Ches. (1752); the Mansion House, Truro (1755); Broughton Hall, Yorks (1755); the Priory, Prior Park, Wilts (before 1760).

59. Leoni had included one on 21 Arlington Street (1738). Henry Joynes (Vanbrugh's clerk of works at Blenheim) placed one in the centre of the garden front at Normanton Park, Rutland, (c.1735–40). Thomas Wright used them on the wings at Shugborough, Staffs (1748), at Nuthall Temple, Notts (1754), and in the wings at Horton House, Northants (1760). He is also a likely candidate for the pair of bows on the south front at Hampden House, Bucks (1744), whose closest comparison is with those at Shugborough. Sir Thomas Robinson, added round-ended bays to Rokeby Park, Yorks (c.1753), and also planned an addition with two round towers to Ember Court, Surrey.

60. Adam used it on the castellated chapel range at Ugbrooke House, Devon (c.1767), and on Wedderburn Castle, Borders (1768), another castellated house; colonnaded, on the Deputy Ranger's House in Green Park (1768); and on the side elevations of the Courts of Justice and Corn Market in Hertford (1768). In the 1770s it became a regular feature of his minor houses: Castle House, Wilts (1770); Ancaster House, Richmond, Surrey (1773); Moreton Hall, Suffolk (1773); Bellevue House, Edinburgh (1774); Langside, Glasgow (1777); Jerviston House, Strathclyde (1782). The one major house at which it appears is Culzean Castle, Ayr (1785). Adam also used it in London at Chandos House (1770) and 20 St James's Square (1771).

61. Giles Worsley, 'Nuneham Park, Oxfordshire', CL (3 Jan. 1984).

62. Julius Bryant, London's Country-House Collections (London, 1993), p. 10.

63. F.J. Ladd, Architects at Corsham Court (Bradford-on-Avon, 1978), pl. 25.

64. As on the refronted Wimpole Hall, Cambs (1742); on the wings and stables at Woburn Abbey from 1748; at Milton House, Northants (1750); and at Stivichall Hall, Warwicks (1755).

65. The Hiorns used it at Wolverley House, Worcs (c.1749), and Kyre Park, Worcs (1753); Joseph Pickford at 61 Church Street, Ashbourne, Derbys (c.1763), the Mansion, Ashbourne (c.1765), and Ogston Hall, Derbys (1767); James Essex at Kenmare House, Cambridge (1768).

66. Franco Barbieri, 'Il Neoclassismo Vicentino: Ottone Calderari', Arte Venete, VII (1953), pp. 63–76.

67. Erich Hubala, 'Il Palladio e l'architettura a Berlino e a Monaco nel 1740–1820, BCISAP, III (1961), pp. 54–6; C.A. Isermeyer, 'Palladio come stimolo al Neoclassismo Europeo', BCISAP, XII (1970), pp. 120–3; Friederich Mielke, 'Palladianismo a Berlino e Potsdam dal diciassettesimo al ventesimo secolo', BCISAP, XXXII pt. 2 (1980), pp. 4–7.

CHAPTER XII

1. D. Stillman, English Neo-classical Architecture (London, 1988), p. 27.

2. John Harris, Sir William Chambers (London, 1970), p. 251, pls. 69, 198.

3. John Newman, Somerset House (London, 1990), p. 15.

4. Ibid., p. 15

5. Harris (1970), p. 70.

6. Eileen Harris, British Architectural Books and Writers (Cambridge, 1990), p. 203.

7. Harris (1970), p. 22.

8. William Chambers, A Treatise on Civil Architecture (London, 1759), p. 19.

9. Harris (1990), pp. 157–8.

10. John Fleming, Robert Adam and his Circle (London, 1962), p. 258.

11. Ibid., p. 273.

12. Ibid., p. 218.

13. Arthur Bolton, The Architecture of Robert and James Adam (London, 1922), I, p. 40.

14. Peter Leach, James Paine (London, 1988), pls. 24 and 30.

15. I am grateful to Mr Francis Russell for showing me a photograph of this unpublished drawing.

16. John Harris, A Catalogue of British Drawings . . . in American Collections (Upper Saddle River, 1971), pl. 208. Intriguingly, C.R. Cockerell's plan of Westbourne House, built for himself by Isaac Ware and later owned by S.P. Cockerell, includes just such a room, used as a library, with apsed colonnaded ends. It would be interesting to know if this was built by Ware, who bought the estate in 1742 and sold it in 1764. Although there is no documentary proof, it seems unlikely to be coincidence that Ware had earlier planned such a room in the Mansion House. It should be noted, however, that on the drawing this room is in a different colour, perhaps suggesting a later addition. If it was designed by Ware it is almost certainly the earliest known example of such a room (John Harris, 'C.R. Cockerell's "Ichnographica Domestica" ', AH, 14 (1971), p. 21, fig. 14b).

17. Giles Worsley, 'Antique Assumptions', CL (6 Aug. 1992).

18. In the introduction to Joseph Gwilt's 1825 edition of Chambers's Treatise on Civil Architecture.

19. Although only one interior design believed to be by Paine survives among the Kedleston drawings, and none of his interiors was carried out, what he intended is known from the plan and section he published in the second volume of his Plans, Elevations and Section of Noblemen and Gentlemen's Houses. While this was not published until 1783 it is unlikely that these designs postdate his involvement at Kedleston and the engravings were probably taken from drawings (believed to be of Kedleston) exhibited at the Society of Arts in 1761 (Leslie Harris, Robert Adam and Kedleston, London, 1987, p. 20).

20. Harris (1987), p. 10.

21. Francis Russell, 'Luton Hoo, Bedfordshire', CL (16 Jan. 1992).

22. Robert and James Adam, Works in Architecture (London, 1778), preface.

23. Harris (1990), p. 85.

24. Paine was not the only contemporary architect to influence Adam. When he arrived in London in 1758 the most important building being erected at the time was undoubtedly Spencer House which had been begun by John Vardy and was then being fitted up. Adam was to attack Stuart's designs furiously but the influence of the house can be traced in his work. An unusual feature of Spencer House was the low hexastyle Doric portico with attached columns on the Green Park front. Could this have given Adam the idea for the similar Doric porticos of the conservatories at Croome Court, Worcs (1760), and Osterley Park, Middx (1763)? In the tea pavilion at Moor Park, Herts (c.1764), Adam was to follow Vardy's use of palm-tree decoration in the Alcove Room of 1757, while it has already been noted that Stuart's Painted Room anticipated Adam's use of the colonnaded apse. A popular motif of his was a pedimented pavilion flanked by pairs of columns or pilasters, the Royal Society of Arts in London of 1772 being a typical example. This was a motif adapted from the north front of Vardy's Spencer House and ultimately derived from the end bays of Campbell's Burlington House.

25. J.M. Crook, The Greek Revival: Neoclassical Attitudes in British Architecture (London, 1972), p. 77.

26. Ibid., p. 71.

27. Giles Worsley, 'West Wycombe Park, Buckinghamshire', *CL* (6 Sept. 1990).
28. There is no precise date for the decoration of these rooms, but there is no reason to think that they were not carried out in the 1750s and early 1760s. Borgnis, who was primarily responsible, died in 1761.
29. D. Wiebenson, *Sources of Greek Revival Architecture* (London, 80).
30. R. Chandler, N. Revett and W. Pars, *Ionian Antiquities* (London, 1769), p. iv.
31. Fleming (1962), pp. 174–5, 332.
32. Gervase Jackson-Stops, 'Spencer House, London', *CL* (29 Nov. 1990). The suggestion that Borra worked at Woburn Abbey in 1751 is almost certainly unfounded. There is no evidence that Borra was employed there and the Palmyra ceiling with which he has been associated was not completed until later in the decade. (Giles Worsley, 'Woburn Abbey, Bedfordshire', *CL* (22 April 1993).
33. Stuart's lack of interest in the structural principles of Greek architecture can be seen in one design for a temple with baseless Doric columns decorating a Pantheon-like structure with a dome and arches between the columns.
34. Giles Worsley, 'The First Greek Revival Architecture', *BM* (April 1985), pp. 226–9.
35. William Chambers, *A Treatise on The Decorative Parts of Civil Architecture* (London, 1791), p. 19.
36. Wiebenson (1969), pp. 80–1.
37. James Stuart and Nicholas Revett, *The Antiquities of Athens* (London, 1762), preface.
38. Ingrid Roscoe, 'Andien de Clermont, Decorative Painter to the Leicester House Set', *Apollo* (Feb. 1986). The decoration does not survive, but designs after Raphael's decoration, believed to be by Clermont, are in the Victoria and Albert Museum, in a volume which includes coloured copies of antique Roman ceilings (V.A.M.E. 2690–92–1948).
39. Giles Worsley, 'Out from Adam's Shadow', *CL* (14 May 1992).
40. Wiebenson (1969), pp. 88–9.
41. Harris (1987), pp. 52–4.
42. John Martin Robinson, 'New Light on Wyatt at Fawley', *CL* (4 July 1991).
43. Adam (1778), preface.
44. Harris (1990), p. 81.
45. *Ibid.*, p. 339.
46. *Ibid.*, p. 87.

CHAPTER XIII

1. Linda Colley, *Britons: Forging the Nation 1707–1837* (New Haven and London, 1992), p. 123.
2. *Ibid.*, p. 125.
3. *Peebleshire*, II, Royal Commission on Ancient and Historical Monuments of Scotland (Aberdeen, 1967), pp. 326–7.
4. Blair Atholl Archives and National Library of Scotland MS 17878 (information from Mr Howard Colvin).
5. John Harris, *The Palladians* (London, 1981), p. 83.
6. Margaret Sanderson, *Robert Adam and Scotland: Portrait of an Architect* (Edinburgh, 1992), pp. 22–3.
7. Plate 59.
8. David J. Griffin, 'Leinster House and Isaac Ware', in *Decantations: A Tribute to Maurice Craig*, ed. Agnes Burnelle (Dublin, 1992), pp. 60–70. It has also been suggested that Ware may have had a hand in the design of the Ballroom at Dublin Castle in 1746–7 (Frederick O'Dwyer, 'The Ballroom at Dublin Castle: The Origins of St Patrick's Hall', in Burnelle, 1992, pp. 160–4).
9. Edward McParland, Alistair Rowan and Ann Martha Rowan, *The Architecture of Richard Morrison and William Vitruvius Morrison* (Dublin, 1989), p. 3.
10. Mills Lane, *Architecture of the Old South: South Carolina* (New York, 1989), p. 64.
11. M.H. Heckscher and L.G. Bowman, *American Rococo, 1750–1775: Elegance in Ornament* (exh. cat., New York, 1992), p. 18.
12. Mills Lane, *Architecture of the Old South: Maryland* (New York, 1991), p. 42.

13. Robert Tavernor, *Palladio and Palladianism* (London, 1991), pp. 182–3.
14. Mills Lane, *Architecture of the Old South: Virginia* (New York, 1989), p. 64.
15. *Ibid.*, p. 62.
16. *Ibid.*, pp. 64–7.
17. Heckscher and Greene Bowman (1992), pp. 1–17.
18. Antoinette F. Downing and Vincent J. Scully, *The Architectural Heritage of Newport, Rhode Island, 1640–1915* (Cambridge, MA, 1952), p. 81, pl. 111.
19. Lane (*South Carolina*), pp. 71–4.
20. Lane (*Virginia*), pp. 78–82, 91; *Maryland*, pp. 48–50.
21. Lane (*Virginia*), p. 90.
22. *Ibid.*, p. 96.
23. *Ibid.*, p. 108.
24. William Howard Adams (ed.), *The Eye of Thomas Jefferson* (Charlottesville, 1981), p. 43.
25. W.H. Pierson, *American Buildings and their Architects* (New York, 1976), p. 289.
26. *Ibid.*, p. 167.
27. S.K. Padovar (ed.), *A Jefferson Profile as revealed in his letters* (New York, 1956), pp. 31, 46.
28. Adams (1981), pp. 234–53.
29. *Architecture in Britain*, p. 550.
30. Lane (*Virginia*), p. 126.
31. Pierson (1976), pp. 244–51.

CHAPTER XIV

1. W.S. Lewis (ed.), *Correspondence of Horace Walpole*, XXXIII (New Haven, 1965), pp. 498–500.
2. Francis Sheppard, Victor Belcher and Philip Cotterell, 'The Middlesex and Yorkshire Deeds Registries and the Study of Building Fluctuations', *London Journal*, v (1979), p. 186.
3. Sheppard *et al* (1979), p. 186.
4. Andrew Byrne, *Bedford Square: An Architectural Study* (London, 1990), pp. 40–1, 155.
5. 'The Adam Brothers and Speculative Building in London', table provided by Frank Kelsall at the *Society of Architectural Historians of Great Britain Adam Symposium*, Architectural Association, London, May 1992 (unpublished).
6. Frank Kelsall, 'Liardet versus Adam', *AH*, 27 (1984), pp. 124–5.
7. J. Parry Lewis, *Building Cycles and Britain's Growth* (London, 1965), p. 22; Sheppard *et al* (1979), pp. 188–9.
8. W. Bonwitt, *Michael Searles: A Georgian Architect and Surveyor* (London, 1987), p. 28.
9. Nancy Briggs, *John Johnson 1732–1814: Georgian Architect and County Surveyor of Essex* (Chelmsford, 1991), pp. 150–3.
10. Sheppard *et al* (1979), p. 189.
11. D.J. Olsen, *Town Planning in London* (New Haven and London, 1982), p. 88.
12. Sheppard *et al* (1979), p. 189.
13. Giles Worsley, 'Nuneham Park, Oxfordshire', *CL* (3 and 10 Jan. 1985).
14. *BDBA*, p. 573.
15. John Fleming, *Robert Adam and his Circle* (London, 1962), p. 188.
16. Eileen Harris, *British Architectural Books and Writers, 1556–1785* (Cambridge, 1990), pp. 329–31.
17. Christopher Gotch, 'The Missing Years of Robert Mylne', *Architectural Review* (Sept. 1951), pp. 179–82.
18. In execution, the austerity of Gorhambury was reduced by adding window-frames.
19. Allan Braham, *The Architecture of the French Englightenment* (London, 1980), pp. 138–41.
20. I am indebted to Mr Howard Colvin for this observation.
21. Harris (1990), p. 283.
22. Harris (1990), p. 282.
23. M.-A. Laugier, *An Essay on Architecture* (Los Angeles, 1977), p. 42.
24. John Soane, *Lectures on Architecture*, ed. A.T. Botton (London, 1929), pp. 52–3.
25. John Summerson, 'The Evolution of Soane's Bank Stock Office in the Bank of England', in *The Unromantic Castle* (London, 1990), pp. 143–56.

26. Hetty Joyce, 'The Ancient Frescoes from the Villa Negroni and their Influence in the Eighteenth and Nineteenth-Centuries', *Art Bulletin* (Sept. 1983), pp. 423–40.

27. Laugier (1977), p. 13.

28. Laugier (1977), p. 51.

29. A.T. Bolton, *The Works of Sir John Soane* (London, 1924), p. 16.

30. Robert and James Adam, *The Works in Architecture of Robert and James Adam* (London, 1773).

31. John Newman, *Somerset House* (London, 1990), pp. 15, 21.

32. Quoted in John Harris, 'Sir William Chambers and his Parisian Album', *AH*, 6 (1963), p. 56.

33. Lewis (1965), xxxiii, pp. 498–9.

34. John Cornforth, 'Berrington Hall, Herefordshire', *CL* (9 Jan. 1992).

35. *Architecture in Britain*, p. 566.

36. Christopher Proudfoot and David Watkin, 'A Pioneer of English Neo-Classicism', *CL* (13 April 1972).

37. Giles Worsley, 'Rustic Idylls', *CL* (31 Aug. 1989).

38. Andrew Ballantyne, 'Function and Meaning', *AH*, 32 (1989), pp. 105–30.

39. Edward Hasted, *The History and Topographical Survey of the County of Kent*, iii (Canterbury, 1790), pp. 664–5.

40. Michael Mansbridge, *John Nash: A Complete Catalogue* (Oxford, 1991), p. 69.

SELECTED BIBLIOGRAPHY

GENERAL

Ackerman, James, *Palladio* (London, 1966).

Campbell, Colen, *Vitruvius Britannicus* (London, 1715–25).

Colvin, Howard, *Biographical Dictionary of British Architects* (London, 1978).

—— (ed.), *History of the King's Works* (London, 1976–82).

Cruickshank, Dan, *A Guide to the Georgian Buildings of Britain and Ireland* (London, 1985).

Girouard, Mark, *Life in the English Country House* (New Haven and London, 1978).

Harris, Eileen, *British Architectural Books and Writers* (Cambridge, 1990).

Harris, John, *The Artist and the Country House* (London, 1979).

——, *The Palladians* (London, 1981).

——, *The Design of the Country House 1620–1920* (London, 1985).

Onians, John, *Bearers of Meaning* (Cambridge, 1988).

Palladio, Andrea, *I Quattro Libri dell'Architettura* (Venice, 1570).

——, *The Architecture of A. Palladio in Four Books* (London, 1715).

——, *The Four Books of Andrea Palladio's Architecture* (London, 1738).

Puppi, Lionello, *Andrea Palladio: The Complete Works* (London, 1989).

Serlio, Sebastiano, *The Five Books of Architecture* (London, 1611).

Summerson, John, *Architecture in Britain 1530–1830* (Harmondsworth, 1977).

——, *The Architecture of the Eighteenth Century* (London, 1986).

Tavernor, Robert, *Palladio and Palladianism* (London, 1991).

Vitruvius, *The Ten Books of Architecture*, ed. M.H. Morgan (New York, 1960).

Wittkower, Rudolf, *Architectural Principles in the Age of Humanism* (London, 1973).

Wittkower, Rudolf, *Palladio and English Palladianism* (London, 1983).

Woolfe, John, and James Gandon, *Vitruvius Britannicus* (London, 1767 and 1771).

CHAPTER I AND II

Bold, John, *Wilton House and English Palladianism* (London, 1988).

——, *John Webb: Architectural Theory and Practice in the Seventeenth Century* (Oxford, 1989).

Downes, Kerry (ed.), *Sir Christopher Wren* (exh. cat., London, Whitechapel Art Gallery, 1982).

Freart, Roland, *A Parallel of the Antient Architecture with the Modern*, trans. John Evelyn (London, 1664).

Gunther, R.T. *The Architecture of Sir Roger Pratt* (Oxford, 1928).

Harris, John, 'Inigo Jones and his French Sources', *Bulletin of the Metropolitan Museum* (May 1961).

Harris, John, *Catalogue of the Drawings Collection of the R.I.B.A.: Inigo Jones and John Webb* (Farnborough, 1972).

——, and A.A. Tait, *Catalogue of Drawings by Inigo Jones, John Webb and Isaac de Caus at Worcester College, Oxford* (Oxford, 1979).

——, and Gordon Higgott, *Inigo Jones: Complete Architectural Drawings* (London, 1989).

Higgott, Gordon, 'Varying with Reason: Inigo Jones's Theory of Design', *AH*, 35 (1992).

Hill, Oliver, and John Cornforth, *English Country Houses: Caroline* (London, 1966).

Kuyper, W., *Dutch Classicist Architecture* (Delft, 1980).

Louw, H.J., 'Anglo-Netherlandish architectural interchange *c.*1600–*c.*1660', *AH*, 24 (1981).

North, Roger, *Of Building*, ed. Howard Colvin and John Newman (Oxford, 1981).

Reiff, Daniel D., *Small Georgian Houses in England and Virginia* (London and Toronto, 1986).

Rubens, Peter Paul, *Palazzi di Genova* (Antwerp, 1622).

Summerson, John, *Inigo Jones* (London, 1966).

——, 'Inigo Jones: Covent Garden and the Restoration of St Paul's Cathedral', in *The Unromantic Castle* (London, 1990).

Wotton, Henry, *The Elements of Architecture* (London, 1624).

CHAPTERS III AND IV

Bold, John, *John Webb: Architectural Theory and Practice in the Seventeenth Century* (Oxford, 1989).

Colvin, Howard, *Catalogue of Architectural Drawings of the 18th and 19th Centuries in the Library of Worcester College* (Oxford, 1964).

——, 'Fifty New Churches', *Architectural Review* (1957).

——, and Maurice Craig, *Architectural Drawings in the Library of Elton Hall by Sir John Vanbrugh and Sir Edward Lovett Pearce* (London, 1964).

Croft-Murray, Edward, *Decorative Painting in England 1537–1837* (London, 1962).

Downes, Kerry, *English Baroque Architecture* (London, 1966).

——, *Hawksmoor* (London, 1970).

——, *Vanbrugh* (London, 1977).

——, *Hawksmoor* (London, 1979).

——, *Sir John Vanbrugh* (London, 1987).

——, *Sir Christopher Wren, The Design of St Paul's Cathedral* (London, 1988).

—— (ed.), *Sir Christopher Wren* (exh. cat., London, Whitechapel Art Gallery, 1982).

Eisenthal, Esther, 'John Webb's Reconstruction of the Ancient House', *AH*, 28 (1985).

Furst, Viktor, *The Architecture of Sir Christopher Wren* (London, 1956).

Harris, John, *William Talman, Maverick Architect* (London, 1982).

——, and A.A. Tait, *Catalogue of the Drawings by Inigo Jones, John Webb and Isaac de Caus at Worcester College, Oxford* (Oxford, 1979).

Lees-Milne, James, *English Country House: Baroque* (London, 1970).

Webb, G.F., 'The Letters and Drawings of Nicholas Hawksmoor relating to the Building of the Mausoleum at Castle Howared', *Walpole Society*, XIX (1931).

Wren, Christopher, *Parentalia* (London, 1750).

CHAPTERS V, VI and VII

Ackerman, James, *The Villa: Form and Ideology of Country Houses* (London, 1990).

Castell, Robert, *Villas of the Ancients* (London, 1729).

Colvin, Howard, *Catalogue of Architectural Drawings of the 18th and 19th Centuries in the Library of Worcester College* (Oxford, 1964).

——, 'A Scottish Origin for English Palladianism?' *AH*, 17 (1974).

Downes, Kerry, *Hawksmoor* (London, 1970).

——, *Vanbrugh* (London, 1977).

——, *Hawksmoor* (London, 1979).

Friedman, Terry, *James Gibbs* (New Haven and London, 1984).

Harris, John, *William Talman, Maverick Architect* (London, 1970).

Harris, John, *Catalogue of the Drawings Collection of the R.I.B.A.: Colen Campbell* (Farnborough, 1973).

Hind, Charles (ed.), *New Light on English Palladianism* (London, 1990).

Honour, Hugh, 'John Talman and William Kent in Italy', *Connoisseur* (August 1954).

Hussey, Christopher, *English Country Houses: Early Georgian 1715–60* (London, 1955).

Morris, Robert, *An Essay in Defence of Ancient Architecture* (London, 1728).

Piggott, Stuart, *William Stukeley* (London, 1985).

Sicca, Cinzia, 'The Architecture of the Wall: Astylism in the Architecture of Lord Burlington', *AH*, 33 (1990).

Summerson, John, 'The Classical Country House in 18th-century England', in *The Unromantic Castle* (London, 1990).

Ware, Isaac, *A Complete Body of Architecture* (London, 1756).

Wilson, Michael I., *William Kent: Architect, Designer, Painter, Gardener, 1685–1748* (London, 1984).

Worsley, Giles, ' The Baseless Roman Doric Column in Mid-Eighteenth-Century English Architecture: A Study in Neo-Classicism', *BM* (May 1986).

——, 'Taking the Ancients Literally: Archaeological Neo-Classicism in Mid-Eighteenth-Century Britain', in Charles Hind (ed.), *New Light on English Palladianism* (London, 1990).

CHAPTER VIII AND XIII

Adams, William Howard (ed.), *The Eye of Thomas Jefferson* (Charlottesville, 1981).

Bence-Jones, Mark, *Burke's Guide to Country Houses: Ireland* (London, 1978).

Colvin, Howard, and Maurice Craig, *Architectural Drawings in the Library of Elton Hall by Sir John Vanbrugh and Sir Edward Lovett Pearce* (Oxford, 1964).

Cornforth, John, 'Was There a Scottish Baroque?' *CL* (15 June 1989).

Craig, Maurice, *The Architecture of Ireland* (London, 1982).

Downing, A.F., and V. Scully, *The Architectural Heritage of Newport Rhode Island 1640–1915* (Cambridge, 1952).

Gifford, John, *William Adam* (Edinburgh, 1989).

Heckscher, M.H., and L.G. Bowman, *American Rococo, 1750–1775* (New York, 1991).

Howard, Deborah (ed.), *William Adam, Architectural Heritage* I, (Edinburgh, 1990).

Lane, Mills, *Architecture of the Old South: South Carolina* (New York, 1989).

——, *Architecture of the Old South: Virginia* (New York, 1989).

——, *Architecture of the Old South: Maryland* (New York, 1991).

Loeber, Rolf, 'Irish Country Houses and Castles of the Late Georgian Period: an Unremembered Past Recaptured', *Irish Georgian Society*, XVI/I (January–June 1973).

Loeber, Rolf, 'Early Classicism in Ireland: Architecture before the Georgian era', *AH*, 22 (1979).

——, *A Biographical Dictionary of British Architects in Ireland 1600–1720* (London, 1981).

Macaulay, James, *The Classical Country House in Scotland 1660–1800* (London, 1987).

McCullough, Niall, and Valerie Mulvin, *A Lost Tradition: The Nature of Architecture in Ireland* (Dublin, 1987).

McParland, Edward, *James Gandon* (London, 1985).

——, Alistair Rowan and Ann Martha Rowan, *The Architecture of Richard Morrison and William Vitruvius Morrison* (Dublin, 1989).

Pierson, W.H., *American Buildings and their Architects* (New York, 1976).

Sanderson, Margaret, *Robert Adam and Scotland, Portrait of an Architect* (Edinburgh, 1992).

CHAPTER IX

Girouard, Mark, 'Elizabethan Architecture and the Gothic Tradition', *AH*, 6 (1963).

Macaulay, James, *The Gothic Revival 1745–1845* (Glawgow and London, 1975).

McCarthy, Michael, *The Origins of the Gothic Revival* (New Haven and London, 1987).

Piggott, Stuart, *William Stukeley* (London, 1985).

Wittkower, Rudolf, *Gothic vs Classic* (New York, 1974).

Worsley, Giles, 'Origins of the Gothic Revival', *Transactions of the Royal Historical Society*, IV (1993).

CHAPTERS X AND XI

Croft-Murray, Edward, *Decorative Painting in England 1537–1837* (London, 1962).

Dixon-Hunt, John, *William Kent: Landscape Garden Designer* (London, 1987).

Harris, John, 'Diverting Labyrinths', *CL* (1 January 1990).

Hind, Charles (ed.), *The Rococo in England* (London, 1986).

Hussey, Christopher, *English Country Houses: Mid Georgian 1760–1800* (London, 1956).

Leach, Peter, *James Paine* (London, 1988).

Mowl, Tim, and Brian Earnshaw, *John Wood* (Bath, 1988).

Snodin, Michael, *Rococo: Art and Design in Hogarth's England* (exh. cat., London, Victoria and Albert Museum, 1984).

Worsley, Giles, 'West Wycombe Park, Buckinghamshire', *CL* (6 September 1990).

——, 'The Vyne, Hampshire', *CL* (9 May 1991).

——, 'Woburn Abbey, Bedfordshire', *CL* (22 April 1993).

CHAPTER XII

Adam, Robert and James, *Works in Architecture* (London, 1778).

Bolton, Arthur, *The Architecture of Robert and James Adam* (London, 1992).

Chambers, William, *A Treatise on Civil Architecture* (London, 1759).

Crook, J.M., *The Greek Revival: Neoclassical Attitudes in British Architecture* (London, 1972).

Fleming, John, *Robert Adam and his Circle* (London, 1962).

Harris, John, *Sir William Chambers* (London, 1970).

King, David, *The Complete Works of Robert and James Adam* (Oxford, 1991).

McKean, Charles (ed.), *The Architecture of Robert Adam: Life, Death and Survival* (Edinburgh, 1992).

Rowan, Alistair, *Catalogue of the Architectural Drawings in the Victoria and Albert Museum: Robert Adam* (London, 1988).

Sanderson, Margaret, *Robert Adam and Scotland, Portrait of an Architect* (Edinburgh, 1992).

Stillman, D., *English Neo-classical Architecture* (London, 1988).

Watkin, David, *Athenian Stuart: Pioneer of the Greek Revival* (London, 1982).

Wiebenson, Dora, *Sources of Greek Revival Architecture* (London, 1969).

Worsley, Giles, 'Out from Adam's Shadow', *CL* (14 May 1992).

——, 'Antique Assumptions', *CL* (6 August 1992).

—— (ed.), *Adam in Context*, London, 1993.

CHAPTER XIV

Bolton, A.T. *The Works of Sir John Soane* (London, 1924).

Briggs, Nancy, *John Johnson 1732–1814: Georgian Architect and County Surveyor of Essex* (Chelmsford, 1991).

Bonwitt, Michael, *Michael Searles: A Georgian Architect and Surveyor* (London, 1987).

Byrne, Andrew, *Bedford Square: An Architectural Study* (London, 1990).

Crook, J.M., *The Greek Revival* (London, 1972).

Gotch, Christopher, 'The Missing Years of Robert Mylne', *Architectural Review* (September 1951).

Hussey, Christopher, *English Country Houses: Late Georgian 1800–1840* (London, 1958).

Laugier, M.-A., *An Essay on Architecture* (Los Angeles, 1977).

Mansbridge, Michael, *John Nash: A Complete Catalogue* (Oxford, 1991).

Meadows, Peter, *Joseph Bonomi, Architect: 1739–1808* (London, 1988).

Ruffinière du Prey, Pierre de la, *John Soane: The Making of an Architect* (Chicago, 1982).

——, *Catalogue of the Architectural Drawings in the Victoria and Albert Museum: Sir John Soane* (London, 1985).

Soane, John, *Lectures on Architecture* (London, 1929).

Stroud, Dorothy, *Humphry Repton* (London, 1962).

——, *Henry Holland* (London, 1966).

——, *Sir John Soane, Architect* (London, 1984).

Summerson, John, *The Life and Work of John Nash, Architect*, (Cambridge, MA, 1980).

Watkin, David, *The Life and Work of C.R. Cockerell* (London, 1974).

Worsley, Giles, *Architectural Drawings of the Regency Period* (London, 1991).

Of Perspectiue

Houses for Tragedies, must bee made for great personages, for that actions of loue, strange aduentures, and cruell murthers, (as you reade in ancient and moderne Tragedies) happen alwayes in the houses of great Lords, Dukes, Princes, and Kings. Therefore in such cases you must make none but stately houses, as you see it here in this Figure; wherein (for that it is so smal) I could make no Princely Pallaces: but it is sufficient for the workeman to see the manner thereof, whereby he may helpe himselfe as time and place serueth: and (as I sayde in the Comicall) hee must alwayes study to please the eyes of the beholders, and forget not himselfe so much as to set a small building in stead of a great, for the reasons aforesayd.   And for that I haue made all my Scenes of laths, couered with linnen, yet sometime it is necessary to make some things rising or bossing out; which are to bee made of wood, like the houses on the left side, whereof the Pillars, although they shorten, stand all vpon one Base, with some stayres, all couered ouer with cloth, the Cornices bearing out, which you must obserue to the middle part : But to giue place to the Galleries, you must set the other shortening Cloth somewhat backwards , and make a cornice aboue it, as you see : and that which I speake of these Buildings, you must vnderstand of all the rest, but in the Buildings which stand far backward the Painting worke, must supplie the place by shadowes without any bearing out : touching the artificiall lights, I haue spoken thereof in the Comicall workes. All that you make aboue the Roofe sticking out, as Chimneyes, Towers, Piramides, Oblisces , and other such like things or Images; you must make them all of thin boords, cut out round, and well colloured : But if you make any flat Buildings, they must stand somewhat farre inward, that you may not see them on the sides.   In these Scenes , although some haue painted personages therein like supporters, as in a Gallery, or doore, as a Dog, Cat, or any other beasts: I am not of that opinion, for that standeth to long without stirring or moouing ; but if you make such a thing to lie sleeping, that I hold withall.   You may also make Images, Victories, or Fables of Marble , or other matter against a wall ; but to represent the life, they ought to stirre.   In the latter end of this Booke I will shew you how to make them.

Illustration from Sebastiano Serlio's *The Five Books of Architecture* (1611).

INDEX

PHOTOGRAPH CREDITS

Worcester College, Oxford/Conway Library: 3, 11, 18, 19, 26, 58, 73, 107, 108, 109, 111, 126, 129

British Architectural Library, R.I.B.A., London: 4, 8, 14, 15, 17, 57, 62, 76, 77, 93, 104, 127 (Devonshire Collection, Chatsworth), 135 (Devonshire Collection, Chatsworth), 181, 205, 223

© The Trustees of Sir John Soane's Museum: 5, 55, 59, 97, 103, 111, 117, 161, 163, 172, 264, 291, 328, 335, 336, 337, 338, 339, 340

Courtesy of the Trustees of the Victoria and Albert Museum: 6 (P. De Bay), 64, 125 (P. De Bay), 249

Country Life Picture Library: frontispiece (Paul Barker), 7, 9, 10, 18 (Julian Nieman), 21, 23, 24, 25, 27 (Tim Imrie Tait), 28, 32, 33, 37 (June Buck), 38 (Julian Nieman), 39, 40, 43, 50, 53 (Tim Imrie Tait), 67, 69, 70, 78, 82, 83, 85, 87, 89, 90, 94, 95, 98, 99, 100, 102, 105, 112, 133, 138 (June Buck), 141, 142, 144, 146, 147, 148, 150, 151, 152, 156, 159 (Eddie Ryle Hodges), 164, 165 (Julian Nieman), 166, 169 (June Buck), 175 (Julian Nieman), 177, 178, 182, 183, 185, 187, 188, 189, 190, 193, 194, 202, 203, 204 (Alex Ramsay), 206, 207, 208, 209, 210, 212, 213 (John Challis), 214, 220, 221, 222, 224, 226, 228, 229 (Julian Nieman), 231 (June Buck), 234, 235, 236, 237, 238, 239, 240, 241 (Tim Imrie Tait), 242 (Tim Imrie Tait), 243, 244, 247, 248, 253 (Julian Nieman), 254, 255, 257, 258, 263, 268, 273, 274, 275, 279, 284 (Julian Nieman), 285, 286, 290, 294, 295, 297 (Julian Nieman), 298 (Julian Nieman), 300, 301, 304, 305, 306, 310, 311, 313, 327 (Tim Imrie Tait), 329 (Julian Nieman), 330, 332, 341 (Tim Imrie Tait), 342, 344, 345, 346, 347, 348

The Worshipful Company of Goldsmiths: 13

The Paul Mellon Centre for Studies in British Art, London: 16, 30, 31, 34, 36, 46, 49, 54, 56, 61, 63, 68, 71, 80, 84, 86, 88, 101, 114, 115, 118, 119, 120, 121, 124, 130, 131, 132, 134, 139, 154, 155, 160, 184, 227, 229, 232, 245, 246, 256, 260, 261, 278, 282, 283, 287, 293, 333, 334, 342

The British Library, London: 20, 162, 350

Christie's Images: 22, 215, 252

Yale Center for British Art, New Haven, Conn., Paul Mellon Collection: 29, 47, 48, 63, 66, 91, 92, 122, 128, 145, 167, 174, 211, 216, 281, 288, 289, 307, 331, 349

The British Museum, London: 35, 269, 276

The Society of Antiquaries, London: 41

A.F. Kersting: 42, 76, 106

Rijksdienst voor de Monumentenzorg, Zeist: 44, 45

Conway Library, Courtauld Institute of Art, University of London: 51, 52, 149, 265, 266, 267, (R.I.B.A.), 296

Devonshire Collection, Chatsworth/Courtauld Institute of Art, University of London (Photographic Survey): 60

Julian Nieman: 74, 75

Bodleian Library, Oxford: 79

National Maritime Museum, London: 96

Centro Italiano di Studii Andrea Palladio: 116

Survey of London: 136

Devonshire Collection, Chatsworth; reproduced by permission of the Chatsworth Settlement Trustees: 137

RCHM, England: 140, 217, 233, 270, 280

Ashmolean Museum, Oxford/Conway Library, Courtauld Institute of Art, University of London: 143, 271

York City Art Gallery: 153

The National Trust Yorkshire, Photographic Library: 156, 173

Courtauld Institute of Art, University of London: 158

Property of the Provost and Fellows of Eton College: 168, 176

Photographic Records Ltd, London: 170, 299

Tim Imrie Tait: 171

Royal Commission on the Ancient and Historical Monuments of Scotland: 179, 180, 302, 303

The Irish Architectural Archive: 186, 191, 312

National Gallery of Ireland, Dublin: 192, 314, 315, 316

Courtesy of the Association for the Preservation of Virginia Antiquities: 195

Colonial Williamsburg Foundation: 196, 197, 200, 321, 322, 326

Prints and Photographs Division, Library of Congress: 198, 325

Courtesy Charleston Library Service: 199

National Archives [U.S.A.], Still Pictures Branch: 201

Dean and Chapter of Westminster Abbey: 218

Canon M.H. Ridgeway/Conway Library, Courtauld Institute of Art, University of London: 225

The National Trust, Photographic Library: 250, 291, 292

Metropolitan Museum of Art, New York: 251

His Grace the Duke of Norfolk/Courtauld Institute of Art, University of London (Photographic Survey): 259

Buckinghamshire Record Office: 262

Pieterse-Davison International Ltd: 277

The National Trust for Scotland: 308

Hugh Doran: 309

Photo Marion Warren, courtesy of the Maryland State Archives: 317

Courtesy Peabody Essex Museum, Salem, MA.: 318

Photo Henry A. Curtis, courtesy of the Redwood Library and Athenaeum: 319

Massachusetts Historical Society: 320

Collection of the Maryland Historical Society, Baltimore: 323

THE architrave is placed upon the capital, the height of which must be half the diameter of the column, that is, a module. It is divided into seven parts. With one the *tenia* or *benda* is made, whose projecture must be equal to its height; then the whole is again divided into six parts, one is given to the *goccie*, which ought to be six, and to the listello under the tenia, which is a third part of the said goccie.

FROM the tenia downwards the remainder is again divided into seven parts; three are to be given to the first fascia, and four to the second. The frize is a module and a half in height. The breadth of the triglyph is one module, and its capital the sixth part of a module. The triglyph is to be divided into six parts; two of which are for the two channels in the middle, one for the two half channels at the ends, and the other three for the spaces between the said channels.

THE *metopa*, or space between triglyph and triglyph, ought to be as broad as it is high. The cornice must be a module and one sixth in height, and divided into five parts and a half, two of which are given to the cavetto and ovolo. The cavetto is less than the ovolo by the width of its listello. The remaining three parts and a half are to be given to the corona or cornice, which is vulgarly called *gocciolatoio*, and to the gola or cima recta and reversa.

THE corona ought to project four parts in six of the module, and have on its soffit, that looks downwards, and projects forward, six drops, or *guttæ*, in length, and three in breadth, with their listelli over the triglyphs, and some roses over the metopæ. The guttæ are round, shaped like bells, and answer to those under the tenia.

THE gola must be an eighth part thicker than the corona, and divided into eight parts; two are to be given to the orlo, and six remain for the gola, whose projecture is seven parts and a half.

THEREFORE the height of the architrave, frize and cornice is a fourth part of the altitude of the column.

THESE are the dimensions of the cornice, according to VITRUVIUS; from which I have deviated in altering some of the members, and making them somewhat larger.

A, *Gola recta.*
B, *Gola reversa.*
C, *Gocciolatoio or Corona.*
D, *Ovolo.*
E, *Cavetto.*
F, *Capital of the Triglyph.*
G, *Triglyph.*

H, *Metopa.*
I, *Tenia.*
K, *Goccie.*
L, *First Fascia.*
M, *Second Fascia.*
Y, *Soffit of the Gocciolatoio.*

Parts of the capital.

N, *Cimacio.*
O, *Abaco.*
P, *Ovolo.*
Q, *Gradetti or Annulets.*
R, *Collarino.*

S, *Astragal.*
T, *Cimbia.*
V, *Shaft of the column.*
X, *Plan of the capital, and the module divided into thirty minutes.*